WEBSTER'S
FAMILY
ENCYCLOPEDIA

WEBSTER'S
FAMILY
ENCYCLOPEDIA

VOLUME 1

1995 Edition

Exclusively distributed by
Archer Worldwide, Inc.
Great Neck, New York, USA

Foreword

Who was Thomas Jefferson and what did he accomplish? What is a capybara and what does it look like? When did Martin Luther King, Jr. die, and who killed him? Where is Samarkand and how many people live there? The answers to these questions—and millions of others—can be found here. In twelve volumes and some 25,000 entries, *Webster's Family Encyclopedia* explores the entire range of human activity—history, sciences, the arts, geography, biography, ideas, beliefs, and pastimes—and puts a wealth of information at your fingertips.

In order to cover all these topics in the space available, contributors were instructed to follow three general rules: (1) to write in simple but precise, non-technical language comprehensible to the general reader; (2) to present all material concisely, without oversimplification; and (3) to be certain that articles were informative and of value. We believe that they have succeeded admirably and that *Webster's* is an up-to-date work that everyone can use for quick, easy, and accurate reference.

The editors would like to thank all of the many contributors, special advisors, researchers, writers, and others whose diligent work has done so much to preserve this encyclopedia's scope, accuracy, and readability.

Notes on using *Webster's Family Encyclopedia*:
1. Articles are in alphabetical order.
2. An asterisk (*) preceding a term in the text indicates that the term has its own entry and that further or related information will be found there. A square (□) indicates that an illustration relevant to the article being read will be found near the term so marked; the term's entry may also contain pertinent information.
3. Population figures given refer, whenever possible, to the city or town itself, rather than to the larger urban area of which it may be a part.
4. Except for a few of the most familiar Chinese names (e.g., Canton, Chiang Kai-shek, Beijing), this encyclopedia follows official Chinese practice in using the pinyin transliteration system. The main article shows the older Wade-Giles system name in parentheses following the pinyin term; the name is also listed in Wade-Giles at its alphabetical place, together with a cross-reference. (Example: **Peking**. *See* Beijing.)

Abbreviations Used in Webster's Family Encyclopedia

AD	After Christ	ht	height	N.M.	New Mexico
Adm.	Admiral	i.e.	that is	NNE	north-northeast
Ala.	Alabama	in	inches	NNW	north-northwest
Apr	April	Ind.	Indiana	Nov	November
AR	Autonomous Republic	Ill.	Illinois	NW	northwest
		Jan	January	N.Y.	New York
at no	atomic number	K	Kelvin	OAS	Organization of American States
at wt	atomic weight	Kans.	Kansas		
Aug	August	kg	kilograms	Oct	October
b.	born	km	kilometers	Okla.	Oklahoma
BC	Before Christ	kph	kilometers per hour	OPEC	Organization of Petroleum Exporting Countries
bp	boiling point				
C	Celsius, Centigrade	kW	kilowatts		
		lb	pounds	Pa.	Pennsylvania
c.	circa	Lt.	Lieutenant	PLO	Palestine Liberation Organization
Calif.	California	Lt. Gen.	Lieutenant General		
Capt.	Captain			Pres.	President
CIS	Commonwealth of Independent States	m	meters	R.I.	Rhode Island
		M. Sgt.	Master Sergeant	S	south, southern
		Mar	March	S.C.	South Carolina
cm	centimeters	Mass.	Massachusetts	SE	southeast
Co.	Company	Md.	Maryland	Sen.	Senator
Col.	Colonel	mi	miles	Sept	September
Conn.	Connecticut	Mich.	Michigan	Sgt.	Sergeant
d.	died	Minn.	Minnesota	sq mi	square miles
Dec	December	Miss.	Mississippi	SSE	south-southeast
Del.	Delaware	mm	millimeters	SSW	south-southwest
E	east, eastern	Mo.	Missouri	SW	southwest
EC	European Community	MP	Member of Parliament	Tenn.	Tennessee
				Tex.	Texas
e.g.	for example	mp	melting point	UN	United Nations
est	estimated	mph	miles per hour	US	United States
F	Fahrenheit	N	north, northern	USSR	Union of Soviet Socialist Republics
Feb	February	NATO	North Atlantic Treaty Organization		
Fl. Lt.	Flight Lieutenant			Va.	Virginia
Fla.	Florida			Vt.	Vermont
ft	feet	NE	northeast	W	west, western
Ga.	Georgia	Neb.	Nebraska	wt	weight
Gen.	General	N.H.	New Hampshire		
Gov.	Governor	N.J.	New Jersey		

EDITORIAL STAFF

Revised Edition
Editor
Stephen P. Elliott

Assistant Editors
Suzanne Stone Burke
Carol B. Dudley
Susan Carter Elliott
Alexander Hellemans
Elizabeth J. Jewell
Dianne Knowles
Rebecca Lyon
Diane Bell Surprenant
David Travers

First Edition
Editor
Alan Isaacs

Subject Editors
Barbara Barrett
John Daintith
Thomas Hill Long
Elizabeth Martin
Judith Ravenscroft
Michael Scott Rohan
Jennifer Speake

Assistant Editors
Robert Hine
Jonathan Hunt
Nada Lyons
Martin Manser
Susan O'Neill
Carol Russell
Mary Shields
Jacqueline Smith
Elizabeth Tootill
Maurice Waite
Rosalind Williams

Illustration and Design
Barbara Barrett
Juliet Brightmore
(consultant)
Jennifer Speake
Robert Updegraff

Picture Research
Jacqueline Smith
Valerie Walker

Artwork
Oxford Illustrators Ltd.

Contributors
J.E. Abbott
Francis Absalom
Joan Ashley
Howard H.R. Bailes
Jill Bailey

Helen Banks
Antoinette Bates
Alison Bideleux
T.J. Boardman
Charles Boyle
O.M.C. Buchan
W.P. Cass
Kathleen Clarke
P.B. Clarke
J.A. Cudden
S.R. Elliot
Martin Elliott
Jane A. Freeman
B.J. Golding
Chris Gray
M.B. Hamilton
P.W. Hanks
G.R. Hawting
Vincent Hetreed
Anne Holloway
Glyn Alyn Hughes
Valerie Illingworth
Yvonne Jacobs
J.B. Katz
Helen Kearsley
Susan Laker
N.R.M. de Lange
David Langford
Marise Larkin
Richard Latham
Bridget Loney
Michael MacCarthy-Morrogh
Iseabail Macleod
Martin Meggs
Denise Mitchell
J.S. Morris
Sa'id Mosteshar-Gharai
Jocelyn Murray
H.M. Nahmad
Ruth D. Newell
Pastor Stuart Olyott
John Oram
Stephanie L. Pain
Ann Palmer

Christopher D. Parker
Kathleen A. Pavelko
I.G. Pears
Volodimir Pechenuk
David A. Ramsay
Elfrida Savigear
Michael Scherk
Kenneth Scholes
Nigel Seller
J.H. Shaw
N. Shiel
Adrian Shubert
Laurel Thomas Silantien
R.L. Sims
Richard Smith
Jane Southern
Stella Stiegeler
B.R. Stratton
Stephanie Stuart
Eric A. Taylor
Ivan Vince
Margaret Wallis
C.S.P. Wolstenholme
Rebecca Woodell
R. Wrigley

Advisors
Stephen Brooks
Jacqueline Bruce
Richard Elms
Clive Farahar
A.M. Genton
Lawrence Hills
Michael Naish
Sally Naish
Michael D. Robson
J.T.R. Sharrock
Margaret Spencer
Mike Torbe
Basil Wright

Computerization
Barry Evans
Sarah Mitchell

A

Aachen (French name: Aix-la-Chapelle) 50 46N 06 06E A spa city in W Germany, in North Rhine-Westphalia near the Belgian and Dutch borders. It is an important industrial center with iron and steel and textile industries. Its technical university was established in 1870. *History*: it was the N capital of Charlemagne's empire and many Holy Roman Emperors were crowned in the cathedral (founded in 796 AD). It was annexed by France in 1801 and passed to Prussia (1815). Extensively damaged during World War II, it was the first major German city captured by the Allies (1944). Population (1991 est): 241,000.

Aalborg. *See* Ålborg.

Aalst (French name: Alost) 50 47N 05 12E A city in N central Belgium, on the Dender River. It possesses the country's oldest town hall (begun 1200). Industries include textiles and brewing. Population (1981 est): 78,860.

Aalto, Alvar (1898–1976) Finnish architect and furniture designer. Aalto established a distinctive "Finnish" style, with his use of timber and high pitched roofs. After World War II he became increasingly individualistic and his hall of residence at the Massachusetts Institute of Technology and the Helsinki Hall of Culture (1958) are among his best work.

Aaltonen, Wäinö (1894–1966) Finnish sculptor. He is known for the portrait sculptures of the Finnish Olympic runner Paavo Nurmi (1924) and of Sibelius (1928).

aardvark (Afrikaans: earth pig) A nocturnal African mammal, *Orycteropus afer*, also called ant bear. It is about 5 ft (1.5 m) long, lives in grassland, and has a long snout, large ears, and a thick tail. Its strong claws are used to dig burrows and tear open the mounds of termites, which are picked up with its long sticky tongue. The aardvark is the only member of its order (*Tubulidentata*).

AARDVARK *This strange animal feeds entirely on termites and ants. It has very few teeth, which are weak and peg-shaped and specialized to cope with its diet.*

aardwolf A nocturnal mammal, *Proteles cristatus*, that lives in open and bushy regions of southern and eastern Africa. It resembles a small striped hyena, about 20 in (50 cm) high at the shoulder, but has small simple teeth suitable for feeding on termites (which form the main part of its diet). It spends the day in burrows, often those deserted by other animals. Family: *Hyaenidae* (hyenas); order: *Carnivora*.

Aarhus. *See* Århus.

Aaron, Hank (Henry Louis A.; 1934–   ) US baseball player. He played for the Milwaukee (later Atlanta) Braves (1954–74) and for the Milwaukee Brewers (1975–76). An outfielder, he was best known for his consistent hitting and was credited with a record career total of 755 home runs. He became a member of the Baseball Hall of Fame in 1982.

Aaron In the Old Testament, the elder brother of Moses, whom he assisted as leader of the Israelites in their journey from Egypt to the Promised Land (Canaan). Although he yielded to the people's demand to build the *golden calf as an idol, he and his descendants were confirmed by Jehovah as priests of the Hebrew nation.

abaca (*or* Manila hemp) A fiber obtained from the leafstalks of a palmlike plant, *Musa textilis* of the Philippines, related to the banana. It is used for ships' ropes and similar objects as it is buoyant and resistant to the action of sea water.

abacus A calculating device consisting of balls strung on wires or rods set in a frame. It is probably of Babylonian origin but its use declined in Europe with the introduction of *Arabic numerals in about the 10th century AD. Until recently it was still in use in the Middle East and Japan.

Abadan 30 20N 48 15E A city in SW Iran, on an island in the Shatt (river) al-Arab. Much of Iran's oil is brought here by pipeline for refining or exporting. Population (1986): 294,000.

Abakan 53 43N 91 25E A city in Russia, the capital of the Khakass autonomous region (*oblast*) at the confluence of the Abakan and Yenisei Rivers. It is the center of a coalmining district. Population (1991 est): 157,000.

abalone A marine *gastropod mollusk belonging to the widely distributed family *Haliotidae*, of rocky coasts, also called ear shell or ormer. Up to 12 in (30 cm) long, their dishlike □shells have a row of holes along the outer edge through which deoxygenated water and waste products are expelled from the body. The large foot is considered a delicacy and the shells are used as mother-of-pearl for ornaments.

abandonment In law, the voluntary relinquishment of property or rights without passing them on to another. For example, when a ship is left crewless and adrift, notice of abandonment can be issued to the insurers and a claim made for a constructive total loss (as opposed to an actual total loss if it sinks).

Abbadids A Muslim dynasty in Andalusia (1023–91). Abbad I (reigned 1023–42) declared Seville's independence from Córdoba (1023) and by war and intrigue enlarged his territory. Abbad II (reigned 1042–69) continued this expansion, but failed to capture Córdoba. He is remembered for his delight in a flower garden planted over his enemies' skulls. Abbad III (d. 1095; reigned 1069–91), poet and king, made Seville an important cultural center. The hostility of Spanish Christians forced him into an alliance with the *Almoravids, who later deposed him (1091) and exiled him to N Africa, where he died.

'Abbasids A powerful dynasty of *caliphs, which ruled Islam from 750 AD to 1258. They were descended from Mohammed's uncle al-Abbas (566–652). In 750 they seized power from the Umayyads in Damascus and moved their capital to Baghdad. The 'Abbasids were known for their imposition of strict religious orthodoxy and their patronage of scholarship. Under *Harun ar-Rashid (786–809) the dynasty was at its peak. By the 10th century its powers were declining as provincial governors asserted their independence of Baghdad, which was still, however, an important commercial, cultural, and intellectual center. Baghdad fell to the Mongols in 1258 and a branch of the 'Abbasids was installed in Cairo until that city fell to the *Ottomans in 1517. The last of the line died in 1538.

Abbas (I) the Great (1557–1628) Shah of Persia (1588–1628) of the Safavid dynasty, who greatly extended Persian territory by defeating the Uzbeks (near Herat, 1598) and the Ottomans (1605, 1618). He created a standing army, established the Persian capital of Isfahan, and was an effective patron of the arts.

Abbas II (1874–1944) The last Khedive of Egypt (1892–1914), who supported nationalist opposition to British influence and was deposed when Britain declared a protectorate over Egypt in 1914.

Abbevillian A culture of the Lower *Paleolithic in Europe. It is characterized by crude stone hand axes made by hammering flakes off a flint with another stone. Named for Abbeville in France, the Abbevillian also appears in Britain but in Africa similar early hand axes are designated *Acheulian.

Abbey Theatre A Dublin theater opened in 1904 and closely associated with the *Irish Literary Renaissance. The Abbey Theatre produced plays by Yeats, Lady Gregory, Synge, George Russell (pseudonym AE) Shaw, and O'Casey and gained an international reputation as a repertory theater dedicated to performing mainly plays by Irish playwrights on Irish subjects. The original playhouse burned down in 1951, but a new theater opened in 1966.

Abbott, Berenice (1898–1991) US photographer. As an assistant to Man *Ray in Paris during the 1920s, she photographed well-known artists and writers. From 1929 her work included a photographic documentation of New York City and, later, of phenomena in the world of science.

ABC Mediation (1915) An unsuccessful attempt by Argentina, Brazil, and Chile to mediate differences between the US and Mexico after the US had sent troops to Vera Cruz, Mexico.

Abd Allah (1846–99) Sudanese leader, known as the Khalifa (caliph). In 1885 he succeeded Muhammad Ahmad (*see* Mahdi, al-) as leader of the uprising against the Egyptian government of the Sudan. He was defeated by *Kitchener in 1898 and was killed in subsequent mopping-up operations.

'Abd al-Malik ibn Marwan (c. 646–705 AD) Fifth *caliph (685–705) of the Umayyad dynasty, who subdued opposition to Umayyad rule of Islam. He defeated the northern Arab tribes in 691 and, with the help of his general al-Hajjaj, overcame resistance in Iraq (692). In 697 he captured Carthage. During his reign, Arabic became the administrative language of the empire and a new Muslim currency was coined.

'Abd ar-Rahman III an-Nasir (891–961 AD) Emir (912–29) and first caliph (929–61) of the Umayyad Arab dynasty of Córdoba. He conquered Muslim Spain and also campaigned against the Christian north: in 924 he took Pampalona, the capital of Navarre, but was defeated by the King of León in 939. Under his rule, Córdoba became a noted center of learning and the arts.

Abdelkader (c. 1807–83) Algerian nationalist, who resisted the French invasion. He became Emir of Mascara in 1832 and gained control of the Oran region. Victories against the French (1835–37) facilitated a further extension of his territories. Defeated in 1841, he withdrew to Morocco and finally surrendered to the French in 1847.

abdomen In mammals (including humans), the region of the body extending from the lower surface of the diaphragm to the pelvis. The abdomen contains the intestines, liver, pancreas, kidneys, gall bladder, and—in females—the ovaries and womb. In arthropods, the abdomen is the posterior section of the body, which is usually segmented.

Abdulhamid II (1842–1918) Sultan of the Ottoman Empire (1876–1909), notorious for the Armenian massacres (1894–96). Following defeat by Russia (1877), he dismissed parliament and suspended the constitution. Thereafter he ruled autocratically, instituting many administrative reforms, especially in education, and opposing western interference in Ottoman affairs. The revolt of the *Young Turks in 1908 brought about his deposition.

Abdul-Jabbar, Kareem (b. Ferdinand Lewis Alcindor; 1947-   ) US basketball player. At 7 ft 2 in in height, he played college basketball (1965–69) at the University of California at Los Angeles (UCLA), during which time the school won three National Collegiate Athletic Association (NCAA) titles. With the Milwaukee Bucks (1969–75) and the Los Angeles Lakers (1975–89), he was named the National Basketball Association (NBA) regular season most valuable player (MVP) six times.

Abdullah (1882–1951) Emir of Transjordan (1921–46) and first King of Jordan (1946–51). He fought with T. E. *Lawrence in the Arab revolt against Turkish rule during World War I. He was assassinated in 1951.

Abdul Rahman, Tunku (1903–73) Malaysian statesman. He was the first prime minister of independent Malaya (1957–63) and of Malaysia (1963–70). He led the Alliance Party to electoral victory in 1955, becoming chief minister and negotiating Malayan independence from Britain (1957) and the formation of Malaysia (1963).

Abel. *See* Cain.

Abelard, Peter (1079–1142) French philosopher. His ill-fated marriage with Heloïse, niece of a canon of Paris, ended when Abelard was castrated by thugs hired by the canon (1118). He retired to a monastery and she became a nun. Abelard turned his formidable powers as a logician to establishing a coherent relationship between faith and reason (*see* scholasticism). A quarrelsome disputant, Abelard was perpetually in trouble with the church authorities; his *Sic et Non* (*For and Against*), for example, outraged opponents by listing points on which acknowledged authorities differed.

abelmosk A flowering plant, *Hibiscus moschatus* (*H. abelmoschus*), native to India. It has large flowers with yellow petals and red centers and grows to a height of 24–71 in (60–180 cm). Abelmosk is cultivated for its seeds, which yield musk used in perfumes, and for its young fruits, which are used as vegetables. Family: *Malvaceae* (mallow family).

Aberdeen 57 10N 2 04W A city, port, and former county of NE Scotland, the administrative center of Grampian Region situated on the North Sea coast between the mouths of the Rivers Don and Dee. Aberdeen is an old cathedral city with a university dating from 1494 (King's College). Fishing has always been important, as has the working of local granite; the "Granite City" provided stone for London's cobbled streets in the 18th century. Other industries include ship building, paper making, textiles, chemicals, and engineering. Aberdeen's proximity to North Sea oil has transformed it into an important service center for the oil industry. Aberdeen has well-known research institutes for fisheries, soils, and animal nutrition. Population (1981): 190,200.

ABERDEEN *Provost Skene's House, dating from the 16th century. Saved from demolition in the early 1950s, it has since been extensively restored.*

Aberdeen, George Hamilton-Gordon, 4th Earl of (1784–1860) British statesman; prime minister (1852–55). He was foreign secretary in Sir Robert *Peel's Conservative government (1841–46). Aberdeen succeeded Peel as leader of the "Peelites" (1850) and became prime minister of a coalition government of Whigs and Peelites.

Aberdeen Angus A breed of polled (naturally hornless) beef cattle, originating from NE Scotland, Short, stocky, and usually black (some have red coats), they are hardy and adapt well to different climates. Angus bulls are commonly mated with dairy breeds to produce a polled beef cross.

Aberdeen terrier. *See* Scottish terrier.

aberration 1. A defect in a lens or mirror that causes blurring or distortion of the image. The three most important types are spherical aberration, chromatic aberration, and *astigmatism. Spherical aberration is caused by rays from the outside of the lens or mirror being brought to a focus at a different point from those nearer to the center. In chromatic aberration, different colors are focused at different points, since the refractive index of glass varies with the wavelength (*see* achromatic lens). **2.** An apparent displacement in the position of a star or other heavenly body resulting from the motion of the observer with the earth in its orbit round the sun.

Abidjan 5 19N 4 00W The capital of the Ivory Coast, off the Gulf of Guinea. A small village until developed by the French in the 1920s, it became the capital in 1934. It is now an important port, linked to the sea by the Vridi Canal. The National University was founded in 1964. Population (1990 est): 2,700,000.

Abilene 38 55N 97 13W A city in N central Kansas. Situated on the Smoky Hill River, it was founded in 1856 and quickly became a distribution hub for cattle from Texas. It is now a major shipping center for the area's grain and livestock and houses the memorabilia of Dwight D. Eisenhower. Population (1990): 6242.

Abilene 32 27N 99 45W A city in central Texas. A major trading center for cotton, grain, and livestock, it has timber mills as well as clothing and food-processing industries. Population (1990): 106,654.

Abjuration, Act of (1581) The declaration of independence by the United Provinces. The Dutch thus renounced their allegiance to *Philip II of Spain. *See also* Revolt of the Netherlands.

Abkhaz Autonomous Republic (*or* Abkhazia) An administrative division in Georgia since 1991 between the Black Sea and the Caucasus Mountains. Most of the population is Abkhazian or Georgian and lives along the narrow subtropical coastal lowland. The region is predominantly agricultural, producing tobacco, tea, and citrus fruits, and the chief mineral is coal. There are several health resorts. *History*: invaded by the Romans, it later gained independence before coming under the Ottoman Turks in the 16th century. It became a Russian protectorate in 1810 and an autonomous Soviet republic in 1921. Area: 3320 sq mi (8600 sq km). Population (1989 est): 526,000. Capital: Sukhumi.

abnormal psychology That branch of *psychology that deals with the basic theory involving psychotic or behavioral disorders, such as *schizophrenia and *phobias and abnormalities due to brain damage and retardation.

Åbo. *See* Turku.

Abolition Movement The 19th century political and moral campaign to abolish *slavery in the US. Soon after the Revolutionary War, opponents of the institution of slavery began to pressure the national government to restrict its legality. In 1787 slavery was prohibited in the Northwest Territory and in 1808 Congress enacted a law that ended the importation of slaves into the US. By the terms of the *Missouri Compromise of 1820, slavery was prohibited in the area of the Louisiana Purchase north of the 36°30" line. Among the early leaders of the Abolition Movement were William Lloyd *Garrison, publisher of the *Liberator* and one of the founders of the New England Anti-Slavery Society; Frederick *Douglass, a prominent orator and publisher; and James Birney, who ran for President as the candidate of the abolitionist Liberty Party in 1840 and 1844. Another abolitionist party, the Free Soil Party, sponsored the candidacy of former Pres. William Van Buren in 1848. During the 1850s, Harriet *Tubman actively aided fugitive slaves to escape to freedom by means of the secret *Underground Railroad route. Perhaps the most influential work of anti-slavery literature was the novel *Uncle Tom's Cabin* written by Harriet Beecher *Stowe. The issue of slavery was finally settled by the *Civil War and the adoption of the 13th Amendment in 1865.

Abomey 7 14N 2 00E A city in S Benin. It was the capital of the Yoruba kingdom of Dahomey until captured by the French (1893). Population (1979 est): 41,000.

Abominable Snowman A creature, also called Yeti (Tibetan: Bearman), that is believed to live at high altitudes in the Himalayas. There have been no authenticated sightings, but gigantic footprints in the snow have been photographed (which may have other natural causes).

Aborigines 1. The dark-skinned hunters and gatherers who inhabited Australia before European settlement. There were about 500 Aboriginal tribes, which were linguistic groups having no social or political unity. The main social units were seminomadic bands. They were a diverse people culturally but, in general, material culture was rudimentary, while kinship organization and terminology were complex. Political affairs were conducted by older men. Male initiation and circumcision were commonly practiced. Aboriginal mythology was generally rich and elaborate and included accounts of creation during the primordial dawn, which they call "Dream Time." There are roughly 136,000 people of Aboriginal descent in Australia. The small proportion who maintain a nomadic way of life are threatened by encroachments upon their lands as these are opened up for mineral exploitation. A movement to protect Aborigines' rights has gathered momentum and in 1971 the first Aborigine MP was elected. **2.** Any indigenous people inhabiting a country, especially as contrasted with invaders or colonizers.

abortion The expulsion or removal of a fetus from the womb before it is capable of independent survival. Abortion may be natural (a miscarriage) or medically induced. Clinical methods for induced abortions include dilatation and curettage, suction by a vacuum aspirator, and the administration of certain drugs. Until 1973 many states severely restricted the use of induced abortion, but the US Supreme Court ruled in the case of *Roe* v. *Wade* that the decision of whether to have an abortion during the first three months of pregnancy should be left to the woman concerned and her physician. *Roe* v. *Wade* was reaffirmed in a 1986 Supreme Court decision. States may, however, restrict induced abortions after the third month. The moral question of abortion continues to be an issue of heated and sometimes violent debate between the opponents of legalized abortion, the "Pro-Life" movement, and the supporters of the present policy, the "Pro-Choice" movement.

Aboukir Bay, Battle of (July 25, 1799) The battle in which Napoleon defeated the Ottoman Turks during his occupation of Egypt. The 7000-strong French army defeated the unruly Turkish force of 18,000.

Abraham In the Old Testament, patriarch and founder of the Hebrew nation, whose story as given in Genesis (11–25) appears to refer to events before 2000 BC. Born at Ur in Chaldaea, he followed a divine command and went first to Haran in N Mesopotamia and then to Canaan, accompanied by Sarah, his wife, and his nephew Lot. After being forced to withdraw to Egypt because of a famine, he returned to Canaan, where God promised him that the land would belong to his descendants. He had eight sons. God tested his obedience by commanding him to sacrifice his son Isaac; when he was about to obey, a ram was substituted and God reaffirmed the promises regarding Abraham's posterity.

Abraham, Plains of A plateau in E Canada, on the W edge of Quebec citadel. Here Gen James Wolfe defeated the French under Gen Montcalm (Sept 13, 1759), leading to British control over Canada.

abrasives Hard rough substances used to wear down the surfaces of less resistant materials. They are widely used in both industry and the home for polishing, grinding, cleaning, and shaping. Abrasives are either natural, such as sandpaper, emery, and pumice, or synthetic, such as silicon carbide and carborundum.

abraxas A mystic word, the Greek letters of which make 365 when read as numbers. Such words are found engraved and sometimes personified as a half-animal half-human deity on gemstones used as charms until the 13th century AD. It is particularly associated with *Gnosticism.

Abruzzi (*or* Abruzzo) A region in E central Italy. It consists of the Apennines in the W and a coastal region in the E. Agriculture is limited, producing mainly cereals. Manufacturing industry is primarily for local needs but there is a large fishing fleet. Area: 4167 sq mi (10,794 sq km). Population (1991): 1,249,388. Capital: L'Aquila.

abscess A pus-filled cavity surrounded by inflamed tissue, usually caused by bacterial infection. Abscesses may form anywhere in the body, including the skin, gums, and internal organs. They may heal without treatment, but usually they require draining and sometimes also antibiotics.

abscission The separation of a plant organ, such as a fruit or a leaf, from its stem. Individual cells at the base of the organ weaken by losing calcium from their cell walls and a sealant layer of cells protects the newly exposed surface. Abscission is controlled by plant hormones (*see* auxin).

absinthe A highly alcoholic drink made from spirits infused with herbs, including aniseed and wormwood. Absinthe has been banned in many countries because of the harmful effects of wormwood, and substitutes, known by different names (e.g. anis, pastis), are drunk instead. Absinthe is pale green and becomes cloudy when diluted with water.

absolute zero The lowest temperature that can theoretically be attained. It is equal to $-273.15°C$ or 0 K. In practice, absolute zero can never be reached, although temperatures of a few thousandths of a degree above absolute zero have been achieved. *See* cryogenics.

absolutism A political system, characteristic of European monarchies between the 16th and 18th centuries, in which the sovereign attempted (with limited practical success) to centralize power in his own person. *Louis XIV of France is often regarded as the typical absolute monarch. Justified by the theory of the *divine right of kings, absolutism was associated in the 18th century with enlightened despotism (*see* Enlightenment) but was challenged by the ideals of the *American and *French Revolutions.

absorption The assimilation of a substance by a solid or liquid, with or without chemical reaction. Moisture, for instance, can be absorbed from air by dehydrating agents, such as sulfuric acid. Certain porous solids, such as charcoal and zeolites, are able to absorb large quantities of gas. The process is distinguished from *adsorption in that the absorbed substance is held in the bulk of the solid rather than on a surface.

abstract art A nonobjective and nonrepresentational form of art. Tendencies to abstraction can be found in almost any age or school of art, particularly oriental and decorative art. However, the widespread use of *photography in the 20th century to create a permanent visual record of people, places, events, etc., made the strictly representational function of painting much less important. This shift of emphasis released artists from the confines of realism, enabling them to explore the wider fields of abstraction. In about 1910 *Kandinsky produced the first abstract watercolor, heralding the free expression of such artists as Jackson *Pollock; in contrast, *cubism led to the geometric abstract style of such painters as Piet *Mondrian and Kasimir *Malevich. A particular characteristic of abstract sculpture is the use of new materials, such as plastic, glass, and steel. *See also* action painting; constructivism; minimal art; op art; orphism; Stijl, de; suprematism.

abstract expressionism. *See* action painting.

Abstraction-Création An international group of abstract geometric artists, active from 1931 to 1936 and based in France under Georges Vantongerloo (1886–1965) and Auguste Herbin (1882–1960). It was also the name of their annual journal and exhibition.

Abu al-Wafa (940–98 AD) Persian mathematician and astronomer, who made notable contributions to *trigonometry. He invented the secant and cosecant functions (the inverse of the sine and cosine), drawing up accurate tables for them and for the sine and tangent functions.

Abu Bakar (c. 1843–95) Sultan of Johore (now in Malaysia) from 1885 to 1895. He became ruler of Johore in 1862, a year after Britain gained control of the state's foreign affairs, and contributed greatly to the maintenance of internal stability, fostering trade and agricultural development.

Abu Bakr (c. 573–634 AD) The first *caliph (632–34), known as as-Siddiq (the righteous). One of the earliest Muslims, Abu Bakr accompanied Mohammed to Medina and became caliph on his death. As caliph he defeated the rebellious tribes and began the invasion of Syria and Iraq.

Abu Dhabi. *See* United Arab Emirates.

Abu Hanifah (700–67 AD) Influential Muslim theologian and teacher of jurisprudence. Of Persian origin, he lived in Kufa (now in Iraq), where he died, perhaps in prison, after refusing to accept a post under the ruling dynasty. He left virtually no writings, but was known as a champion of the use of reason and analogy in law. His teachings form the basis of one of the two orthodox schools of the *Sunnites.

Abuja 9 10N 7 06E A city in central Nigeria. Agriculture is the most important activity with some local manufacturing. It became Nigeria's federal capital in 1982. Population (1992 est): 298,000.

Abu Nuwas (c. 762–c. 813 AD) Arab poet. Although he learned his craft from older poets and from the Bedouins, he abandoned traditional poetic forms and became popular for sophisticated lyrics celebrating the pleasures of wine and erotic affairs with women and boys. A favorite at the Abbasid court of *Harun ar-Rashid at Baghdad, he is portrayed in the *Arabian Nights* as a free-thinking pleasure-seeker.

Abu Simbel A monumental rock-cut temple complex constructed about 1250 BC by Pharaoh Ramses II in *Nubia. Four colossal statues of Ramses, each 66 ft (20 m) high, at the entrance were raised to escape inundation by Lake Nasser (1968).

Abutilon A genus of tropical and subtropical perennial herbs and shrubs (over 100 species). The plants reach a height of 12–60 in (30–150 cm) and have drooping stems with bell-shaped flowers. Some species are grown as ornamental plants. *A. avicennae* is cultivated in China for fiber (China jute). Family: *Malvaceae* (mallow family).

Abydos An ancient city in Upper Egypt, founded before 3000 BC and continuously occupied until Roman times. It was a principal center of *Osiris worship. The most impressive remaining structure is Seti I's Great Temple (c. 1300 BC), with shrines for six deities and the god pharaoh. The Table of Abydos, a king list carved on its walls, provides information about earlier pharaohs.

abyssal zone The ocean depths lying below 1000 m. It is the zone of greatest ocean depth, lying seaward of the continental slope (*see* continental shelf). Since no light penetrates to these depths, they contain relatively little marine life and the temperature never rises above 34°F (4°C). The ocean depths below 19,500 ft (6000 m), the deep-sea trenches, are sometimes classified separately as the **hadal zone.**

Abyssinian cat A breed of short-haired cat, many individuals of which are descendants of one exported to the UK from Abyssinia in the 19th century. They have slender bodies and wedge-shaped heads with large ears. The reddish-brown coat has black or brown markings and the eyes are green, yellow, or hazel. The Red Abyssinian is a rich copper-red.

Acacia A genus of tropical and subtropical trees and shrubs (over 700 species), particularly abundant in Australia (*see* wattle). Acacias have clusters of yellow or white flowers, produce long flattened pods, and usually have compound leaves consisting of many small leaflets. In some species the leaflets do not develop and the leafstalks assume their function, being broad and flattened. These species are often very spiny. Acacias yield a number of useful products: gums (including *gum arabic), tannins, dyes, and woods suitable for furniture. Many are grown as ornamental plants. Family: *Leguminosae*.

Académie Française The French literary academy founded by Cardinal de Richelieu in 1634 (incorporated 1635) to preserve the French literary heritage. Its membership is limited at any one time to 40 "immortals," who have included Corneille, Racine, and Voltaire. It is continuously engaged in the revision of the official French dictionary.

Academy, Greek The college founded (c. 385 BC) near Athens by Plato, which continued in various guises until its dissolution by Justinian in 529 AD. It is famed mainly for contributions to philosophy and science. At first metaphysics and mathematics predominated but in the mid 3rd century BC philosophical skepticism became the overriding tendency.

Academy of Motion Picture Arts and Sciences An organization founded in Hollywood in 1927 to raise the artistic and technical standards of the film industry. It is responsible for the annual presentation of the Academy Awards, popularly known as Oscars, for excellence in acting, writing, directing, and other aspects of film production.

Acadia A former French colony in E Canada centered on present-day Nova Scotia. The original French settlement was destroyed by the British in 1613. Conflict over Acadia between French and British continued until 1763, when it fell finally to the British. Many Acadians were deported by the British and resettled in Louisiana, where their descendants, called Cajuns, still live. Longfellow's poem *Evangeline* tells their story.

Acadia National Park A national park on Mount Desert Island and part of Isle au Haut and the mainland along the N Atlantic coast of Maine. Established in 1919 as Lafayette and in 1929 as Acadia, it includes Cadillac Mountain 1530 ft (465 m). Area: 116.5 acres (47.2 hectares).

Acanthus A genus of perennial herbaceous plants (about 50 species), mostly native to the Mediterranean region: *A. mollis* and *A. spinosus* are the species most commonly planted in temperate gardens. Growing to a height of 40–60 in (1–1.5 m), they have tough leaves, often spiny and with deeply cut margins, and spikes of purple and white flowers. The fruit—a capsule—explodes to disperse the seeds. Family: *Acanthaceae*.

acanthus A decorative element of classical architecture. It is mainly found on the capitals of Corinthian and Composite columns, and normally comprises heavy carvings of stylized leaves.

a cappella (Italian: in the church style) A marking on a piece of music for several voices, indicating that it is to be sung unaccompanied.

Acapulco 16 51N 99 56W A seaside resort in S Mexico, on the Pacific Ocean. Known as the Riviera of Mexico, it has fine sandy beaches and many hotels. Population (1980): 301,902.

Accademia The principal art gallery in Venice, opened in 1756 to display work by Venetian artists. Formerly a monastery, it houses masterpieces by such painters as Bellini, Titian, and Canaletto in a collection with items dating from the 13th century.

ACANTHUS *The spiky leaf of Acanthus spinosus inspired the decorative architectural motif used on Corinthian and Composite columns.*

acceleration The rate of change of a body's velocity. Linear acceleration is the rate of change of linear velocity. It is measured in such units as meters per second per second. Angular acceleration is the rate of change of angular velocity and is measured in such units as radians per second per second.

acceleration of free fall (g) Formerly called acceleration due to gravity; the acceleration of a falling body when air resistance is neglected. Caused by gravitational attraction between the body and the earth, it varies slightly at different points on the earth's surface. Its standard value is 32 ft (9.806 m) per second.

accelerator principle The economic principle that investment will accentuate economic booms and *depressions. As income rises, businesses gain confidence in the expected future level of demand and increase their investment in plant and equipment; this pushes up employment in the capital-goods industries and heightens the boom. The converse applies to a slump.

accelerators Large machines used for accelerating beams of charged particles (electrons, protons, neutrons, etc.) to very high speeds primarily for research in *particle physics. The particles are accelerated by electric fields either in a straight line, as in the *linear accelerator, or in a circle, as in the *cyclotron, *synchrotron, and *synchrocyclotron. The beam is confined to its path by magnetic fields. The energies of the particles are measured in millions of electronvolts (MeV) or giga-electronvolts (1000 MeV = 1 GeV), some modern accelerators attaining several hundred GeV. Particle accelerators are used by directing a beam of particles at a stationary target or, for greater energy, by colliding two beams of particles together. Accelerators are also used to create artificial isotopes and in *radiotherapy. The first accelerator was a linear accelerator, produced in 1932 by *Cockcroft and *Watson.

accentor A small sparrow-like songbird belonging to an Old World family (*Prunellidae*; 12 species), usually restricted to northern and mountain regions. It has a red or brownish-gray plumage with gray underparts, often streaked or striped. Accentors feed on insects or—in winter—seeds and berries. The family includes the *dunnock (hedge sparrow).

accessory In criminal law, a person who incites another to commit a crime but is not present when the crime is committed is an accessory before the fact. (An abettor is distinguished from an accessory before the fact by being present at the commission of a crime.) A person who assists another whom he knows has committed a crime is an accessory after the fact.

Accius, Lucius (170–c. 85 BC) Roman tragic dramatist, admired for his melodramatic plots and lively rhetorical style. About 700 lines survive from over 40 of his plays, mainly on Greek mythological themes. He also wrote treatises on poetry and grammar.

accomplice In law, a person concerned with one or more other persons in committing a crime, either as a principal or an *accessory.

accordion A portable musical instrument invented in Berlin in 1822. A member of the reed-organ family, the accordion is a boxlike instrument in which bellows operated by the left arm force air through reeds mounted in end panels. In the modern **piano accordion** a small piano-like keyboard played by the right hand supplies the melody, while buttons operated by the left hand produce chords. The instrument is supported in front of the player's body by straps.

accountancy The profession of preparing, verifying, and interpreting the accounts of a business. The main branches are bookkeeping, auditing, financial accounting, and cost accounting. Bookkeeping is concerned with the preparation of records of all the financial transactions undertaken by a firm or a self-employed person, usually on a day-to-day basis. The books of account kept by a firm usually include a cash book to record all payments and receipts, a nominal ledger in which all transactions with named clients, suppliers, etc., are recorded, a purchase and a sales ledger, and sometimes purchase and sales day books. Auditing is the process of verifying that the bookkeeping and the preparation of accounts have been carried out accurately and truthfully. In most countries, including the UK and the US, auditing is carried out by an independent firm of accountants, which is required to certify that a company's accounts are a true record of its transactions during the past year. Financial accounting consists of analyzing a firm's transactions and summarizing them in the firm's annual accounts. These will normally consist of a profit and loss account and a balance sheet. The former lists the total sales, total purchases, opening and closing value of the inventory (or work in progress), and the expenses, enabling the profit or loss in the period to be calculated. The balance sheet lists the firm's assets and liabilities. Cost accounting identifies the costs of production at all stages of a manufacturing process. Unlike financial accounting it can be used to measure economic performance and the relative efficiency of the constituent parts of a business.

Accra 5 32N 0 12W The capital of Ghana, a port on the Gulf of Guinea. It is built on the site of three 17th-century trading fortresses founded by the English, Dutch, and Danish. It became the capital of the Gold Coast in 1877. Following the opening of a railway to the agricultural hinterland (1923) it developed rapidly into the commercial center of Ghana. The University of Ghana was founded in 1948 at Legon, just outside Accra. Population (1988 est): 949,000.

acetaldehyde (CH_3CHO) A colorless liquid *aldehyde with a pungent smell, formed by the oxidation of *ethanol. On further oxidation it becomes acetic acid.

acetic acid (CH_3COOH) The *acid contained (3% to 6%) in vinegar. It can be made from alcohol but for industrial purposes is commonly made from *acetaldehyde and is used in the manufacture of plastics.

acetone (*or* dimethyl ketone; CH_3COCH_3) A colorless inflammable liquid used as a solvent, for example in nail-polish remover and in the manufacture of rayon.

acetylcholine A chemical that transmits impulses between the ends of two adjacent nerves and is confined largely to the parasympathetic nervous system. Acetylcholine is released on stimulation of the nerve and diffuses across the gap of the *synapse to stimulate the adjacent nerve. It is rapidly converted to an inactive form by the enzyme cholinesterase, permitting the passage of a further impulse.

acetylene (*or* ethyne; C_2H_2) A colorless toxic inflammable gas. The two carbon atoms are joined by a triple bond and it forms the basis of a series of compounds called *alkynes. Acetylene is made by the action of water on calcium carbide and is widely used as a starting material for many organic compounds. Because of its high flame temperature (about 1864°F [3300°C]) it is used in oxy-acetylene welding.

Achaea A region of ancient Greece occupying the N coast of the Peloponnesus and SE Thessaly. The 12 towns of the region formed the **Achaean League** in the 4th century BC. Dissolved in the late 4th century, it was revived by the ten surviving cities in 280 BC and included non-Achaean cities, such as Sicyon. The League finally disintegrated when Achaea was annexed by Rome in 146 BC. Its NW part approximates the modern department of Achaea.

Achaeans An ancient Greek people mentioned by Homer as being among the besiegers of *Troy. They were probably related to the *Dorian Greeks but also seem to have had associations with *Mycenaean culture.

Achaemenians An ancient Persian dynasty founded by Achaemenes in the 7th century BC. Cyrus I (reigned c. 645–602 BC), Cambyses I (c. 602–559 BC), *Cyrus the Great (559–530 BC), who founded the Achaemenian (or Persian) Empire, and *Cambyses II (529–521 BC) belonged to the senior branch of the family. *Darius I (522–486 BC) headed the junior line, which included *Xerxes I (486–465 BC). The Achaemenian dynasty ended in 330 BC, when Alexander the Great defeated Darius III (336–330 BC).

Achebe, Chinua (1930–   ) Nigerian novelist of the Ibo tribe. His first novel, *Things Fall Apart* (1958), deals with the arrival of missionaries and colonial government in the Ibo homeland. The conflict between traditional African society and western values is a central theme in all his work. *A Man of the People* (1966) is a satirical attack on corrupt politics in modern Africa. His other works include a collection of short stories; a book of poems, *Beware Soul Brother* (1971); and a novel, *Anthills of the Savannah* (1987).

achene A small dry *fruit having a single seed that is attached to the fruit wall at one point only. The fruit does not open at maturity (i.e. the fruit is indehiscent) and the seed is thus retained until germination. Lettuce fruits are examples of achenes.

Achernar A conspicuous blue star, apparent magnitude 0.5 and 114 light years distant, that is the brightest star in the constellation Eridanus.

Acheron A river in N Greece, in Greek mythology the chief river of the underworld. In Dante, it is the river across which the souls of the dead are ferried to hell by *Charon.

Acheson, Dean (Gooderham) (1893–1971) US lawyer and statesman. Serving in a variety of government posts including leading delegate to the Bretton Woods Conference (1944) and undersecretary of state (1945–47), he became influential in shaping foreign policy. As secretary of state in *Truman's cabinet

(1949–53), his foreign policy aimed at the containment of Soviet communism. This led him to play a leading role in developing the Truman Doctrine, the *Marshall Plan, and the *North Atlantic Treaty Organization. After 1953 he continued advising American presidents. His memoir, *Present at the Creation*, was awarded the 1970 Pulitzer Prize.

Acheulian A culture of the Lower *Paleolithic. It is characterized by hand axes made by hammering flakes off a flint with a hammer of wood, antler, or bone, thus producing a more regular and effective tool than the *Abbevillian hand axe. Named after St Acheul near Amiens (N France) the Acheulian occurs widely in Eurasia and also in Africa where it apparently originated and survived longest (until about 58,000 years ago). Acheulian sites provide the earliest evidence of man's use of fire and are often associated with *Homo erectus* remains (*see* Homo).

Achilles In Greek mythology, the greatest Greek warrior in the Trojan War. The son of Peleus, King of Thessaly, and Thetis, a sea nymph, he was dipped by his mother in the River Styx as a child, which made his whole body invulnerable except for the heel by which she had held him. After a quarrel with *Agamemnon he ceased fighting until the death of his friend *Patroclus at the hand of *Hector. Achilles then slew Hector and was himself later killed by Paris, who shot a poisoned arrow into his heel.

achromatic lens A combination of lenses used to eliminate chromatic *aberration in an optical system. The simplest type has two lenses of different powers made from different kinds of glass. The chromatic aberration of one lens is cancelled by the chromatic aberration of the other lens.

acids and bases Acids are chemical compounds containing hydrogen that can be replaced by a metal atom to produce a *salt. They have a sour taste and turn litmus red. When dissolved in water they dissociate into ions. Hydrochloric acid (HCl), for instance, gives chloride ions and hydrogen ions: $HCl + H_2O \rightarrow Cl^- + H^+ + H_2O$. The hydrogen ion is associated with a water molecule, a combination referred to as a hydroxonium ion (H_3O+).

Strong acids dissociate completely in water; hydrochloric acid, sulfuric acid (H_2SO_4), and nitric acid (HNO_3) are common examples. Such compounds are extremely corrosive, sulfuric and nitric acids being particularly so because they are also powerful oxidizing agents. **Weak acids** do not dissociate completely. Many of these are organic compounds, usually carboxylic acids, which contain the carboxylate group $-CO.OH$. A large number occur naturally: for example, acetic acid (CH_3COOH) in vinegar, citric acid ($C_3H_4(OH)(COOH)_3$) in citrus fruits, and lactic acid ($C_2H_4(OH)COOH$) in milk.

Bases are compounds that react with acids to form salts and water. Bases that dissolve in water, known as **alkalis**, produce hydroxide ions (OH^-). Many are metal hydroxides, such as sodium hydroxide (NaOH) and potassium hydroxide (KOH). Ammonia is also a base, reacting with water molecules to form ammonium ions and hydroxide ions: $NH_3 + H_2O \rightarrow NH_4^+ + OH^-$. The neutralization of an acid by a base in solution is a reaction in which hydrogen and hydroxide ions combine to give water. In chemistry the simple concept of acids and bases has been extended to include the concept of an acid as any compound that can donate a proton and a base as a proton acceptor. This (the Brönsted-Lowry theory) can be applied to reactions in nonaqueous solvents. A further extension of the terms (Lewis theory) defines an acid as an acceptor of an unshared electron pair and a base as a pair donor. *See also* pH.

acmeism A movement in Russian poetry in the 1910s and 1920s that asserted the value of precision against what was seen as the abstract vagueness of the symbolist movement. Because it was apolitical it met with official hostility, and several of its members, including *Akhmatova and *Mandelstan, were persecuted.

acne A skin condition, common in adolescence, affecting the face, chest, and back. Acne is caused by overactivity and inflammation of the sebaceous glands: oily sebum accumulates in the hair follicles, producing pustules and blackheads. Acne usually disappears by the late twenties; severe cases can be treated with antibiotics.

Aconcagua, Mount (Spanish name: Cerro Aconcagua) 32 40S 70 02W A mountain in W Argentina, in the Andes, regarded as being the highest point in the W hemisphere. It is of volcanic origin. Height: 22,835 ft (6960 m).

MOUNT ACONCAGUA

aconite A European herbaceous plant, *Aconitum napellus*, also known as monkshood. Growing to a height of 40 in (1 m), its flowers are usually purplish-blue and hood-shaped; the bulbous roots yield poisonous *alkaloids, including aconitine, which have been used in medicine as *narcotics and analgesics. The genus, which is restricted to N temperate regions, also includes wolfsbane (*A. lycotonum*). Family: *Ranunculaceae* (buttercup family).

acornworm A wormlike marine invertebrate animal, 2–71 in (5–180 cm) long, that burrows in soft sand or mud. Its front end is acorn-shaped, with the mouth at the base. It filters food particles from sea water, which enters the mouth and passes out through gill slits along the length of the body. Chief genera: *Balanoglossus, Saccoglossus*; phylum: *Hemichordata*.

acouchi (*or* acushi) A small, long-legged *rodent belonging to the genus *Myoprocta* (about 5 species). Acouchis have the same habits and lifestyle as the closely related agoutis but are smaller, measuring up to 18 in (45 cm) long. They have a thin, white-tipped tail and lack the colored rump hairs of agoutis.

acoustics The branch of physics concerned with the production, propagation, reception, properties, and uses of sound. It has several subdivisions. The most important, architectural acoustics, is concerned with the design of public auditoriums so that sounds can be heard in all parts of them with the maximum clarity and the minimum distortion. *Ultrasonics is the study of very high frequency sound, especially as it is used in the investigation of matter and in industrial processes. The structure and function of sound sources, such as the voice, loudspeakers, etc., and sound receptors, such as the ear, microphones, etc., also form part of the study of acoustics. Other fields include speech communication and the design of machines that can understand spoken instructions.

acquired character. *See* Lamarckism.

acquired immune deficiency syndrome (AIDS) A sexually transmitted, contagious disease of viral origin. The disorder is characterized by a marked decrease of helper-induced T-lymphocyte cells, resulting in a general breakdown of the immune system. AIDS manifests itself by the occurrence of opportunistic infections, such as persistent Herpes simplex, diffuse pneumonitis, mycobacterial tuberculosis, or by Kaposi's syndrome (tumors involving the skin and mucous membranes). Other sarcomas and a host of persistent disorders also occur. The World Health Organization estimates that, as of 1994, more than 2.5 million people worldwide were infected. The disease, which is always fatal and for which there is no cure, is found most frequently in homosexuals and intravenous drug users. The etiological agent, which can be transmitted by blood, sperm, or saliva, is the human T-cell leukemia virus type III (HTLV-III). The virus has been found in AIDS patients, but also in healthy individuals.

acquittal In criminal law, the clearing of an accused person of the charge against him, usually by court verdict. Acquittal prevents a person from being prosecuted for the same offense again. Anyone charged as an *accessory to a crime is automatically acquitted if the principal is acquitted.

Acre (Arabic name: 'Akko) 32 58N 35 06E A city in N Israel, on the Mediterranean coast. Acre was held by the Crusaders for many years and was in Turkish hands for several centuries. Allocated to the Arabs under the UN plan for *Palestine, it fell to the Jews in May 1948, and became part of Israel. Its notable structures include walls and a mosque from the 18th century, and caravanserais. It is a fishing port and a center for light industry. Population: 33,000.

acrolith A statue made, especially in ancient Greece, of marble for the flesh and gilded wood for the clothing. This method was a cheaper substitute for chryselephantine (gold and ivory) statuary. The acrolith's purpose was usually religious or monumental.

acromegaly A rare disease in which a noncancerous tumor of the pituitary gland secretes abnormally large amounts of *growth hormone. This causes enlargement of the face, hands, feet, and heart. The tumor can be destroyed by X-rays or surgically removed.

acropolis (Greek: high town) In ancient Greek towns, the isolated rocky plateau on which stood the religious and administrative nucleus of the town and which served as a citadel in time of war. *Mycenae and *Corinth have imposing examples, but the most famous is the Acropolis of Athens, which is still adorned by remains of buildings erected by *Cimon, *Themistocles, and *Pericles after the sack of Athens by the Persians (480 BC). These buildings include the *Propylaea, *Parthenon, Erectheum, and the reconstructed temple of Athena Nike.

acrylics Synthetic materials produced by *polymerization of acrylonitrile (vinyl cyanide; CH_2:CHCN). Acrylic resins are used in paints and plastics, a common one being Perspex. Acrylic fiber is widely used in textiles, mainly for knitwear, furnishing fabrics, and carpets. The fibers are strong, absorb little water, and resist most substances encountered in use, although they become plastic in hot water or steam. Modacrylic is acrylic fabric or yarn with more than 15% of other fibers added.

Acta The ancient Roman *Acta Senatus* (*Senate Business*) were official records of *Senate proceedings compiled by a senator chosen by the emperor. The *Acta Diurna* (*Daily News*) constituted a popular gazette of political and social news, instituted by Julius Caesar in 59 BC and continuing until 300 AD. The emperor's official enactments were also known as *Acta*.

Actaeon A mythological Greek hunter, son of the god Aristaeus and Autonoe, daughter of Cadmus, King of Thebes. Ovid, in his *Metamorphoses*, relates how Actaeon accidentally caught sight of the goddess Artemis bathing naked and was turned by her into a stag and killed by his own hounds.

ACTH (adrenocorticotrophic hormone) A peptide hormone, secreted by the anterior lobe of the pituitary gland, that stimulates the cortex of the adrenal glands to produce three types of *corticosteroid hormones. Secretion of ACTH is stimulated by physical stress and is regulated by secretions of the *hypothalamus of the brain.

actinides A group of related chemical elements in the periodic table ranging from actinium (atomic number 89) to lawrencium (atomic number 103). They are all radioactive and include a number of *transuranic elements. Chemically, they resemble the *lanthanides, having unfilled inner electron shells.

actinium (Ac) A highly radioactive metal that occurs naturally in uranium minerals. It is the first of the actinide series of elements and is chemically similar to the lanthanide elements. It was discovered in 1899 by A. L. Debierne (1874–1949). At no 89; at wt (227); mp 615°F (1050°C); half-life of ^{227} Ac 21.6 yrs.

actinium series One of three naturally occurring series of radioactive decays. The actinium series is headed by uranium-235 (known as actino-uranium), which undergoes a series of alpha and beta decays ending with the stable isotope lead-207. *See also* thorium series; uranium series.

actinomycetes Bacteria belonging to the order *Actinomycetales*. They have rigid cell walls and often form branching filamentous moldlike colonies. Some may cause diseases in plants and animals, particularly *Mycobacterium tuberculosis*, which causes tuberculosis, and *M. leprae*, which causes leprosy; others are relatively harmless parasites inhabiting the gastrointestinal tract. Many are found in soil, where they decompose organic matter. Certain species produce valuable *antibiotics.

action painting A modern style, also called abstract expressionism, in which paint is sprayed, splashed, or dribbled over a large canvas to form an unpremeditated and usually abstract design. Jackson *Pollock invented it in 1947 to give free rein to his own emotions. It was later also used by Willem *de Kooning to produce figurative pictures. Together with color-field painting (*see* Rothko, Mark), action painting was the dominant style in the US in the 1950s and made New York, for the first time, the most advanced center of modern art.

action potential The change in electric potential on the surface of a nerve cell that occurs when the cell is stimulated. It results from sodium and potassium ions moving across the cell membrane. The electrochemical impulse travels along the nerve fiber, and in this way information is transmitted through the *nervous system. *See also* neuron; synapse.

Actium, Battle of (31 BC) The decisive land and sea battle that ended the civil war in ancient Rome. Octavian, later *Augustus (the first Roman emperor), defeated the forces of *Mark Antony and *Cleopatra.

activated charcoal Charcoal that has been processed to increase its power of absorption by heating it to drive off absorbed gas. It then has a high capacity for further absorption of gas. Uses of activated charcoal include removing impurities from gases and liquids and as filters in gas masks.

active galaxy Any galaxy, including *Seyfert galaxies, certain *radio galaxies, and *quasars, in which there is an unusually large release of energy, often from the center of the object. It has been suggested that the source of such violent activity is a supermassive *black hole.

act of God In law, an occurrence due to a sudden, violent natural cause, such as a storm, which could not reasonably have been guarded against and loss from which could not have been avoided or predicted.

Acton, John Emerich Edward Dalberg-Acton, 1st Baron (1834–1902) British historian, born in Naples. As a Whig MP (1859–66) he formed a close friendship with Gladstone. Acton mobilized liberal Roman Catholic opinion against the doctrine of papal infallibility promulgated in 1870. Appointed professor of modern history at Cambridge (1895) he planned the *Cambridge Modern History*.

Actors' Studio An actors' workshop founded in New York in 1947 by Elia *Kazan and others. Under its director Lee Strasberg (1901–82), who joined it in 1950, it became famous for its emphasis on "method" acting, which was developed from the theories of *Stanislavsky. Film actors influenced by it include Marlon *Brando, Rod Steiger, and James *Dean.

Acts of the Apostles The fifth book of the New Testament, written by Luke about 63 AD as a sequel to his Gospel. Starting with the ascension of Christ, it deals with the rise and spread of the Christian Church from a single Jewish congregation at Jerusalem, where Peter is prominent, to Paul's first missionary journey and his eventual imprisonment at Rome.

actuary A mathematician employed by an *insurance company to calculate the premiums payable on policies. The calculations are based on statistically determined risks and eventualities (e.g. sickness, life expectancy).

acupuncture A traditional Chinese system of healing in which thin metal needles are inserted into selected points in the body. The needles are stimulated either by manual rotation or electrically. Acupuncture is used in the Far East to relieve pain and in China as an anesthetic for surgical operations. The traditional explanation of its effectiveness, dating back to 2500 BC, relates to balancing the opposing life forces *yin and yang. Recent research in the West suggests that the needles may activate deep sensory nerves, which cause the pituitary and midbrain to release endorphins (natural pain killers; *see* encephalins).

Adad A Babylonian and Assyrian weather god. He was worshiped as both creator and destroyer of life: his summer rains ensured a good harvest but his storms and floods brought terror and death. His father was Anu, god of the heavens.

Adalbert (c. 1000–72) German churchman, Archbishop of Bremen. From a noble Saxon family, he became a trusted and powerful adviser to Emperor Henry III. He was active in the evangelization of Scandinavia, the Orkneys, Iceland, and Greenland until his exile from Henry IV's court in 1066.

Adam, Adolphe-Charles (1803–56) French composer. He composed over 60 operas but is primarily remembered for his romantic ballet *Giselle* (1841), the earliest full-length ballet in the traditional repertoire.

Adam and Eve In the Old Testament, the first human beings. According to Genesis (2.7–3.24), Jehovah (*or* Yahweh) created Adam from dust in his own image and put him in the Garden of Eden. His wife Eve was created from one of his ribs. Tempted by the serpent (the devil) to eat the forbidden fruit of the Tree of Knowledge of Good and Evil, Eve succumbed to the temptation and induced

Adam to eat the fruit also. They became aware of their guilt and were expelled from Eden. Their sons included *Cain and Abel.

Adam de la Halle (c. 1240–90) French poet and musician. He traveled with his patron Robert II of Artois and became famous at the court of Charles of Anjou in Naples, where he died. His *Jeu de la feuillée* and *Jeu de Robin et Marion*, the first comic opera, combined popular songs with a sequence of realistic narrative scenes.

adamellite A variety of *granite consisting of roughly equal proportions of potassium feldspar and sodic plagioclase feldspar, with one or more ferromagnesian minerals.

Adamov, Arthur (1908–70) French dramatist of the *Theater of the Absurd. Born in Russia, Adamov went to Paris in 1924. The experimental forms of his plays owe much to the images and logic of dreams, which include *La Parodie* (1947) and *Le Ping Pong* (1955). His later, more political, work included anti-Gaullist sketches. He committed suicide in Paris.

Adams, Abigail (1744–1818) US first lady; wife of John *Adams, 2nd president and mother of John Quincy Adams, 6th president. She married John Adams at the age of 20 and bore him five children. A strong supporter of her husband's political career, she was an advocate of women's rights and a chronicler of the customs of her day.

ABIGAIL ADAMS *First lady, wife of Pres. John Adams, mother of Pres. John Quincy Adams, and recorder of her times.*

Adams, Brooks (1848–1927) US historian, brother of Henry *Adams. He held that the success of a civilization is closely allied with its economics, and he applied Darwin's theory of survival of the fittest to the development of societies. His notable works include *The Law of Civilization and Decay* (1895) and *America's Economic Supremacy* (1900).

Adams, Charles Francis (1807–86) US diplomat; ambassador to Britain (1861–68). He was the grandson of John Adams and the son of John Quincy Adams. He was influential in keeping Britain neutral during the US Civil War and attempted to prevent British-built ships from joining the Confederate fleet, protesting against the dispatch of the *Alabama* (1862). He represented the US in the subsequent *Alabama* claims for compensation against Britain (1871).

Adams, Henry (1838–1918) US historian. After completing Harvard, he served as secretary to his father, Charles Francis Adams, in Washington and Britain. He returned to Harvard in 1870 to teach and edit the *North American Review*. After working as a radical political journalist, he became disillusioned with active politics and turned to fiction and history, writing a long history of early democracy in America (1889–91). His most influential works were *Mont Saint Michel and Chartres* (1913), a study of the unity of art and religion in the middle ages, and his autobiography, *The Education of Henry Adams* (1918).

Adams, James Truslow (1878–1949) US historian. A conservative, he extolled oldtime values and believed in interpreting facts and their interrelations. *The Founding of New England* (1921) earned him a Pulitzer Prize. Other works include *The Epic of America* (1931) and *The Living Jefferson* (1936).

Adams, John (1735–1826) US statesman; first vice president (1789–97) and second president of the US (1797–1801). A graduate of Harvard College and a lawyer in his native Massachusetts, he early became prominent in opposing British rule, attacking the Stamp Act, and serving on patriot committees. As a delegate to the first and second Continental Congresses (1774–78), he supported George *Washington as commander of the army and the passage of the Declaration of Independence. He was the main author (1780) of the Massachusetts constitution. With Benjamin *Franklin and John *Jay, he represented the US in the peace negotiations with Britain that ended the Revolutionary War (1783) and was subsequently US minister to Britain (1785–88). As vice president he played a pivotal role in the Senate, breaking the many tie votes of the era. Succeeding Washington as president, his disputes with Alexander *Hamilton, unpopular legislation, and conflicts with Vice President Thomas *Jefferson over US policy toward Revolutionary France all contributed to the loss of his personal popularity and that of his Federalist party. Adams was defeated by Jefferson in the election of 1800 and retired to his home in Quincy, Mass.

Adams, John Quincy (1767–1848) US statesman; sixth president of the US (1825–29), son of John *Adams. Educated in Europe (1778–80), he returned to the US, where he followed his father's example, attending Harvard and becoming a lawyer. A diplomat under Washington and his father, he was elected (1803) to the Senate, from which he resigned in 1808. His expertise in diplomacy was subsequently used as minister to Russia (1809–14), in negotiating the Treaty of Ghent to end the War of 1812, as minister to Britain (1815–17) and as President *Monroe's Secretary of State (1817–25). At the State Department he obtained Florida (1819) and helped promulgate the *Monroe Doctrine. In the disputed election of 1824, in which Andrew *Jackson had more electoral votes, Adams was elected president by the House of Representatives, thanks to the support of Henry *Clay. During his term Adams concentrated on internal improvement projects, but neglected politics. As a result he lost the election of 1828 to Jackson. Adams reentered politics as a representative in the House (1831–48), where he adamantly opposed the extension of slavery.

Adams, Richard (1920–   ) British novelist. He worked in the civil service from 1948 to 1974. His children's book *Watership Down* (1972), an epic treatment of the adventures of a community of rabbits, became an international bestseller. His later novels include *Shardik* (1974), *The Plague Dogs* (1977), and *The Girl in a Swing* (1980).

JOHN ADAMS *Second president (1797–1801) who also served his country as its first vice president.*

Adams, Samuel (1722–1803) US politician. A propagandist of revolution against Britain, he led the *Stamp Act agitation of 1765. His protests against British troops in Boston led to the Boston Massacre (1770) and he helped to plan the *Boston Tea Party (1773). He signed the Declaration of Independence (1776), served in the *Continental Congress until 1781, and was then governor of Massachusetts (1794–97).

Adams-Onís Treaty (or Transcontinental Treaty; 1819) An agreement between the United States and Spain that, in essence, gave Florida and the Oregon Territory to the US and Texas to Spain. Formulated by Secretary of State John Quincy Adams and Spain's Luis de Onís, the treaty erased any Spanish claims to land east of the Mississippi River in return for possession of Texas.

Adana 37 00N 35 19E A city in S Turkey, the fourth largest in the country. The prosperity of this important agricultural and industrial center comes from the surrounding fertile valleys, where much cotton is grown, and its position on the Anatolian-Arabian trade routes. It has a university (1973). Population (1990): 916,150.

adaptive radiation The process by which a uniform population of animals or plants evolves into a number of different forms over a period of time. The original population increases in size and spreads to occupy different habitats. It forms several subpopulations, each adapted to the particular conditions of its habitat. In time—and if the subpopulations differ sufficiently—a number of new species will be formed from the original stock. The Australian marsupials evolved in this way into burrowers, fliers, carnivores, herbivores, and many other different forms.

Addams, Jane (1860–1935) US social worker and reformer. She co-founded Hull House, a settlement house, in Chicago in 1889 and led the nation in attempts to improve living conditions in the slums and to reform child labor laws. She led pacifist and women's rights groups and shared the Nobel Peace Prize in 1931. Among her notable works is *Twenty Years at Hull House* (1910).

addax A rare African antelope, *Addax nasomaculatus*, about 40 in (1 m) high at the shoulder, that lives in small herds in the Sahara Desert. It has a grayish hide with a white patch on the face, long spirally twisted horns, and broad hooves suitable for running over loose sand.

adder A widely distributed European *viper, *Vipera berus*, about 31 in (80 cm) long, common in heathland areas. It is usually grayish with a broad black zigzag line along its back and black spots on its sides. Although venomous, its bite is rarely fatal. It is one of the three species of snakes found in Britain. The name adder is also given to a highly venomous Australian snake (death adder) of the cobra family and to some harmless North American snakes. *See also* puff adder.

addiction. *See* drug dependence.

Addington, Henry, 1st Viscount Sidmouth (1757–1844) British statesman; prime minister (1801–04), replacing Pitt the Younger. Addington was attacked for his management of the Napoleonic Wars and resigned. As home secretary (1812–21) he introduced stern measures against radical and working-class movements and he has been held responsible for the *Peterloo Massacre.

Addis Ababa 9 02N 38 43E The capital of Ethiopia, on a central plateau 8000 ft (2440 m) above sea level. It became the new capital of Ethiopia in 1889 and was capital of Italian East Africa (1936–41). Growth in the 20th century has been rapid. It is the country's administrative center and chief market place. Its major industries produce cement, tobacco, textiles, and shoes. A railroad line links the city with the port of Djibouti on the Gulf of Aden. It is also an important pan-African center. The National University was established in 1961. Population (1989 est): 1,732,000.

Addison, Joseph (1672–1719) British essayist and poet. In 1703 he published "The Campaign," a poem to celebrate Marlborough's victory at Blenheim. He began to contribute to Richard *Steele's journal, the *Tatler*, and in 1711 Addison and Steele founded the *Spectator*, for which Addison wrote essays famous for their clarity, wit, and elegance. He is also remembered for the tragedy *Cato* (1713).

Addison's disease A rare disease of the adrenal glands, first described by Thomas *Addison, characterized by a reduced secretion of corticosteroid hormones. This leads to weakness, intestinal upsets, darkening of the skin, low blood pressure, and collapse. Formerly fatal, Addison's disease can now be readily treated with synthetic steroids.

addition reaction A chemical reaction in which atoms or molecules combine to form a single molecule. It is frequently encountered in organic *chemistry, since many substances readily add to the double or triple bonds in alkenes, alkynes, aldehydes, etc. *Aromatic compounds are less susceptible, while *alkanes do not undergo addition. *See also* polymerization; substitution reaction.

additive process. *See* color.

Adelaide 34 56S 138 36E The capital of South Australia, on the Torrens River. Founded in 1837, the city was laid out in wide straight streets with extensive parklands separating the city from its suburbs. The University of Adelaide was founded in 1874. It is an important commercial and industrial center with harbor facilities at Port Adelaide. Industries include the manufacture of cars and textiles, oil refining, and electronics. Population (1991 est): 1,057,500.

Adélie Land. *See* Terre Adélie.

Aden 12 50N 45 03E The economic capital of Yemen, on the **Gulf of Aden**, an arm of the Indian Ocean connecting the main body with the Red Sea. Taken by the British in 1839, Aden was an important coaling station on the route to India through the Suez Canal (opened 1869). It became part of the Federation of Saudi Arabia in 1963 and was the scene of fighting between rival nationalist groups until 1968, when it became the capital of the independent republic of South Yemen. It was designated the economic when the two Yemens united in 1990. Economic activity centers on the port, which suffered from the closure of the Suez Canal (1967–75), and an oil refinery. Population (1986 est): 318,000

Adenauer, Konrad (1876–1967) German statesman. He was a successful Rhineland politician until the Nazi government forced him out of public life (1934) and imprisoned him (1934, 1944). In 1946 Adenauer re-emerged as chairman of the Christian Democratic Union (CDU) and became the first chancellor of the Federal Republic of Germany (1949–63). He presided over the German economic revival but was personally more concerned with foreign policy. He established that West Germany was part of W Europe, did much to restore its international prestige, and built up Franco-German friendship.

adenoids Two masses of tissue situated at the back of the nose. They consist of lymphatic tissue, which destroys disease-causing microbes in the throat. In children they are normally large, and when associated with recurrent throat infections or persistent breathing through the mouth are usually removed surgically. This operation is often combined with tonsillectomy (removal of the tonsils) as the tonsils tend to be infected at the same time.

adenosine triphosphate. *See* ATP.

adhesives Substances used for bonding materials together. Adhesives are usually colloidal solutions that set to a hard film adhering to the surfaces of the materials. There are many different types. Animal glues are forms of collagen (a protein) produced by boiling bones, hides, horns, etc., and drying the resulting jelly. They are water soluble and usually contain additives to preserve them. Vegetable glues (mucilages) are also water-soluble substances, such as starch, or gums, such as gum arabic or tragacanth. Other natural adhesives include water-glass, pitch, and rubber latex. In addition many synthetic resins are used as adhesives. **Thermoplastic adhesives** (polymers, such as polystyrene, asphalt, and polyvinyl compounds) remain soluble after setting and melt when heated; these are used where flexible bonding is needed, for example in attaching the soles of shoes, safety glass, sticky tape, etc. **Thermosetting adhesives** (condensation polymers, such as *epoxy resins) are insoluble, chemically inert, and will not melt. They are set by heat or by an added catalyst (hardener). They are used for bonding wood, paper, textiles, plastics, etc.

adiabatic process Any process in which heat neither enters nor leaves a system. Usually, such a process changes the temperature of the system. An example is the sudden compression of a gas, causing its temperature to rise. The compression is assumed to take place so quickly that the gas loses none of its acquired heat.

Adige River A river in Italy, rising in the N and flowing mainly SE, entering the Adriatic Sea near Po. Navigation is difficult because of its rapid current. Length: 220 mi (354 km).

Ádi Granth The sacred canonical scriptures of *Sikhism, compiled in 1604 by Arjun Mal (1581–1606). It consists of about 6000 hymns, mostly the work of the first five *gurus, together with the writings of some Bhakta saints and Muslim Sufis (*see* Sufism). The Sikhs do not venerate images but the *Ádi Granth* has itself become the object of worship.

Adirondack Mountains A mountain range in N New York state. It consists of a glaciated plateau rising to 5344 ft (1629 m) at Mount Marcy. Its scenic gorges, waterfalls, and many lakes make it a popular tourist area.

adjutant stork A large carrion-eating *stork, *Leptotilos dubius*, occurring in Asia and similar to the related *marabou. It has a white plumage with dark-gray back, wings, and tail, a short neck, and a heavy pointed bill. Its head and neck are naked and a bald pouch hangs from the throat. Order: *Ciconiiformes*.

ADJUTANT STORK *Standing about 5 ft (1.5m) tall, these grotesque birds congregate with vultures around animal carcasses, which provide their food.*

Adler, Alfred (1870–1937) Austrian psychiatrist, whose theories concerning the psychology of the individual introduced the concept of the inferiority complex. Initially an associate of Sigmund *Freud, Adler's views diverged from Freud's and by 1911 he had founded his own school of thought. Adler viewed each individual as an unique entity striving to compensate for feelings of inferiority resulting from physical or social disabilities (*The Neurotic Constitution*, 1912) and regarded sex as simply an opportunity to express dominance. Adler emphasized the importance of education and, in 1921, opened the first of his child-guidance clinics in Vienna.

Adler, Felix (1851–1933) German-born, US educator, who founded the Society for Ethical Culture (1876). Through the resulting ethical movement and in books, such as *An Ethical Philosophy of Life* (1918), he proclaimed the importance of morality in human affairs and advanced the view that moral considerations arose independently of any religious creeds. He instigated many educational and social reforms.

administrative law The law regulating the organization, responsibilities, and powers of a country's administrative bodies, such as the civil service, customs and excise, and social services. Many countries enforce this law through special courts, but in *common law countries it is dealt with in the ordinary courts.

Admiralty Court. *See* maritime law.

Admiralty Islands A group of about 40 islands in the SW Pacific Ocean, in Papua New Guinea in the Bismarck Archipelago. Copra and pearls are exported. The main island is Manus with the chief town, Lorengau. Area: about 800 sq mi (2000 sq km).

Adonis In Greek mythology, a youth from Cyprus, loved by *Aphrodite for his great beauty. *Zeus decreed that his time should be divided between Aphrodite on earth, Persephone, queen of the underworld, and himself. He was celebrated in many festivals as a vegetation god, his death and resurrection representing the seasonal decay and regeneration of nature.

adoption In law, the process whereby the natural parent's legal rights and obligations toward an unmarried *minor are transferred to another adult. The need for a male heir has traditionally been one of the prime motives for adoption and the welfare of the adopted child was not the main consideration. This was reflected in Roman Civil law, which subsequently influenced the adoption laws of a number of European and Latin-American countries. The increased effectiveness of birth control, the legalization of abortion, and the social acceptance of one-parent families has decreased the number of children available for adoption in recent years. However, greater emphasis, including publicity on television, has been given to finding adoptive homes for children with special needs, e.g. older children, children of mixed race, and the physically or mentally handicapped.

Adowa (Adwa *or* Aduwa) 14 02N 38 58E A town in N Ethiopia. Emperor Menelik II defeated the Italians nearby in 1896, halting their expansion into Ethiopia until 1935. It is a market center for agricultural produce, including grains, honey, and coffee. Population: 16,430.

adrenal glands Two small pyramid-shaped *endocrine glands in man and other mammals, one at the upper end of each of the kidneys. Each gland has an outer cortex, controlled by hormones secreted by the pituitary gland, and an inner medulla, controlled directly by the nervous system. The cortex secretes three classes of steroid hormones that regulate the balance of salts and water, the use of carbohydrates, and the activity of the sex glands (*see* corticosteroid). The medulla produces the hormones *adrenaline and *noradrenaline. *See also* Addison's disease; Cushing's syndrome.

adrenaline (*or* epinephrine) A hormone secreted by the central core (medulla) of the adrenal glands. A *catecholamine derived from the amino acid tyrosine, adrenaline increases heart rate, raises blood pressure, and increases the level of blood glucose. Its release is triggered by stress in preparation by the body for "fight or flight." Adrenaline is also secreted by nerve endings of the sympathetic nervous system. *See also* noradrenaline.

adrenocorticotrophic hormone. *See* ACTH.

Adrian, Edgar Douglas, 1st Baron (1889–1977) British physiologist, whose work was largely concerned with the electrical properties of the nervous system. He developed techniques for recording nerve impulses from single nerve fibers and later studied the electrical activity of the brain. He shared a Nobel Prize (1932) with Sir Charles *Sherrington.

Adrian IV (Nicholas Breakspear; c. 1100–59) Pope (1154–59). The only English pope, also known as Hadrian IV, he was unanimously elected after a career of papal service, leading the mission to the Scandinavian churches (1152). His claim that the Holy Roman Empire was held by papal grant occasioned a major quarrel with Emperor *Frederick Barbarossa, whom he refused to crown until Frederick had done homage for his office. Adrian also intervened in the internal politics of France and Sicily.

Adrianople, Battle of (378 AD) The battle in which the Eastern Roman emperor *Valens was defeated and killed defending Adrianople (now Edirne, Turkey) against the Visigoths. The Huns had driven the Visigoths across the Danube in 376 AD, prompting them to attack the Romans at Adrianople.

Adriatic Sea A northern arm of the Mediterranean Sea, extending between Italy and Yugoslavia and its former republics of Slovenia, Croatia, and Bosnia-Herzegovina for about 465 mi (750 km). Its principal ports are Brindisi, Bari, Venice, Trieste, and Rijeka. The coasts are strikingly different: the Italian is flat and sandy, the other is rocky and irregular with many off-shore islands.

adsorption The production of a layer of atoms or molecules of a substance on a solid or liquid surface. The adsorbed atoms or molecules may be strongly held by chemical bonds (**chemisorption**), in which case the adsorbed layer is usually only one molecule thick. Adsorption may also occur through weaker physical forces (**physisorption**), often giving rise to several molecular layers.

adult education Education of all kinds for adults, but usually the various forms of education provided for adults once their formal education has ceased. Adult education may be specifically vocational or assist in general cultural development.

adultery Voluntary sexual relations between a married person and someone who is not that person's husband or wife. In some jurisdictions, also, a distinction is made between double and single adultery, the former being committed where both parties are married to other persons, the latter where only one is so married. In some states, adultery is a crime. Adultery is rarely relied on as a grounds for divorce since no-fault divorce became popular.

advaita (Sanskrit: nondualism) The Hindu philosophical view, derived from the *Upanishads, that the individual soul and ultimate reality are indivisibly one; the apparent separation of subject and object, or spirit and matter, is only illusion. Realization of this truth leads to liberation. Some thinkers see all phenomena, including the self, as altogether unreal; others maintain that the existence of the soul is qualified by, or dependent upon, *Brahman, who alone is fully real. Chief among the proponents of *advaita* is the 8th century philosopher *Shankara.

Advent (from Latin: *adventus*, coming) The first season of the *church year, leading up to *Christmas. It begins on the Sunday nearest St Andrew's Day (Nov 30). From the 6th century it has been observed as a solemn preparation for celebrating Christ's birth and for his Second Coming.

adventists Several Protestant Christian denominations that stress a belief in the imminent Second Coming of Christ. In the US adventism began in 1831 with the millenarian preaching of William Miller (1782–1849), who predicted the Second Coming for 1843–44, but postponed the date when his prediction proved false. In the UK a similar movement was founded in 1832 as the Catholic Apostolic Church. There have been numerous adventist movements, the Seventh-Day Adventists being the principal church today.

advertising The publicizing of a product or service, usually in order to increase sales. In some cases it is used to discourage sales (e.g. of cigarettes) or to promote noncommercial activities (e.g. highway safety). Although some 3% of the US *gross national product is spent on advertising, there is no evidence to show that advertising actually persuades people to buy things they do not want. Consumer advertising seeks to sell one branded product at the expense of others (e.g. toothpaste), to publicize a manufacturer's name when his product is the same as everyone else's (e.g. gasoline), or to persuade people that a category of products (e.g. wool) should be bought in preference to some other category (e.g. man-made fibers). Trade advertising is restricted to specific sections of the public (e.g. doctors or caterers). Advertisements may be informative, assisting purchasers to make a choice between products, or persuasive, in which case it may exaggerate some aspect of a product by appealing to the purchaser's image of himself. Advertising is carried by newspapers, by television and radio, by public transportation, and at the point of sale. The industry is largely in the hands of advertising agencies, which work closely with their clients researching, copywriting, and producing the advertisements as well as reserving space in the press and time for broadcasting.

Adygei An autonomous region (*oblast*) in Russia. It was formed in 1922 for the Muslim Adyghian people. It has valuable forests and oil and natural-gas deposits. Area: 2934 sq mi (7600 sq km). Population (1991 est): 437,000. Capital: Maikop.

Adzhar Autonomous Republic (*or* Adzharia) An administrative division in Georgia, on the Black Sea. It is mainly mountainous with a subtropical coastal plain. A popular holiday region, it is also the country's main producer of tea and citrus fruits. Industries include shipyards and oil refining. Area: 1160 sq mi (3000 sq km). Population (1991 est): 382,000. Capital: Batumi.

Aechmea A genus of herbaceous plants (over 140 species), native to South America, where they grow upon the branches of trees (but are not parasitic). From the center of a rosette of spiny-toothed leaves, 12–24 in (30–60 cm) long, grow flower stalks bearing showy red or yellow flowers, often with blue tips. Some species, for example *A. fulgens* and *A. fasciata*, are cultivated as ornamental greenhouse plants. Family: *Bromeliaceae* (pineapples, etc.).

Aedes A genus of mosquitoes, widespread in the tropics and subtropics, that are important as vectors of diseases of man and livestock including yellow fever and dengue (transmitted by *A. aegypti*) and Rift Valley fever (transmitted by *A. cabalus*).

Aegae (modern name: Vergina) The capital, with *Pella, of ancient Macedon (*see* Macedonia). During the 1970s archaeological work on a nearby mound revealed tombs believed to be those of *Philip II of Macedon and his immediate family. Treasures found here include magnificent wall paintings, golden jewelry, and silver vases.

Aegean civilizations The prehistoric settlements on the islands of the Aegean Sea (between mainland Greece and Asia Minor). At the beginning of the Bronze Age (c. 3000 BC) an influx of immigrants to the *Cyclades islands (S Aegean) brought a high level of sophistication and prosperity, which can be seen from the excavations on Thera (*or* Santorini). The subsequent civilization of *Minoan Crete was at its greatest between the 17th and 15th centuries BC. At the end of the 15th century the related *Mycenaean civilization of mainland Greece began to assert its supremacy, lasting until about 1200.

Aegean Sea A section of the NE Mediterranean Sea, lying between Greece and Turkey and containing many islands, including the Cyclades, Dodecanese, and N Sporades.

Aegina (Modern Greek name: Aíyina) A Greek island in the Aegean Sea, one of the largest in the Saronic group lying SSW of Piraeus. It achieved its greatest prosperity in the 5th century BC but fell to Athens (458), which later expelled all its inhabitants. Today it serves as a holiday resort for Athenians. Area: 33 sq mi (85 sq km).

Aegina, Gulf of. *See* Saronic Gulf.

Aegis In Greek mythology, a breastplate worn by Zeus and his daughter Athena. At its center was an image of *Medusa, which petrified enemies.

Aelfric (c. 955–c. 1020) Anglo-Saxon prose writer and Abbot of Eynsham from 1005. His *Catholic Homilies* (990–92), collections of sermons, and his *Lives of the Saints* (996–97) were important contributions to the spread of learning in the 10th century. He also wrote a Latin grammar, thus acquiring his nickname, Grammaticus.

Aeneas A legendary Trojan leader, son of *Anchises and *Aphrodite, and hero of Virgil's *Aeneid*. After the Greek victory in the Trojan War, he sailed away from burning Troy with his family and other survivors and was shipwrecked near Carthage. He fell in love with *Dido but abandoned her to continue his divinely ordained voyage to Italy, where he founded what was to become Rome.

Aeneas Silvius. *See* Pius II.

Aeolian harp A musical instrument named for the Greek wind god *Aeolus, consisting of a wooden resonating box strung with gut strings of varying thicknesses. When hung in the open air it produces chordal sounds that vary according to the wind pressure.

Aeolus The Greek god of the winds and ruler of Aeolia. In Homer's *Odyssey* he gave Odysseus a bag containing contrary winds; Odysseus' companions untied it, causing his ship to be blown back to Aeolia.

Aepyornis A genus of extinct flightless birds (ratites), also called elephant birds because of their huge size and bulk. They are known only from fossil bones and eggs found in Madagascar.

aerobe An organism that requires free oxygen for oxidation of foodstuffs to release chemical energy in the process of *respiration. Most living organisms are aerobes; exceptions include certain yeasts and bacteria. These organisms, called **anaerobes,** produce chemical energy by a series of reactions in which free oxygen is not required. **Obligate anaerobes** never use oxygen for respiration, while **facultative anaerobes** normally use oxygen but are able to switch to anaerobic respiration when free oxygen is deficient.

aerodynamics The study of the behavior and flow of air around objects. As air is a viscous fluid any object moving through it experiences a drag. Aerodynamics is important in the design of vehicles traveling at more than 31 mph (50 kph), buildings and bridges, engines, furnaces, as well as aircraft (*see* aeronautics) and missiles. Proposed cross-sections of models of such objects are often tested in wind tunnels or in water, smoke or colored dyes being used to trace the flow of the fluid around the surface and to measure the lift and drag forces. This enables the best streamlined shapes to be found in order to avoid *turbulence.

aeronautics The science and history (*see also* aircraft) of flight. An object flying through air is subject to four basic forces: its own weight (vertically downward as a result of gravity), lift (to counterbalance its weight and keep it in the air), thrust (to force it through the air), and drag (resulting from friction between the body and the air). Birds and insects use their wings to provide both lift and thrust; man, in his heavier-than-air, fixed-wing craft, uses an airfoil to provide the lift and an *internal-combustion engine (propeller or jet) to provide the thrust (*see also* gliders). *Helicopters use rotating airfoils to provide lift, while *rockets use no lift surfaces, the jet of expanding gas providing both lift and thrust. Man's lighter-than-air craft (*see* airships; balloons) use helium or hydrogen to reduce the craft's weight in relation to the volume of air it displaces to such an extent that the lift is provided by buoyancy. The use of airfoils as lift surfaces depends on *Bernoulli's theorem, according to which the total energy of a flowing fluid remains constant; thus, if the velocity of the fluid increases, its pressure decreases in proportion. An airfoil is a wing so shaped that (at subsonic speeds) air is accelerated over its rounded leading edge and curved upper surface, causing a reduced pressure above it. A smaller reduction in air velocity on its underside causes a slightly increased pressure below it. The combination of these pressure differences provides the lift. The design of practical aircraft wings has to take into account a number of complex factors, including suitable streamlining to avoid *turbulence in the airflow, stability over different angles of attack, the provision of suitable control surfaces (flaps, ailerons, etc.), and adequate strength and rigidity. At supersonic speeds these forces are somewhat altered (*see* sound barrier) and the airfoil has to be more sweptback and more streamlined. At hypersonic speeds (i.e. in excess of five times the speed of sound) the *aerodynamics changes again and blunter noses and even smaller wings are needed.

aerosol A colloidal suspension of particles of liquid or solid in a gaseous medium. Fog, mist, and smoke are common natural examples. By means of pressurized packages, aerosols can be produced from a huge range of substances, including insecticides, paints, hairsprays, etc. In these, the substance is mixed with an easily liquefied gas (often a fluorinated or chlorinated hydrocarbon), which acts as a propellant when the pressure is released. Fears have been expressed that fluorinated hydrocarbons, being lighter than air, could cause chain reactions in the upper atmosphere, which could destroy the *ozone layer. As this layer protects life on earth from the sun's ultraviolet radiation, measures have been encouraged worldwide to ban the use of fluorinated hydrocarbons in aerosols. *See* colloids.

Aeschines (c. 397–c. 322 BC) Athenian orator, who was an opponent of *Demosthenes. He was part of the Greek embassy to Philip of Macedon that in 350 negotiated peace, for which Demosthenes tried unsuccessfully in 343 to convict him of treason. In 330 Aeschines was defeated in his attempt to prevent Demosthenes being awarded a crown for his services to Athens and he retired to Rhodes.

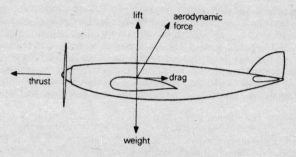

forces acting on aircraft

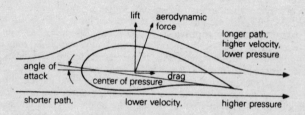

cross-section of air foil

AERONAUTICS *The forces acting on an aircraft. The airfoil cross-section shows how the lift, which keeps it in the air, results from the passage of the airfoil through the air, causing a lower pressure above it and a higher pressure below it.*

Aeschylus (c. 525–456 BC) Greek tragic dramatist, the first of the great trio of Athenian tragedians that included Sophocles and Euripides. He wrote over 80 plays, of which only 7 survive: *The Persians* (472), *Seven Against Thebes* (467), the *Oresteia* trilogy (*Agamemnon, Libation Bearers*, and *Eumenides*, 458), *Suppliant Women* and *Prometheus Bound*. His introduction of a second actor, allowing dialogue and action independent of the chorus, and his innovations in costume and scenery, transformed the conventions of drama. His deeply religious plays dramatize the perpetual conflict between human passions and divine will.

Aesculapius The Greek god of medicine, son of Apollo and Coronis. He was taught medicine by the centaur Chiron. The sick, believing in Aesculapius' power to cure them through dreams, came to sleep in his temples, the chief of which were at Epidaurus and on the island of Cos.

Aesop The supposed author of a collection of Greek fables, said by Herodotus to be a slave from Samos who lived in the 6th century BC. Originating in popular folklore, the fables are anecdotal stories whose animal characters are used to illustrate a moral point. The Roman poet Phaedrus popularized them in the 1st century AD, and the French poet LaFontaine wrote more sophisticated versions in the 17th century.

Aesthetic movement A British literary and artistic movement of the late 19th century, summarized in the slogan "art for art's sake." Reacting against the ugliness of industrialism and against contemporary utilitarian social philosophies, its followers sought to create beauty for its own sake, self-consciously divorcing art from life. Their artistic precursors were the *Pre-Raphaelite Brotherhood, formed in 1848, whose emphasis on pure aesthetics was continued by Swinburne, William Morris, and others, culminating in the work of Oscar Wilde, Aubrey Beardsley, and the other contributors to the periodical *The Yellow Book* (1894–97).

aesthetics The philosophical study of art and critical judgments about art. It includes questions concerning the nature of beauty and general questions about ascribing value—what we mean when we say that a work of art is good and how we arrive at standards of judgment. Objective views hold that beauty or value is in the object and that aesthetic judgments are true or false. Subjective views see value as something an observer brings to the work of art—it may be purely a matter of personal preference or, as *Kant held, something that can be universally agreed on. There are also various approaches to evaluation, including analytical views that discuss the standards and logic of evaluation, and those that consider the social or moral significance of art.

Aeth-. For names beginning Aeth *see* Eth-.

Aetius, Flavius (d. 454 AD) Roman general. After a checkered early career, he became virtual ruler of the western Empire, dominating the emperor, Valentian III (reigned 425–55). Aetius defeated the Huns under Attila at the *Catalaunian Plains (451) but was powerless to halt their invasion of Italy. He was subsequently murdered by Valentian.

Aetolia A region of ancient Greece N of the Gulf of Corinth. In 326 BC the tribes of Aetolia formed the **Aetolian League**, a federation that became a leading military power in Greece. In 27 BC Aetolia was included in the Roman province of Achaea. It forms part of the modern department of Aetolia and Acarnania.

Afars A Cushitic-speaking people of the Horn of Africa, also known as Danakils. They are mainly nomads, herding goats and camels. Their social organization is complicated, with patrilineal kinship groups, age sets each under the authority of a chief, and a class division between the Asaimara (red men) nobles and the Adoimara (white men) lower class. Afars are nominally Muslim but the influence of earlier Cushitic beliefs persists.

Afars and the Issas, French territory of the. *See* Djibouti, Republic of.

Affenpinscher A breed of toy dog, also called monkey terrier. Small but sturdy, it has small erect ears, a short tail, and a short usually black coat with long hair on the legs and face. Height: 9–11 in (23.5–28 cm).

Afghan hound A breed of large dog having long legs, large drooping ears, and a very long, silky coat, which may be of any color. The Afghan probably originated in ancient Egypt and was later used in Afghanistan to hunt leopards and gazelles. Height: 27–29 in (68–73 cm) (dogs); 24–26 in (61–66 cm) (bitches).

Afghani, Jamal ad-Din al- (1838–97) Muslim religious and political reformer. Of obscure origins, al-Afghani lived at various times in Istanbul, Egypt, Paris, India, and Persia. He argued for the unity of all Muslims and resistance to European interference in the Muslim countries. He has been seen as a forerunner of Arab nationalists.

Afghanistan, Democratic Republic of A state in central Asia. The country is mountainous, the Hindu Kush range rising over 20,000 ft (6000 m). The only lower-lying areas are along the Amu Darya (ancient name: Oxus) River in the N and the delta of the Helmand River in the SW. The population consists of mixed ethnic groups, the largest being the *Pathans and the Tadzhiks. *Economy*: largely agricultural, with stock raising (especially of fat-tailed sheep) having particular importance. There has been industrial development in recent years, especially since the discovery of natural gas in the N. The first natural-gas power station was opened in 1972. Textiles are important, especially carpet making, and attempts are being made to develop the considerable mineral resources and improve communications. Building of asphalt roads was carried out through the 1980s with US and Soviet help. There are still no railroads, although plans have been investigated for a line connecting Kabul with Iran. Main exports include Persian lambskins, fruit, cotton, wool, carpets, and natural gas. *History*: Before the opening up of international sea routes in the 15th century Afghanistan was an important center on the overland routes across central Asia. For centuries under the rule of different powers, including the Mongol, Genghis Khan, in the 13th century, it became an independent kingdom in 1747. During the 19th century Afghanistan became involved in the struggle between Britain and Russia for influence in central Asia. Following two wars with Britain (1839–42 and 1878–80) it became a buffer state between British India and Russia, with Britain controlling its foreign policy. In 1919, under the leadership of *Amanollah Khan, Afghanistan attempted to free itself of British influence, which led to further fighting between the two countries. This third Afghan War led to the recognition of Afghanistan as an independent state in 1921. In 1926 Amanollah declared himself king. He was deposed in 1929 by a brigand chief, Habibullah, who was, in turn, defeated by Nader Khan. When the latter was assassinated in 1933 he was succeeded by his son, King Zahir. During the years following World War II there has been considerable friction with Pakistan over the question of an independent Pathan state in Pakistan. In 1973 the monarchy was overthrown by Mohammed Daud, a cousin of King Zahir, and in 1977 a constitution was approved setting up a republic with Daud as president. In 1978 he was killed in a military coup and a new government under Nur Mohammed Taraki was set up by members of the Marxist People's Democratic Party. Two further coups occurred in 1979; in the second Babrak Karmal was brought to power with Soviet aid. Soviet military occupation of Afghanistan provoked worldwide condemnation and US withdrawal from the 1980 Olympic Games in Moscow. The US increased arms supplies to the Afghan rebels.

By the mid 1980s the total Soviet military and economic investment in Afghanistan over the course of the conflict was high and continued to mount. In 1984 the USSR boycotted the Los Angeles Olympics, despite US efforts to urge Soviet participation. Resistance in Afghanistan to the Soviet Union and Babrak Karmal's puppet government continued, and by the mid 1980s the military situation was stalemated. In 1986 the USSR announced that it would gradually withdraw its troops. The flood of millions of Afghan refugees into neighboring Pakistan created a growing social and political problem for that nation. With the breakup of the USSR in 1991, aid ceased, as it did from the US. Afghanistan's Communist government toppled in 1992, and an interim coalition government came to power. Conflicts among the many rival factions in the country continued to cause unrest through 1993, although an interim constitution was agreed upon. Joint official languages: Pushtu and Dari Persian. Official currency: afghani of 100 puls. Area: 250,000 sq mi (657,500 sq km). Population (1989 est): 15,600,000. Capital: Kabul.

aflatoxin. *See* Aspergillus.

Africa The second largest continent in the world. Linked to SW Asia by the Isthmus of Suez, it is of irregular triangular shape with more than two thirds of its area lying to the N of the equator, which runs across the center of the continent. Except for Australia, its relief is the most uniform of all the continents, consisting principally of two well-defined physical regions: a S tableland and a lower but still elevated plain in the N. A notable feature of the NE is the *Great Rift Valley, which contains the most extensive system of freshwater lakes in the world after North America, as well as the continent's highest point, Mount *Kilimanjaro. Madagascar, the fourth largest island in the world, lies off the SE coast but there are few island groups. The principal rivers are the Nile, Niger, Zaïre, and Zambezi. Africa's climate and vegetation vary considerably from the arid desert of the Sahara to the tropical rainforest of the Congo basin. The inhabitants of Africa are principally of Negroid origin, although the originators of the Berber language group remain dominant in N Africa and the Sahara and there are a few Cushite-speaking peoples in the NE. *History*: Africa's long history has been substantiated by Louis *Leakey's finds of hominoid man at Olduvai Gorge. The earliest African civilization was established in Egypt in about 3400 BC. Also in N Africa the Phoenicians founded Carthage (9th century BC), later conquered by the Romans (146 BC). From the 7th century AD Arab influence was strong and Islam spread with the trans-Saharan and East African coastal trade. Several African kingdoms and empires emerged during this period, notably the Sudanese empires of Ghana, Mali, and Songhai. From the 15th century European exploration and exploitation began, initiated by the Portuguese. Slaves, ivory, and gold were exported from Africa from the 17th to the late 19th centuries, during which time the Atlantic slave trade was active, over 10 million slaves being shipped to the plantations of America and the West Indies. This enforced migration considerably changed the composition of the American and West Indian populations. From 1880 to 1912 most of Africa was partitioned by the European powers, which imposed political boundaries upon the continent that bore no relationship to former political and social organizations; this resulted in longstanding problems. In the 1950s there was movement toward independence and Africa now consists chiefly of independent nations. Famine and political and social unrest have characterized modern Africa. In 1983 the worst drought in 100 years caused severe crop loss and consequent shortages of food and consumer and industrial goods. A declining balance of trade, resulting from poor exports and the oil glut, forced many African nations to borrow from the International Monetary Fund (IMF) and from Western lenders. In the 1980s Africa saw the worst fiscal crisis since the beginning of its independence movement. Under pressure from the IMF and the lending nations, governments of many African states imposed austere economic measures on their people. In the early 1990s the critical political issues were the growing power of fundamentalist Muslims in northern Africa and the progress toward black majority rule in South Africa. Area: about 11,700,000 sq mi (30,300,000 sq km). Population (1991 est): 817,000,000.

African art The traditional art of the peoples of sub-Saharan or Black Africa. Among these peoples the visual or plastic arts were not distinguished one from another or from the religious and cultural life of the community. Artists, however, were professionals who enjoyed a respected and sometimes priestly and hereditary status, working on commission or with royal patronage. They produced ceremonial masks, figures for use in the ancestor cults, weapons, furnishings, and everyday utensils. Carving and sculpture in wood, ivory, copper alloys, terracotta, and clay were the dominant forms, but artistic skills extended to textiles, basketry, leatherwork, and wall and body painting; they also included the mastery of sophisticated techniques, such as the *cire perdue process of bronze-casting. Most of the extant examples of traditional art are less than 200 years old, but these are often representative of much earlier developments. Art flourished in the area of West Africa roughly extending from Senegal and Mali in the N, through the countries bordering the Atlantic, to N Angola and Zambia and E to the chain of great lakes. Within this area a large number of styles are evident. The Dogon of Mali are noted for their stylized rectangular wooden masks. The Yoruba of Nigeria and Dahomey (now Benin) made naturalistic human heads and figures, and similar figures in brass and terracotta were produced at the Yoruba center, Ife, in Nigeria, as early as the 12th century. The skill in casting metal passed from Ife to Dahomey, where the Edo people produced brass reliefs and sculpture. The Baule of the Ivory Coast made finely polished masks and figures; they and the Ashanti of Ghana are the only African people to have used gold leaf to cover sculptures and other carved wooden objects. In the Congo region, ancestral figures, masks, fetishes, and other decorated objects were made in great profusion, chiefly in human and animal forms that were rendered not naturalistically but symbolically, as part of a magical or religious view of reality. It was this quality in African art that perhaps most appealed to many 20th century western artists, including Picasso, Modigliani, and Epstein, upon whom it has had a profound effect.

African hunting dog A large, long-legged, wild dog, *Lycaon pictus*, also called the Cape hunting dog, that is widespread south of the Sahara. It is about 24 in (60 cm) high at the shoulder and has a heavy head, large ears, and a short coat mottled in black, yellow, and white. These dogs hunt in packs, chasing their prey (usually gazelle and young wildebeest) until it tires and can be pulled down.

African languages A geographical classification of the heterogeneous languages spoken in the African continent. The *Hamito-Semitic group extends across N Africa from Mauritania to Somalia. The *Nilo-Saharan group is spoken in many dialects in central Africa, and the *Niger-Congo languages, many of them *Bantu languages, cover most of the area S of the Sahara. In S Africa the *Khoisan languages survive. There are up to a thousand indigenous languages of the continent as well as the European languages (*English, *Afrikaans, *French, *Portuguese) imported by colonizers. *Malagasy, a language of *Austronesian origin, is spoken in Madagascar. *Swahili is an important lingua franca in East Africa. Certain African languages are unique in using click sounds in their phonology; predominance of certain consonantal groups (kp, gb, mb, nd) is also common in Africa.

African violet A flowering plant, *Saintpaulia ionantha*, native to tropical East Africa. The plants have rosettes of hairy, often deeply ridged, leaves, bear clusters of pink, blue, purple, or white flowers, and grow to a height of 4–6 in (10–15 cm). Many varieties and hybrids have been developed as ornamentals. Family: *Gesneriaceae*.

Afrikaans. *See* Afrikaner.

Afrikaner A South African of Dutch or *Huguenot descent. The Afrikaners comprise about 60% of the Republic's white population. Formerly called "Boers" (farmers), they have undergone considerable urbanization since the 1930s. In the 18th and 19th centuries they led a seminomadic life, resisting governmental control from Cape Town. Their two independent states, the South African Republic and the Orange Free State, came under British rule after the second *Boer War. Their language, Afrikaans, derives, but is distinct from Dutch and together with English has been an official language of South Africa since 1925. *See also* Great Trek.

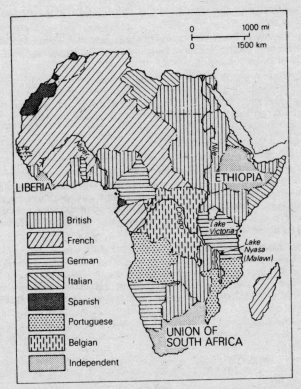

AFRICA *In the scramble for Africa the European powers annexed most of the continent. The map shows the positions in 1914.*

Afro-Asiatic languages. *See* Hamito-Semitic languages.

Agade. *See* Akkad.

Agadir 30 30N 9 40W A port in SW Morocco, on the Atlantic coast. Its growth has followed the development of the port and inland resources. An earthquake in 1960 destroyed much of the town and killed about 12,000 people. Population (1982): 110,479.

Aga Khan IV (1936–) Imam (leader) of the *Ismaili sect of Muslims (1957–), succeeding his grandfather Aga Khan III.

agama A common African broad-headed lizard belonging to the family *Agamidae* (50 species). 12–18 in (30–45 cm) long, agamas have a thick body and a tapering tail and feed on insects. The common agama (*Agama agama*) is variously colored: dominant males have a brick-red head, blue body and legs, and banded tail; other males are duller colored, like the females.

Agamemnon King of Mycenae and commander of the Greek army in the Trojan War. His quarrel with Achilles is the main theme of Homer's *Iliad*. After his return from Troy with Cassandra, the captured daughter of King Priam, he was murdered by his wife Clytemnestra and her lover Aegisthus. The subsequent vengeance of his son Orestes is the central theme of *Aeschylus' *Oresteia* trilogy.

Agana 13 28N 144 45E The capital of Guam in the W Pacific Ocean, in the Mariana Islands. The University of Guam was established here in 1952. Population (1990): 1139.

Agapanthus A genus of herbaceous plants native to South Africa and cultivated for ornament in greenhouses and tropical gardens. *A. africanus* (African lily) has long, strap-shaped leaves and large clusters of blue, funnel-shaped flowers borne on a tall stalk. There are many cultivated varieties and hybrids. Family: *Amaryllidaceae*.

agar-agar A gelatinous substance obtained from seaweed. A solution in water sets to a firm jelly, which is used for growing bacteria.

agaric A fungus belonging to a large family (*Agaricaceae*) found throughout the world. The group includes many edible mushrooms, such as the white mushroom (*Agaricus bisporus*) and field mushroom (*A. campestris*), as well as the poisonous death cap (*see* Amanita). The visible part of the fungus consists of a stipe (stalk) bearing a cap with gills on the undersurface. Class: *Basidiomycetes*. *See also* fly agaric; mushroom.

Agassiz, Jean Louis Rodolphe (1807–73) Swiss natural historian. Agassiz's early work centered on the study of extinct species, fossilization, and glaciation. His later theories on animal species were contrary to those of Charles Darwin. In his *Essay on Classification* (1859) he argued that organisms were immutable and independent of each other and that there was no possibility of evolution from one source. As professor of zoology at Harvard University, his innovative teaching methods revolutionized the study of natural science in the US. His son **Alexander Agassiz** (1835–1910) was a marine zoologist and mining engineer. His copper mine became noted for its modern and enlightened management. He was a benefactor to various biological institutions and founded his own research station, from which he mounted expeditions to study marine fauna and the sea bed.

agate A banded or concentrically patterned form of *chalcedony. The banding is due to intermittent deposition in rock cavities and the colors, ranging from white, milky blue, yellow, and brown to red, are due to traces of mineral or organic coloring matter. Being hard, it is used for mortars for grinding. It is also used for ornamental purposes, for which the stone may be artificially dyed.

Agathocles (361–289 BC) Tyrant (317–304) and King (304–289) of Syracuse. After seizing power he gained control of E Sicily but fled to Africa after his defeat (311) by the Carthaginians. By 304 he had brutally pacified the Sicilian opposition and took the title of king. He died without establishing a dynasty.

Agave A genus of plants (about 300 species) of the S US and tropical America, many of which are widely grown for ornament. Agaves have a basal tuft of thick fleshy, sometimes toothed, leaves and a cluster of flowers that—in some species—grows on a tall stalk (up to 40 ft [12 m] high). Growth is slow—it may be 60 or more years before flowers are produced; after flowering the plant dies. Several species are commercially important as a source of fiber, especially *sisal; the fermented juice of others is used as an alcoholic drink (pulque) or distilled to produce spirits (*see* tequila). Family: *Agavaceae* (or *Amaryllidaceae*). *See also* century plant.

Agee, James (1909–55) US poet, novelist, and film critic. After graduating from Harvard he published a book of poems, *Permit Me Voyage* (1934), and wrote influential film reviews for various magazines. *Let Us Now Praise Fa-

mous Men (1941), in collaboration with the photographer Walker Evans, is a bitter account of the lives of Alabama sharecroppers. He also produced two autobiographical novels, *The Morning Watch* (1951) and *A Death in the Family* (1957, Pulitzer Prize), and several filmscripts.

AGAVE *The leaves of this plant are coated with wax. Only 2–3 grow per year and they store large reserves of food materials.*

Agency for International Development (AID) US government agency that carries out economic assistance programs to developing countries to help develop resources, increase productivity, increase quality of life, and promote economic and political stability. Established by the Foreign Assistance Act of 1961.

Age of Reason. *See* Enlightenment.

age set A recognized group of persons, usually males initiated at the same time, that is an important feature of the organization of many primitive societies. Each age set may pass through a series of stages (age grades) to which are assigned various functions requiring abilities dependent upon age, such as physical strength, experience, and wisdom. Typically there will be one or more grades of warriors and of elders who exercise political and often ritual authority. *See also* initiation rites.

Agesilaus II (444–360 BC) King of Sparta (c. 399–360). A noted general, he achieved some success against the Persians in Asia Minor (396–395) and against the Boeotians at Coronea (394). His subsequent diplomatic activities contributed to Sparta's disastrous defeat by the Thebans at Leuctra (371). Xenophon wrote a memoir of Agesilaus.

agglomerate A rock composed of a mixture of coarse angular fragments and finer-grained material formed by volcanic explosions; it is usually found in or near the volcanic vent.

Agha Mohammad Khan (1742–97) Shah of Persia (1796–97), who founded the Qajar dynasty (1796–1925). The chief (1758) of one of the clans of the Qajar tribe, he made himself ruler of the whole of Persia and was crowned in 1796. He was the first ruler to make Tehran his capital.

Agincourt, Battle of (Oct 25, 1415) The battle that took place during the *Hundred Years' War at Agincourt (now in the Pas-de-Calais), in which the French were defeated by an English army led by Henry V. The decisive English victory, which owed much to their outstanding archers, was achieved with not more than 1600 dead; the French may have lost as many as 6000 men.

aging (*or* senescence) The degenerative process in an organism that precedes death. In man aging is characterized by a gradual decline in the efficiency of the repair mechanisms of the body tissues, leading to increased susceptibility to disease; it is also associated with a reduction and then loss of fertility. In some elderly people there is marked physical and mental deterioration (senility). There are several theories to account for the aging process. Some maintain that it is due to the accumulation of errors in metabolism brought about by faulty protein synthesis in the cells; others that aging—particularly in plants after flowering and some animals after reproduction—is a genetically programmed event.

Agnes, St (4th century AD) Roman virgin and martyr. Nothing certain is known about her life, but according to legend she was martyred under Diocletian for refusing to marry and subsequently resisting plans to make her a prostitute. Feast day: Jan 21. Emblem: a lamb.

Agnesi, Maria Gaetana (1718–99) Italian mathematician and philosopher. A child prodigy, Agnesi became the first woman to occupy a chair of mathematics when she was appointed to that at Bologna University in 1750. On the death of her father in 1752, she devoted herself to religion and charitable work. The curve $x^2y = a^2 (a - y)$ is known as the "Witch of Agnesi" because she called it a *versiera* (Latin: turning), a word also meaning witch in colloquial Italian.

Agnew, Spiro T(heodore) (1918–   ) US Republican politician; vice president (1969–73), who gained notoriety for his attacks on the critics of President Nixon. A lawyer, he was elected governor of Maryland in 1966 before becoming Nixon's running mate. He was accused of taking bribes as governor and vice president, and in 1973 a federal tax case forced him to resign his office. He was given a suspended prison sentence and fined $10,000.

Agnon, Shmuel Yosef (Samuel Josef Czaczkes; 1888–1970) Jewish novelist, born in Galicia, who settled in Palestine in 1907. His treatment of contemporary Jewish themes in *The Day Before Yesterday* (1945) and other works was influenced by folklore and traditional religious literature. In 1966 he shared the Nobel Prize.

agnosticism The philosophical view that doubts the existence of God and other spiritual phenomena and claims that even if they do exist it is impossible to know anything about them. Although this position occurs sporadically throughout history, the term was apparently coined by T. H. *Huxley in 1869. Agnosticism was subsequently enthusiastically embraced by rationalists, who hesitated on philosophical or social grounds to adopt outright *atheism. Agnosticism is now frequently loosely used to mean neither knowing nor caring about the supernatural world.

Agora A central feature of ancient Greek town planning. Similar to the Roman *forum, the primary function of the agora was as the town market. In addition, however, it also became the main social and political meeting place. Together with the acropolis, it normally contained the most important buildings of the town.

agoraphobia. *See* phobia.

agouti A rabbit-sized rodent belonging to a genus (*Dasyprocta*; 13 species) of Central and South American forests. Agoutis have long legs, small ears, and a very short hairless tail. The hair on the rump is often long and brightly colored and can stand erect when the animal is alarmed. Agoutis feed on leaves, roots, and berries and are commonly eaten by the Indians. Family: *Dasyproctidae* (agoutis and pacas); suborder: *Hystricomorpha*.

Agra 27 09N 78 00E A city in India, in Uttar Pradesh on the River Jumna. Former capital of the Mogul Empire (1566–69 and 1601–58), it fell to the British in 1803 and from 1835 until 1862 was capital of the North-West Provinces. Notable buildings include the celebrated *Taj Mahal and a fine 16th century fort. Its university was established in 1927. A major commercial, industrial, and communications center, it produces carpets. Population (1991): 899,195.

agranulocytosis The condition resulting from a deficiency or absence of certain white blood cells (called granulocytes). Agranulocytosis may be caused by an allergic reaction to drugs, cytotoxic drugs (which damage the bone marrow), and severe infection. Symptoms include weakness, fever, and a sore throat; treatment includes withdrawal of the suspect drug, fresh-blood transfusions, and antibiotics.

Agricola, Georgius (George Bauer; 1494–1555) German physician and mineralogist. Working as a physician in several mining towns, he carried out a systematic study of mining and minerals; this study consistently discounted the traditional "magical" attributes of minerals, describing instead their observable physical properties. His publications concerning these properties culminated in his *De re metallica* (1556), which for two centuries was the standard text on mining and metallurgy.

Agricola, Gnaeus Julius (40–93 AD) Roman governor of Britain and father-in-law of his biographer Tacitus. Sent to govern Britain in 78, after holding previous legionary posts there, he followed a policy of Romanization, exploration, and expansion. He circumnavigated the mainland and advanced the Roman frontiers in annual campaigns, reaching the Scottish Highlands before his recall in 84.

Agricultural Adjustment Act (1933) A law that established the Agricultural Adjustment Administration, an agency to promote recovery from the Depression among US farmers; part of the New Deal. By controlling farm production and therefore surplus products, prices could be fixed and farmers' incomes increased. This was done by fixing quotas, rewarding underproduction, and penalizing, through taxation, overproduction. The law was declared unconstitutional by the Supreme Court in 1936.

Agricultural Research Service (ARS) US government agency that administers research programs in animal and plant protection and production; soil, air, and water use and improvement; farm product processing, storage, and distribution; and human nutrition. Its headquarters are in Beltsville, Md.

agricultural revolution The name given to the changes in agriculture in Britain that took place mainly in the 18th century. The open-field system of strip farming was replaced by larger enclosed fields, hedged and ditched, in which improved agricultural methods and new implements could be used; the quality of cattle and sheep was improved by scientific stock breeding. This resulted in a greater production of food for the growing industrial population (*see* industrial revolution), although it meant hardship for those farmers who were displaced by *enclosure.

agriculture The study of farming. Settled farming probably dates back to the 10th millennium BC, when in many regions of the world it began to replace man's activities as a hunter and gatherer of food. The domestication of cattle, goats, sheep, and pigs, together with the cropping of wheat, barley, rice, etc., enabled settled communities to evolve and primitive civilizations to flourish in such regions as the fertile river basins of the Tigris, Euphrates, and Nile.

Farming has developed in various ways in different parts of the world, depending largely on climatic conditions, the type of land, and the local system of land tenure. Many areas are suitable only for *livestock farming whereas in many others large-scale *arable farming is possible. In some cases the most economically successful farms are mixed arable and livestock.

Until the end of the 19th century farming was based on energy derived from man and his draft animals. Some parts of the world still use such traditional methods; however, during the 20th century, especially in developed countries, the *tractor has become the primary energy source. In this century, too, there has been great success in improving breeds of plants and animals, improving soil fertility (*see* fertilizers), increasing mechanization, and control of plant and animal pests, measures that have enormously increased the quantity and quality of food produced. These measures are now being applied in the developing world, where they are bringing about the Green Revolution that is needed to feed the world's growing population.

However, misuse of modern intensive farming methods can cause such problems as soil erosion, while pollution by excessive use of fertilizers, weedkillers, insecticides, etc., can seriously damage the environment. The reconciliation of optimum food production with conservation of the environment is one of the principal tasks of the UN *Food and Agriculture Organization.

Agriculture, Department of (USDA) US executive department, headed by the Secretary of Agriculture, a cabinet position. It oversees farm income; develops foreign markets; combats hunger and malnutrition; directs environment, conservation, and rural development projects; conducts agricultural research; and ensures standards of quality in the daily food supply. Established in 1862, the department includes the Farmers Home Administration, the Agricultural Cooperative Service, the Food and Nutrition Service, *Agricultural Research Service, and the Forest Service.

Agrigento 37 19N 13 35E A seaport in Italy, in S Sicily. Founded about 580 BC, it has famous ancient temples and is the birthplace of the philosopher Empedocles. Sulfur mining is the main occupation. Population: 49,213.

agrimony A herbaceous perennial plant of the genus *Agrimonia* (especially *A. eupatoria*), native to Europe but grown in most temperate regions. Up to 40 in (1 m) tall, it has a spike of small yellow flowers and toothed oval leaves that yield a yellow dye. Family: *Rosaceae*.

Agrippa, Marcus Vipsanius (?63–12 BC) Roman general and close associate of Emperor *Augustus, whose daughter Julia was his third wife. After military successes in Gaul (38 BC) Agrippa became consul (37 BC). He played an important part in the defeat of Mark Antony at *Actium (31 BC) and greatly contributed to the military successes of Augustus.

Agrippina the Elder (?13 BC–33 AD) The daughter of *Agrippa, wife of *Germanicus Caesar, and mother of Emperor *Caligula. A courageous and high-minded woman, she accompanied her husband on his campaigns. After his death she incurred the hostility of Tiberius, who exiled her to Pandataria, where she died in suspicious circumstances. Her daughter, **Agrippina the Younger** (15–59 AD), was notorious for her political intrigues. She probably murdered her uncle, Emperor Claudius, who was also her third husband, to make way for the succession of her son, Nero. She exerted considerable political influence early in Nero's reign, but after they had quarreled he had her murdered.

agronomy The management of land, especially for the production of arable crops. Agronomy involves the determination of the nature of a soil and how its fertility may be improved by such processes as drainage, irrigation, the application of natural and artificial fertilizers, and husbandry techniques (e.g., *crop rotation). Equally important is the breeding of crop plants that are better suited to a particular soil.

Aguascalientes 21 51N 102 18W A city in central Mexico. The commercial center for a region producing fruit and vegetables, its industries include ceramics production, tanning, and railroad engineering. There are medicinal hot springs nearby. Population (1980): 293,152.

Agulhas, Cape 34 50S 20 00E A cape in South Africa, in W Cape Province. It is the most southerly point of the African continent and has a lighthouse (1849).

Ahad Ha'am (Asher Ginsberg; 1856–1927) Hebrew essayist and an influential Zionist thinker. Born in Russia, he moved to London in 1908 and participated in negotiations leading to the *Balfour Declaration. In 1922 he settled in Palestine. Critical of political *Zionism, he looked to nationalism to achieve the moral and cultural regeneration of the Jewish people. His adopted name means "One of the People."

Ahaggar Mountains (*or* Hoggar Mts) A plateau area in S Algeria, in the central Sahara. It averages about 2950 ft (900 m) but reaches 9573 ft (2918 m) at Mount Tahat and consists chiefly of rocky desert.

ahimsa (Sanskrit: noninjury) The ethical practice, strictly observed in *Jainism but also of fundamental importance in *Hinduism and *Buddhism, of not causing harm to any living thing. Because of the belief in reincarnation, these religions respect all forms of life as being parts of the cycle of rebirth. Vegetarianism is consequently widespread in Asia. The doctrine of nonviolence (*see* satyagraha) as applied by Mohandas *Gandhi to political conflicts was derived from the principle of ahimsa.

Ahmadabad (*or* Ahmedabad) 23 03N 72 40E A city in central India, in Gujarat. Founded in 1411, it is one of India's leading industrial centers; it is a major rail center and its textile industry (established 1859–61) is one of the largest in the country. Its university was established in 1949. Population (1991): 2,872,865.

Ahmadiya A religious sect founded in the Punjab by Mirza Ghulam Ahmad of Qadiyan (1839–1908), who was of Muslim background. His teaching combined elements of Islam, Christianity, and Hinduism. He taught that Jesus was buried in Srinigar and that he himself was the messiah and *Mahdi. In 1918 the Ahmadiya split into two groups, the larger regarding Mirza Ahmad as a prophet, the smaller regarding him only as a reformer, and so remaining closer to orthodox Islam. Both groups are based in Pakistan, but have communities elsewhere.

Ahmad Shah Durrani (c.1723–73) Afghan ruler (1747–73), who founded the Durrani dynasty. Ahmad was commander in India for the Persian *Nader Shah. When Nader died (1747), Ahmad succeeded him as shah and built an empire that was bordered by the Oxus River, Tibet, the Indus River, and Persia. After his death, the empire collapsed.

Ahmed III (1673–1736) Sultan of the Ottoman Empire (1703–30). After a successful war against Russia (1711–13) Ahmed suffered defeat at the hands of Austria and by the Peace of Passarowitz (1718) the Ottomans lost Hungary and parts of Serbia. In 1730 he was deposed and died in captivity. His reign is often known as the Tulip Age because of the flower's contemporary popularity.

Ahmose I King of Egypt (c. 1570–1546 BC), who founded the 18th dynasty. He liberated Egypt from the *Hyksos, retaking Memphis, and reasserted Egyptian power in Nubia and Palestine. After more than a century of alien domination, he reorganized the administration of his reunited country, and encouraged trade and commerce.

Ahmose II King of Egypt (570–526 BC) of the 26th dynasty, who was described by the Greek historian Herodotus. He came to power in a military coup but ruled for 44 years in peace and prosperity.

Ahriman In *Zoroastrianism, the evil spirit created, and ultimately to be overcome, by *Ahura Mazda. According to Zoroastrian dualism he is the essence of untruth, greed, anger, and jealousy and, hence, the cause of suffering in the world.

Ahura Mazda The supreme deity of *Zoroastrianism, creator of all things good and just. He represents the creative principle, living in eternal light, and is opposed to Ahriman, the destructive principle, living in darkness.

ai. *See* sloth.

AIDS. *See* Acquired Immune Deficiency Syndrome.

Aid to Families with Dependent Children (AFDC) US government welfare program that provides supplemental funds for low-income families with dependent children.

Aiken, Conrad (1899–1973) US writer and critic. Influenced by T. S. *Eliot, whom he knew at Harvard, he was a prolific writer of poetry including *Selected Poems* (1929), which was awarded a Pulitzer Prize and "Preludes to Definition," contained in *Collected Poems* (1953). His fiction includes both short stories and novels, among which are the novels *Blue Voyage* (1927) and *Great Circle* (1933) in which he dealt with his parents' deaths. His critical writings comprise *Collected Criticism* (1958). An autobiography, *Ushant*, appeared in 1952.

Aiken, Howard Hathaway (1900–73) US mathematician, who pioneered the construction of electronic computers. His Mark I, built in 1944 and later used by the US Navy, anticipated the modern digital computer.

aikido A Japanese form of unarmed combat, primarily for self-defense by means of dodging an attacker and leading him in the direction in which his momentum takes him before subduing him without injury. Like other *martial arts it emphasizes the need for a calm frame of mind and total physical control. It has developed into a competitive sport in which two people fight in one or two one-minute rounds. *See also* judo; jujitsu.

Ailanthus. *See* tree of heaven.

Ailey, Alvin (1931–89) US dancer and choreographer. He formed his own modern dance group, the Alvin Ailey Dance Theatre, in 1958 after studying with such dancers as Martha Graham, Hanya Holm, and Lester Horton. His best-known works include *Revelations* (1960), *Creation of the World* (1960), *Roots of the Blues* (1961), *Labyrinth* (1963), *Pas de Duke* (1976), and *Phases* (1980).

Ain River A river in E France, flowing SSW from the Jura Mountains to join the River Rhône 18 mi (29 km) above Lyons. Length: 118 mi (190 km).

Ainu A Caucasoid people living on certain islands of Japan and Russia (Hokkaido, Sakhalin, Kurile Islands). Traditionally a hunting and food-gathering people, distinct from the surrounding Mongoloid peoples, they are now few in number and much changed in both appearance and culture. They were once noted for their profusion of body hair, but intermixture has made them resemble the Japanese and their traditional culture has largely disappeared. They speak a language that is not related to any other known language.

air. *See* atmosphere.

aircraft Any machine capable of flying. The attempts by humans to fly fall into two categories: those using lighter-than-air machines (*see* airships; balloons) and those using heavier-than-air machines. The latter include wing-flapping, birdlike devices, rotating wing machines (*see* helicopters), and fixed-wing air-craft, first *gliders and then powered airplanes. By the end of the 19th century it was clear to all but the most eccentric that man was both too weak and too heavy to emulate birds. Flapping wings combine both thrust and lift (*see* aeronautics) in one device; man needs to separate these two components, obtaining lift from a fixed wing and thrust from an engine. 19th-century experience of gliding, especially by Otto *Lilienthal, provided the Wright Brothers with the information they needed to build their first powered aircraft. The power source was provided by the Otto-Daimler *internal-combustion engine. By 1907 the Wrights were able to remain airborne for 45 minutes; in 1909 the Frenchman Louis *Blériot flew across the English Channel, and in the same year the French rotary Gnome engine revolutionized aircraft-engine design (this engine and its derivatives powered many early aircraft, including several used in World War I). By the beginning of the war, aircraft were sufficiently advanced to be used for reconnaissance and their usefulness as bombers soon became evident. Fast maneuverable fighters to shoot down the slower heavily laden bombers were an obvious subsequent development. By the end of the war aerial combat was established as an integral part of modern warfare, both sides being equipped with a range of fighters, bombers, and reconnaissance aircraft.

After the war and during the 1920s, air shows and flying clubs run by ex-wartime pilots using World War I aircraft sprang up all over the world, popularizing the concept of flying and heralding the age of civil aviation. Private airlines were founded in the 1920s, and during the 1930s a worldwide network of commercial routes developed. The Atlantic was first flown nonstop from New York to Paris in 1927 by Charles *Lindberg and by 1939 there was a transatlantic flying-boat service, using Class C Short flying boats with in-flight refueling.

Between the wars all the main countries of the world were also building up their air forces, those with expansionist aspirations more quickly than the others. By the outbreak of World War II aircraft of all kinds were poised for aerial combat. During the war the main US bombing force consisted of 12,700 Boeing B17s, 18,000 Consolidated B24 Liberators, and toward the end of the war, a fleet of Boeing B29 Superfortresses. Germany entered the war with 370 Dornier Do 17s and the Heinkel He 111, some 7300 of which had been made by the end of the war. The Junkers 88 entered service in 1940 and at the end of the war (1945) the Arado Ar 234 jet bomber was used for the first time.

The US fighter pilots had some 10,000 Lockheed P38 Lightnings and 15,000 P51 Mustangs during the war. Dominant British fighters were the Supermarine Spitfire and the Hawker Hurricane, the latter being slightly slower than the main German fighter, the Messerschmitt Me Bf109. Later British fighters included the De Havilland Mosquito. The British jet-powered Gloster Meteor entered service in 1944, as did the German Messerschmitt Me 262 jet.

By the end of war the practicality of the *jet engine had been established and it has dominated aircraft design ever since. However, the first postwar generation of civil aircraft used the jet engine to drive propellers. The highly successful

AIRCRAFT (CIVIL)

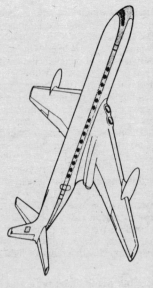

Vickers Viscount *Introduced into service in 1950, it was the first successful turboprop airliner. Powered by four engines, it carried 60 passengers.*

De Havilland Comet I *The first jet airliner, it went into service in 1952. Crashes due to metal fatigue caused its withdrawal and in 1958 it was replaced by the Comet IV.*

Boeing 747 *Nicknamed the "jumbo jet," this wide-bodied jetliner, which can carry up to 500 passengers, has been in service with many airlines since 1970.*

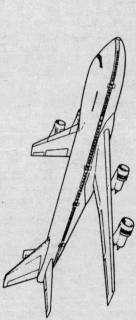

Concorde *The first supersonic airliner, it was built by the French and British in cooperation. Powered by four engines, it came into service in 1976.*

44

AIRCRAFT (CIVIL)

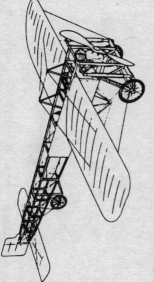

Wright Brothers' Flyer *The first powered flight at Kitty Hawk, North Carolina, on Dec 17, 1903, lasted 12 seconds.*

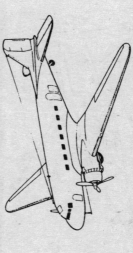

Blériot XI. *Louis Blériot's 30-minute flight from Calais to Dover on July 25, 1909, was the first cross-channel flight.*

Handley Page 42E Hannibal *In 1928 the British airline, Imperial Airways, bought eight HP42 aircraft. The 24-seater Hannibal had a top speed of 100 mph (160 km/hr).*

Douglas DC3 *Introduced in 1936, it was widely used in World War II as the Dakota transport. Its Pratt and Whitney 1200 hp engines gave it a maximum speed of 200 mph (320 km/hr).*

AIRCRAFT (MILITARY)

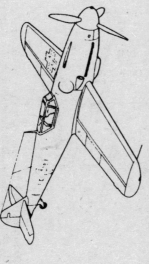

Messerschmitt 109 *German fighter, designed in 1935. The latest version (the 109G) had an 1800 hp engine enabling it to fly at 430 mph (692 kph).*

Hawker Siddeley Harrier *British VTOL aircraft developed in 1969. Two movable nozzles direct the thrust of its engine downwards for vertical take-off.*

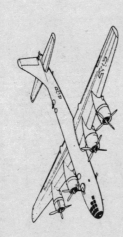

Boeing B-29 Superfortress *This enormous US bomber entered the war in 1943 and was used to drop the atom bombs on Japan.*

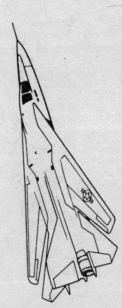

General Dynamics F-111 *US fighter and fighter-bomber, the first warplane to have swing wings (1967). It is powered by a Pratt and Whitney TF30 turbo fan.*

47

AIRCRAFT (MILITARY)

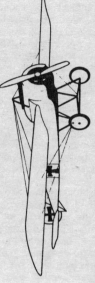

Fokker Eindecker E111 *German fighter, in service from 1915. It had a top speed of 83 mph (133 km/hr) and the first machine gun synchronized to fire through the propeller.*

Supermarine Spitfire *British fighter. Originally powered by a Rolls-Royce Merlin engine, it later had the Griffon engine, giving it a top speed of 450 mph (724 kph).*

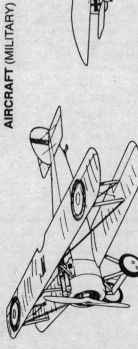

Sopwith Camel *A highly maneuverable fighter, first delivered in 1917. Its 130 hp Clerget engine gave it a top speed of 113 mph (181 km/hr).*

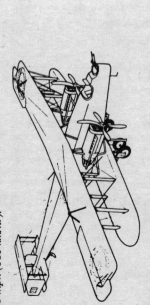

Handley Page 0/400 *The largest World War I bomber. Its twin 360 hp engines enabled it to carry 2000 lbs (907 kg) of bombs.*

Boeing 707 (with its four engines in pods suspended below the wings) followed in 1954 and the French Caravelle (with two rear-mounted engines) in 1959.

The first aircraft to break the *sound barrier were military and nearly all modern warplanes are supersonic and armed with missiles. Examples include the US McDonnell Douglas Phantom, Convair Hustler, and General Dynamics Swingwing F111; the British Hawker Hunter and Avro Vulcan; the French Mirage; and the Soviet MiGs. The first supersonic passenger aircraft (SST) to fly was the Soviet Tupolev Tu-144 in 1968. This was followed a year later by the Anglo-French Concorde, which despite opposition from conservationists, is now in service. However, long- and medium-range passenger services are likely to be dominated for most of the remainder of this century by the wide-bodied (jumbo) jets, such as the Boeing 747 and the European Airbus.

aircraft carrier A naval vessel with a large flat deck for launching and landing warplanes. The first flight from the deck of a ship was made in 1910, and the first true aircraft carrier, *Argus*, was completed for Britain's navy in 1918, too late for action in World War I. Carriers played a dominant role in World War II, despite early predictions that *battleships would be the most important warships. Carriers were especially effective in the war against the Japanese, where they were instrumental in destroying the Japanese fleet. After World War II, carriers came to be regarded chiefly as tactical units, although they saw considerable action in the Korean and Vietnam Wars. The USS *Enterprise*, the first nuclear-powered carrier (1961), displaced 76,000 tons and steamed more than 270,000 mi (432,000 km) before requiring refueling. The introduction of larger and heavier aircraft required the refitting of carriers. Because of the increased range of aircraft, the enormous cost of carriers, and the development of sophisticated missiles, there have been few aircraft carriers built since the late 1970s, and indications are that their size, cost, low speed, and vulnerability will preclude their extensive use in the future.

air-cushion vehicle. *See* Hovercraft.

Airedale terrier The largest breed of terrier, originating in Yorkshire, England. It has a long, squarish muzzle, a short tail, and a tan-colored, wiry coat with a black saddle region. A powerful and intelligent dog, the Airedale has been used as a guard dog, for hunting, and as a police dog. Height: 23–25 in (58–61 cm) (dogs); 22–23 in (56–58 cm) (bitches). □dog.

airfoil. *See* aeronautics.

Air Force, Department of the US government military department within the Department of *Defense. Directed by the Secretary of Defense, it consists of the Air Staff, which furnishes professional assistance to the Secretary and Chief of Staff, and the field organization, which consists of the major commands, separate operating agencies, and direct reporting units. It was established by the National Security Act of 1947.

Air Force, United States (USAF) US branch of military service. Part of the Department of *Defense since 1947, it is directed by the Secretary of the Air Force and supervised by a professional staff under the chief of staff. Beginning as the Aeronautical Division of the Army Signal Corps in 1907, it evolved into the Army's Air Service division by 1918. By 1926 it was known as the Air Corps and, during World War II, as Army Air Forces. In 1956 the Air Force was given responsibility for land-based missile systems and, in 1965, satellite development.

air sac In zoology, a thin-walled, air-filled sac that functions in the breathing mechanism of birds, some insects, and some lizards. In birds there are five pairs in the spaces between the internal organs and around or in some bones. They are connected with the air passages and enable a constant supply of air to the lungs during flight.

airships. *See* dirigibles.

air space In international law, the space above a country over which that country is sovereign. Under the Outer Space Treaty (1967), outer space is not subject to national appropriation.

Aisne River A river in N France. Rising in the Argonne Forest, it flows mainly NW joining the Oise River near Compiègne. It was a major battleground of *World War I. Length: 175 mi (282 km).

Aistulf (d. 756) King of the Lombards (749–56). Aistulf captured Ravenna (751) and then threatened Rome. The pope sought the aid of *Pepin, King of the Franks, who twice defeated Aistulf at Pavia (755, 756).

Aix-en-Provence (Latin name: Aquae Sextiae) 43 31N 5 27E A city in S France, in the Bouches-du-Rhône department. The capital of Provence in the Middle Ages, it has a Gothic cathedral and a university (1409). The artist Cézanne was born here. An agricultural center, it trades in olive oil and fruit. Population (1975): 117,119.

Aix-la-Chapelle. *See* Aachen.

Aix-la-Chapelle, Congress of (1818) Meeting of the Quadruple Alliance (Great Britain, Austria, Prussia, and Russia) and France at Aix-la-Chapelle (now Aachen). The Alliance reaffirmed the political reorganization of Europe established by the Congress of *Vienna (1814–15) and restored France's status as an independent power: it withdrew its occupying forces and admitted France into what thus became the Quintuple Alliance.

Aix-les-Bains (Latin name: Aquae Gratiane) 45 41N 5 55E A spa and resort in E France, in the Savoie department. Situated in a picturesque valley, it is noted for its hot sulfurous springs. Population (1975): 22,293.

Ajaccio 41 51N 8 43E The capital of Corsica, a port on the Gulf of Ajaccio. Napoleon I was born here and his home is now preserved as a museum. Tourism is the principal industry. Population (1982 est): 55,300.

Ajanta 20 30N 75 48E A village in W India, in Maharashtra. It is renowned for its Buddhist caves hewn out of the granite cliffs. Dating from the 1st century BC to the 7th century AD, they consist of monasteries and temples, some of which contain remarkable paintings illustrating the life of the times.

Ajax A legendary Greek hero, son of Telamon, King of Salamis. Described in Homer's *Iliad* as great in stature and in courage, he fought *Hector in single combat. He became insane with rage after being defeated by Odysseus in the contest for the armor of the dead *Achilles. *Sophocles' play *Ajax* depicts the hero recovering his sanity, only to be driven by shame to suicide.

Ajmer(Ajmere *or* Ajmir) 26 29N 74 40E A city in India, in Rajasthan. It contains the white marble tomb of a Muslim saint and a Mogul palace. A focal point of road and rail routes, it is a commercial and industrial center. Population (1991): 401,930.

Akashic records The "pictures" of all past events, emotions, and thoughts, believed by occultists to be retained in supersensory fluid called Akasha. Clairvoyants and mediums claim to have access to these records.

Akbar (I) the Great (1542–1605) The third Mogul emperor (1556–1605). After establishing his authority, Akbar embarked on the extension of his rule over all N India by a series of military campaigns in Punjab, Rajput, Gujarat, Bengal, Kashmir, and Sind. Late in his reign he conquered the Deccan, further to the south. As ruler he was noted for his able administration, the development of trade, reforms of taxation, the abolition of extortion, and his tolerance toward non-Muslims. *See also* Mogul art.

Akhenaton (*or* Ikhnaton) King of Egypt (1379–1362 BC) of the 18th dynasty, one of whose wives was *Nefertiti. He replaced the traditional *Amon cult with the monotheistic worship of the sun god, *Aton, and built a new capital Akhetaton (*see* Tell el-Amarna). Internal disorder during his reign enabled the Hittite king, *Suppiluliumas, to remove N Syria from Egyptian control.

Akhmatova, Anna (Anna Andreevna Gorenko; 1889–1966) Russian poet. Her first books, *Evening* (1912) and *Beads* (1914), consisting chiefly of short, intensely lyrical, love poems, were immediately successful. She was married to Nikolai Gumiliov (1886–1921), founder of *acmeism, from 1910 until 1918. After the Revolution she wrote on public as well as personal themes, but her essential style remained unchanged. Her works were banned from 1922 until 1940, and she was again denounced in 1946. In the 1960s, however, her work was restored to favor.

Akiba ben Joseph (died c. 135 AD) One of the outstanding teachers of early rabbinic Judaism. He came to scholarship late in life, but became a master of biblical interpretation and law. He supported the revolt of *Bar Kokhba and was martyred by the Romans.

Akihito (Tsugu Akihito; 1933–   ) Emperor of Japan (1989–   ). Invested as crown prince in 1952, he became the first heir to the throne to marry outside the court nobility when he married Michiko Shoda in 1959. He represented Japan at the coronation of Britain's Queen Elizabeth II in 1953 and from that time made numerous international visits for Japan. He succeeded his father, Emperor Hirohito, in January 1989 and had his formal coronation in an elaborate traditional ceremony in 1990. Akihito named his imperial era *Heisei* ("achieving peace") and was the first emperor to begin his reign as a "symbol of the state" rather than as a "living god."

Akkad The capital city and dynastic name of a S Mesopotamian kingdom established about 2300 BC, N of *Sumer. Akkad, the site of which is still unidentified, was founded by *Sargon, who extended his rule over most of Mesopotamia. The Semitic language of Akkad, Old Akkadian, spread to much of the Middle East, developing later into the languages of both *Babylonia and *Assyria. About 2150 BC, barbarian invasions brought about Akkad's decline and the short-lived reascendancy of *Ur.

Akron 41 04N 81 31W A city in Ohio. It is the main center of the US rubber industry, specializing in tires; other industries include plastics and chemicals. Its university was established in 1870. Population (1990): 223,019.

aksak A type of musical meter, found in the vigorous asymmetrical dance rhythms of the E Mediterranean, deriving from Turkish sources. *Bartók recorded examples of these rhythms in Bulgaria and named them Bulgarian rhythms.

Aksum (*or* Axum) 14 05N 38 40E An ancient town in N Ethiopia. It was capital of the Christian Aksumite Empire (1st–6th centuries AD). According to tradition, the *Ark of the Covenant was brought here from Jerusalem. The old town is now a popular tourist attraction.

Aktyubinsk 53 43N 91 25E A city in Kazakhstan, on the Ilek River. Founded (1869) as a Russian fort, it is now an industrial center. Population (1987 est): 248,000.

Alabama A state in the SE, on the Gulf of Mexico. Alabama borders Tennessee on the N, Georgia on the E, Florida on the S, and Mississippi on the W. A small portion of S Alabama flanks the Gulf of Mexico, where an inlet forms the important port of Mobile. Except for the forested uplands in the NE it consists of an undulating plain, drained by the Alabama and Tombigbee Rivers. The iron and steel industry, based on deposits of iron ore, coal, and limestone around the state's largest city, Birmingham, is the most important industry. Other industries include the production of oil, metal goods, chemicals, plastics, and defense and space projects. Cotton production has decreased since the boll weevil blight (1915) but remains a principal crop along with peanuts, soybeans, and corn; the raising of cattle and poultry is also important. Industry, however, supplies the greatest portion of the state's revenue. Diversification of agriculture and increased industrialization have helped to improve Alabama's standard of living, although it remains economically one of the poorest states. It has, nonetheless, a rich rural culture, particularly among its large African-American community. *History*: first explored by the Spanish in the 16th century. Settlement, however, was begun by the French. It passed to the British (1763) after the French and Indian Wars. In 1783 it came under US control and with an area to the S added in the Louisiana Purchase (1803) became a state in 1819. Following the War of 1812 and statehood, the demand for cotton brought a wave of settlement from neighboring states. The wealthier settlers established slave-based plantations in the fertile bottomlands. Because of the dominance of "King Cotton," the slave-owning planters were a crucial influence in firing anti-Union sentiments before the Civil War. Following secession from the Union (1861), the state sent most of its white male population to fight against the North. The period since its readmittance (1868) has been marked by troubled race relations. A 1954 Supreme Court decision declaring school segregation unconstitutional, resulted in increased racial tension and violence. Montgomery, the capital, became the scene of numerous outbreaks of unrest, including a year-long boycott of public buses by African Americans. The Alabama Freedom March in 1965 marked a milestone in the social protest movement of the late 1950s and 1960s. An indication of change in the area of race relations was reflected in the 1982 gubernatorial race, in which former governor George Wallace received 80 percent of the African-American vote. Area: 51,609 sq mi (133,677 sq km). Population (1990): 4,040,587.

Alabama claims Compensation claimed by the US government from Britain for damage caused by the *Alabama* and other warships of the *Confederate states in the Civil War (1861–65). Britain was accused of violating its neutrality by allowing these ships to be built or equipped in its shipyards. In 1871 the dispute was referred to arbitration by Italy, Switzerland, and Brazil. Britain was found liable and ordered to pay more than $15 million. This was the first major settlement of an international dispute by arbitration.

alabaster A pure, fine-grained form of *gypsum. It is white or delicately shaded and often translucent and attractively veined. It has long been worked ornamentally, for carvings, etc., but weathers too easily for external use. The alabaster of Volterra, Tuscany is well known.

Alain-Fournier (Henri-Alban Fournier; 1886–1914) French novelist. The son of a country schoolmaster, he became a literary journalist in Paris and was killed in World War I. The mood of his one completed novel, *Le Grand Meaulnes* (1913), is nostalgic and almost mystical; set in the French countryside of his childhood, it describes a young man's search for a girl he has glimpsed only briefly.

Alamogordo 32 54N 105 57W A city in S New Mexico. The first atom bomb was exploded in a test near here on July 16, 1945. Population (1990): 27,596.

Alamo, the A mission in San Antonio, Texas. During the Texas revolution it was defended from February 24 until March 6, 1836, by fewer than 200 Texan volunteers (including Davy *Crockett), who were all massacred during the on-slaught of 4000 Mexican troops led by *Santa Anna. Six weeks later a victory at San Jacinto secured Texan independence.

Alanbrooke, Alan Francis Brooke, 1st Viscount (1883–1963) British field marshal. He joined the Royal Field Artillery in 1902, serving as a staff officer in World War I. In World War II, after service in France, he became commander in chief of the home forces. Appointed Chief of the Imperial General Staff in 1941, he advised Churchill at all his conferences with Roosevelt and Stalin.

Åland Islands (Finnish name: Ahvenanmaa Islands) A group of over 6000 islands and islets under Finnish administration, at the entrance to the Gulf of Bothnia. Capital: Mariehamn.

Alarcón, Pedro Antonio de (1833–91) Spanish novelist. He began his career as a poet and journalist, but his literary reputation is based on his later novels, especially *The Three-Cornered Hat* (1874), which was used by Manuel de *Falla as the basis for a ballet.

Alarcón y Mendoza, Juan Ruiz de (1581–1639) Spanish dramatist. Born in Mexico, he became one of the leading dramatists of the Golden Age of Spanish drama. His best-known play is *La Verdad Sospechosa* (?1619), a satirical comedy. He apparently ceased to write after being appointed to the Council for the Indies in 1626.

Alaric I (c. 370–410 AD) King of the *Visigoths. Alaric served in the Roman army as the commander of the Gothic auxiliary forces before his election as King of the Visigoths. After failing to reach a peaceful agreement with the Roman imperial administration, he invaded Greece and Italy. Alaric died shortly after his forces sacked Rome (410).

Alaska The largest state in the US, occupying the extreme NW corner of the North American continent. Alaska juts out into the sea, which surrounds it on three sides. The Pacific Ocean lies to the S, the Bering Sea, the Bering Strait, and the Chukchi Sea to the W, and the Arctic Ocean to the N. Alaska borders Canada on the E (the Yukon Territory and British Columbia), which separates it from the coterminous "lower 48" states. It is a mountainous volcanic area; from the coast extend the Seward Peninsula in the S and the Alaska Peninsula further north. Alaska has roughly four physiographical regions. The Pacific mountain system, including the Coast Ranges and the Alaska Range (where Mt McKinley, the highest peak in North America, rises to over 20,000 ft (6100 m), dominates the S. The central region consists of uplands and lowlands. The Rocky Mountains extend into Alaska toward the N, forming the Brooks Range. The North Slope reaches down from the Brooks Range to the Arctic Ocean. There are numerous rivers, the chief of which is the Yukon flowing W into the Bering Sea. It has an indented coastline with many islands. One third of the state lies within the Arctic Circle. The economy is based principally on the state's rich mineral wealth. The discovery of oil (1950) and subsequent finds (1968) have made oil production a major industry and there are abundant supplies of natural gas. Coal, gold, and copper are all mined. Fishing, especially salmon, and forestry are also major industries. Agricultural development is hindered by the short growing season and severe climate. Fur trapping has declined in importance although sealskins (from the offshore Pribilof Islands) remain an important export. Conflict between further development and the preservation of the natural landscape has become a major problem. *History*: first settled by Russians following voyages by the Dane Vitüs Bering (1728, 1741), it was under the trade control of the Russian American company until 1867 when it was purchased by the US (it became known as Seward's Folly after the secretary of state who had led the negotiations). A number of gold rushes in the late 19th century helped to swell the sparse population. It became the 49th state in 1959. Environmental issues are under continuous debate in Alaska. The most famous was that of the Alaska Pipeline, an oil pipeline running 789 mi (1270 km) through the state. Opposed because of the supposed detrimental effect it would have on the state's ecology, the pipeline was eventually approved and was completed in 1977. In 1989, a 260,000 gallon oil spill from the tanker, *Exxon Valdez*, into Prince William Sound caused a renewal of environmental groups' efforts. Area: 586,412 sq mi (1,518,800 sq km). Population (1990): 550,043. Capital: Juneau.

Alaska Highway A road from Dawson Creek, Canada to Fairbanks, Alaska, built for defense against Japan (1942). Open throughout the year, it now serves tourism and economic development. Length: 1523 mi (2437 km).

Alaskan Boundary Dispute (1898–1903) A disagreement between the US and Canada over access from the Pacific Ocean across US-owned Alaska, to the Klondike gold fields in Yukon Territory, Canada. Canada claimed possession of the inlets and strip of land along the coast; the US claimed the same area as part of its purchase of Alaska from Russia in 1867. Due to inadequate surveying, both sides felt they had legitimate claims. An international panel of six settled the question in favor of the US.

Alaskan malamute. *See* husky.

Alaskan North Slope A low-lying plain in N Alaska, from the Arctic Ocean S to Brooks Range. It is a main source of oil, discovered during the 1960s, in Alaska.

Alaska Purchase (1867) The sale of Alaska by Russia to the US for $7,200,000. Negotiated by Secretary of State William H. *Seward at the urging of settlers in the California-Washington territories, the purchase of this unsurveyed land was often referred to as "Seward's Folly" or "Seward's Ice Box."

Alaska Range A mountain range in S Alaska, arcing NE from the N end of the Aleutian Range at the base of the Alaska Peninsula and then SE to the SW Yukon Territory, Canada, border. Mt. McKinley, 20,320 ft (6194 m), the highest point in North America, is here.

Alastor In Greek legend, the son of Neleus and brother of Nestor, killed by Heracles on the island of Pylos. The name was also applied to the personified spirit of vengeance that could possess a man.

Alba, Fernando Alvarez de Toledo, Duke of (*or* Alva; 1507–83) Spanish general, who successfully commanded Hapsburg forces against Protestants in Germany and the French in Italy. Philip II of Spain placed him in command of the Netherlands (1567–73), where his ruthless attempts to subdue the Dutch Protestants made him very unpopular, both in Spain and the Netherlands, and led to his recall. He led the successful expedition against Portugal (1580–81). *See also* Revolt of the Netherlands.

Albacete 39 00N 1 52W A city in SE central Spain, in Murcia. A market center, it is famous for the manufacture of cutlery and daggers. Its notable buildings include the 16th-century cathedral. Population (1986 est): 127,000.

albacore A fast-swimming *tuna fish, *Thunnus alalunga*, found in warm seas. It has very long pectoral fins and reaches up to 40 in (1 m) in length. It is the chief source of tuna for canning.

Alban, St (3rd century AD) The first English martyr. A pagan soldier, he protected a Christian priest and was converted by him. On admitting this to the Roman authorities, he was scourged and beheaded on a site subsequently dedicated to him as the Abbey of St Albans in the city of St Albans in Hertfordshire, England. Feast day: June 22 or 17. Emblem: a stag.

Albania, Republic of (Albanian name: Shqiperia) A country in SE Europe, occupying part of the Balkan Peninsula on the Adriatic Sea. It consists of a mountainous interior, rising to over 9000 ft (2700 m), with extensive forests and fertile coastal lowlands. The people, of whose origins little is known, belong to two main groups, the *Ghegs (N of the River Shkumbi) and the *Tosks (S). *Economy*: mainly agricultural, organized into state farms and collectives, although industrial development is increasing (the principal industries being agricultural processing, textiles, oil products, and cement). There have been recent attempts to develop the rich mineral resources, especially oil, lignite, copper, chromium, limestone, salt, and bauxite, as well as the rich natural-gas deposits. Main exports include crude oil, bitumen, chrome ore, copper wire, tobacco, fruit, and vegetables. *History*: became independent in 1912 after more than four centuries of Turkish rule. Following a civil war, in which Italy intervened, Albania became a republic in 1925 and a monarchy in 1928, when its president, Ahmed Beg Zogu (1895–1961), was proclaimed as King Zog. After occupation by Italy and Germany during World War II, another republic was set up in 1946, with a communist-controlled assembly. It aligned itself with the Soviet Union but after the death of Stalin relations between the two countries weakened and in 1961 diplomatic relations were broken off. Meanwhile Albania, alone among the other East European communist states, maintained close relations with China. In recent years, however, the alliance has cooled, and in 1978 Albania suspended commercial relations with China; a trade agreement signed in 1983 suggested an easing of tensions between the two countries. Fiercely communist, Albania maintained a hostile stance toward both the USSR and the US, denouncing the arms race and US-Soviet domination of Third World countries. Albania expressed enthusiastic support for the Argentines during the Falkland Islands crisis of 1982. Enver *Hoxha, as first party secretary, was the country's dictatorial leader from 1946 until his death in 1985. Hoxha was succeeded by Ramiz Alia. As reforms swept across eastern Europe in the late 1980s and early 1990s, elections in 1991 brought about a coalition government of Communists and Democrats. In 1992, an all-Democrat government was elected; Sali Berisha, leader of the Albanian Democratic Party, succeeded Alia as president. Albania signed a cooperation pact with the US in 1993 as economic problems continued to plague the country. Official language: Albanian. Currency: lek of 100 qintars. Area: 11,101 sq mi (28,748 sq km). Population (1990): 3,270,000. Capital: Tirana. Main port: Durrës.

Albanian An Indo-European language, the only modern representative of a distinct branch of this linguistic group, spoken by two million Albanians and known by them as Shqiptar. It is divided into two main dialects, *Gheg and *Tosk.

Albany 42 40N 73 49W The capital of New York state, located on the Hudson River. Founded in 1614 by the Dutch, it is one of North America's oldest cities and has several notable public buildings, including the state capitol (1879). Economic growth accelerated with the building of the Erie Canal (1825) and today its main industries are brewing, the manufacture of electrical goods and textiles, and printing and publishing. Population (1990): 101,082.

Albany Congress (1754) A meeting of representatives from the American colonies to form a common defense and to discuss Indian affairs. Delegates from New Hampshire, Massachusetts, Rhode Island, Connecticut, New York,

Pennsylvania, and Maryland worked to gain the loyalty of the Iroquois Indian tribes, previously allied with the French. Agreements reached were short-lived. Benjamin Franklin's resultant Albany Plan of Union, although not ratified by any of the colonies, was a model draft of the future US Articles of Confederation and US Constitution.

albatross A large seabird belonging to a family (*Diomedeidae*; 14 species) that occurs mainly in southern oceans. It has a stout, hooked bill; usually a white or brown plumage, often with darker markings on the back, wings, or tail; and very long narrow wings (the wandering albatross, *Diomedea exulans*, has the largest wingspan of any bird, reaching up to 12 ft (3.5 m). Albatrosses can glide for hours over the open sea, feeding on squid and cuttlefish; they come ashore only to breed. Order: *Procellariiformes* (*see* petrels).

ALBATROSS *The waved albatross (Diomedea irrorata) breeds on the Galapagos Islands.*

albedo A measure of the reflecting power of a nonluminous object, such as a planet or natural satellite or a surface feature on such a body. It is the ratio of the amount of light reflected in all directions from the object to the amount of incident light. Clouds, snow, and ice have high albedos while volcanic rocks have very low albedos.

Albee, Edward (1928–) US dramatist. His early one-act plays, notably *Zoo Story* (1960) and *The Death of Bessie Smith* (1960), analyze contemporary social tensions using techniques of the *Theater of the Absurd. His first three-act play, *Who's Afraid of Virginia Woolf?* (1962), which dramatizes the love-hate relationship of an academic couple, was very successful. Later plays include *A Delicate Balance* (1967) and *Seascape* (1975), both of which were awarded Pulitzer Prizes.

Alberoni, Giulio (1664–1752) Spanish-Italian cardinal and statesman, who rose to prominence during the War of the Spanish Succession. In 1713 he was appointed consular agent for Parma at the court of Philip IV of Spain and in

1715 became prime minister of Spain and a cardinal. An ambitious foreign policy, which angered England, France, and Holland, resulted in his banishment to Italy (1719).

Albers, Josef (1888–1976) German abstract painter, designer, and poet. His successful career as an influential art teacher and theoretician began at the *Bauhaus school of design and after 1933 continued in the US, where he painted a famous series of abstract paintings entitled *Homage to the Square*.

Albert I (1875–1934) King of the Belgians (1909–34). As commander in chief of the Belgian army, Albert led his country's heroic but unsuccessful resistance to the German invasion (1914) and contributed to the Allied victory in World War I. After the war he did much to encourage industrial reconstruction and currency reform.

Albert (I) the Bear (?1100–70) The first Margrave of Brandenburg (1150–70), who took the title following conquests that brought him Havelland in E Europe. Further campaigns extended his territories, in which he sponsored land-reclamation schemes and missionary work.

Albert II Alcibiades (1522–57) Margrave of Brandenburg, prominent in the conflict between Emperor Charles V and the German Protestants. A Protestant, he nevertheless supported Charles until 1551, when he turned his coat and joined Maurice of Saxony and the French. Defeated by Charles' brother Ferdinand, in 1553, he was outlawed and fled to France.

Albert III (1443–1500) Duke of Saxony jointly with his brother Ernest (1441–86) from 1464 until 1485, when the Saxon lands were divided between them. He campaigned for the Holy Roman Emperor and in 1488–89 restored imperial authority in Holland, Flanders, and Brabant. He died while repressing a rebellion in Friesland, where he was governor (1498–1500).

Albert, Lake. *See* Mobutu, Lake.

Albert, Prince (1819–61) Prince Consort of the United Kingdom and younger son of Ernest I, Duke of Saxe-Coburg-Gotha. In 1840 he married his cousin Queen Victoria and became her chief adviser. Although he was initially unpopular, his devotion to duty and his active patronage of the arts, science, and industry eventually won him respect. He is perhaps best remembered for his organization of the *Great Exhibition (1851). He died of typhoid.

Alberta A province of W Canada, mostly on the Great Plains. It consists mainly of a plateau, rising to the foothills of the *Rocky Mountains in the SW. The undulating S prairie and parkland further N support profitable ranches and grain farms. Alberta is Canada's largest oil and gas producer, possesses vast coalfields, and includes the Athabasca tar sands, one of the world's largest oil reserves. Manufacturing is based on agriculture and mineral resources. Lumbering, construction, and tourism are also important. *History*: first explored in the 18th century, Alberta became Canadian territory in 1869. The arrival of the railroad from E Canada (1883) facilitated agricultural settlement, and Alberta grew rapidly (especially 1900–14), becoming a province in 1905. Alberta's government tends to be controlled by one party for long periods, notably by the Social Credit Party (1935–71). Calgary, Alberta, hosted the 1988 Winter Olympic games. Area: 248,799 sq mi (644,389 sq km). Population (1991): 2,545,553. Capital: Edmonton.

Albert Canal A canal in Belgium, completed in 1939. It links the Meuse River at Liège with the Scheldt River at Antwerp. Length: 80 mi (130 km).

Alberti, Leon Battista (1404–72) Italian Renaissance architect. Alberti, who was also a painter, writer, musician, and scientist, is known mainly for being among the first Renaissance architects fully to grasp the principles of classical architecture. As his innovative façade of Sta Maria Novella in Florence demonstrates, he adapted these rules to 15th-century requirements. He built relatively little, his most significant buildings being the churches of S Sebastiano and S Andrea in Mantua and the incomplete Tempio Malatestiano in Rimini. His abiding influence upon architecture was through his treatise *De re aedificatoria* (*On Architecture;* 1452) soon translated into several European languages.

LEON BATTISTA ALBERTI *The west front of Sta Maria Novella (Florence).*

Albert of Brandenburg (1490–1545) German churchman, Cardinal Archbishop and Elector of Mainz. Although a religious liberal, a patron of the arts, and a friend of *Erasmus, he is chiefly remembered as the object of Luther's attacks for his sale of indulgences. In later life he supported the *Counter-Reformation.

Albertsville. *See* Kalemie.

Albertus Magnus, St (c. 1200–80) German bishop, philosopher, and Doctor of the Church. Provincial of the German Dominicans (1254–57) and for a short time Bishop of Regensburg, he taught constantly throughout his life. His best-known pupil was *Aquinas. An outstanding scholar, he wrote extensively on logic, natural and moral sciences, scripture, and theology. Feast day: Nov 15.

Albi 43 56N 2 08E A city in S France, the capital of the Tarn department on the Tarn River. A center of Catharism, it gave its name to the Albigensian heresy (*see* Albigenses). Notable buildings include the Gothic cathedral and the 13th-century archbishop's palace, which is now a museum housing works by Toulouse-Lautrec (a native of Albi). An agricultural market, it has textile, glass, and cement industries. Population (1975): 49,456.

Albigenses Followers of the Christian heresy of Catharism (*see* Cathari), who flourished in southern France in the 12th and 13th centuries. The Albigenses, named for the town of Albi in Languedoc, were the object of the Albigensian Crusade, launched in 1208 and led by Simon de *Montfort. They were finally suppressed by the Inquisition, which operated in the area from 1233.

albinism An inherited disorder in which tyrosinase, one of the enzymes required for the formation of the pigment *melanin, is absent. Albinos have abnormally pale skin, fair hair, and pink or light-blue irises. The condition can be eased by the use of spectacles to treat the lens abnormalities common in albinos and by protection of the skin and eyes from direct sunlight. Albinism, which can affect all human races, is also seen in wild and domestic animals.

Albino horse A horse exhibiting the characteristics of albinism and bred to maintain the color type. Albinos have pinkish sensitive skin, pure-white hair, and blue eyes. Defective eyesight is common, lessening its usefulness as a riding horse.

Albinoni, Tomaso (1671–1750) Italian composer and court musician to the Duke of Mantua. His works, which influenced J. S. Bach, include 50 operas, a violin concerto, and two oboe concertos. The *Adagio* for organ and strings often attributed to Albinoni was in fact composed by his Italian biographer Remo Giazotto.

Alboin (died c. 573) King of the Lombards (c. 565–c. 573). He succeeded to lands in central Europe and then conquered N Italy, establishing the kingdom of Lombardy (572), with his capital at Pavia.

Ålborg (*or* Aalborg) 57 03N 09 56E A city and seaport in Denmark, in N Jutland. Founded in 1342 AD, it has a Gothic cathedral and a 16th-century castle. A university was established in 1974. Its industries include ship building and textiles. Population (1988 est): 155,000.

albumins A class of proteins that are soluble in both water and dilute aqueous salt solutions. Serum albumins are constituents of blood; α-lactalbumin is found in milk; and ovalbumin is part of egg white. Preparations of albumins are used in therapeutic transfusions.

Albuquerque 35 05N 106 38W A city, in New Mexico, on the Rio Grande. The state's largest city, it is situated in a rich agricultural area and food canning and the manufacture of livestock products are its principal industries. It is the home of the University of New Mexico (1892). Population (1990): 384,736.

Albuquerque, Alfonso de (1453–1515) Portuguese governor in India (1509–15). He was already a veteran soldier when he led his first expedition to India (1503). By a series of conquests he established Portuguese influence in the Indian Ocean based on three strongholds—Goa, Ceylon, and Malacca. He led the first European fleet to sail into the Red Sea and took Hormuz in 1515. Private enemies at the Portuguese court sought to discredit him and he was recalled, dying at sea.

Al Bu Sa'id The ruling dynasty of Oman since 1749 and of Zanzibar from 1749 to 1964. In 1749 Ahmad ibn Sa'id, the dynasty's founder, seized power over Oman and Zanzibar. In 1856 Oman and Zanzibar were divided. Zanzibar continued under Bu Sa'idi rule under the British protectorate (1890–1963), but the dynasty was overthrown when Zanzibar was incorporated into Tanzania (1964). The present ruler of Oman is Qaboos ibn Sa'id.

Alcaeus (6th century BC) Greek lyric poet. A member of the aristocracy of the island of Lesbos and a friend of *Sappho, he went into exile when the tyrant Pittacus gained power and wandered for many years in Thrace and Egypt. His work, only fragments of which survive, was greatly admired by *Horace.

Alcatraz An island, in W California in San Francisco Bay. It was the site of a notorious maximum security prison from 1934 until 1962.

alcázar (Arabic *al-qasr*: castle, palace) A Spanish fortress built during the conflicts between Moors and Christians in the 14th and 15th centuries. The most renowned is the Alcázar of *Seville, built by King *Pedro the Cruel. The word remains an element in certain placenames, e.g. Alcázar de San Juan.

Alcázar de San Juan 39 42N 3 12W A town in S central Spain, in New Castile on La Mancha plain. It is associated with Cervantes' *Don Quixote*. Population: 26,963.

alchemy A pseudoscience combining practical *chemistry with magical or mystical views of man and his relationship to the universe. Originating independently in China and Egypt, probably before the 3rd century BC, alchemy remained a legitimate branch of science and philosophy in Asia, Europe, and the Islamic lands for over 1500 years and is the ancestor of modern chemistry. It had three principal goals, the emphasis on which varied from place to place: the elixir of life (to ensure immortality), the panacea (or universal medicine), and the means of transmuting base metals into gold (*see* philosopher's stone). In China, *Taoism, which highly esteemed long life, fostered alchemical experimentation in search of the elixir. In Europe, concentration upon gold-making brought alchemy into disrepute.

Alcibiades (c. 450–404 BC) Athenian general and politician. Brought up by *Pericles, he was the pupil and lover of *Socrates. Alcibiades encouraged Athenian imperialism during the *Peloponnesian War (431–404) until, accused of desecrating monuments in Athens, he defected to Sparta (415). He regained Athenian favor (410) and was a successful commander until defeat, the fault of a subordinate, forced him into exile (406). He was murdered in Phrygia.

Alcmeon (c. 500 BC) Greek pioneer in medical science, from Croton (S Italy). Following *Pythagoras' experimental tradition, Alcmeon used dissection and vivisection to investigate human sense organs. He discovered the optic nerve and located the center of sensation in the brain.

Alcmaeon In Greek mythology, the son of Amphiarus, one of the *Seven Against Thebes, and Eriphyle. He killed his mother to avenge the death of Amphiarus, and was pursued by the Furies. His first wife was Arsinoë, daughter of King Pegeus of Psophis, but on his wanderings he married the daughter of the river god Achelous, and was pursued and killed by Pegeus and his sons. His own sons later avenged his death by killing Pegeus.

Alcmaeonids An aristocratic family prominent in virtually all ancient Athenian political crises, usually on the radical side. In 632 BC Megacles (an Alcmaeonid) violated the sanctuary of Athena by having a political opponent treacherously murdered there. The oracle of Delphi placed a hereditary curse on the family, banishing it from Athens. The Alcmaeonids returned under Solon, withdrew under Pisistratus, and returned again after the expulsion of Hippias (511/510 BC). *Cleisthenes was an Alcmaeonid; *Pericles and *Alcibiades had Alcmaeonid mothers.

Alcock, Sir John (William) (1892–1919) British aviator. He served with the Royal Naval Air Service in World War I and in 1919, accompanied by **(Sir) Arthur Brown** (1886–1948), was the first to fly the Atlantic Ocean. They flew from Newfoundland to Ireland, in 16 hours 27 minutes.

Alcoholics Anonymous (AA) A voluntary organization started in the US in 1934 to help alcoholics to help themselves. Members, who must have an honest desire to stop drinking, help one another on the basis of group therapy by sharing their experiences of alcoholism. There are local autonomous groups in over 90 countries. An associated organization, AL-ANON, provides support for the close relatives of alcoholics.

alcoholism An illness caused by physical and psychological dependence on alcohol (*see also* drug dependence). The incidence of alcoholism varies between different societies: it is most common in countries where alcohol is readily available and where heavy drinking is socially acceptable. Alcoholism causes mood changes, deterioration in personal standards and habits, and periods of memory loss. Continued heavy consumption will eventually lead to cirrhosis of the liver, heart disease, and damage to the nerves. Sudden withdrawal may produce specific symptoms: tremor, delusions, and hallucinations. Treatment, which is lengthy and difficult, includes initial alcohol withdrawal (with appropriate sedation) accompanied and followed by adequate psychological support. Drugs such as disulfiram (Antabuse), which cause vomiting after drinking alcohol, may assist the treatment. Nonmedical solutions to problems of alcoholism include group therapy in the company of other alcoholics (*see* Alcoholics Anonymous).

alcohols The class of organic compounds that includes *ethanol (ethyl alcohol; C_2H_5OH) and *methanol (methyl alcohol; CH_3OH). Ethanol is the common alcohol found in intoxicating drinks and is often called simply "alcohol." Alcohols contain at least one hydroxyl group and have the general formula ROH, where R is a *hydrocarbon group. They react with *acids to give *esters and water. Primary alcohols oxidize to form *aldehydes and secondary alcohols to form *ketones.

alcohol strength The measurement of the percentage volume of *ethanol (ethyl alcohol) in alcoholic drinks in order to calculate government duty on them. In the US, 100° proof is 50% alcohol by volume. Until 1980, the UK used a similar system for spirits, but with 57.06%, measured at 59°F (15°C), as the standard (100° proof), pure alcohol being 175° proof. France and Italy formerly used the Gay-Lussac scale, which simply states the percentage volume of alcohol, measured at 59°F (15°C). The **OMIL** (International Organization of Legal meterology) system, now used throughout the European Economic Community (EEC), is based on percentage volume of alcohol at 68°F (20°C). Thus a bottle of liquor labeled in the EEC "35% vol" is approximately equivalent to 61° proof in the former UK system or 70° proof in the US system.

Alcott, Amos Bronson (1799–1888) US philosopher, educator, reformer, and writer; father of Louisa May Alcott. He had several schools in Connecticut, Boston, and Philadelphia, before founding the Temple School (1834) in Boston. Here he attempted to develop the well-rounded student, intellectually, emotionally, and physically. He also founded Fruitlands (1843), an experimental community in Harvard, Mass., and advocated transcendentalism throughout his later life. Among his works are *Ralph Waldo Emerson* (1865) and *Concord Days* (1872).

Alcott, Louisa May (1832–88) US novelist. Daughter of the social theorist Bronson Alcott, her education was supplemented by instruction from *Thoreau, *Emerson, and her neighbor Nathaniel *Hawthorne. Her first book, *Flower Fables* (1854), was written when she was 16 to raise money for her family. *Hospital Sketches* (1863) recounted her experiences as a nurse in the Civil War. *Little Women* (1868–69), her most famous book, was, like her subsequent children's books, largely autobiographical. Other works include *An Old Fashioned Girl* (1870), *Little Men* (1871), and *Jo's Boys* (1886).

Alcuin (c. 735–804 AD) English theologian and educator, who inspired the Carolingian renaissance. He became the religious and educational adviser to Charlemagne after meeting him in 781. He established important libraries and developed a method of teaching based on *Boethius, St *Augustine, and the study of grammar. Among his pupils was Rabanus Maurus (c. 780–856). He compiled numerous educational manuals and was also a poet. His letters are important sources for the study of Carolingian society.

Aldanov, Mark (M. Aleksandrovich Landau; 1886–1957) Russian novelist. He emigrated to France in 1919 and to the US in 1941. His best-known work is a trilogy about Revolutionary France, comprising *Saint Helena* (1924), *The Ninth Thermidor* (1926), and *The Devil's Bridge* (1928). *The Fifth Seal* (1936) was an anti-Soviet satire and *The Tenth Symphony* (1931), a portrait of Beethoven's Vienna.

Aldebaran A conspicuous *red giant, apparent magnitude 0.9 and 68 light years distant, that is the brightest star in the constellation Taurus. It is both a visual *binary star and an irregular *variable star.

aldehydes A class of organic chemicals that contain the -CHO group. They are prepared by the oxidation of alcohols and are themselves oxidized to form carboxylic acids. Most are liquids; common aldehydes are *formaldehyde and *acetaldehyde.

Alden, John (1599–1637) English colonist in America. He sailed to America on the *Mayflower* in 1620 and is said to have been the first Pilgrim to set foot in the new land at Plymouth, Mass. He was a signer of the *Mayflower Compact*, co-founded Duxbury, Mass., and served as deputy governor of Massachusetts twice (1623–41; 1650–86). He is immortalized in Henry Wadsworth Longfellow's poem "The Courtship of Miles Standish" (1858) for courting Priscilla Mullins (whom he did in fact marry) for his friend Miles Standish.

alder A tree or shrub belonging to a genus (*Alnus*; about 30 species) of the N hemisphere. The leaves are roundish and toothed; the flowers grow as separate male and female catkins on the same tree. The fruit is a woody cone containing small winged nuts. The black alder (*A. glutinosa*), about 65 ft (20 m) high, is found in wet places throughout Europe and Asia and in N Africa. Its timber is used in general woodworking. Family: *Betulaceae* (birch family).

alderfly An insect, also known as a fish fly, having two pairs of delicate finely veined wings and long antennae. Up to 2 in (50 mm) long (including the wings), alderflies live near fresh water, feeding on smaller insects and laying their eggs on reeds. The larvae, which are also carnivorous, live in the water and crawl out to pupate in burrows in the soil. Family: *Sialidae*; order: *Neuroptera* (lacewings, etc.).

Alderney (French name: Aurigny) 49 43N 2 12W The third largest of the Channel Islands, separated from the French coast by the dangerous Race of Alderney channel. Its economy is based on dairy farming and tourism. Area: 3 sq mi (8 sq km). Chief town: St Anne.

Aldington, Richard (1892–1962) British poet, novelist, and biographer. In 1913 he married his fellow Imagist poet Hilda *Doolittle. He suffered shell shock in World War I; *Death of a Hero* (1929) and *The Colonel's Daughter* (1931) are his best-known novels. Among his frequently controversial biographies are studies of D. H. Lawrence (1950) and T. E. Lawrence (1955).

Aldiss, Brian W(ilson) (1925–   ) British novelist. Most of his novels and short stories are science fiction and he has written a history of the genre in *Billion Year Spree* (1975) and *Trillion Year Spree* (1986). His novels include *The*

Malacia Tapestry (1976). He edited many science-fiction anthologies, and his individual collections include *The Saliva Tree* (1966) and *Last Orders* (1977).

aldol An organic compound that contains a *hydroxyl group (OH) and an *aldehyde group (CHO) bound to adjacent carbon atoms. A common aldol is **acetaldol** ($CH_3CHOHCH_2CHO$), which is used as a sedative and hypnotic drug.

aldosterone A steroid hormone that acts on the kidney tubules to regulate the content of salts and water in the body. Derived from cholesterol, aldosterone is produced by the cortex of the adrenal glands in response to changing blood volume, changing levels of sodium and potassium, and the presence of the pituitary hormone *ACTH.

Aldrich, Thomas Bailey (1836–1907) US novelist and poet. He left school at 13 and began writing for magazines while working in New York as a clerk. He is known for his light verse and short stories and his autobiography, *The Story of a Bad Boy* (1870).

Aldrich-Vreeland Currency Act (1908) US law that created the National Monetary Commission and paved the way for the Federal Reserve Act of 1913. Aimed at alleviating the bank failures and currency shortages of 1907, the bill provided for relief in such cases by authorizing temporary emergency currency issuance by organized bank groups. Meanwhile, the commission was to study banking conditions and recommend reforms.

Aldridge, Ira Frederick (1804–67) US actor. The first great black tragedian, he made his debut as Othello in London in 1826 and made several successful European tours in Shakespearean roles.

Aldrin, Buzz (Edwin Eugene A., Jr.; 1930–) US astronaut. A graduate of West Point (1951), he served in Korea as an Air Force pilot before entering the astronaut program at the National Aeronautics and Space Administration (NASA) in 1963. He was part of the two-man crew on the Gemini XII flight in 1966 and was the second man to walk on the moon during the 1969 flight of Apollo 11.

ale. *See* beer.

aleatoric music Music that incorporates elements of chance in its structure. The term from Latin *alea*, a game of dice, was first used in the 1950s to describe John *Cage's experiments in determining compositional procedures of pitch, rhythm, structure, and dynamics by the use of the *I Ching.

Alegría, Ciro (1909–61) Peruvian novelist, imprisoned and finally exiled to Chile and the US from 1934 until 1948 for his political activities. His works embody his deep knowledge of, and sympathy for, the Peruvian Indians: his best-known novel, *Broad and Alien Is the World* (1941), deals with the resistance of an Indian tribe to the usurping white man.

Alekhine, Alexander (1892–1946) French chess player, born in Russia. He became world champion by defeating *Capablanca (1927), losing the championship in 1935, but holding it again from 1937 until his death. He regarded chess as an art, the aesthetic merits of which were more important to him than winning.

Alemán, Mateo (1547–?1614) Spanish writer, famous for his picaresque novel *Guzman de Alfarache* (1599–1604), the scurrilous adventures of a youth who runs away from home and is finally condemned to the galleys, where he repents. The book became popular throughout Europe. Alemán himself was often imprisoned for debt and emigrated to Mexico in 1607.

Alençon 48 25N 0 05E A city in NW France, the capital of the Orne department situated at the confluence of the Sarthe and Briant Rivers. The former capital of the duchy of Alençon, it is famed for its lace (especially point of d'Alençon). It serves an agricultural area. Population (1975): 34,666.

Aleppo (Arabic name: Halab) 36 14N 37 10E A city in NW Syria. The Crusaders tried in vain to capture it, and from 1516 to 1919 Aleppo was part of the Ottoman Empire. After World War II, it was incorporated into independent Syria. It is now an industrial center and the terminus of a pipeline from Iraq; its university was founded in 1960. Population (1975 est): 778,523.

Alessandria 44 55N 8 37E A city in N Italy, in Piedmont on the Tanaro River. It is a railroad center and has an important engineering industry. The surrounding district is agricultural. Population (1980 est): 101,075.

Ålesund (*or* Aalesund) 62 28N 6 11E A seaport in W Norway. Founded in the 9th century AD, it is an important trading center, especially for fishing in northern waters. Population (1981 est): 34,630.

Aletsch Glacier The largest glacier in Europe, in Switzerland in the Bernese Oberland, lying SE of the Aletschhorn mountain. Length: 16 mi (26 km).

Aleut A native of the Aleutian Islands and W Alaska, similar to the *Eskimo in culture. Aleuts hunted seals, whales, and walrus, using skin-covered boats called bidarkas, which were like *kayaks but often two-manned. They also fished for salmon and in some areas hunted caribou and bear. They produced fine basketry and worked stone, bone, and ivory. Their population was considerably reduced during the Russian administration of the area and today their culture has been much changed by the impact of the modern world. Their language is closely related to Eskimo. It has three dialects, the two principal ones being Attuan and Unalaskan.

Aleutian Islands A chain of volcanic Alaskan islands lying between the Bering Sea and the Pacific Ocean, divided politically between Russia and the US. The chief settlements are on Unalaska. Russian exploitation of supplies after 1741 greatly reduced the population, but fishing and seal, otter, and fox hunting are now regulated. There are strategic US military stations on the islands and underground nuclear tests have been made.

alewife A small silvery fish, *Pandopus pseudoharengus*, up to 12 in (30 cm) long. It occurs chiefly in the Atlantic coastal waters of North America but has recently become established in the Great Lakes. It is an important food fish and is also used in the manufacture of fertilizers. Family: *Clupeidae* (herrings).

Alexander (1876–1903) King of Serbia (1889–1903); the last of the *Obrenović dynasty. Alexander's arbitrary rule, including the abolition of the liberal constitution in 1894, and his unpopular marriage in 1900 led to his assassination, and that of his wife, by a group of army officers.

Alexander I (c. 1077–1124) King of the Scots (1107–24), who ruled the highlands of Scotland while his brother and successor David ruled the lowlands. He was noted for his reform of the Scottish church and his foundation of the monastery of Scone (1114). He aided Henry I of England's campaign against Wales (1114).

Alexander I (1777–1825) Emperor of Russia (1801–25), succeeding his unstable father Paul I. Alexander made some educational and administrative reforms but was more concerned with foreign policy. France's defeat of Russia at *Friedland in 1807 forced Alexander to agree to the Treaty of *Tilsit, which lasted until Napoleon's unsuccessful invasion of Russia in 1812. After Napoleon's defeat, Russia controlled the *Congress Kingdom of Poland.

Alexander turned to religious mysticism, hoping to establish a new Christian order in Europe by means of the Holy Alliance (1815) with Austria and Prussia. Toward the end of his life he withdrew into seclusion.

Alexander II (1198–1249) King of the Scots (1214–49). Hoping to regain the northern counties of England, he supported the unsuccessful *Barons' War (1215–17) against King John. In 1221 he married Joan, the sister of Henry III of England, and gave up his claims to English territory in 1237, when the present border between England and Scotland was fixed.

Alexander II (1818–81) Emperor of Russia (1855–81). After the conclusion of the *Crimean War (1856) Alexander embarked upon a program of modernization. He emancipated the serfs (1861) and reorganized administration, the army, the judicial system, local government, and education. These reforms were not wholly successful because Alexander lacked personnel able to implement them. He presided over Russian expansion into Central Asia and the victorious war against Turkey (1877–78). The end of his reign saw the growth of radical opposition and he was killed by a bomb thrown into his coach.

ALEXANDER (III) THE GREAT *A detail of a mosaic at Pompeii, which shows Alexander on his horse Bucephalus pursuing the fleeing Darius III (d. 330) of Persia. Alexander's decisive victory was fought at Gaugamela in 331.*

Alexander (III) the Great (356–323 BC) King of Macedon (336–323), who between 334 and his death conquered most of the world known to antiquity. Alexander, who was a pupil of Aristotle, inherited a plan to invade Persia from his father Philip II; having secured his position in Macedon and Greece, he put this plan into action. In 333 he defeated the Persian king *Darius III at Issus; in 332 he reduced Tyre in his greatest victory. Alexander then proceeded to conquer Egypt and Babylon (331). Moving on to Media and then east into central Asia, he finally embarked on the Indian expedition (327–325). He crossed the Indus River and conquered the Punjab. Forced to turn back by his reluctant army, he died at Babylon shortly after the marathon return journey. In the administration of his empire Alexander adopted a novel policy of appointing subject races to posts of responsibility, which some historians have called idealism and others, opportunism. His outstanding gifts as a general, however, are indisputable.

Alexander III (Rolando Bandinelli; c. 1105–81) Italian pope. Elected in 1159, he was immediately challenged by the antipope Victor IV, who was supported by *Frederick Barbarossa. He eventually forced Frederick to reconcile himself with the Church at the Peace of Venice in 1177. He imposed penance on *Henry II of England for the murder of Thomas *Becket. He called and presided at the third *Lateran Council, which conferred the exclusive right of papal elections on the cardinals.

Alexander III (1241–86) King of the Scots (1249–86). He married (1251) Margaret, daughter of Henry III of England. Under his leadership, the Scots defeated the Norwegians at the battle of Largs (1263) and by the Treaty of Perth (1266) gained the Isle of Man and the Hebrides from Norway.

Alexander III (1845–94) Emperor of Russia (1881–94). Owing to the assassination of his father, Alexander II, and the influence of the lawyer K. P. Pobedonostsev (1827–1907), Alexander's reign showed extreme conservatism. He increased police powers, persecuted revolutionaries, permitted education to decline, and encouraged the russification of subject races. Under him, Russia made its last conquests in Central Asia and the Middle East.

Alexander VI (Rodrigo Borgia; c. 1431–1503) Pope (1492–1503), notorious for his immorality, nepotism, and extravagance. Father of four illegitimate children, he used papal wealth to further the career of his son, Cesare *Borgia, who pursued Alexander's territorial ambitions in Italy. He was a generous patron of artists and was responsible for demarcating the respective areas of influence of Spain and Portugal in the New World.

Alexander Archipelago A chain of islands in the US, off the SE coast of Alaska. They consist of the summits of a submerged mountain chain and their rugged densely forested terrain supports an abundance of wildlife.

Alexander Nevsky (c. 1220–63) Prince of Novgorod (1236–63) and Grand Prince of Vladimir (1252–63). Alexander's fame rests on his defeat of the Swedes (1240) near the Neva River (thus acquiring his name Nevsky) and of the Teutonic Knights (1242) on Lake Peipus. Despite the opposition of many Russians, he accepted the overlordship of the invading Mongols, thereby saving N Russia from certain devastation.

Alexander of Hales (c. 1170–1245) English scholastic philosopher, born at Hales (Gloucestershire). He became professor of theology in Paris and in 1236 a Franciscan. He is renowned for his efforts to combine the newly rediscovered *Aristotelianism, as mediated by the Arabic thinkers, such as *Averroes, with the Platonist tradition mediated by St *Augustine of Hippo.

Alexander of Tunis, Harold, 1st Earl (1891–1969) British field marshal. In World War II he commanded the evacuation of British forces from Dunkirk. He became commander in chief in the Middle East (1942) and directed the offensive that defeated the Germans in N Africa (1943). He ended the war as Allied supreme commander in the Mediterranean and was subsequently governor general of Canada (1946–52).

Alexander Severus. *See* Severus Alexander.

Alexandria (Arabic name: al-Iskandariyah) 31 13N 22 55E The chief seaport and second largest city in Egypt, between Lake Mareotis and the Mediterranean Sea. It handles most of Egypt's trade and the chief export is cotton; industries include oil refining and cotton ginning. The University of Alexandria was established in 1942. *History*: founded in 332 BC by Alexander the Great, partly on the island of Pharos, which was linked to the mainland by a breakwater, it remained the Egyptian capital for over a thousand years. It was a Greek and Jewish cultural center with a famous library (*see* Alexandria, Library of) and in 30 BC fell to the Romans, becoming their most important regional capital. It declined following the discovery of the Cape of Good Hope passage and the removal of the capital to Cairo. It was bombarded by the British in 1882, Pompey's Pillar being one of the few ancient monuments to escape destruction. Two obelisks that also survived, *Cleopatra's Needles, were removed and one is now in London, the other in New York. During World War II the city suffered many air raids but since then has seen rapid expansion. Population (1990 est): 3,190,000.

Alexandria 38 48N 77 03W A city and port in E Virginia on the Potomac River, S of Washington, D.C. Established in 1749, Alexandria's historic sites include Christ Church. The *Alexandria Gazette* (1784), the oldest daily newspaper in the United States, is still published here. Manufactures include wood products and chemicals. Population (1990): 111,183.

Alexandria, Catechetical School of A Christian theological school at Alexandria from the late 2nd to the 4th century AD. Its early teachers, *Clement and *Origen, dominated the School's approach, which was a Platonic mystical philosophy that stressed divine transcendence, the deity of Christ, and a Trinitarianism that was almost tritheism. Athanasius was typically Alexandrian in opposing the Arian and related heresies.

Alexandria, Library of The greatest library of the ancient world, which in its heyday may have contained more than 700,000 items. A composite library, museum, and school, it was founded in the 3rd century BC by *Ptolemy I Soter and his son, *Ptolemy II Philadelphus. Large parts were destroyed in fires, notably in 97 BC, and it was finally destroyed by the Arabs in 696 AD. The survival of much of classical Greek literature is due to the work of its scholars.

alexandrine A verse meter consisting of a line of 12 syllables usually with major stresses on the sixth and final syllables. The name is derived from 12th-century French poems about Alexander the Great. It was the dominant verse form in 17th-century French poetry and was used by *Racine and *Corneille.

Alexis (1690–1718) The son and heir of *Peter the Great of Russia. Alexis' unhappy relations with his father progressively worsened and in 1716 Alexis fled to Vienna. Peter lured him back and condemned him to death for treason. He died before his execution.

Alexius I Comnenus (1048–1118) Byzantine emperor (1081–1118), who founded the Comnenian dynasty. Seizing the throne in a coup, Alexius revived the weakened Byzantine state, defeating the Normans and Seljuq Turks, who were encroaching on Byzantine territory, and introducing administrative reforms. However, in the second half of his reign, the Empire was threatened by the advance of the Crusaders. His achievements were celebrated in the *Alexiad* of his daughter *Anna Comnena.

alfalfa A perennial flowering plant, *Medicago sativa*, also called lucerne. Growing to a height of 40 in (1 m), it resembles clover, having clusters of small purple flowers. Native to Europe, it is widely grown as forage for cattle and because of its ability to fix nitrogen. Family: *Leguminosae*.

al-Farabi, Mohammed ibn Tarkhan (d. 950) Muslim philosopher, physician, mathematician, and musician, of Central Asian origin. He is acknowledged to be one of the greatest Muslim thinkers and his works on medicine and music became standard treatises. But it was his contribution to Arabic philosophy that earned him renown. A staunch believer in the truth of Islam, Al-Farabi strove to bring the whole of Greek philosophy into conformity with its doctrines.

Alfieri, Vittorio, Count (1749–1803) Italian poet and dramatist. He abandoned a military career in order to travel widely throughout Europe (1767–72). After the success of his first play, *Cleopatra* (1775), he devoted himself entirely to literature. He wrote 28 plays, of which his 19 tragedies, among them *Saul* and *Mirra*, depict romantic heroes struggling against tyranny and oppression. He also wrote poetry and an autobiography, *La vita* (1804).

Alfonsín, Raúl (1926–   ) Argentine statesman; president (1983–89). A lawyer, he was a member of the Radical Party, serving as president of the party from 1965. His election to the presidency ended the almost-40-year reign of the Peronist Party. An advocate of civil and human rights, Alfonsín fought corruption in the government and military and attempted to ease Argentina's economic distress and stormy relations with other countries in the aftermath of Argentina's unsuccessful attempt to occupy the Falkland Islands. He was succeeded by the Peronist, Carlos Menem.

Alfonso (V) the Magnanimous (1385–1458) King of Aragon (1416–58) and, as Alfonso I, of Sicily (1416–58) and Naples (1443–58). During the 1420s he helped Queen Joanna II of Naples (1371–1435; reigned 1414–35) to resist the claims of Louis III of Anjou (1403–34) to the Neapolitan throne. After her death he seized the throne himself and his court at Naples became a brilliant center of Renaissance culture.

Alfonso VI (d. 1109) King of León (1065–1109) and of Castile (1072–1109). In 1085 Alfonso took Toledo from the Muslims but in the following year suffered defeat by the Almoravids of N Africa, with whom conflict continued until 1108. Alfonso's marriage to Constance of Burgundy brought cultural ties with France and he supported the introduction of Cluniac monasticism to León. His reign is also notable for the exploits of El Cid.

Alfonso VIII (d. 1214) King of Castile (1158–1214), famous for his defeat of the Moors at Navas de Tolosa (1212). He married Eleanor, a daughter of Henry II of England; their daughter was *Blanche of Castile.

Alfonso (X) the Wise (c. 1221–84) King of Castile and León (1252–84). He made his court at Toledo, a center of learning and a haven for Arab and Jewish, as well as Christian, scholars. He compiled a legal code, the Seven Divisions of the Law, but it never came into effective use. He also failed in an attempt (1257) to become the first Spanish Holy Roman Emperor.

Alfonso XIII (1886–1941) King of Spain from birth until 1931. Alfonso, who came of age in 1902, ruled during a turbulent period of social unrest and political instability and several attempts were made on his life. The dictatorship (1923–30) of Miguel *Primo de Rivera undermined his reign and he abdicated in 1931 following Republican victories in municipal elections.

Alfred the Great (849–99) King of Wessex (871–99). He prevented the Danish conquest of England, defeating them at Edington (878) after a campaign of guerrilla warfare. After his victory he allowed the Danes to keep their conquests in Mercia and East Anglia provided that Guthrum, their king, converted to Christianity. Alfred built a navy of warships to defend the south coast against further Danish invasions (885–86; 892–96) and protected Wessex with a chain of fortifications. He took London (886), thus gaining control of all England except the Danish areas. Alfred did much to revive learning, translating important Latin works into English. He also devised a legal code.

Alfvén, Hannes Olof Gösta (1908–   ) Swedish astrophysicist. A specialist in *plasma physics, his original work includes studies of sunspots, cosmic rays, and the aurora. His work on the interaction of plasma with magnetic fields (magnetohydrodynamics) forms the basis of several proposed systems for harnessing nuclear fusion power; he shared the 1970 Nobel Prize for this work.

algae A vast group of simple plants (about 25,000 species) that contain the green pigment chlorophyll (and can therefore carry out photosynthesis) but have no true stems, roots, or leaves (*see* Thallophyta). They range from single-celled organisms to the giant seaweeds. Most algae are aquatic, although some live in damp places on land—on rocks, trees, or in soils. A few are parasitic or associate with other organisms (*see* lichen). Reproduction is extremely variable and may involve asexual means, such as cell division, fragmentation, or spore production, and/or sexual means by gamete production. The more advanced algae often alternate between sexual and asexual phases. Algae provide a valuable food source for aquatic herbivorous animals and many are used as fertilizers and in industry. There are generally considered to be seven divisions of algae (*see* red algae). Some of the unicellular forms are alternatively classed as *Protozoa.

Algarve The most southerly region of Portugal, bordering on Spain and the Atlantic Ocean. It became a Moorish kingdom in 1140 and was the last stronghold of the Moors in Portugal, being reconquered in 1249. Sparsely populated inland, its fertile coastal belt is densely populated and produces chiefly grain, figs, almonds, and olives; fishing is also important. Tourism is a flourishing industry. It is part of the modern district of Faro. Chief town: Faro.

algebra The branch of mathematics that uses symbols to represent unknown quantities. The first treatise on the subject was written by Diophantus of Alexandria in the 3rd century AD and the name derives from the Arabic *al-jabr*, a term used by the mathematician al-Khwarizmi to denote the addition of equal quantities to both sides of an equation and later adopted as the name for the whole subject. Algebra was used in ancient Babylon, Egypt, and India and brought to Europe by the Arabs. In classical algebra, symbols, such as x and y, represent ordinary numbers and the central part of the subject is the study of algebraic equations. Modern, or abstract, algebra is concerned with any system of quantities that obey a particular set of general rules and relationships. Such systems may or may not obey the *commutative laws or even the *associative laws that hold in arithmetic.

Algeciras 36 08N 5 27W A port in S Spain, in Andalusia on the Bay of Gibraltar. Founded in 713 AD, it was destroyed by Alfonso XI of Castile (1311–50; reigned 1312–50) in 1344. The present town was rebuilt in 1760. In 1906 it was the site of the Algeciras Conference, a meeting of European powers to solve their dispute over Morocco. Its exports include oranges and cork. Population (1991): 101,063.

Alger, Horatio (1832–99) US novelist and churchman, known for his stories of the rise from "rags to riches." Born in Massachusetts and educated for the ministry, Alger wrote his first novel in 1864 and followed with more than 135 others, all with the theme of riches achieved by virtuous, hard-working young men. His works include *Ragged Dick* (1867), *Tattered Tom* (1871), and *The Young Miner* (1879).

Algeria, Democratic and Popular Republic of A country in N Africa, on the Mediterranean Sea. It consists chiefly of the N Sahara Desert, with the Atlas Mountains in the N and small fertile areas near the coast. The inhabitants, who live almost entirely in the N, are mainly Arabs and Berbers. *Economy*: mainly agricultural although industrialization has proceeded rapidly since independence, financed by the discovery of oil (the main export) and natural gas in the desert areas. *History*: a former province of the Roman Empire, Algeria was subjugated in the 7th century by the Arabs, who introduced Islam. Overrun by

Turks in the 16th century, it became a pirate state in the 18th century under the domination of *deys*, independent rulers who preyed on Mediterranean shipping. Algeria was annexed by the French in the 19th century and in 1881 the N section became part of Metropolitan France. A war of independence, waged by the *Front de Libération nationale (FLN), lasted from 1954 to 1962 when independence was granted by de Gaulle, following referenda held in both Algeria and France. A republic was set up under Ahmed *Ben Bella but was overthrown in 1965 by a Council of Revolution. Col. Houari *Boumédienne became president and in 1976 was elected for a further six years in office. In the same year a new constitution was adopted in which the one-party principle was reaffirmed, the FLN being the only political party permitted in Algeria. Following Boumédienne's death in December 1978, Col. Chadli Benjedid became the new president. A new constitution was adopted in 1989. Although Benjadid's administration was not as strict as that of his predecessor, he tightened the reins when violence erupted between the Islamic Salvation Front (a fundamentalist party) and the government in 1991. Elections later that year brought surprising fundamentalist victories. Benjadid resigned in early 1992, and an army-controlled ruling council, led by Mohamed Boudiaf, instituted emergency rule in a move to prevent a takeover by the fundamentalists. Official language: Arabic; French is also widely spoken. Official religion: Islam. Currency: dinar of 100 centimes. Area: 919,595 sq mi (2,381,745 sq km). Population (1990 est): 25,715,000. Capital and main port: Algiers.

Algiers (Arabic name: al-Jaza'ir; French name: Alger) 36 45N 3 05E The capital of Algeria, an important port in the N of the Mediterranean Sea. Its main exports include wine, citrus fruits, and iron ore. The University of Algiers was founded in 1879 and the University of Science and Technology in 1974. *History*: originally founded by the Phoenicians, it was re-established by the Arabs in the 10th century. Overrun by Turks in the 16th century, it became a base for Barbary pirates until taken by the French in 1830. During World War II it was the headquarters of the Allied forces in N Africa and for a time the seat of the French government-in-exile. It was the scene of several uprisings during the Algerian struggle for independence from France (1954–62). Population (1986 est): 1,500,000.

algin (sodium alginate) A slimy substance extracted from seaweed. It is used as a thickener in such foods as ice cream and in industrial compounds.

Algirdas (*or* Olgierd; d. 1377) Grand Duke of Lithuania (1345–77). A pagan ruler, Algirdas was nevertheless tolerant of the Orthodox Church. He fought the Poles, Mongols, and Teutonic Knights and extended Lithuania eastward.

Algol (*or* Winking Demon) A white 2nd-magnitude star in the constellation Perseus. Its regular variations in brightness have been known for centuries. It is the prototype of the **Algol variables**, a class of eclipsing *binary stars: Algol revolves around its fainter companion in 2.87 days.

ALGOL (*algo*rithmic *l*anguage) A computer-programming language. It is used to express mathematical and scientific problems in a way that can be processed by computer. ALGOL is a high-level language, i.e. statements made in it resemble English and algebraic formulae rather than a computer notation. *See* program.

Algonquian A group of North American Indian languages, including *Cree, *Cheyenne, *Blackfoot, and others spoken by tribes living to the S and E of Hudson Bay and in the eastern woodland zone. The Algonquian peoples lived by hunting and fishing and roamed widely in small family groups. They moved their possessions by means of toboggans and crafted their clothing from the hides of animals, such as deer, caribou, and moose. Their religion involved a belief in a single creator god, and they relied on the protective and curative powers of medicine men, who possessed considerable authority within Algonquian society. The Algonquians were eventually driven from their original homelands in the middle of the 17th century by the neighboring *Iroquois.

Algonquin The language and name of a North American Indian people of Quebec and Ottawa in Canada. The *Algonquian language group was named for it. Algonquin culture was similar to that of other Algonquian-speaking tribes of the area.

Algren, Nelson (1909–81) US novelist. He trained as a journalist in Chicago, where most of his fiction is set, and briefly became a migrant worker during the Depression. In his novels, such as *Never Come Morning* (1942), he portrayed the underworld of American city life in an intense naturalistic style. *The Man with the Golden Arm* (1949), about drug addiction, brought him international fame.

Alhambra A castle on a hilly terrace outside *Granada (Spain), built between 1238 and 1358. It was the last stronghold of the Muslim kings of Granada. Combining citadel and palace, it is an outstanding example of Moorish architecture, with magnificent courts and gardens. The name derives from Arabic *alhamra*, the red, an allusion to the red stucco used on the walls.

ALHAMBRA *The arcade around the Court of the Lions features the horseshoe arches characteristic of Moorish architecture.*

Al Hudaydah. *See* Hodeida.

Ali (c. 600–67) The cousin of *Mohammed and his son-in-law by marriage to *Fatimah. Born at Mecca, he was the second, or perhaps the first, person to embrace Islam. He became the fourth caliph in 656, but faced much opposition and was murdered in 661 at Kufa, Iraq. His tomb is venerated at Najaf. According to *Shiite Muslims, Ali was the only legitimate successor of Mohammed and only his descendants are recognized as *imams.

Ali, Muhammad (Cassius Marcellus Clay; 1942–   ) US boxer. A gold medalist in the 1960 Olympic Games, he became professional world heavyweight champion (1964). On becoming a Black Muslim he changed his name and was soon afterward stripped of his title for three years because of his refusal to be inducted into the army. Defeated (1971) by Joe *Frazier, he again became champion in 1974 by defeating George Foreman, losing the title briefly in 1978 to Leon Spinks. His defeat of Spinks later that year made him the only boxer to become champion three times. In 1980 he was defeated by Larry Holmes in his bid to regain the world title. He is renowned for his extroverted personality.

MUHAMMAD ALI *A familiar display of clowning amuses a Philippine official (right) before Ali's defeat of Joe Frazier in Manila, 1975.*

Alicante 38 21N 0 29W A port in SE Spain, in Valencia on the Mediterranean Sea. Exports include wine, olive oil, and fruits and it serves as an outlet for Madrid. Industries include oil refining, textiles, chemicals, soap, and tobacco. It is a popular tourist resort. Population (1991): 261,255.

Alice Springs 23 42S 133 52E A city in central Australia, in S Northern Territory. It is a major center for beef cattle and mineral transportation, linked by air, road, and rail with Adelaide and by air and the Stuart Highway with Darwin. It is also a base for tourism. Population (1991): 22,759.

alien A person born in a foreign country who has not qualified as a US citizen.

Alien and Sedition Acts (1798) Four laws enacted ostensibly to prevent domestic subversion but actually to check the threat posed to the *Federalist Party by Thomas Jefferson's Republican Party. The Naturalization Act delayed voting rights for the immigrants upon whom the Republicans depended for support. The Alien Act and Alien Enemies Act authorized deportation of aliens suspected of threatening the government and the Sedition Act prohibited criticism of the government, thereby nullifying the First Amendment. The Alien Act expired in 1800 and the Sedition Act in 1801. The Alien Enemies Act was never enforced. The Naturalization Act was repealed in 1802.

alienation A pathological feeling of self-estrangement and loss of moral purpose. Hegel used the term to refer to a condition in which an individual's freedom of choice and action appears to him to have become an independent force constraining him. Marx made special use of the concept of alienated labor, believing that when men are forced to sell their labor to employers they are alienated from their own productive abilities. In contemporary common usage the term is applied loosely to situations in which people feel alienated from society, considering themselves to be "outsiders" with no sense of belonging to a community. In this meaning it overlaps the concept of *anomie.

Aligarh 27 42N 78 25E A city in N India, in Uttar Pradesh. An agricultural trading center, it is the site of the notable Aligarh Muslim University (founded as a college in 1875). Population (1991): 479,978.

alimony In law, a money allowance that a court may order a husband to pay to his wife for her support and that of any children, if, through separation or divorce, he is no longer living with her. Only occasionally are such payments awarded against the wife, because in general she has no legal obligation to maintain her husband. With easier and earlier divorces now granted, the courts have tended to lower alimony in cases where the wife is earning or is able to earn the same income as the husband.

Ali Pasa, Mehmed Emin (1815–71) Grand Vizier (chief minister) of the Ottoman Empire five times between 1852 and 1871. He represented the Ottomans at the Congress of Paris (1856) following the Crimean War and was an advocate of Ottoman friendship with France and Britain. He was one of the architects of the period (1839–76) of Ottoman reform known as the Tanzimat (Reorganization).

aliphatic compounds Organic chemical compounds that are not *aromatic. They include the *alkanes, *alkenes, and *alkynes as well as some cyclic compounds (cycloalkanes).

Aliutor. *See* Paleo-Siberian languages.

alizarin (1,2 dihydroxy-anthraquinone; $C_{14}H_6O_2(OH)_2$) An orange-red crystalline solid, formerly extracted from madder root and used in dyeing. It is almost insoluble in water but dissolves in alcohol. Alizarin is now made from *anthracene and yields a wide variety of dyes.

alkali. *See* acids and bases.

alkali metals The elements forming group I of the *periodic table: lithium, sodium, potassium, rubidium, cesium, and francium. All are soft, silvery-white *metals with low densities, melting points, and boiling points. In chemical reactions they tend to form positive ions and have a valence of 1. They are highly reactive, form soluble salts with nonmetals, generally release hydrogen on contact with water, and react with air to form oxides. The oxides and hydroxides are alkalis.

alkaline-earth metals The elements forming group II of the *periodic table: beryllium, magnesium, calcium, strontium, barium, and radium. They are similar to the *alkali metals in appearance and chemistry, but are harder, have higher melting and boiling points, and are somewhat less reactive. They have a valence of 2. The **alkaline earths** are the oxides of these metals.

alkaloids A group of nitrogen-containing basic compounds that are produced by plants and have diverse effects on the body. Many alkaloids are used as medicinal drugs, including quinine, reserpine, morphine, scopolamine, and atropine. Others, such as strychnine and coniine (from hemlock) are poisons. Caffeine, nicotine, and LSD are also alkaloids.

alkanes (*or* paraffins) A series of hydrocarbons, which contain only single bonds between the carbon atoms. They have the general formula C_nH_{2n+2}. The first four members of the series methane (CH_4), ethane (C_2H_6), propane (C_3H_8), and butane (C_4H_{10}) are gases, higher members are liquids or waxes. They are obtained from natural gas or oil and they and their substitution products have many uses.

alkanet A herbaceous plant of the genus *Anchusa*, native to Eurasia but widely grown for ornament (*A. azurea* is a common garden plant). It may reach a height of 20–48 in (50–120 cm), with clusters of small blue or white flowers and narrow or oval leaves. Family: *Boraginaceae*.

A similar and related plant, *Pentaglottis sempervirens*, is also called alkanet.

alkenes (*or* olefins) Hydrocarbons that contain at least one carbon–carbon double bond in their molecules. The simplest types, with one double bond, have the general formula C_nH_{2n}; ethylene (*or* ethene, C_2H_4) is the first member of this series. The alkenes are more reactive than the *alkanes, undergoing addition and polymerization reactions. They are obtained by cracking petroleum and their main use is as starting materials in industrial chemistry.

Al Khalil. *See* Hebron.

al-Khwarizmi, Muhammed ibn Musa (c. 780–c. 850 AD) Arabic mathematician, who introduced the Hindu decimal system and the use of zero into Arabic mathematics. He also extended the work of Diophantus on algebraic equations in a book the title of which included the word *al-jabr* ("transposition"), from which the modern word "algebra" is derived.

Al-Kindi, Abu Yusuf Ya'qub ibn Ishaq (died c. 870) Muslim Arab philosopher, born in al-Kufa (now in Iraq). He was dubbed "philosopher of the Arabs" as he was the only Arabic philosopher of pure Arab stock. He made the whole field of Greek science his own and was among the first Arabic scholars to interest himself in philosophy from a scientific rather than a theological viewpoint.

alkynes (*or* acetylenes) Hydrocarbons that contain at least one carbon–carbon triple bond in their molecules. The simplest types, with one triple bond, have the general formula C_nH_{2n-2}; acetylene (*or* ethyne, C_2H_2) is the first member of this series. The alkynes, like the *alkenes, undergo addition and polymerization reactions. They are extremely reactive, tending to explode under pressure, and are difficult to use in large quantities.

Allah (Arabic, probably from *al-ilah*: the god) The Islamic name of God. Allah was worshiped in pre-Islamic Arabia as early as the 3rd century BC. In Mecca he was given special rank as "the god," but lesser tribal gods continued to be worshiped alongside him until *Mohammed proclaimed the rigorous monotheism of Islam. As formulated by Mohammed, Allah is the one omnipotent and omniscient God, the same God as worshiped by Jews and Christians. He is eternal, the creator of the universe, the judge of men, merciful and compassionate. His word is embodied in the *Koran.

Allahabad 25 57N 81 50E A city in N India, in Uttar Pradesh at the confluence of the Ganges and Jumna Rivers. It is principally an administrative and educational center; its university was established in 1887. There is an annual religious festival and a much larger one every 12 years. A former center of the independence movement, it was the home of the Nehru family. Population (1991): 806,447.

Allegheny Mountains A mountain range extending from North Carolina to Pennsylvania. Part of the Appalachian Mountains, it consists of well-rounded uplands rising to 4860 ft (1480 m) at Spruce Knob. It forms the watershed between the Atlantic Ocean and the Mississippi River and was for many years a frontier zone between French settlers in the Mississippi Basin and English colonists along the coast.

Allegheny River A river rising in N Pennsylvania, flowing NW through New York and SW through Pennsylvania before joining the Monongahela River at Pittsburgh to become the Ohio River. Length: 235 mi (524 km).

allegory A verse or prose narrative in which characters and events in the plot refer to a deeper, usually moral, meaning. It is an ancient and universal form, similar to but usually longer than the *fable and the parable. Examples of allegory include the French *Roman de la rose* (13th century), Bunyan's *The Pilgrim's Progress* (1678), Swift's *Gulliver's Travels* (1726), and Orwell's *Animal Farm* (1945).

Allegri, Gregorio (1582–1652) Italian composer. He was appointed a singer in Pope *Urban VIII's chapel in 1629. An important composer of church music, his works include a *Miserere* for nine voices, two volumes of concertinos, and two volumes of motets.

allele Any one of the various alternative forms of a *gene that can occur at the same site on a *chromosome. In *Drosophila* fruit flies, for example, several alternative eye colors are possible depending on which of the various alleles of the gene for eye color is present in the individual.

allemande A 16th-century processional dance in 4/4 time originating in Germany. Popular in France and in England under the name almand or almain, it reappeared in the 18th century as an elaborate figure dance for couples, in 2/4 time. A stylized version of the early dance was frequently used by Bach, Couperin, and other contemporary composers to open a suite. The name is also applied to a lively German-Swiss folk dance resembling the *Ländler*.

Allen, Bog of (Irish name: Moin Almkaine) An area of peat bogs in the Republic of Ireland, covering much of the central plain. The peat is used for fueling power stations and for domestic use. Area: 370 sq mi (958 sq km).

Allen, Ethan (1739–89) American soldier, who pursued the independence from New York of the Green Mountain region (now Vermont), which was claimed by both New York and New Hampshire. Between 1770 and 1775 he commanded the *Green Mountain Boys, which with Benedict *Arnold's forces captured Fort Ticonderoga (1775), the first American victory in the American Revolution. He was held captive by the British (1775–78). Vermont declared its independence but was not recognized by the Continental Congress. Allen did much to ensure Vermont's independence but died before it achieved statehood in 1789.

Allen, Woody (Allen Stewart Konigsberg; 1935–) US film actor and director. His performances are witty portrayals of social inadequacy and embarrassment. His films include *Play It Again, Sam* (1972) and *Annie Hall* (1977); he also directed *Interiors* (1978), *Manhattan* (1979), *Zelig* (1983), *Broadway Danny Rose* (1984), *Hannah and Her Sisters* (1986), *Radio Days* (1987), *Alice* (1990), and *Husbands and Wives* (1992). The breakup of his relationship with actress Mia Farrow, who starred in many of his films, resulted in court battles.

Allenby, Edmund Henry Hynman, 1st Viscount (1861–1936) British field marshal. After experience in the Boer War, he commanded the Third Army in France in World War I. In 1917, appointed commander in chief of the Egyptian Expeditionary Force against the Turks in Palestine, he captured (Dec 9) Jerusalem (as a "Christmas present" for the British people) and then went on to devastate the Turks at Megiddo (1918). He ended his career as high commissioner in Egypt (1919–25).

Allende (Gossens), Salvador (1908–73) Chilean statesman; president of Chile (1970–73), the first Marxist to come to power through free elections. A founder of the Chilean Socialist Party, Allende governed a coalition of left-wing parties. His nationalization policies created much opposition and he was overthrown and killed by a military coup.

Allentown 40 37N 75 30W A city in the US, in Pennsylvania. It has important steel and machinery industries. Population (1990): 105,090.

allergy An abnormal reaction by the body that is provoked by certain substances, including pollen, dust, certain foods and drugs, fur, molds, etc. Normally all foreign substances (antigens) entering the body are destroyed by *antibodies without further trouble. Allergic people, however, become hypersensitive to certain antigens (called allergens), so that whenever they are subsequently encountered they stimulate not only the normal antibody reaction but also the specific symptoms of the allergy. Allergic conditions include *hay fever, some forms of *asthma and *dermatitis, and *urticaria. Treatment includes the use of *antihistamines, corticosteroids, and *desensitization.

Alliance for Progress A program initiated in 1961 by Pres. John F. Kennedy to maintain democracy, improve economic conditions, and further social development in 22 Latin American countries. Largely financed by the US, the program has had disappointing results.

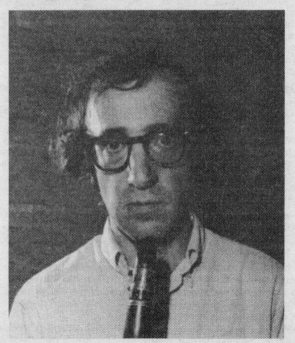

WOODY ALLEN *He is an enthusiastic amateur jazz clarinetist.*

Allied Powers The nations united in opposition to the *Central Powers in World War I and to the *Axis Powers in World War II. In World War I the Allies were initially Britain, France, and Russia, bound by the Treaty of London (1914), and later included Italy, Japan, and Portugal; the US was an associated power from 1917. In World War II the chief Allies were Britain, France (1939–40, 1944–45), the Soviet Union (from June, 1941), the US (from December, 1941), and China.

Allier River A river in central France. Rising in the Cévennes, it flows NNW through the fertile Limagne area, joining the Loire River near Nevers. Length: 250 mi (403 km).

alligator A large, broad-snouted □reptile belonging to the genus *Alligator* (2 species). Each side of the jaw contains 17–22 teeth, which are all covered when the mouth is closed. The American alligator (*A. mississippiensis*) is mainly black and lives in rivers of the SE US, reaching a length of 16–20 ft (5–6 m); the rare Chinese alligator (*A. sinensis*) of the Yangtze River is smaller. They dig burrows in which they hibernate during cold weather. Order: *Crocodilia* (*see* crocodile).

Allingham, Margery (1904–66) British detective-story writer. Her mild-mannered likable detective Albert Campion appeared in a popular series of novels begun in the 1920s and ending with *Cargo of Eagles* (1968). *Tiger in the Smoke* (1952), *The China Governess* (1963), and *The Mind Readers* (1965) are among her most acclaimed books.

Allium A genus of herbaceous plants (about 450 species), including the *onion, *shallot, *garlic, *leek, *chive, etc. They have bulbs, those of several species being widely used in temperate regions for food and flavoring, and in many the flowers are replaced by small bulbs (bulbils), by means of which the plants can be propagated. Family: *Liliaceae* (or *Alliaceae* according to some authorities).

allopathy Literally, the use of drugs or other means to induce a reaction in the body that will counteract—and therefore relieve—the symptoms of a disease. The term is used by practitioners of *homeopathy to describe the orthodox system of medicine.

Allosaurus A large bipedal dinosaur of the Jurassic and Cretaceous periods (200–65 million years ago). Up to 34 ft (11 m) long, it had large, strong hind limbs, a well-developed tail, small forelegs, and thick, protective knobs of bone over the eyes. Although fairly slow, it hunted prey, possibly in groups, and was equipped with sharp claws, powerful jaws, and sharp, pointed teeth. Order: *Saurischia*.

allotropes Two or more different physical forms of the same element or compound. Allotropes have different arrangements of atoms in their crystals or molecules and occasionally quite different chemical behavior. Diamond and graphite, for example, are allotropes of carbon.

alloy A blend of a metal with other metals or nonmetals, formed by mixing the molten substances and allowing the mixture to cool and solidify. An alloy is usually harder than any of its constituents. The first alloy was probably *bronze, which was used in Europe in about 2000 BC. *Steel and *brass are the most widely used alloys. Alloys of aluminum are also widely used, especially in the aircraft industry. Some metals, such as lead and aluminum, will not mix when they are melted together because their different densities make them separate into two layers. However, many metals do combine to form alloys, which may consist of intermetallic compounds, solid solutions, heterogeneous mixtures, or any combination of these forms. In general, intermetallic compounds tend to be hard and brittle: iron carbide, which strengthens iron to form *steel is an example. Solid solutions, on the other hand, are usually soft and ductile: cartridge-case *brass is a typical example.

Most alloys melt over a range of temperatures unlike a pure metal, which has a specific melting point. **Eutectic alloys** are an exception to this rule, they consist of solid solutions having the lowest melting point of all the possible mixtures of the components. They are used in fuses and other safety mechanisms.

All Saints' Day A Christian feast commemorating all saints, whether known or unknown. In the Eastern Churches it has always been observed on the first Sunday after Pentecost. In the West its date varied until fixed as Nov 1 by Gregory III. *See also* Halloween.

All Souls' Day A Christian feast in the Western Church commemorating all Christians who have died (the "faithful departed"). It is observed on Nov 2. Requiem masses, containing the *Dies Irae*, are celebrated.

allspice (*or* pimento) A widely used aromatic spice, so named because it combines the flavors of several different spices. It is derived from the powdered dried unripe berries of an evergreen tree, *Pimenta dioca*, which is native to Central America and the West Indies and grows to a height of 30 ft (9 m). Family: *Myrtaceae*.

Allston, Washington (1779–1843) The earliest US Romantic painter. He studied at Harvard University before training at the Royal Academy (1801–03) in England. He finally settled in Boston in 1818. The drama of his early landscapes and biblical subjects was replaced by a quieter mood in such later works as *Moonlight Landscape* (Boston). He also wrote poetry and one novel.

Alma Ata 43 19N 76 55E (name until 1921: Verny) Capital city of Kazakhstan. Situated in the foothills of the Trans-Alay Alatau (mountains), it is one of the region's most beautiful cities. Industries include food and tobacco processing, and it has a thriving film industry. Its museum is housed in the former Russian Orthodox cathedral, the world's second highest wooden building. It has many educational institutions. *History*: founded in 1854 as a fort, it soon became a trade center. The completion of the Turkistan-Siberian railroad in 1930, on which it is situated, resulted in its rapid growth. Population (1991 est): 1,156,000.

almanac A calendar of the months and days of the year containing astronomical and other miscellaneous data. It usually includes information about eclipses, phases of the moon, positions of the planets, times of sunset and sunrise and of high and low tides, as well as religious and secular holidays. A well-known example is *The Old Farmer's Almanac*. Modern almanacs include official government publications listing national statistics.

Almeida, Francisco de (c. 1450–1510) Portuguese colonialist. The first viceroy of Portuguese India (1505–09), Almeida consolidated Portuguese rule there and expanded its power in the Indian Ocean. He organized further voyages of discovery that reached Madagascar and fought the Arabs on the African coast.

Almería 36 50N 2 26W A port in S Spain, in Andalusia on the Gulf of Almería. It was a thriving town under the Moors (8th–15th centuries) and has a fine 16th-century cathedral. Exports include grapes and oranges. Population (1986 est): 157,000.

Almohads A fundamentalist reforming Muslim movement that ruled much of N Africa and Spain (1130–1269). Comprising the Masmudah Berber tribe, the Almohads recognized Ibn Tumart (d. 1130) as their leader in 1121 and he directed them against the ruling *Almoravids, taking the title of mahdi. On his death he was succeeded by Abd al-Mu'min (d. 1163), who completed the conquest of N Africa and Spain from the Almoravids. The Almohads regarded Muslims who did not follow them as unbelievers and Abd al-Mu'min became their *caliph. His descendants ruled the state until the fall of Marrakech to the Marinid Berber dynasty in 1269.

almond A tree, *Prunus amygdalus*, native to SW Asia but widely grown in warm regions for its nuts. The edible nuts are produced by a variety called sweet almond; the nuts of the bitter almond yield aromatic almond oil, used as a flavoring. Almond trees grow to a height of 23 ft (7 m); they have attractive pink flowers and are grown for ornament in cooler regions. Family: *Rosaceae*. *See also* Prunus.

Almoravids A military Muslim missionary movement that ruled much of N Africa and Spain in the 11th and 12th centuries. The Almoravids were founded by Ibn Yasin (d. 1059) and after his death Yusuf ibn Tashufin (d. 1107) conquered NW Africa and invaded Spain. At the battle of Zallaqah (1086) he defeated the rising Christian power of León and Castile and Muslim Spain now came under Almoravid control. After Yusuf's death in Marrakech, the Almoravid capital that he had founded, his state was ruled by his descendants until 1147, when it fell to the *Almohads.

Alnico An *alloy of aluminum, nickel, and cobalt. It is a ferromagnetic material and is used to make permanent magnets.

Aloe A genus of succulent herbaceous plants (about 200 species), all native to Africa. A stem is usually absent, the toothed, fleshy leaves forming a basal rosette, up to 16 in (40 cm) in diameter. The flowers are red or yellow and some species are ornamental (e.g. *A. variegata*); the juice of some species, especially *A. vera*, is used as a purgative (bitter aloes). Family: *Liliaceae*.

Aloysius, St (Luigi Gonzaga; 1568–91) Italian patron of youth. A noble, he entered the Society of Jesus against his father's wishes in 1585 and studied philosophy and theology. Famous for his simple piety and charity, he died while tending plague victims in Rome. Feast day: June 21.

alpaca A shaggy-coated, hoofed mammal, *Lama pacos*, traditionally domesticated and bred in the South American Andes. Its dark, fine, high-quality fleece reaches nearly to the ground from its shoulder height of 35 in (90 cm) and is shorn every two years, each animal yielding about 7 lb (3 kg). Alpacas thrive at high altitudes, keeping to damp grassy plateaus. Family: *Camelidae* (camels).

Alp Arsian (c. 1029–1072) Sultan of Turkey (1063–72) of the Seljuq dynasty. He succeeded his uncle *Toghril Beg. His victory over the Byzantines at Manzikert in 1071 opened Asia Minor to Muslim penetration for the first time.

alphabets Writing systems in which each symbol represents a speech sound (*see* phonetics). Many *pictographic writing systems developed as far as ideography and even *syllabaries, but the breakthrough to true alphabetic phonetic writing took place, it seems, only on the E shores of the Mediterranean around 2000 BC. From this *Semitic alphabet all the major alphabets in use today—Roman, Greek, *Cyrillic, Hebrew, Arabic, and *Devanagari—are ultimately derived.

It is hard now to appreciate the achievement of identifying speech sounds separately from meaning and of analyzing syllables into vowels and consonants. It meant that the number of symbols required to record a language was reduced from many thousands to between 20 and 40. Moreover, it became possible to write down unfamiliar or foreign words without reference to their sense.

Correspondence between conventional *spelling and speech sounds is rarely exact. Speech sounds change continually over the centuries, while spelling forms tend to become conventionalized and static. In Greek, for example, where the alphabet has been used to represent the language for almost 3000 years, the letters ι, η υ, ει, and οι, which originally represented different sounds, now all represent the sound /i:/; by contrast, γ, which used to represent a single

North Semitic				Greek		Etruscan	Latin		Modern Capital
early Phoenician	early Hebrew (cursive)	Moabite	Phoenician	early	classical	classical	early	classical	Roman
⊀	⊀	⊀	⊀	◁	A	A	A	A	A
�9	�9	�9	ᒑ	8	B			B	B
1	٦	1	1	1	Γ	>		C	C
△	۹	△	۹	Δ	△		ᗡ	D	D
ᒾ	ᒾ	ᒾ	ᒾ	ᒷ	E	Ǝ	Ǝ		E
Y	Y	Y	٩	⅃		ᒾ	٦	F	F
									G
I	⚏	I	⚏	I	⚏	⁊			
⊟	⊠	⊟	⊟	B	H	⊟	⊟	H	H
⊕	⊘	⊗	⊗	⊗	θ	⊙			
⍭	⊀	₂	⁊	⟨	I	I	١	I	I
									J
↓	⅄	⅄	⅄	⅄	K	⅄	⅄	K	K
∟	∤	∟	∟	٦	∧	⅃		L	L
⅀	⅄	⅋	⅋	⌒	M	⌒	⌒	M	M
⅁	⅁	⅁	⅁	⅁	N	⅄	И		N
∓	⅀	∓	⅋		≡	⋈			
O	O	O	O	O	O	O		O	O
？	⅄	⅂	⅂	⅂	Π	٦	Γ	P	P
	⅄	⼞	⼞	M		M			
	Y	φ	φ	φ		Q			Q
⅁	⅀	⅃	⅃	⅃	P	⅄		R	R
W	⌄	W	W	⟩	Σ	⅄	⅄	S	S
+	×	×	ⴕ×	×	T	ⴕ		T	T
					Y	∨	∨		U
									V
									W
				×				X	X
								Y	Y
								Z	Z

ALPHABETS *The letters of the modern Roman alphabet have developed from the ancient North Semitic script. This script in its Aramaic form was also the ultimate source of the Arabic alphabet and probably of the Brahmi alphabet, from which the numerous scripts of modern India are derived.*

sound, now represents four quite distinct sounds, depending on the letters adjoining it. On the other hand, Czech and Turkish, both of which have adopted or revised a modified version of the Roman alphabet within the last hundred years, display great regularity between sound and spelling. These two and many other languages that have taken over the Roman alphabet use accents and other diacritics to indicate sounds for which there is no standard Roman alphabet symbol.

With the passage of time, however, the use of diacritics itself becomes conventionalized and unsystematic.

From time to time, attempts have been made to develop alphabets that record speech sounds absolutely regularly and systematically. The most important of these is the *International Phonetic Alphabet.

Alpha Centauri A conspicuous nearby *multiple star in the constellation Centaurus. The two brightest components form a yellow visual *binary star that is seen as the third brightest star in the sky, magnitude −0.27. The much fainter third component, **Proxima Centauri**, is the nearest known star, lying 4.3 light years away.

alpha decay A spontaneous radioactive disintegration in which a nucleus ejects an *alpha particle. This process reduces the mass number of the nucleus by four and its atomic number by two. An example is the decay of uranium-238 into thorium-234.

alpha particle The nucleus of a helium-4 atom, consisting of two protons and two neutrons. It is extremely stable and is emitted by some radioactive nuclei in the process known as *alpha decay.

alphorn A musical instrument used in Switzerland for calling cattle. Made of wood, it is commonly 6.5 ft (2 m) long or more. Its mouthpiece is similar to that of a cornet. Being valveless, it plays only harmonics.

ALPHORN *The instrument is constructed from long wooden staves bound together with birch bark. Instruments similar to the alphorn are used in Poland and Scandinavia as well as in Switzerland.*

Alpine orogeny The period of mountain building that occurred mainly during the Tertiary period, beginning about 65 million years ago. The regions most affected extend from S Europe and N Africa across S Asia to Indonesia, resulting in the formation of the Alps, Atlas Mountains, and Himalayas, and across a belt bordering on the Pacific Ocean. It is the most recent *orogeny and is probably still continuing in some parts of the world.

Alps The highest mountain range in Europe. It extends some 500 mi (800 km) in an arc roughly E–W through France, Switzerland, Italy, and Austria, and rises to 15,771 ft (4807 m) at Mont Blanc near the W end. Several major rivers rise here, including the Rhône, Rhine, Drava, and Po. The snowline varies between 7874 ft and 9843 ft (2400 m and 3000 m) and many of the lower slopes are used as pasture in summer, while in winter the Alps are Europe's major skiing area. There are several road and rail routes across the chain, including a number of tunnels. *See also* Maritime Alps.

Alsace (German name: Elsass) A planning region and former province in NE France, separated from Germany to the W by the Rhine River. It is a fertile agricultural area and has important potassium deposits. *History*: it was often a scene of conflict between France and Germany. Under Roman occupation from the 1st century AD, it became a Frankish duchy in the 5th century and was part of the Holy Roman Empire from the 10th to the 17th centuries. Its cities, which became effectively independent in the middle ages, were important centers of the Reformation in the 16th century. The French gained control of Alsace in 1648, after the Thirty Years' War, but it was lost to Germany in 1871, after the Franco-Prussian War, and linked with *Lorraine to form the German imperial territory of **Alsace-Lorraine**. This existed until it reverted to France in 1919. It came under German control again in World War II and was restored to France in 1945. Area: 3208 sq mi (8310 sq km). Population (1991 est): 1,630,000.

Alsatian dog. *See* German shepherd dog.

alsike A perennial Eurasian *clover, *Trifolium hybridum*, also called Swedish or Alsatian clover, with typically three-lobed leaves and a pink flower head about 0.4 in (1 cm) in diameter. Capable of fixing atmospheric nitrogen, it is often used to improve the nitrate level in soil. Family: *Leguminosae*.

Altaic languages A family of languages comprising languages of the *Turkic, *Mongolian, and *Manchu-Tungus groups. Named for the Central Asian Altai Mountains, languages of this family are spoken in N China, Mongolia, Kazakhstan, Kyrgyzstan, Tajikistan, Turmenistan, Uzbekistan, Afghanistan, Iran, and Turkey. The genetic relationship between the various Altaic languages is debatable, but certain common features are discernible, notably sound harmony. The connection of *Japanese and *Korean with this family is questionable.

Altai Mountains A mountain system in Asia, extending from Siberia, Russia, into China and Mongolia. It rises to 14,783 ft (4506 m) at Belukha in Russia and has important lead, silver, and zinc reserves.

Altair A conspicuous white star, apparent magnitude 0.77 and 16.5 light years distant, that is the brightest star in the constellation Aquila.

Altamira Upper *Paleolithic cave site in N Spain, recognized in 1879. Doubts as to the authenticity of the 150 magnificent polychrome paintings of animals on the cave's ceiling were eventually settled by Henri *Breuil in 1901. Bison, painted in red ocher with black manganese manes, tails, and hooves, are the chief species depicted. *See also* Magdalenian.

Altdorf 46 53N 8 38E The town in central Switzerland where William Tell engaged in his legendary exploits.

Altdorfer, Albrecht (c. 1480–1538) German artist, who was one of the first European painters to paint landscapes for their own sake. His masterpieces, few of which survive, show his love of forested mountains, depicted in minute detail, and include *The Battle of Issus* and *St George* (both Alte Pinakothek, Munich). He worked in Regensburg, where he became city architect and a member of the council.

alternating current (ac) Electrical current that periodically reverses its direction. It is the form of current that is produced when a coil of wire rotates in a magnetic field and, as this is the way in which current is produced in *power stations by *electric generators, it is the form of current most widely used. The electromotive force (emf), E, produced by a generator is equal to $E^1\sin \omega t$, where E^1 is the maximum emf, ω is the angular velocity of rotation, and t is the time. Thus the current has the form of a sine wave, with a frequency $\omega/2\pi$.

The chief advantage of ac is that the voltage can be stepped up with a transformer before transmission to minimize energy losses in the lines and then reduced to a safer level by another transformer for domestic use. In most European countries the ac supply has a frequency of 50 hertz, is transmitted at several hundreds of kilovolts, and is used at 220 volts. In the US the supply frequency is 60 hertz and the voltage is 110 volts.

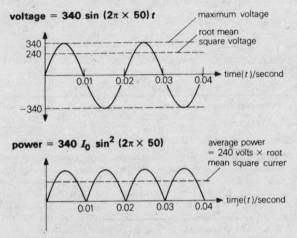

voltage = 340 sin (2π × 50) t — maximum voltage / root mean square voltage

power = 340 I_0 sin² (2π × 50) — average power = 240 volts × root mean square current

ALTERNATING CURRENT *The voltage and power waveforms in a 240-volt, 50-hertz supply. The current ($I = I_o \sin (2\pi \times 50) t$) has a similar waveform to the voltage.*

alternation of generations A phenomenon occurring in the *life cycles of many plants and some animals (particularly *coelenterates) in which there is an alternation between two distinct forms (generations), which differ from each other in structure, reproduction, and also often in habit. In plants the generation reproducing sexually is the gametophyte and the asexual generation is the sporophyte. Either phase may be predominant in a particular species; for example, the gametophyte is dominant in mosses and the sporophyte in flowering plants. In coelenterates, sedentary asexual polyps alternate with free-living sexual medusae.

alternative energy The investigation and use of new sources of power, based on natural energy flows in the environment. Most countries now rely heavily on *fossil fuels (oil, coal, and natural gas) and nuclear power for their energy needs. However, reserves of fossil fuels are declining and, although dates for their total exhaustion vary, their price must rise as they become increasingly scarce. The estimates of reserves of recoverable uranium are also uncertain and there is opposition to the development of nuclear breeder reactors, mainly on the grounds of safety and environmental hazard from waste disposal. Fusion reactors are still in the experimental stage. Although nuclear power is still regarded as the main option, it is also necessary to explore the alternatives. Renewable energy sources are those that do not use up finite mineral resources. Of these *solar power, *wind power, and *wave power are being most seriously investigated in several countries. *Hydroelectric power is already in use and has limited potential for further expansion. A number of other alternatives are of interest. Tidal power is the use of water raised by the tide and collected behind a barrage to generate electricity in a similar way to hydroelectric generation. There are few sites where the tidal rise makes this a feasible project. The Severn estuary in Britain, which has an average tidal rise of 29 ft (8.8 m), is said to form the best site in Europe.

Geothermal power comes from the heat beneath the earth's crust. In Iceland naturally heated water is taken from rocks near the surface, but in most places geothermal power is not feasible.

Biomass energy, methane generated from sewage, refuse, or specially cultivated organisms, has also been considered. As with many of the other alternative energy sources it is most suitable for small-scale, specialized uses. Governments all over the world are examining alternative energy sources in order to reduce their dependence on fossil fuels.

Althing The parliament of Iceland, the oldest in the world, founded in about 930 AD. Since independence in 1944 it has been the country's sovereign legislature. It has 60 members in two houses of equal power.

Althusius, Johannes (1557–1638) German political philosopher. He became professor of law at Herborn Calvinist college (1594), where he wrote his most famous work, *Politics Methodically Arranged and Illustrated by Holy and Profane Examples* (1603). Althusius attempted a systematic approach to political science, based on the concept of contracts between different groupings in society.

Altichiero (c. 1330–c. 1390) Italian painter. Influenced by *Giotto, Altichiero is credited with the foundation of the Veronese school. His only surviving works in Verona are the late frescoes in S Anastasia but there are also cycles in the Basilica of S Antonio and the Oratorio di S Giorgio in Padua.

altimeter A device for measuring altitude in one of two ways. A **pressure altimeter** consists of an aneroid *barometer calibrated in meters (or feet) above sea level. A **radio altimeter** consists of a device that measures the time taken for a radio or radar signal to reach the ground and return.

altitude The angular distance of an astronomical body above or below an observer's horizon. It reaches a maximum of 90° when the body is directly overhead. It is used with the angular distance **azimuth**, which is measured eastward along the horizon from the direction of N, to specify the position of an astronomical body on the *celestial sphere.

alto A high adult male singing voice produced by falsetto. Range: that of the *countertenor and *contralto.

altocumulus cloud (Ac) A medium type of *cloud appearing as globular masses in bands across the sky.

altostratus cloud (As) A medium type of *cloud appearing as a grayish sheet, sometimes thin enough for the sun to be seen through it. It usually heralds rain.

altruism. *See* egoism.

aluminum (Al) A light, silvery-white metal first isolated by Wöhler in 1827. Although it is the most abundant metal in the earth's crust, its extraction is difficult and energy consuming. The main source is *bauxite, an impure hydrated oxide. The metal is extracted by electrolysis of the oxide dissolved in a flux of low melting point with the mineral cryolite. Its most important uses depend on its lightness (relative density 2.70), ductility, and good electrical conductivity. It is used in electrical power cables, kitchen utensils, and many industrial applications. Pure aluminum is soft, but its alloys with copper, magnesium, and other elements have considerable strength. This combined with their low densities makes such alloys important in aircraft construction. Compounds include alum ($K_2SO_4Al_2(SO_4)_3.24H_2O$) and the oxide ($Al_2O_3$), which occurs naturally as corundum and *ruby and is used as an abrasive, a gem, and in *lasers. The hydroxide ($Al(OH)_3$) is used in glass manufacture and as an antacid in medicine. At no 13; at wt 26.9815; mp 399°F (660.4°C); bp 1001°F (1800°C).

alums Crystalline hydrated double sulfates of monovalent and trivalent metals. The typical example is potash alum (often called simply alum; ($K_2SO_4.Al_2(SO_4)_3.24H_2O$), which is used as a mordant, size for paper, styptic, and astringent. Other related substances exist in which the potassium and aluminum ions are replaced by other monovalent or trivalent ions respectively. For example, **chrome alum** is $K_2SO_4.Cr_2(SO_4)_3$. It is a dark-purple substance used in dyes, printing, and tanning.

alunite (*or* alumstone) A mineral consisting of potassium and aluminum sulfate and aluminum hydroxide, $K_2SO_4.Al_2(SO_4)_3.4Al(OH)_3$. It is a source of alum and a potential source of potash. It is usually found associated with volcanic rocks altered by sulfurous gases.

Alvarado, Pedro de (c. 1485–1541) Spanish conquistador, who accompanied Hernán Cortés in his conquest of Mexico, becoming governor of Tenochtitlán (Mexico City). He conquered parts of Guatemala (1523–24) and El Salvador (1524). In 1534 he embarked on an expedition to take Ecuador but was bought off by a rival.

Alvarez, Luis Walker (1911–88) US physicist, who works at the University of California. Working with F. *Bloch he made the first measurement of the neutron's magnetic moment and won the Nobel Prize (1968) for research on short-lived fundamental particles. During World War II, he worked on the development of the atom bomb.

Alvárez Quintero brothers Spanish dramatists, Serafin (1871–1938) and Joaquin (1873–1944) Alvárez Quintero. In collaboration, they wrote nearly 200 popular plays, set mainly in their native Andalusia. Simple entertainment was their chief aim, although *El Amor que pasa* (1904) and *Malvaloca* (1912) were more serious works.

Alvars A group of wandering poets and mystics, fervently devoted to Vishnu, which flourished in S India in the 7th–10th centuries AD. Almost exclusively male, they worshiped ecstatically, with song and dance. Their 4000 hymns in the Tamil language, collected in the 10th century, sing the praises of Vishnu and his various incarnations.

alveolus. *See* lung.

Alyattes (d. 560 BC) Fourth King of Lydia (c. 617–560), which he made a major power. Alyattes extended his kingdom as far as the Halys River (585) following a war against Media that was ended by the combatants' fear at the sight of the sun's eclipse. Alyattes, who was buried in a huge round tomb near Sardis, was succeeded by his son Croesus.

Alypius (4th century AD) Greek writer, from Alexandria in Egypt. His *Introduction to Music* is the chief surviving guide to classical Greek music, preserving its notation and complex scale system.

Alyssum A genus of low-growing herbaceous plants (about 150 species), mostly native to S Europe but widely grown in gardens. Alyssums have small flowers grouped in terminal clusters. Varieties of sweet alyssum (*A. maritimum*), 4–6 in (10–15 cm) high, have white or pink flowers and are grown as annuals. Perennial alyssums include *A. saxatile*, which grows to a height of 12 in (30 cm) and has yellow flowers. Family: *Cruciferae*.

Alzheimer's disease (*or* presenile dementia) A degenerative disease that affects nerve cells of the brain. It causes speech disturbances, progressive loss of mental faculties, and other symptoms of senility although it may occur in middle age. Its cause is unknown and there is no cure. Named for the German neurologist Alois Alzheimer (1864–1915).

Amadeus (VIII) the Peaceful (1383–1451) Count of Savoy (1391–1434). Amadeus became duke in 1416, when Savoy was made a duchy by Emperor Sigismund. Amadeus abdicated in 1434 and in 1439 was elected antipope as Felix V by the schismatic Council of *Basle. He resigned in 1449.

Amagasaki 34 42N 135 23E A port in Japan, in S Honshu on Osaka Bay. An industrial center, it has metal, chemical, and textile industries. Population (1990): 498,999.

Amalasuntha (*or* Amalasuentha; 498–535 AD) The daughter of Theodoric, King of the Ostrogoths, and regent (526–34) for her son Athalaric (516–34). After Athalaric's death she shared the throne with her cousin and second husband, Theodahad (d. 536), who, having banished her, was party to her murder.

Amalekites In the Old Testament, a nomadic tribe living in SW Palestine and the Sinai, who were descended from Esau. They attacked the Israelites on their journey out of Egypt and remained their enemies until finally suppressed during the reign of Hezekiah.

Amalfi 40 37N 14 36E A seaport and resort in Italy in Campania on the Gulf of Salerno. A major port in the 10th century, its maritime code of law was recognized in the Mediterranean area until the latter half of the 18th century.

Amana Society Residents of seven villages in E central Iowa, on the N shore of the Iowa River, SW of Cedar Rapids. Founded as the Amana Church Society in 1855, it was a communistic cooperative society run by elders of the Community of True Inspiration, a sect founded in Germany in 1714. Reorganized as the Amana Society, a cooperative stock company, in 1932, its members share in profits from its industries, mainly agricultural, and are given medical care benefits.

Amanita A genus of widely distributed mushroom fungi (about 100 species). Several species are extremely poisonous, including the deadly destroying angels (*A. vena* and *A. virosa*), the *death cap, and the *fly agaric. Some species are harmless and sometimes eaten, for example panther cap (*A. pantherina*). Family: *Agaricaceae* (*see* agaric).

Amanollah Khan (1892–1960) Emir (1919–26) and King (1926–29) of Afghanistan. Amanollah obtained Afghan independence from Britain in 1919. He introduced a policy of westernization and declared Afghanistan a kingdom in 1926. In 1929 a revolt forced him into exile in Switzerland.

Amaranthus A genus of herbaceous plants (50–60 species) native to tropical and subtropical regions but now widely distributed (*see* pigweed). The small, petal-less flowers grow in long, drooping spikes. Several species are grown for ornament, including *A. caudatus* (love-lies-bleeding), 24–40 in (60–100 cm) tall with dark-red flowers, *A. tricolor* (Joseph's coat), with purple flowers and red, yellow, and green leaves. Family: *Amaranthaceae*.

Amaravati school A style of Indian religious sculpture that originated in Amaravati in S India in the 2nd century BC and flourished until the 3rd century AD. A series of bas-reliefs of the life of Buddha have survived from Amaravati, showing the school's fusion of naturalism with elegance. The style spread through Ceylon to SE Asia.

Amarillo 35 14N 101 50W A city in N Texas. Expansion followed the arrival of the railroad (1887) and the discovery of gas (1918) and oil (1921). Today Amarillo has meat-packing, flour-milling, oil-refining, and rubber industries. Population (1990): 157,615.

Amarna Tablets *Cuneiform inscriptions found at Tell el-Amarna (Middle Egypt) in 1887. Most of the tablets were written about 1350 BC. They record administrative correspondence between the pharaoh and his vassal kings in Palestine and Syria.

Amaryllis A perennial herbaceous plant, *Amaryllis belladonna*, also called belladonna lily, native to South Africa but widely cultivated for ornament. Growing from bulbs, it has strap-shaped leaves and a 18 in (45 cm) long stem bearing a cluster of 5–12 funnel-shaped sweet-scented flowers, usually rose-pink and often veined. Family: *Amaryllidaceae*.

Amaterasu In Japanese mythology, the sun goddess, supreme among the *kami* (spirits). She was the daughter of *Izanagi, born either from his eye or from a mirror held by him. She was symbolized by a mirror, which she gave to her grandson Ninigi, forerunner of the Japanese emperors, as part of the imperial regalia. It is still preserved at the Shinto shrine at Ise (S Honshu).

Amati A family of violin makers in Cremona, Italy. **Andrea Amati** (c. 1520–c. 1578) developed the design that became the standard modern violin. His sons **Antonio Amati** (?1550–1638) and **Girolamo Amati** (1551–1635) worked as a team. Girolamo's son **Niccolò Amati** (1596–1684) was the family's greatest craftsman and taught Andrea *Guarneri and *Stradivari. They also made violas and cellos.

Amazon River (Portuguese name: Rio Amazônas) The largest river system and the second longest river in the world, it is the chief river of South America. Rising as the Río Marañón in the Andes, in Peru, it flows generally W–E to enter the Atlantic Ocean in NE Brazil. Its drainage basin extends over much of Brazil, and parts of Venezuela, Colombia, Ecuador, Peru, and Bolivia. It is covered by a mantle of tropical rain forest (selva) and provides valuable forest products including rubber, quinine, and nuts. Navigable to oceangoing vessels as far as Iquitos, 2300 mi (3700 km) upstream, the river and its tributaries provide an essential communications system. New roads, including the Trans-Amazonian Highway, are now opening up the hinterland. Length: 4000 mi (6440 km). Drainage basin area: about 2,250,000 sq mi (5,827,500 sq km).

Amazon ant A *slave-making ant of the genus *Polyergus* (especially *P. rufescens* or *P. lucidus*). Amazon ants, which have long, sharp, sickle-shaped mandibles, raid nests of *Formica* ants to steal eggs and larvae that hatch to become workers in their own colony. Amazon ants cannot feed or brood without slave workers.

Amazons (Greek: breastless ones) A mythical nation of female warriors who were believed by the ancient Greeks to live in Pontus, near the Black Sea. Trained for war and hunting, the Amazons got their name from their habit of removing the right breast to facilitate the drawing of bows. They intervened in the *Trojan War against the Greeks, but Achilles killed their queen, Penthesilea. The Athenians said that at one time they invaded Attica but were defeated by *Theseus, who took their queen Hippolyte captive.

Ambartsumian, Viktor A (mazaspovich) (1908–   ) Soviet astrophysicist, who taught at the University of Leningrad before becoming director of the Byurakan Observatory. He wrote the first classic Russian textbook of theoretical astrophysics. His most notable work was the description of radio sources as explosions in the core of galaxies.

amber A translucent or opaque yellow fossil resin exuded by coniferous trees; insects and leaves are often preserved in the mineral, having been trapped on the sticky surface prior to hardening. It is found predominantly in Tertiary deposits around the S Baltic coast. It is used for beads, ornaments, and amber varnish.

ambergris A waxy substance found in the intestines of sperm whales. It contains mainly cholesterol, with fatty oils and steroids and has a musky scent. It is used in making perfumes.

Ambler, Eric (1909–) British novelist. He began writing suspense novels in the 1930s, skillfully creating an atmosphere of fear and tension appropriate to the times. These novels, which include *The Dark Frontier* (1936), *The Mark of Dmitrios* (1939), and *Journey into Fear* (1940), were set mostly in W Europe; in later novels, such as *A Passage of Arms* (1959), he used more exotic settings. Other works include *The Nightcomers* (1956), *The Light of the Day* (1965), and *In Care of Time* (1981).

ambo A raised platform in early churches with a reading stand for the reading of the Bible during services. It was most popular in Italy, although even there it began to be replaced by the pulpit during the 14th century.

Amboise 47 25N 1 00E A town in France, in the Indre-et-Loire department on the Loire River. Its fine Gothic chateau was damaged during World War II but has since been restored. Population (1975): 11,116.

Ambon (*or* Amboina) 03 41S 128 10E An Indonesian island off SW Ceram. Produce includes cloves, nutmegs, and copra. Area: 386 sq mi (1000 sq km). Chief town: Ambon.

amboyna A tropical Asian tree, *Pterocarpus indicus*, that reaches a height of about 30 ft (9 m) and yields reddish, beautifully grained wood used for furniture. Family: *Leguminosae*.

Ambrose, St (c. 339–97 AD) Italian bishop of Milan and Doctor of the Church. Born at Trier, he was appointed a provincial governor in 370 with his headquarters at Milan. After becoming a priest, he was made Bishop of Milan in 374 and was famous as a preacher and for his breadth of scholarship. He championed orthodoxy and the rights of the church against the civil power. Feast day: Dec 7.

ambrosia beetle A wood-boring beetle, *Trypodendron lineatum*, that tunnels into the wood of dying and fallen trees. It carries its food supply—a type of fungus—with it into the tunnels, and this produces black spores that color infected wood distinctively. Family: *Scolytidae* (bark beetles).

Amenemhet III King of Egypt (c. 1842–1797 BC) of the 12th dynasty. He regulated the lake of El *Faiyum to irrigate S Egypt, and built the Labyrinth (later described by the Greek historian Herodotus) nearby as an administrative center.

Amenhotep III King of Egypt (c. 1417–1379 BC) of the 18th dynasty. He controlled Palestine and Syria through vassal kings and maintained good relations with *Babylon. Many of the monumental buildings at *Karnak, *Luxor, and elsewhere in Egypt were erected by him. He was the father of *Akhenaton.

America. *See* United States of America.

American Academy and Institute of Arts and Letters US honorary association devoted to fostering art, literature, and music. Originally, the institute (1898) and the academy (1904) were separate, but merged in 1977 to include a total elected membership of 250, with 75 from other countries admitted as honorary members. Awards are given annually, the most prestigious and highest honor being the Gold Medal.

American Bar Association US association of attorneys. Membership is voluntary, but only members of state bars are admitted. Founded in 1878, the organization promotes uniformity of the law, coordinates state and local activities, and promotes constant education in the law through maintenance of a library and the work of special committees.

American Civil Liberties Union (ACLU) A US organization that protects and promotes civil rights and liberties. Founded in 1920 by a group headed by Roger Baldwin, it sponsors protests, public declarations, test cases in law courts, and other measures against what it believes are violations of civil liberties.

American eagle. *See* bald eagle.

American Expeditionary Force (AEF) US troops under Gen. John J. Pershing sent to Europe during World War I. Following a presidential directive, the AEF kept its identity as a separate unit and was not integrated into the Allied forces, but played a key part in the defeat of Germany.

American Federation of Labor (AFL) US labor organization founded by Samuel Gompers in 1886. Organized to oversee and coordinate the specialized craft and trade (skilled worker) unions, it advocated better working conditions and higher wages through strikes and collective bargaining. In 1955 it merged with the Congress of Industrial Organizations (CIO).

American Federation of Labor-Congress of Industrial Organizations (AFL-CIO) A federation of US labor unions formed by the amalgamation in 1955 of the two major US unions—the AFL and CIO. It is currently composed of about 110 national and international unions giving a US membership of about 14.5 million and an affiliated membership of 55,000. Delegates from the member unions attend a biennial convention to decide policy. Committees contribute recommendations on subjects ranging from civil rights to safety and occupational health. Affiliated members must conform to requirements laid down by the AFL-CIO but remain autonomous within these limits.

American Fur Company US fur trading company established by John Jacob Astor in 1808. The company soon monopolized the fur market across America and by 1810 had established the Pacific Fur Company at Ft. Astoria, Oregon, to compete with Canada for the China fur trade. Although Astoria was lost during the War of 1812, Astor's American Fur Company had grown, by 1834, into the largest US fur company. Company explorations eased the way for settlers.

American Import Duties Act. *See* Townshend Acts.

American Indian Movement (AIM) A militant movement, organized in 1968 to promote civil rights for Indians in the US and Canada. Its objectives are the reformation of the Bureau of Indian Affairs and the observance of past treaties. The dramatization of these goals was carried out in 1972, when members took over the Washington, D.C. headquarters of the Bureau of Indian Affairs and in 1973, when they occupied the historic site of an Indian massacre (1890) at Wounded Knee, South Dakota.

American Indians A diverse group of peoples of North, Central, and South America and the Caribbean Islands. In many respects they resemble the Mongoloid peoples of Asia, which has led to their classification as a subtype of the *Mongoloid race. However, their physical diversity, and the possession of certain features not common among Mongoloids, suggest other origins. Their ancestors probably migrated to the Americas from Asia via Alaska between 10,000 and 20,000 years ago. They have coarse dark and usually straight hair, a skin coloration ranging from copper-brown to a yellowish-brown, dark eyes, and sparse body hair. They speak a great variety of languages and their traditional cultures range from that of primitive hunters and gatherers to the elaborate and complex civilizations of the *Aztecs, *Mayas, and *Incas.

AMERICAN INDIANS *These South American Indians in Xingu (Brazil) cover their bodies with elaborate paintings.*

American Library Association (ALA) US organization that promotes universal library services. Established in 1876, its open membership, numbering about 35,000, is responsible for standardization of library systems, and of library education, and accreditation of library schools.

American literature The literature in English of the British colonies of North America and after 1776, of the United States. The earliest colonial literature consisted mainly of religious and political tracts. The first notable poets were Anne Bradstreet (1612–72) and Edward Taylor (1642–1729), both of Massachusetts. The intellectual dominance of New England was continued into the early 18th century by the theologian and metaphysician Jonathan Edwards (1703–58). The period of the American Revolution was dominated by political writers, such as Benjamin Franklin and Thomas Paine. Influential writers of the early 19th century included Washington Irving, James Fenimore Cooper, and Edgar Allan Poe and American literature came to its full maturity in the works of the New England writers Nathaniel Hawthorne, Ralph Waldo Emerson, and Herman Melville, the poets Walt Whitman and Emily Dickinson, and the humorist Mark Twain. The influence of English literature on the early development of American literature was now reciprocated, notably in the works of the novelist Henry James and the poets T. S. Eliot and Ezra Pound, all of whom went to live in Europe. They were followed in the 1920s by Ernest Hemingway and F. Scott Fitzgerald. The tradition of portraying American life has transcended changes in style and has included such important writers as Edith Wharton, Willa Cather, Stephen Crane, Theodore Dreiser, Sinclair Lewis, and John Dos Passos. Other writers who achieved a transatlantic reputation include the dramatists Eugene O'Neill, Tennessee Williams, and Arthur Miller and the poets Robert Frost,

Robert Lowell, and John Berryman. The vitality of 20th-century American literature is most evident in the novel, the later practitioners of which include such writers as William Faulkner, John Steinbeck, Henry Miller, Thomas Wolfe, Norman Mailer, Saul Bellow, John Updike, and Thomas Pynchon.

American Medical Association (AMA) US federation of state medical associations that promotes educational and ethical standards in the medical profession. Established in 1847, with a current membership of over 200,000, it coordinates and disseminates scientific information to the profession and health information to the public.

American Revolution (1775–83) The conflict in which the 13 colonies of North America gained independence from Britain. American resentment at Britain's authoritative rule focused in the mid 18th century on taxation. Protests against such legislation as the *Stamp Act (1765) and *Townshend Acts (1767) culminated in the *Boston Tea Party (1773), to which Britain responded with the punitive *Intolerable Acts (1774). The First *Continental Congress was summoned at Philadelphia and, after attempts by both sides at negotiation had failed, the first shots of the war were fired at *Lexington and Concord (April, 1775). In the autumn the Americans invaded Canada, taking Montreal and besieging Quebec until forced to withdraw to Ticonderoga in Spring, 1776. On July 4 the Second Continental Congress issued the *Declaration of Independence. Gen Howe landed on Long Island in August and defeated the newly appointed American commander in chief, Washington, near White Plains. At the beginning of January, 1777, however, Washington dealt a counterblow at Princeton before settling in winter quarters at Valley Forge. Britain's strategy in 1777 was based on a plan for Burgoyne to march S from Canada and join forces with Howe at the Hudson River. Burgoyne duly arrived at the Hudson (August) but Howe had left New York by sea, landed at Chesapeake Bay, and defeated Washington at Brandywine, taking Philadelphia (September). Burgoyne, meanwhile, was forced to surrender his army at *Saratoga, a defeat that proved a turning point by bringing France into the war on the American side. In 1778 the British began an offensive in the S that resulted in several American defeats. Howe's successor, Clinton, took Charleston, South Carolina, and Cornwallis defeated Gates at Camden (1780). In early 1781 the Americans won decisively at Cowpens (Jan 17) but lost the battle of Guilford Court House (Mar 15). Cornwallis now moved into Virginia, establishing a base at Yorktown. There besieged by an American-French force under the Comte de Rochambeau (1725–1807) and Washington, on Oct 19 Cornwallis surrendered. Ultimate American victory was now assured although conflict continued, chiefly at sea. The British navy had been threatened throughout by American privateers and the activities of such commanders as John Paul *Jones, but the main threat at sea came from America's European allies—the French, Spanish (from 1779), and Dutch (from 1780), who gained control of the English Channel and threatened invasion. In 1783 Britain acknowledged American independence in the Treaty of *Paris.

American River A river rising in the Sierra Nevada Mountains in NE California, flowing SW to join the Sacramento River at Sacramento. The California Gold Rush (1849) was precipitated by John A. Sutter's discovery of gold (1948) at one of the river's head streams. Length: 30 mi (49 km).

American Samoa. *See* Samoa.

American Tobacco Case (1911) US Supreme Court case (*US* v. *American Tobacco Co.*) decided against the American Tobacco Company. The company was ordered to reorganize to allow for fairer competition in the tobacco industry. The decision did not break the tobacco monopoly completely and thus weakened current antitrust laws.

America's Cup A sailing race held periodically off Newport, Rhode Island, in which US yachts are challenged for a cup won by the US *America* off the Isle of Wight in 1851. The US retained the cup until 1983, when it was won by the Australian entry *Australia II*.

americium (Am) The fourth transuranic element, synthesized (1944) by G. T. Seaborg and others by addition of neutrons to plutonium followed by β-decay. It forms the oxide (AmO_2) and such trihalides as $AmCl_3$; it is strongly radioactive. At no 95; at wt 243; mp 584°F (994°C).

amethyst A gemstone comprising a purple variety of *quartz. Its color is due to impurities, particularly iron oxide. The best crystals are found in Brazil and the Urals. It is used for jewelry. Birthstone for February.

Amhara A descendant of the invading Semitic conquerors of the Cushitic peoples of Ethiopia. They occupy the southern area of the central highlands of Ethiopia over which, with the Tigré, they have exercised political dominance until the present day. Their society is hierarchical and largely feudal. The emperors were believed to be descended from the biblical king *Solomon. They are a Christian people, who belong to the Coptic Church. Amharic is the language of the Amharas and the principal and official language of Ethiopia. It is derived from a language related to Ethiopic or Ge'ez, the liturgical language of the Ethiopian Church, and is written in Ge'ez characters. It is similar to *Semitic languages in grammar but its vocabulary is largely *Cushitic.

Amherst, Jeffrey, Baron (1717–97) British soldier prominent in the French and Indian War (1754–63) in North America. In 1758 he took the fortress of Louisburg and became commander in chief in America. He captured Crown Point and Ticonderoga in 1759. By 1760 he had conquered Montreal. He was governor general of British North America from 1760 to 1763.

Amici, Giovanni Battista (1786–1863) Italian astronomer, microscopist, and optical instrument maker. He is best known as the inventor of the *achromatic lens. With his own microscopes he discovered many details of orchid pollination and seed development; in astronomy, he studied double stars and Jupiter's moons, as well as designing improved mirrors for reflecting telescopes.

Amiens 49 54N 2 18E A city in NE France, the capital of the Somme department situated on the Somme River. Known as Samarobriva in pre-Roman times, it was the ancient capital of Picardy. The Peace of Amiens (1802), which marked a respite in the Revolutionary and Napoleonic Wars, was signed here. Its fine gothic cathedral survived the damage of both World Wars. An important railroad junction, Amiens' industries include textiles, tires, and chemicals. Population (1986 est): 155,000.

Amin Dada, Idi (c. 1925–) Ugandan politician; president (1971–79). He rose rapidly in the army, becoming commander in 1966. He overthrew Milton *Obote to become president. A flamboyant and unpredictable personality, his prestige was severely damaged by the successful Israeli commando raid (1976) on Entebbe airport to rescue passengers hijacked by Palestinian terrorists. He and his government were notorious for their brutality; Amin was overthrown in a Tanzanian-backed coup after which he went into exile.

Amindivi Islands. *See* Lakshadweep.

amines A class of basic organic compounds derived from ammonia (NH_3), in which one (primary amines), two (secondary amines), or three (tertiary amines) of the hydrogen atoms are replaced by organic radicals or groups. *See also* amino acids.

amino acids A group of organic acids characterized by having at least one carboxyl group ($-$COOH) and at least one amino group ($-$NH$_2$). About 20 different amino acids comprise the basic constituents of *proteins, the arrangement and types of amino acids determining the structure and hence the function of the protein molecule. Certain essential amino acids cannot be manufactured by the body and must be supplied in the diet. In man these are: arginine, histidine, isoleucine, leucine, lysine, methionine, phenylalanine, threonine, tryptophan, and valine.

Amirante Islands An archipelago of sparsely populated coral islands in the W Indian Ocean, belonging to the Seychelles. They are leased to private companies, usually for coconut plantations.

Amis, Kingsley (1922–) British novelist and poet, one of the *Angry Young Men of the 1950s. Educated at Oxford, he taught at Swansea and Cambridge universities and in the US. His first novel, *Lucky Jim* (1954), a comic satire on middle-class academic life, was a popular success. In later novels, such as *I Want It Now* (1968), *Ending Up* (1974), and *Jake's Thing* (1979), his humor became progressively darker. He published several volumes of poetry, contributed to the important verse anthology *New Lines* (1956), and edited the *Oxford Book of Light Verse* (1978). He was awarded the Booker Prize (1986) for *The Old Devils*.

Amish US and Canadian Protestant sect, a conservative faction of the *Mennonites. The Amish disagreed with certain Mennonite beliefs on conformity, or lack of it, broke away, and settled in North America, mainly Pennsylvania and Ontario, Canada. Jakob Ammann, a Mennonite bishop in Switzerland, made the initial break in the 1690s, and by 1727 his followers had begun to settle in Pennsylvania. The Amish live conservatively, dress uniformly, and are self-sufficient, depending on farming as a livelihood and, usually, avoiding modern conveniences.

Amistad Case A US Supreme Court case (1840) that ruled that a slave who escapes illegal bondage is considered free. In 1839 illegally enslaved Africans being transported to the Caribbean on the Spanish ship *Amistad* mutinied, killing two crew members. A US ship then seized the *Amistad* off Long Island and imprisoned the slaves until sympathetic supporters insisted that the case be brought to trial. John Quincy Adams defended them in 1840 before the Supreme Court, which declared them free.

Amman 31 57N 35 56E The capital of Jordan. Amman was the capital of the biblical Ammonites, and there are some Greek and Roman remains. Under the British mandate in Palestine, the town grew from a small village, and in 1946 it became the capital of independent Jordan. The city has had large influxes of refugees following fighting in the Arab-Israeli Wars (1948, 1967, and 1973); in 1970 tension resulting from the refugee presence led to fighting on the streets of Amman between Jordanian forces and Palestinians. The university was founded in 1962. Amman is now an important communications center, with some manufacturing industry. Population (1986): 972,000.

Ammanati, Bartolommeo (1511–92) Florentine mannerist architect and sculptor. Beginning as an assistant of *Sansovino in Venice, Ammanati later worked with *Vasari in Rome on the Villa Giulia. In Florence he was responsible for the Ponte Sta Trinità and the garden façade of the Palazzo Pitti; as a sculptor he is best known for the Neptune fountain in the Piazza della Signoria.

ammeter An instrument for measuring electric current. The two most common types are the moving-coil and the moving-iron ammeters. The moving-coil ammeter is more sensitive but will measure only alternating current. The moving-iron ammeter will measure both alternating and direct current but is less sensitive and its scale is nonlinear. Some modern instruments are electronic and have a digital display.

ammonia (NH_3) A colorless, toxic gas used for the manufacture of fertilizers, nitric acid, explosives, and synthetic fibers. When dissolved in water, ammonia produces an alkaline solution of ammonium hydroxide (NH_4OH), an unstable compound that cannot be isolated from solution.

ammonite A *cephalopod mollusk belonging to the subclass *Ammonoidea* (over 600 genera), abundant during the late Paleozoic and Mesozoic eras, becoming extinct 100 million years ago. Their fossilized remains have either straight or coiled shells, some up to 80 in (200 cm) in diameter, containing many chambers, which provided buoyancy for the free-swimming animal. □fossil.

Ammonites An ancient Semitic tribe who were descended from Ben-ammi, the son of Lot, and lived E of Jordan. They worshiped the god Moloch and often warred against the Israelites.

amnesia Loss of memory resulting from such causes as head injuries, drugs, hysteria, senility, or psychological illness. The memory loss may be for events before the injury or disease (retrograde amnesia) or for events after it (anterograde amnesia). In some cases specific areas of the brain show pathological changes. Treatment is related to the cause.

Amnesty International An organization, founded by Peter Benenson in the UK in 1961, aiming to defend freedom of speech, opinion, and religion in all parts of the world. Its work consists of campaigns for the release of "prisoners of conscience," against torture, and for human rights and it is concerned for the welfare of refugees. It has some 100,000 members in 75 countries and is funded by voluntary contributions.

amniocentesis The removal for examination of a small quantity of the fluid (amniotic fluid) that surrounds an unborn baby in the mother's womb. The specimen may be taken by needle through the abdominal wall or, later in pregnancy, the opening of the womb. Tests on the amniotic fluid may reveal the presence of certain diseases or congenital disorders in the baby (e.g. Down's syndrome or spina bifida). If serious abnormality is detected, the possibility of abortion at an early and safe stage can be considered. Amniocentesis is particularly useful when there is a family history of serious congenital disease. *See also* prenatal diagnosis.

Amoeba A genus of free-living, microscopic animals (□*Protozoa*). They occur widely in soil, fresh water, and salt water and their flexible cells assume various shapes. The common amoeba (*A. proteus*) may be up to 0.02 in (0.5 mm) long. Amoebas move by extending their cytoplasm into broad lobes (pseudopodia), which are also used to engulf food particles (e.g. bacteria and other protozoans) and liquids. They reproduce by binary *fission and under adverse conditions form cysts with a thick protective wall surrounding the cell. Some related forms are parasitic, including *Entamoeba histolytica*, which causes amoebic dysentery in man. Class: *Sarcodina*.

Amon The supreme Egyptian deity. Originally a local god of Thebes, he acquired major status in the ascendancy of the 18th (Theban) dynasty in about 1570 BC. He became associated with the rival god *Ra and as Amon-Ra became the national god. Great temples were built to him at Luxor and Karnak (c. 1400 BC). Except during the brief reign of *Akhenaton, Amon-Ra remained supreme god until the Assyrians captured Thebes in 663 BC.

Amorites Semitic nomads of Palestine and Syria, who invaded the centers of civilization of Mesopotamia during the late 3rd millennium and 2nd millennium BC. They occupied *Babylonia, assimilated its culture and established numerous small kingdoms. Many Babylonian kings, including *Hammurabi, were of Amorite stock. *Mari and *Aleppo were important centers under Amorite control.

amortization 1. The discharging of a debt (e.g. a mortgage) through (usually equal) periodic payments of principal and interest. **2.** The depreciation of an asset through wear or obsolescence. The value of a fixed asset purchased by a company is not charged in full to its profit and loss account in the year in which it is purchased. Instead it is amortized over its useful life in the accounts, i.e. only a certain portion of its cost is charged to the profit and loss account each year.

Amos (early 8th century BC) An Old Testament prophet of Judah. The Book of Amos contains his prophecies delivered in Israel. He denounces the luxury and injustice of the privileged nation and predicts God's judgment by means of an Assyrian invasion and natural calamities.

amount of substance A quantity proportional to the number of particles, such as atoms or ions, in a substance. The constant of proportionality is *Avogadro's number. Amount of substance is measured in *moles.

Amoy. *See* Xiamen.

ampere (A) The *SI unit of electric current equal to the current that when passed through two parallel infinitely long conductors placed 1 meter apart in a vacuum produces a force between them of 2×10^{-7} newton per meter of length. This 1948 definition replaced all former definitions including that of the international ampere based on the rate of deposition of silver from a solution of silver nitrate. Named for A. M. *Ampère.

Ampère, André Marie (1775–1836) French physicist, who was a professor at Bourg and later in Paris. He is remembered for his fundamental work on the physics and mathematics of electricity and electromagnetism. He introduced the important distinctions between electrostatics and electric currents and between current and voltage, demonstrated that current-carrying wires exert a force on each other, and gave an explanation of magnetism in terms of electric currents. The unit of electric current is named for him.

Ampère's law The strength of the magnetic field at any point produced by a current (I) flowing through a conductor of length l is proportional to Il/d^2 where d is the distance between the point and the conductor. Named for A. M. *Ampère.

amphetamine A stimulant drug that produces a feeling of alertness and well-being, increases muscular activity, and reduces fatigue and appetite. Because of the risk of addiction, particularly when combined with barbiturates ("purple hearts"), amphetamine is now rarely prescribed. It is occasionally used to treat obesity and narcolepsy (a tendency to fall asleep at any time). Trade name: Benzedrine. *See also* drug dependence.

amphibian An animal belonging to the class *Amphibia*, which contains over 2500 species of frogs, toads, newts, salamanders, and caecilians. Adult amphibians breathe through lungs and have adapted to a wide range of habitats; however they require damp surroundings in order to minimize loss of body fluids through their thin, moist, and usually scaleless skin. Generally amphibians lay their eggs in ponds or rivers, often migrating long distances to do so. The eggs hatch into aquatic tadpole larvae that breathe using gills and develop into adults by a complete bodily transformation known as *metamorphosis.

amphiboles A group of rock-forming minerals, mostly complex hydrous fer-romagnesian silicates. The anthophyllite-cummingtonite subgroup contains anthophyllite, gedrite, cummingtonite, and grunerite; the hornblende subgroup contains tremolite, actinolite, hornblende, edenite, hastingsite, and kaersutite; the alkali amphibole subgroup contains glaucophane, nebeckite, richterite, and katophorite. Amphiboles are common in igneous and metamorphic rocks and often occur in fibrous or acicular forms, including some forms of *asbestos.

amphioxus A small slender fishlike animal, also called lancelet, belonging to the subphylum *Cephalochordata* (about 30 species). Up to 2 in (5 cm) long, they occur in shallow coastal waters, living mostly in burrows with the front end protruding. Food particles are filtered from the water, which enters the mouth and leaves through gill slits; there is a supportive rodlike *notochord and a nerve cord running the length of the body. Amphioxus is thought to resemble the primitive ancestors of other chordate animals, including vertebrates. Genera: *Branchiostoma; Asymmetron. See also* Chordata.

amphisbaena A wormlike lizard, also called worm lizard, belonging to the family *Amphisbaenidae* (120 species) occurring in tropical and subtropical America and Africa and the Mediterranean region. Up to 24 in (60 cm) long, amphisbaenas are specialized for burrowing having reduced eyes, a small head with thick skull bones, and, except for one genus (*Bipes*), no legs. They feed on insects and larvae.

amphitheater An elliptical or circular building with tiers of seats surrounding an arena, designed by the Romans as a setting for gladiatorial and wild-beast shows, mock sea battles, etc. Small, wooden amphitheaters were built throughout the Roman world. The earliest stone amphitheater is that at Pompeii (c. 70 BC). The largest is the *Colosseum in Rome but there are also impressive remains of amphitheaters in Arles, Nîmes, Capua, Verona, and in Sicily and N Africa.

Amphitrite The Greek goddess of the sea. Poseidon chose her to be his wife when he saw her dancing with her sister Nereids. She rejected him and fled to the island of Naxos, but he sent a dolphin to reclaim her. She bore him three sons, Triton, Rhodos, and Benthesicyma.

Amphitryon In Greek mythology, a grandson of Perseus who was betrothed to Alcmene, daughter of the King of Mycene. While he was away at war, Zeus assumed his appearance and seduced Alcmene, who conceived *Heracles from the union.

amphora An ancient Greek two-handled vase used as a container for liquids and fruit, and sometimes as an urn for holding ashes of the dead or for prize awards. The most important are the Black Figure vases (600–480 BC) of black-painted red earthenware, depicting mythological scenes. Other undecorated types, sometimes tapering to a pointed base, were in general use for transporting oil and wine until Roman times.

amplifier A device for increasing the magnitude of some quantity by using power from an external source. The term usually refers to an electronic device for intensifying an electrical signal in an alternating-current circuit, with an external steady voltage supply. Originally built with *thermionic valves, but now almost exclusively with *transistors, amplifiers are designed to multiply the input (current, voltage, or power) by a specific factor, known as the gain. Often an amplifier consists of several stages, the output from one stage becoming the input to the next stage. This method is used in the more complex and specialized type of amplifier used in sound-reproduction systems.

AMPHORA *A Greek form of the 6th century* BC.

amplitude modulation. *See* modulation.

Amr ibn al-As (d. 663 AD) Arab soldier, who led the Muslim conquest of Egypt. Following the conquest of Syria he led the invasion of Egypt; Alexandria fell in 642. Having helped *Mu'awiyah I secure the caliphate (661), he governed Egypt until his death.

Amritsar 31 35N 74 56E A city in NW India, in Punjab. Founded in 1577 by the fourth guru of the Sikhs, Ram Das, it has become the center of the Sikh faith. It was the scene of a massacre (1919), in which hundreds of Indian nationalists were killed when fired upon by troops under British control. In June 1984 about 1000 people died when the Sikh shrine, the Golden Temple, was fortified by Sikh extremists and stormed by the army. The dead included the Sikh extremist leader Sant Jarnail Bhindranwale. The subsequent assassination of Indira Gandhi later in the year was a reprisal for this event. A commercial, cultural, and communications center, it manufactures textiles and silk. Population (1991): 709,456.

Amsterdam 52 21N 4 54E The official capital of the Netherlands, in North Holland province on the Amstel and IJ Rivers. The government seat is at The Hague. Linked to the North Sea by canal (1876), it is a major seaport. It is also an important financial and industrial center, possessing a renowned diamond cutting and polishing trade. Industries include ship building, dairy produce, tobacco, and brewing. The city is mostly built on piles and linked with a radial system of canals and approximately 1000 bridges. Notable buildings include the 13th-century Oude Kerk (Old Church), the 15th-century Nieuwe Kerk (New Church), and a royal palace (1665). It possesses two universities, the Rijksmuseum, containing a superb collection of Dutch and Flemish paintings, and the Stedelijk Museum with its leading modern-art collection. *History*: chartered in 1300, it joined the Hanseatic League in 1369. During the 17th century it prospered as a seaport; it gained significantly through Antwerp's loss of trade following the closure of the Scheldt River under the Treaty of Westphalia (1648). It became the capital in 1808. Population (1992 est): 702,500.

Amu Darya River A river in central Asia. Rising in the Pamirs, it flows mainly NW through the Hindu Kush, Turkmenistan and Uzbekistan to join the Aral Sea through a large delta. It forms part of the border between Afghanistan and Turkmenistan, and it is important for irrigation. It is navigable for over 800 mi (1450 km). Length: 1500 mi (2400 km).

Amundsen, Roald (1872–1928) Norwegian explorer, the first person to reach the South Pole. In 1897 he became first mate on the *Belgica*, which was engaged in Antarctic exploration. After sailing the *Northwest Passage in the *Gjöa* (1903–06), he abandoned his plan to reach the North Pole on hearing of *Peary's success (1909). He himself beat *Scott to the South Pole in 1911. In 1926 he flew a dirigible over the North Pole with Umberto *Nobile. Amundsen died while searching for Nobile following the latter's dirigible crash in the Arctic Ocean.

Amundsen Sea A small section of the S Pacific Ocean, bordering on Ellsworth Land in Antarctica.

Amur River (Chinese name: Heilong Jiang *or* Hei-Lung Chiang) A river in NE Asia. Rising in N Mongolia, it flows generally SE and NE through Mongolia, Russia, and China, to the Sea of Okhotsk. It forms the border between Russia and Manchuria and was the scene of much Sino-Soviet friction in the 1960s and 1970s. Length: 2700 mi (4350 km).

amyl alcohol ($C_5H_{11}OH$) A colorless oily liquid *alcohol that has eight *isomers: pentan-1-ol, pentan-2-ol, etc. It is obtained from *fusel oil and is used as a solvent.

amylase A digestive enzyme that breaks down starch and glycogen into maltose. It is present in saliva (as ptyalin) and in pancreatic juice.

Anabaptists (from Greek: rebaptizers) Any of various radical religious groups originating in several continental countries during the *Reformation. They were called Anabaptists because they rejected infant baptism in favor of baptizing adults when they professed their faith. Persecuted by Roman Catholics and Protestants, they were accused of fanaticism, heresy, and immorality. Modern research has shown them in a somewhat more favorable light. They believed in pacifism, common ownership of goods, millenarianism, and held radical political views. Prominent leaders were the German Thomas Münzer (c. 1490–1525), killed after the Peasants' Revolt, and *John of Leiden. Their modern descendants, such as the *Mennonites, number more than 500,000 in all.

anabolism. *See* metabolism.

anaconda A nonvenomous South American *constrictor snake, *Eunectes murinus*. Up to 33 ft (10 m) long, it is typically dark green with oval black spots and lives in swamps and rivers, feeding on fish and small caymans and also hunting deer, peccaries, and birds along the water's edge.

Anacreon (6th century BC) Greek lyric poet. He fled from his native island of Teos before the Persian invasion, and lived at Samos and then Athens, under the patronage of Hipparchus. His work, only fragments of which survive, consisted chiefly of love lyrics and drinking songs, written in a formal and restrained style.

anaerobe. *See* aerobe.

anagnoresis (Greek: recognition) A literary term referring to the moment of recognition of a previously unsuspected truth. The concept was defined in Aristotle's *Poetics*. It is considered an essential part of the plot of tragedy, in which the protagonist's recognition of his tragic flaw occurs at the climax and leads to his downfall. The best-known example occurs in Sophocles' *Oedipus Rex* when Oedipus discovers that he has unknowingly killed his father and married his mother.

Anaheim 33 50N 117 56W A city in S California near Los Angeles. It is a major tourist center, containing the famous Disneyland opened in 1955. Population (1990): 266,406.

ANACONDA *This enormous snake spends most of the time in water, although it may climb trees to bask or search for prey. Like other boas, it bears live young.*

analgesics A class of drugs that relieve pain. **Narcotic analgesics**, such as *morphine, are powerful pain killers that act directly on the brain. Some anesthetics also have analgesic properties. *Aspirin and paracetemol are examples of **antipyretic analgesics**, which also reduce fever. These drugs are not addictive but are less potent than the narcotics. *See also* drug dependence, narcotics.

analog computer. *See* computer.

analytic geometry The study of geometrical relations by algebraic methods. Geometrical figures are placed in a *coordinate system, each point in the figure being represented by its coordinates, which satisfy an algebraic equation. Also known as coordinate geometry or Cartesian geometry, after its inventor, René *Descartes.

anamorphosis A perspective technique used in painting and drawing to distort an image or object seen from a normal viewpoint. The image's true form is only recreated when viewed from an angle or through a special device, such as a peephole. A famous example is the elongated skull in Hans Holbein's *Ambassadors* (1533; National Gallery, London).

Ananda (5th century BC) The first cousin, favorite disciple, and personal attendant of the Buddha. At his insistence a Buddhist order was founded to admit women.

anaphylaxis A form of *allergy that follows the interaction of the foreign substance (allergen) with antibody that is bound to the surface of certain cells (mast cells). This leads to the release of bradykinin, *histamine, and other chemicals, which cause the symptoms. Symptoms are either local (such as asthma) or general (shock and collapse). The latter usually follows injection of the allergen (such as penicillin) and is a medical emergency; it is treated with injections of corticosteroids and adrenaline.

anarchism A political theory advocating abolition of the state and all governmental authority. Most anarchists believe that voluntary cooperation between individuals and groups is not only a fairer and more moral way of organizing society but is also more effective and orderly. Anarchism aims at maximizing personal freedom and holds that societies in which freedom is limited by coercion and authority are inherently unstable. *Proudhon thought that anarchism could be achieved by peaceful change, but *Bakunin believed that violent means were necessary. As an influential political force, anarchism was defeated in Russia by communism but persisted in Europe, especially in Spain until the end of the Civil War (1939).

Anastasia (1901–?1918) The youngest daughter of *Nicholas II of Russia. Although she was believed to have been executed after the Russian Revolution, a Mrs. Anna Anderson claimed from 1920 that she was Anastasia. In 1961 her claim was officially rejected.

Anasatasius I (c. 430–518 AD) Byzantine emperor (491–518). Anastasius instituted thorough financial and administrative reforms and built a defensive wall to protect Constantinople. His adherence to the heretical *Monophysite doctrine was unpopular.

Anatolia. *See* Asia Minor.

Anatolian languages An extinct subgroup of the *Indo-European language family, which included Palaic, Luwian, Lydian, and Lycian. Originally spoken in Asia Minor, some date back to 2000 BC. The classification is sometimes used in a geographical sense to include all the languages of ancient Asia Minor, some of non-Indo-European origin. There is some confusion about the relation of the Anatolian languages to *Hittite and a precise classification of the relations between these and Indo-European has not been achieved. *See also* Indo-Hittite languages.

anatomy The study of the structure of living organisms. Early studies of human anatomy were made by the Greek physician Galen, in the 2nd century AD, but it was not until the 16th century that the prejudice against dissecting human cadavers was overcome and anatomists—notably *Vesalius—made valuable contributions to the science. In the 17th century William *Harvey discovered the circulation of blood and the development of the microscope enabled advances in the detailed structure of the body to be made by such microscopists as *Malpighi, *Leeuwenhoek, and *Swammerdam. In the 20th century anatomy received a valuable tool with the development of the electron microscope, which greatly extended the investigation of microscopic structure. Today anatomy explores structure within the context of function (*see* physiology). Specialized branches of anatomy include embryology (the study of development), *histology (tissues), and *cytology (cells).

Anaxagoras (c. 500–428 BC) Greek philosopher, born at Clazomenae (Asia Minor). In about 480 he moved to Athens, but because of his influence on *Pericles, he was eventually (450) banished on a trumped-up charge of impiety. He diverged from some other early Greek philosophers by stating that the physical universe was made up of an infinite number of substances and that matter was infinitely divisible. He was also the first to explain solar eclipses.

Anaximander (c. 610–c. 546 BC) Greek philosopher, born in Miletus (Asia Minor). He was one of the earliest thinkers to develop a systematic philosophical view of the physical universe. He held that it came from something unlimited, not just one particular kind of matter, and maintained that the earth lay unsupported at the center of the universe. He also had an evolutionary view of the origin of life, holding that it arose in the sea, and that man evolved from some more primitive species.

Anaximenes (died c. 528 BC) Greek philosopher, who lived in Miletus (Asia Minor). He believed that the universe fundamentally consisted of air or vapor; different degrees of condensation correspond to different degrees of density in matter. He held that air, being constantly in motion, possessed life and that its motion accounted for changes in physical objects.

ancestor worship In many primitive societies, the propitiation of the spirits of dead forebears, usually with the object of persuading them to exert their powers on behalf of their descendants in hunting, warfare, etc. Ancestor cults can also be socially important in reinforcing the authority of living elders, who, as guardians of the ancestral shrines, are the spirits' mouthpieces. Festivals for the dead involving visits to the tombs, food offerings, and sacrifices were features of ancient Greek and Roman religion. An ancestor cult formed an important part of traditional Chinese religion and also survives in the Buddhist family altar (*butsudan*) in Japanese households.

Anchieta, José de (1534–97) Portuguese poet and scholar. He became a Jesuit in 1551, and in 1553 joined a mission in Brazil. He helped protect the Indians from slavery and was one of the founders of the city of São Paulo. As well as his chiefly religious poetry and historical works he wrote a grammar of the Indian language, Tupí, and descriptions of the Indian culture.

Anchises In Greek mythology, a Trojan nobleman, father of *Aeneas by *Aphrodite. He was blinded for boasting of his relationship with the goddess. Carried from burning *Troy on Aeneas' back, he died in Sicily.

anchor Any device used for mooring a vessel to the bottom of a body of water. In ancient times a heavy stone was used, attached to the vessel by a rope. Today various patent anchors are in use. They are designed for different kinds of bottom—sandy, rocky, muddy, etc.—and usually dig into the bottom with their bladelike flukes. Depending on the size of the vessel, the anchor rode, or attachment to the vessel, may be entirely of heavy chain, as in the case of larger boats and ships, or of a short length of chain to which a rope, usually of nylon, is attached.

Anchorage 61 10N 150 00E A city and major port in S Alaska at the head of Cook Inlet. Founded in 1914 as the terminus of the Alaska Railroad, its main industries are defense projects and the development of natural resources, especially coal and gold. Population (1990): 226,338.

anchovy A small herring-like fish belonging to the tropical and warm-temperate family *Engraulidae* (100 species). 4–10 in (10–25 cm) long, anchovies have a large mouth extending behind the eye, a small lower jaw, and a pointed snout. They live in large shoals, chiefly in coastal waters, and are widely fished for food, bait, and animal feeds.

Anchusa. *See* alkanet.

ancien régime The social and political system of France prior to the *French Revolution.

Ancona 43 37N 13 31E A seaport in central Italy, the capital of Marche on the Adriatic Sea. It dates from 1500 BC, when it was founded by the Dorians. Its industries are connected with ship building, engineering, and sugar refining. Population (1991 est): 103,000.

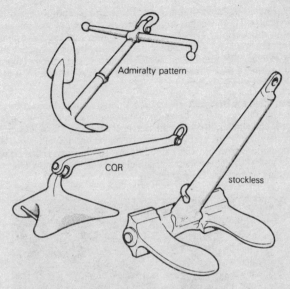

ANCHOR *Three common forms of anchor.*

Andalusia (Spanish name: Andalucia) The southernmost region of Spain, bordering on the Atlantic Ocean and Mediterranean Sea. It occupies chiefly the river basin of the Guadalquivir and is one of Spain's most fertile regions producing citrus fruits, olives, and wine. Under Roman control after the 2nd century BC, the region was named Andalusia (after its 5th-century Vandal settlers) by the Muslims, who invaded the region in the early 8th century; much evidence of the Muslim occupation remains. In the 15th century Castile finally recovered Andalusia from the Muslims. After the *Moriscos (Christians of Moorish descent) were expelled in 1609 the region's prosperity diminished. It is now popular with tourists, who are attracted by the great Moorish buildings found especially in Córdoba, Seville, and Granada.

Andalusian horse A breed of large, strong horse developed in Spain in the 15th century. Andalusian horses are usually gray (but sometimes bay or black), with a long silky mane and tail and a high stepping movement. Docile and attractive, they are often used in parades and bullfighting. Height: 15.75–16.75 hands (1.60–1.70 m).

Andaman and Nicobar Islands A Union Territory of India, comprising two island groups in the E Bay of Bengal. The Andaman forests support plywood and match industries. Coconuts, rubber, and coffee are also important. The Nicobar Islands 75 mi (120 km) S of the Andaman Islands, produce coconuts, arecanuts, and fish. *History*: the Andaman Islands were an Indian penal colony until 1945. Both groups were occupied by Japan (1942–45) and transferred to India (1947). Area: 3215 sq mi (8293 sq km). Population (1991): 279,111. Capital: Port Blair.

Andamanese The indigenous inhabitants of the Andaman and Nicobar Islands in the Bay of Bengal. They are of negrito racial type. Their traditional culture, surviving only in southern areas among the Jarawa and Onge tribes, was based upon gathering shellfish, fishing, and hunting, using single outrigger canoes, nets, lines, and bows and arrows. Tools and weapons were often made from large shells. There was no method known to them of making fire. Social organization was simple. Tribes were divided into hunting bands, several of which might acknowledge a common chief. Trading between coastal and inland bands was extensive. Ritual initiation was important and various taboos were a prominent feature of their ritual life. Their language, Andamanese, is almost extinct and has no known relations.

Andersen, Hans Christian (1805–75) Danish author, famous for his fairy tales. The son of a shoemaker, he attempted to become an actor in Copenhagen. A benefactor enabled him to attend the university there in 1828; he subsequently traveled widely in Europe and wrote novels, plays, and travel books. His international reputation, however, was earned by the 168 fairy tales that he wrote between 1835 and 1872. These include such classics as "The Snow Queen," "The Little Mermaid," and "The Ugly Duckling."

HANS CHRISTIAN ANDERSEN

Anderson, Carl David (1905–91) US physicist, who worked at the California Institute of Technology. He shared the 1936 Nobel Prize for showing (1932) that cloud-chamber tracks were made by *positrons, whose existence had been predicted by Dirac. In 1935 Anderson discovered the first *meson, thinking it was the particle predicted by *Yukawa. In fact Anderson's meson is now known as the muon, whereas Yukawa's particle is known as the pion (discovered by *Powell).

Anderson, Marian (1902–93) US singer. Having established a reputation as a contralto abroad, she was refused permission, because of her race, by the

Daughters of the American Revolution (DAR) to use Washington, D.C.'s Constitution Hall for a recital in 1939 and was later sponsored by Eleanor Roosevelt in a concert at the Lincoln Memorial. In 1955 she became the first African American to sing a leading role with the Metropolitan Opera. She was awarded the Presidential Medal of Freedom (1963) and a Congress-authorized gold medal for her contribution to the arts (1978).

Anderson, Maxwell (1888–1959) US playwright. A journalist, he had his first play, *White Desert*, produced on Broadway in 1923. He wrote about war, corruption, and injustice. *What Price Glory?* (1924) and, later, *Key Largo* (1939) and *Storm Operation* (1944) dealt with the disillusionment of war. *Both Your Houses* (1933), a satire on Congress, won the Pulitzer Prize. Other works include *Saturday's Children* (1927), *Winterset* (1935), *High Tor* (1937), *Knickerbocker Holiday* (1938; with Kurt *Weill), and *The Eve of St. Mark* (1942).

Anderson, Robert (1805–71) US Union soldier in the Civil War. In charge of Ft. Sumter, South Carolina, he, with inadequate supplies, withstood a 2-day attack (1861) by the Confederates before surrendering the fort. This was the first battle of the Civil War.

Anderson, Sherwood (1876–1941) US author. Born in a small town in Ohio, he held a variety of jobs before abandoning job and family in 1906 to become a writer. He was encouraged by Theodore *Dreiser, Carl *Sandburg, and other Chicago writers and by Gertrude *Stein in Paris. He finally settled in Virginia as a newspaper owner; there he in turn encouraged *Faulkner and *Hemingway. *Winesburg, Ohio* (1919), his best-known book, is a series of tales about the stunted lives of a small-town community. His novels included *Poor White* (1920), *Many Marriages* (1923), *Dark Laughter* (1925), and *Beyond Desire* (1933). Other works include story collections, *The Triumph of the Egg* (1921) and *Death in the Woods* (1933), and the autobiographical *Story Teller's Story* (1924).

Andes (Spanish name: Cordillera de los Andes) A mountain system in W South America. It extends N for about 4500 mi (7250 km) from Cape Horn to the Isthmus of Panama, reaching 22,835 ft (6960 m) at Mount Aconcagua and separating a narrow coastal belt from the rest of the continent. Comprising a series of parallel mountain ranges, it is chiefly of volcanic origin and contains several active volcanoes, including *Cotopaxi; earthquakes are common phenomena. It is rich in mineral wealth; the chief metals extracted include gold, silver, platinum, mercury, copper, and lead.

andesite A group of volcanic rocks comprising the fine-grained equivalent of *diorite. They consist mainly of plagioclase-feldspar and one or more ferromagnesian minerals, and many andesites are porphyritic. They are found associated with basalts and rhyolites in island arcs and orogenic regions. The Andesite Line is the geographic boundary between continental andesitic rocks and oceanic basalts, traced through the Pacific.

Andhra Pradesh A state in E central India, on the Bay of Bengal. The coastal plain rises westward over the Eastern *Ghats into the *Deccan plateau. Rice, sugar cane, cotton, tobacco, and pulses are farmed. Large forests provide teak, bamboo, and fruit trees. Manganese, iron ore, mica, and coal are mined. A few industries exist, such as textile, machinery, and shipbuilding, which has been developed with cheap hydroelectricity. *History*: the Andhra people and culture have flourished since the 1st century BC. From 1700 local rulers gradually lost control to France and Britain. A center of 20th-century Indian nationalism, the Telegu-speaking area of *Madras became Andhra Pradesh state in 1953. Further boundary adjustments were made in 1956 and 1960. Area: 106,258 sq mi (275,281 sq km). Population (1991): 66,354,559. Capital: Hyderabad. Chief seaport: Vishakhapatnam.

Andorra, Coprincipality of (Catalan name: Valls d'Andorra; French name: Les Vallées d'Andorre) A small country in the E Pyrenees, between France and Spain, a principality until 1993. It is mountainous with peaks reaching heights of about 9500 ft (almost 3000 m). *Economy*: tourism is an important source of revenue supplementing the primarily agrarian economy (wheat, potatoes, livestock raising, and tobacco). *History*: records of Andorra's existence as a state date from 1278, when it was placed under the joint overlordship of the Bishop of Urgel in Spain and the Comte de Foix in France. The latter's rights passed in the 16th century to the French crown and are now held by the president. Andorra pays dues in alternate years of 960 francs to France and 460 pesetas to the bishopric respectively. In 1993, voters adopted Andorra's first constitution, establishing a parliamentary government. The former co-princes retained rights over Andorra's security and other powers. Andorra is a tax haven, and immigration has been substantial in recent years. Official language: Catalan; French and Spanish are also spoken. Official currencies: French and Spanish currencies are both in use. Area: 179 sq mi (465 sq km). Population (1990): 51,000. Capital: Andorra la Vella.

Andrássy, Gyula, Count (1823–90) Hungarian revolutionary and statesman. In the *Revolution of 1848 Andrássy supported Lajos *Kossuth. With Ferenc *Deák he negotiated the Dual Monarchy of *Austria-Hungary (1867) and was Hungary's first constitutional prime minister (1867–71). From 1871 to 1879 he was the Austro-Hungarian foreign minister and strove to halt Russian expansion into the Balkans.

André, John (1751–80) British soldier. While serving as adjutant to the commander in chief of British troops in the American Revolution, he negotiated with the treacherous Benedict *Arnold, the commander of West Point, for its surrender. He was captured by Washington's army and tried and executed as a spy.

Andrea del Sarto (Andrea d'Agnolo; 1486–1530) A leading Florentine Renaissance painter, whose work, through its influence on his pupils *Pontormo, Giovanni Battista Rosso (1494–1540), and *Vasari, became a starting point for Tuscan *mannerism. He was able to combine Florentine draftsmanship with a Venetian feeling for color and atmosphere and his compositions resemble relief sculpture. Andrea spent most of his life in Florence, producing a series of frescoes in the cloister of the Scalzi and the SS Annunziata. Among his most important paintings are several representing the Holy Family, some portraits, and the *Madonna of the Harpes* (1517; Uffizi).

Andrew, St In the New Testament, one of the 12 Apostles. Originally a fisherman in partnership with his brother Simon Peter, he was a disciple of John the Baptist before following Jesus. Apparently crucified, he is the patron saint of Scotland and Russia. Feast day: Nov 30.

Andrew II (1175–1235) King of Hungary (1205–35). Andrew was forced by his recalcitrant barons to accept the *Golden Bull in 1222, which limited royal powers. He participated in the fifth Crusade (1218).

Andrić, Ivo (1892–1975) Serbian writer. He wrote his first major book, *Ex Ponto* (1918), while imprisoned by the Austrians as a Yugoslav nationalist. He later served abroad in the Yugoslav diplomatic service, but his native Bosnia provided the settings and themes for his novels, notably *Bosnian Story* (1945) and *The Bridge on the Drina* (1945). He was awarded the Nobel Prize in 1961.

Androcles The hero of a story by Aulus Gellius (?125–165? AD). Androcles was an escaped slave who removed a thorn from the paw of a lion. The lion later recognized the recaptured slave in the arena and spared him; both were freed. The story was satirized in the play, *Androcles and the Lion*, by G. B. *Shaw.

androgens A group of steroid hormones that influence the development and function of the male reproductive system and determine male secondary sexual characteristics, such as the growth of body hair and deepening of the voice at puberty. The major androgens are *testosterone and androsterone, produced by the testes in higher animals and man, and also in small amounts by the adrenal glands and ovaries in mammals. Natural and synthetic androgens are used in medicine to treat conditions caused by androgen deficiency. Some androgens promote the growth of muscle and bone. These—the anabolic steroids—have been used for their body-building effects in debilitated patients and in athletes.

Andromache In Greek mythology, the wife of Hector, the chief Trojan warrior. She appears in Homer's *Iliad*. After the fall of Troy she became the slave of Neoptolemus, son of Achilles, and bore him three sons. After his death she married Helenus, brother of Hector.

Andromeda A constellation in the N sky near Cassiopeia. The brightest star is the 2nd-magnitude Alpheratz. The constellation contains the spiral **Andromeda galaxy**, which is the largest of the nearby galaxies in the *Local Group.

Andropov, Yuri Vladimirovich (1914–84) Soviet statesman and general secretary of the Soviet Communist Party (1982–84) and president of the Soviet Union (1983–84). He was ambassador to Hungary (1953–57) during the 1956 uprising and headed the KGB (1967–82).

Andros, Sir Edmund (1637–1714) British colonial governor of Dominion of New England. Appointed by the Duke of York (later James II) as governor of New York in 1674, he was recalled in 1681, but returned in 1686 to govern the consolidated Dominion of New England, which by 1688 included the New England colonies, New York, and New Jersey. Although he carried out his duties for England admirably, the colonists were disgruntled and rebelled in 1689 when James II was dethroned in England. Sent back to England for trial, Andros was acquitted and later returned to govern Virginia (1692–97).

androsterone. *See* androgens.

anechoic chamber A room used in acoustical experiments that is designed to absorb nearly all the sounds produced in it. Its walls, floor, and ceiling are constructed from insulating and absorbent materials.

Aneirin (6th century AD) Welsh poet. His poem "Y Gododdin," preserved in the manuscript *Book of Aneirin* (c. 1250), celebrates the heroes of an expedition sent from Edinburgh to recapture Catterick from the Saxons. Out of 300 warriors only one survived.

anemia A reduction in the number of red cells or the quantity of red pigment (*see* hemoglobin) in the blood. It may be due to loss of blood, for example after an accident or operation or from chronic bleeding of a peptic ulcer, or lack of iron, which is necessary for the production of hemoglobin. **Hemolytic anemias** are caused by increased destruction of the red blood cells, as may occur in certain blood diseases (e.g. *sickle-cell disease and *thalassemia) and malaria or because of the presence of toxic chemicals. Anemia can also result from the defective production of red cells, such as occurs in **pernicious anemia** (when it is due to deficiency of *vitamin B_{12}).

The main symptoms of anemia are extreme tiredness and fatiguability, breathlessness, pallor, palpitations, and poor resistance to infection. The treatment depends on the cause.

anemometer An instrument for measuring the velocity of a fluid, often the velocity of the wind. In one type, the fluid drives a small windmill or set of cups, the rate of rotation of which is a measure of the velocity of the fluid. Two other common types of anemometers are the *Pitot tube and the *Venturi tube.

Anemone A genus of herbaceous perennial plants (about 150 species) mostly native to N temperate regions. The leaves are segmented and the flowers lack true petals (the sepals function as petals). The Eurasian wood anemone (*A. nemorosa*), 4–6 in (10–15 cm) high, has white flowers. Many species are cultivated as ornamentals for their brightly colored flowers, including the poppy and Japanese anemones (*A. coronaria* and *A. japonica*). Family: *Ranunculaceae*.

aneroid barometer. *See* barometer.

anesthesia A state of insensitivity to pain. Anesthesia occurs in certain diseases of the nervous system, but the term usually refers to the state induced artificially for surgical operations. It may be produced by anesthetic drugs or other means, including *hypnosis and *acupuncture. Alcohol and opium derivatives have been used as anesthetics for centuries, but it was not until the 1840s that the first anesthetic gases—ether, nitrous oxide, and chloroform—were used to induce **general anesthesia** (total unconsciousness). This procedure now involves premedication (including administration of sedatives) to prepare the patient for surgery, followed by induction of anesthesia by injecting a short-acting barbiturate (usually sodium thiopentone). Anesthesia is maintained by inhalation of an anesthetic gas. **Local anesthesia** is usually used for dental surgery and also for other operations when the medical state of the patient makes general anesthesia unadvisable. Procaine and lignocaine are widely used local anesthetics. **Spinal anesthesia** (epidural or subarachnoid) produces loss of sensation in a particular part of the body by injecting a local anesthetic into the space around the spinal cord. It may be used, for example, during a difficult childbirth.

aneurysm A swelling in the wall of an artery, due to a weakness in the wall. The most common cause in the western world is now *atherosclerosis. Aneurysms may rupture, causing fatal hemorrhage. Treatment consists of surgical removal of the aneurysm and its replacement with a graft.

Angara River A river in Russia in SE Siberia. It flows mainly NNW from Lake Baikal to the Yenisei River. Length: 1150 mi (1840 km).

Angel Falls (Spanish name: Salto Angel) The highest cataract in the world, in SE Venezuela on a tributary of the Río Caroní. Height: 3211 ft (979 m).

angelfish 1. A fish of the tropical marine family *Chaetodontidae*, having a narrow oval laterally compressed body, a small mouth, and often an elongated snout. Up to 28 in (70 cm) long, angelfish are solitary, living around coral reefs, and feeding on small invertebrates. They are usually patterned in a variety of brilliant colors. **2.** A South American *cichlid fish of the genus *Pterophyllum*, especially *P. scalare*, which is valued as an aquarium fish.

Angelica A genus of tall perennial herbs (about 70 species) distributed in the N hemisphere and New Zealand. They grow up to 7 ft (2 m) tall and have umbrella-like clusters of white or greenish flowers. The Eurasian species *A. archangelica* yields an oil used in liqueur and perfume making, and its stems are candied to make the confectionary angelica. *A. sylvestris* (wild angelica) is native to Europe and Asia and introduced in Canada. Family: *Umbelliferae*.

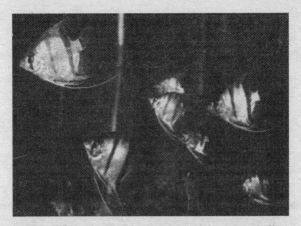

ANGELFISH *The Amazonian angelfish (Pterophyllum scalare) is a favorite aquarium fish. After an elaborate courtship, eggs are deposited and stick to water plants. They hatch in about 48 hours.*

Angelico, Fra (Guido di Pietro; c. 1400–55) Italian painter of the early *Renaissance, born in Vicchio (Tuscany). In the early 1420s he became a Dominican monk in Fiesole. His order transferred in 1436 to St Mark's Convent, Florence, where he painted several frescoes, including a famous *Annunciation*. From 1445 to about 1450 he painted fresco cycles in the Vatican but only the *Scenes from the Lives of SS Stephen and Lawrence* has survived. His other major work is *The Coronation of the Virgin* (Uffizi). He was an exclusively religious painter, whose spiritual serenity is reflected both in his art and his "angelic" nature (hence his popular name).

Angell, Sir Norman (1874–1967) British author, economist, and Labor politician. He received the Nobel Peace Prize in 1933 for his opposition to totalitarianism and his influential antiwar book *The Great Illusion* (1910).

angels (Greek: messengers) In Christianity, Judaism, and Islam, supernatural beings who were created at the same time as the material universe and whose primary role was to praise and serve God. Many, however, followed *Lucifer in his rebellion, becoming devils in *hell. In both Old and New Testaments angels appear as emissaries from God to man. *Dionysius the Areopagite systematized angelology into nine orders in the celestial hierarchy, the rank of angel being the lowest of these. Later medieval theologians debated such questions as the nature of angels' bodies, but since the 17th century angelology has been generally ignored. In art, angels are usually depicted as winged human figures. *See also* archangels.

Angers 47 29N 0 32W A city in W France, the capital of the Maine-et-Loire department on the Maine River. The former capital of Anjou, it has many fine buildings, including a 13th-century moated chateau, a cathedral (12th–13th centuries), and the 15th-century Logis Barrault (Barrault House). Its varied manufactures include wine, textiles, and agricultural machinery. Population (1975): 142,966.

Angevins Two dynasties descended from the rulers of the medieval French duchy of *Anjou. Founded by Fulk I (d. 938), his successors as Counts of

Anjou, notably Fulk III Nerra (972–1040) and *Geoffrey Martel, expanded the county in France during the 10th and 11th centuries. The marriage in 1128 of Geoffrey Plantagenet, Count of Anjou, to *Matilda, daughter of Henry I of England, gave rise to the accession to the English throne in 1154 of their son as Henry II, the first *Plantagenet King of England. The so-called Angevin empire, which stretched from the River Tweed to the Pyrenees, was broken up by *Philip II Augustus of France in the early 13th century and in 1246 Louis VIII's brother Charles became Count of Anjou. Charles conquered Naples and Sicily, where as *Charles I he founded a second Angevin dynasty. The Angevin claim to Naples and Sicily passed to the French crown in 1486.

angina pectoris Chest pain caused by a reduction in the supply of blood to the heart due to narrowing of the coronary blood vessels supplying the heart. It is usually associated with *atherosclerosis, is brought on by exercise, and can herald a heart attack. Treatment includes rest and administration of glyceryl trinitrate and drugs to reduce blood pressure.

angiosperm Any flowering plant. Angiosperms comprise a vast group of diverse, leafy, green plants (about 250,000 species) in which the seeds are formed within an ovary, which becomes the *fruit. They are thought to have evolved from the cone-bearing *gymnosperms in the Jurassic period (about 180 million years ago), rapidly radiating and becoming the dominant plants in the mid-Cretaceous (about 100 million years ago). They include many trees and shrubs but most are herbaceous. The 300 families are grouped into two classes: the *monocotyledons and *dicotyledons.

Angkor A ruined city in Cambodia, founded about 880 AD as capital of the *Khmer empire. It was rediscovered, covered by jungle, in 1860. Angkor was the center of a sophisticated irrigation system, with huge reservoirs (barays) for controlling water supplies to the surrounding rice fields. Its temples, decorated with extensive relief sculpture, were intended to emulate mountains in dressed stone; chief of these are the Angkor Wat (early 12th century) and Bayon (c. 1200).

anglerfish A marine fish, also called goosefish, belonging to the order *Lophiiformes*. Anglerfish are generally small and have flat bodies, large heads, and wide mouths. The first ray of the spiny dorsal fin is modified to form a "fishing line" ending with a fleshy flap of skin—the "bait," which is often luminous in deep-sea species. Fish, invertebrates, and even seabirds are lured and snapped up by the huge mouth. In some deep-sea species, the male is parasitic on the female, becoming permanently anchored by the mouth and dependent upon her for nourishment.

Angles A Germanic tribe originating from the Angeln district of Schleswig, which together with the *Saxons and *Jutes invaded and conquered most of England during the 5th century AD. They settled in *Northumbria, *Mercia, and *East Anglia. England is named for them.

Anglesey (Welsh name: Ynys Môn; Latin name: Mona) A low-lying island in the United Kingdom, off the NW coast of Wales, linked to the mainland by road and rail bridges over the Menai Strait. The chief agricultural activity is sheep rearing. Tourism, especially along the coast, is developing in importance. Recent industrial developments include the building of an aluminum smelter. Area: 272 sq mi (705 sq km). Chief town: Beaumaris.

Anglican Communion The fellowship of episcopal Churches in communion with the see of Canterbury. Until 1786, when the consecration of bishops for foreign sees was legalized, it consisted of the Churches of England, Ireland, and Wales and the Episcopal Church of Scotland. In 1787 the Protestant Episcopal

Church of the US was founded and thereafter Anglican dioceses were formed in all parts of the British Empire and elsewhere. Total membership is estimated at 65 million.

Anglo-Burmese Wars The wars that resulted in the British annexation of Burma (now Myanmar). In the first Anglo-Burmese War (1824–26), Burmese forces provoked the British-Indian forces into war by crossing into Bengal to attack Arakanese refugees and Britain captured, and kept, Rangoon. The aggressive action of a British naval officer provoked the second war (1852), which resulted in the annexation of Lower Burma. In the third war (1885), which occurred when the French, encouraged by the Burmese king, threatened British interests in Burma, Britain gained Upper Burma.

Anglo-Japanese Alliance (1902–23) The alliance between Britain and Japan contracted to maintain their interests in China and Korea respectively against Russian encroachment. The alliance brought Japan into World War I but subsequently lapsed as Britain sought friendship with the US, Japan's rival in the Pacific.

Anglo-Saxons The Germanic conquerors of Britain during the 5th century AD (*see* Angles; Saxons; Jutes). They first established a number of separate kingdoms, principally *Northumbria, *Mercia, and *Wessex, but eventually England was unified under an Anglo-Saxon dynasty. Kings ruled with the assistance of a *witan or council of wise men. Popular government and justice at the local level took the form of *hundred courts. They were eventually converted to Christianity. The Anglo-Saxons developed a rich art and literature. Their language is also known as Old English. *See also* English.

Angola, People's Republic of A country in SW Africa, on the Atlantic Ocean situated mainly to the S of the Congo River. The Cabinda district, however, lies to the N of the Congo and is separated from the rest of the country by a section of Zaïre. The country consists of a narrow coastal plain and a broad dissected plateau that reaches heights of over 6500 ft (2000 m). The inhabitants are almost all Negroes (mainly of Bantu origin) with small numbers of mixed race and a rapidly decreasing white population. *Economy*: agriculture is now being reorganized on a state-run and cooperative basis and the main crops are sugar cane and coffee. Angola is rich in mineral resources and diamonds have long been an important source of revenue. There is considerable oil production, especially offshore from Cabinda, and this has opened up new possibilities for industrial development. Hydroelectricity is being harnessed from the short steep river systems descending to the coastal plains and these schemes will provide irrigation as well as power. Main exports include oil, coffee, diamonds, and iron ore. The economy was severely disturbed by the civil wars (1974–76) and one effect was the withdrawal of Portuguese technicians, but these were replaced to some extent by Cubans. *History*: discovered and settled by the Portuguese in the late 15th century, the area remained a Portuguese colony (apart from a brief period of Dutch occupation from 1641 to 1648) until 1951 when it became an overseas province of Portugal. During the 1950s and 1960s there was a rise in nationalism and three main independence movements emerged: the MPLA (Popular Movement for the Liberation of Angola), the FNLA (National Front for the Liberation of Angola), and UNITA (National Union for the Total Independence of Angola). After its own change of government in 1974 Portugal agreed in principle to independence for Angola but, owing to lack of internal unity and opposition from the remaining white population, civil war broke out. The various groups took over different parts of the country and in November 1975, Portugal granted independence to the "Angolan people" rather than to any one group. The People's Republic of Angola was declared by the MPLA, with its capital in

Luanda, and a coalition of the FNLA and UNITA formed a People's Democratic Republic of Angola, based on Huambo. The MPLA was supported by the Soviet Union and Cuba and the FNLA by the US and certain W European countries. Eventually, with further help from Cuba, the MPLA gained control in 1976 but opposition continued. In 1979 Dr. José Eduardo dos Santos was elected president following the death of Dr. Antonio Agostinho Neto (1922–79). Despite all movements toward peace—a US-mediated ceasefire in 1988; the beginning of the removal of Cuban troops in 1989; independence granted by South Africa for neighboring Namibia and the removal of South African forces from southern Angola as part of a peace accord in 1990; and free, multiparty elections held in 1992—fighting between the ruling MPLA and the minority UNITA under Jonas Savimbi continued well into the 1990s. Official language: Portuguese. Official currency: kwanza of 100 lwei. Area: 481,351 sq mi (1,246,700 sq km). Population (1992 est): 8,900,000. Capital and main port: Luanda.

Angora goat A breed of goat, originating in Turkey, whose long silky hair is regularly sheared and used commercially to make *mohair. Mohair is now also obtained from several other goat breeds derived from the Angora.

Angora rabbit A breed of domesticated rabbit, originating in France in the 17th century, of which there are now both English and French varieties. The long wool, which is usually white but can be black or blue, is periodically shorn and spun for use in clothing manufacture (**Angora wool**).

angostura A bitters made from distilled herbs and plants. Angostura bitters originated in Ciudad Bolívar (formerly Angostura) in Venezuela as a tonic and febrifuge but its manufacture was transferred to Trinidad in 1975.

Angoulême 45 40N 0 10E A city in SW France, the capital of the Charente department on the Charente River. The site of a 12th-century cathedral, its varied manufactures include paper, refrigerators, felt, and iron. Population (1975): 50,500.

Angoulême, Charles de Valois, Duc d' (1573–1650) French soldier. An illegitimate son of Charles IX, he was imprisoned (1605–16) for conspiring against Henry IV. He subsequently rose through the influence of Richelieu and then Mazarin to several important military commands, including that of the siege of Huguenot-held La Rochelle (1627).

Angry Young Men A group of British novelists and dramatists in the 1950s whose attitudes included dissatisfaction with postwar British society and disrespect for the so-called "Establishment" and its traditional institutions. Many of them came from working-class or lower-middle-class backgrounds. The phrase "angry young man" was first applied to the dramatist John *Osborne. Among other writers associated with this group were the novelists Kingsley *Amis, John *Wain, Alan Sillitoe, and John *Braine.

Ångström, Anders Jonas (1814–74) Swedish physicist and astronomer. He was a founder of spectroscopy, his work on solar spectra leading to the discovery (1862) of hydrogen in the sun. He also studied geomagnetism. The **angstrom**, a unit of wavelength equal to 10^{-10} m (one tenth of a nanometer), is named for him.

Anguilla 18 14N 63 05W A West Indian island in the E Caribbean Sea, in the Leeward Islands. Formerly part of the UK Associated State of St Kitts-Nevis-Anguilla, it became a separate British dependency in December 1980. Its economy is based chiefly on stock raising, salt production, boat building, and fishing. Area: 35 sq mi (90 sq km). Population (1988 est): 7000. *See also* St Kitts-Nevis.

angular momentum The product of the *moment of inertia of a body and its angular velocity about an axis. It is an important quantity in physics since the total angular momentum of a closed system is conserved.

angular velocity. *See* velocity.

angwantibo A small rare nocturnal prosimian primate, *Arctocebus calabarensis*, also called the golden potto, found in West African forests. It is 9–12 in (23–30 cm) long, has pale-brown fur and large eyes, and moves through the trees, feeding chiefly on insects. Family: *Lorisidae*.

Anhui (*or* Anhwei) A province in E China. The Yangtze River in the S and the Huai River in the N are linked by ancient waterways, which provide transport and irrigation. Main products are tea, rice, soybeans, silk, and steel. Area: 54,000 sq mi (13,986 sq km). Population (1990): 56,180,813. Capital: Hefei.

Anhwei. *See* Anhui.

anil A small shrub, *Indigofera anil*, native to India and the original source of the blue dye *indigo, which is now produced synthetically. Family: *Leguminosae*.

aniline (*or* phenylamine; $C_6H_5NH_2$) A colorless, oily, nonflammable liquid *amine. It is used to make dyes, plastics, and drugs and is made by the reduction of nitrobenzene obtained from *coal tar.

animal A living organism belonging to the kingdom *Animalia*. Animals are typically mobile and feed on *plants, other animals, or their remains. Their body *cells lack the rigid cellulose wall of plant cells and they require specialized tissues, such as bone, for protection and support. Because of their activity, animals have specialized organs for sensing the nature of their environment; information from the sense organs is transmitted and coordinated by means of a nervous system. Individuals of the same species have a consistent body form; growth occurs in all regions of the body and ceases at a certain stage of development, usually when sexual maturity has been attained.

There are over one million species of animals, grouped into about 30 phyla (authorities differ in their classification of the lesser phyla). *See also* life; taxonomy.

animal behavior. *See* ethology.

animal worship. *See* totemism.

animism 1. The belief that the physical world is permeated by a spirit or a vital principle sometimes called the *anima mundi*. Georg Ernst *Stahl was its leading proponent. 2. In anthropology, all forms of belief in spiritual agencies. Two main classes of such beings are distinguished: the souls of the dead (*see* ancestor worship) and other personalized supernatural entities.

anise An annual Egyptian herb, *Pimpinella anisum*, growing to a height of up to 30 in (75 cm) and having umbrella-like clusters of small yellow-white flowers. It·is extensively cultivated in subtropical areas for the licorice-flavored oil (principally anthole) extracted from its small seeds, which is widely used in certain foods, beverages, and liqueurs. Family: *Umbelliferae*.

Anjou A former province in W central France, approximating to the present-day Maine-et-Loire department. Anjou was inherited by the future Henry II of England in 1151 and remained under English rule until the early·13th century, when it was lost to France. Permanently annexed to the French crown in 1480, it ceased to exist as a province in 1790. *See also* Angevins.

Ankara 39 55N 32 50E The capital of Turkey, in the W central region of the country. There is evidence of human settlement from very early times, and it has

phylum (approx. no. species)	important classes	representative members
Protozoa (30 000)	Sarcodina	Amoeba
	Ciliata	Stentor
	Flagellata	Trypanosoma
	Sporozoa	Plasmodium
Porifera (5000)		sponges
Coelenterata (9000)	Hydrozoa	Hydra, Portuguese man-of-war
	Scyphozoa	jellyfish
	Anthozoa	sea anemones, corals
Platyhelminthes (9000)	Turbellaria	planarians
	Trematoda	flukes
	Cestoda	tapeworms
Nematoda (10 000)		roundworms
Mollusca (100 000)	Gastropoda	snails, slugs
	Bivalvia	mussels, oysters, cockles
	Cephalopoda	squids, octopus

phylum (approx. no. species)	important classes	representative members
Annelida (9000)	Oligochaeta	earthworms
	Polychaeta	lugworms
	Hirudinea	leeches
Arthropoda (>1 000 000)	Arachnida	spiders, scorpions
	Crustacea	lobsters, crabs, woodlice
	Insecta	beetles, wasps, ants, flies, bugs
	Myriapoda	centipedes, millipedes
Echinodermata (6000)	Asteroidea	starfish
	Echinoidea	sea urchins
	Holothuroidea	sea cucumbers
Chordata (55 000)	Chondrichthyes	sharks, rays
	Osteichthyes	bony fish (salmon, carp, eels, perch, etc.)
	Amphibia	frogs, toads, newts, salamanders
	Reptilia	lizards, snakes, crocodiles, turtles
	Aves	birds
	Mammalia	mammals, including man

ANIMAL *A simplified classification of the animal kingdom (major phyla only are listed).*

long been an important trading town. Conquered by Alexander the Great in the 4th century BC, it later came within the Roman and Byzantine Empires. It was attacked by Persians and Arabs, and in the 11th century it was defeated by the Turks. It became the capital of modern Turkey in 1923 and since then has expanded considerably; it has three universities including the Middle East Technical University (1956). Population (1990): 8,800,000.

ankylosaur A heavily armored dinosaur of the late Cretaceous period, which ended 65 million years ago. Ankylosaurs were low and flat and their backs were covered with hard protective bony plates. *Euoplocephalus* (or *Ankylosaurus*) reached a length of 16 ft (5 m), weighed 3 tons, and its plated tail ended in a large bony knob. Order: **Ornithischia.*

An Lu Shan (703–57 AD) Chinese military governor, who in 756 declared himself emperor of a new Yan dynasty. Tang imperial troops opposed him but An Lu Shan seized the capital Chang An and the emperor was forced to flee. An Lu Shan was murdered shortly afterward but only in 763 did the imperial army succeed in putting down the rebellion.

Annaba (former name: Bône) 36 57N 7 39E A large port in E Algeria, on the Mediterranean Sea. An early center of Christianity, it held the bishopric of St Augustine (396–430 AD). In 1832 it was captured by the French. Mineral exports are important, particularly phosphates and iron ore. Industries include flour milling and iron and steel processing. Population (1987): 305,526.

Anna Comnena (1083–1148? AD) Byzantine historian. The daughter of Emperor **Alexius I Comnenus, Anna married (1097) Nicephorus Bryennius (?1062–1137) and conspired (1118) to depose her brother John II (1088–1143; reigned 1118–43) in favor of her husband. She was banished to a convent, where she wrote the *Alexiad*, an account of her father's achievements and of the early Crusades from a Byzantine point of view.

Anna Ivanovna (1693–1740) Empress of Russia (1730–40). A niece of **Peter the Great, Anna married (1710) Frederick William, Duke of Courland (d. 1710). She was elected by the Supreme Privy Council to become empress on the condition that she accept a number of provisions curtailing her powers. In practice, however, she became an autocrat, whose administration was run by her German advisers. In the Russo-Turkish War (1736–39) she regained Azov.

Annam A region in central Vietnam, long ruled from Hue. The Chinese, who had occupied it in 111 BC, were driven out in 939 AD, and it was a powerful independent state until becoming a French protectorate in 1884. In 1949 it became part of independent Vietnam.

Annapolis 38 59N 76 30W The capital of Maryland, on the Severn River. Founded in 1648, it was here that Congress received George Washington's resignation as commander in chief of the Continental Army and ratified the peace treaty ending the American Revolution (1783). The US Naval Academy was established here in 1845 and the many historic buildings and riverside setting make it a popular tourist resort. It is also a minor seaport and has seafood industries. Population (1990): 33,187.

Annapolis Convention (1786) A meeting at Annapolis, Md., to discuss interstate commerce. Although 13 states had been asked to attend, only representatives from Virginia, Delaware, Pennsylvania, New Jersey, and New York were there. It was decided to reconvene in Philadelphia the next year to discuss, on a broader scale, the revisions needed in the Articles of Confederation. Thus, the Annapolis Convention paved the way for the Constitutional Convention (1787).

Annapolis Royal 44 44N 65 32W A town and port in E Canada, in Nova Scotia. One of the first settlements in Canada (1632), it was Nova Scotia's capital until 1749. A market town, it attracts many tourists.

Annapurna, Mount 28 34N 83 50E A massif in NW central Nepal, in the Himalayas. Its highest peak **Annapurna I**, at 26,504 ft (8078 m), was first climbed in 1950 by a French team.

Ann Arbor 42 18N 83 43W A city in Michigan. A research and educational center, it is the site of the University of Michigan (1817) and its manufactures include chemicals and precision instruments. Population (1990): 109,592.

Ann, Cape A peninsula in NE Massachusetts jutting into the Atlantic Ocean, NE of Gloucester and N of Massachusetts Bay. Gloucester, on the S shore is the main town on the cape. Fishing, boating, and tourism are important to the economy.

Anne (1665–1714) Queen of England and Scotland (Great Britain from 1707) and Ireland (1702–14). Anne, the last Stuart monarch, was the daughter of the Roman Catholic James II but was herself brought up as a Protestant. Following the overthrow (1688) of James, she supported the accession of her Protestant brother-in-law, William III, whose heiress she became. She married (1683) Prince George of Denmark (1653–1708); none of her children survived childhood. Anne therefore agreed to the Act of *Settlement (1701), which provided for the Hanoverian succession after her death. Anne was greatly influenced by the Duke and Duchess of *Marlborough. In 1710, however, having quarreled with the Marlboroughs and faced with a country dissatisfied with the leadership, Anne returned to her earlier principles.

Anne (Elizabeth Alice Louise) (1950–   ) Princess of the United Kingdom, sixth in line of succession to the throne, the only daughter of *Elizabeth II and Prince Philip. An accomplished horsewoman, in 1973 she married Lt. Mark Phillips, a gold medalist in the equestrian events in the 1972 Olympic Games. Their son Peter was born in 1977 and daughter Zara in 1981. They were divorced in April 1992. In December 1992, she married naval commander Timothy Laurence.

annealing. *See* heat treatment.

annelid worm An invertebrate animal belonging to a phylum (*Annelida*) of about 9000 species, widely distributed in salt water, fresh water, and on land. The body is characteristically a muscular cylinder divided into many fluid-filled segments. Annelids vary greatly in form and habit and are divided into three classes: the Polychaeta, or bristleworms (*see* ragworm; lugworm; fanworm); the Oligochaeta (*see* earthworm; tubifex), and the Hirudinea (*see* leech).

Anne of Austria (1601–66) The wife (1615–43) of Louis XIII of France, whose antipathy toward her was aggravated by that of his chief minister Cardinal de Richelieu. After her husband's death she was regent (1643–51) for her son Louis XIV and chose her lover *Mazarin to succeed Richelieu.

Anne of Bohemia (1366–94) The first wife (from 1382) of Richard II of England and daughter of Emperor Charles IV. Her household extravagance was a cause of dissension between Richard and parliament. She died of the plague.

Anne of Brittany (1477–1514) Duchess of Brittany (1488–1514), succeeding her father Francis I (1435–88; ruled 1458–88). Her marriages to Charles VIII of France (1491) and to his successor Louis XII (1499) initiated the union of Brittany with France, in spite of Anne's desire to preserve Breton autonomy.

Anne of Cleves (1515–57) The fourth wife of Henry VIII of England. The marriage (January, 1540) was arranged to effect an alliance with German Protestant rulers but Henry found Anne unattractive and quickly divorced her (July, 1540).

Annigoni, Pietro (1910–   ) Italian painter. One of the most famous 20th-century artists to use the techniques of the Old Masters, Annigoni has worked chiefly in *tempera and *fresco. He is best known for his portraits of President Kennedy (1961) and Queen Elizabeth II (1955 and 1970). In later years he devoted himself to a fresco cycle of the life of Christ in the Church of S Michele Arcangelo, in Ponte Buggianese, near Florence.

annihilation The conversion of a particle and its antiparticle into electromagnetic radiation (annihilation radiation) as a result of a collision. The energy of the radiation is equivalent to the combined mass of the two particles. *See also* antimatter.

annual rings (*or* growth rings) A pattern of rings visible in a cross section of a tree trunk, produced by different rates of wood growth corresponding to the seasonal fluctuations in climate in temperate regions. Each year the wood produced in spring consists of large cells corresponding to vigorous growth; autumn wood has small cells as growth slows down, and in winter growth ceases. The number of rings gives an estimate of the age of the tree. *See also* dendrochronology.

annuals Plants that complete their life cycle—from germination, flowering, and seed production to death—within one year. Many annuals are used for bedding plants (e.g. marigolds) and flower extensively in the summer months. *Compare* perennials.

annuity A form of pension in which an institution, such as an *insurance company, makes a series of periodic payments to a person (annuitant) or his or her dependents over a number of years (term), in return for money paid to the institution either in a lump sum or in installments. An immediate annuity begins at once and a deferred annuity after a fixed period. An annuity certain is for a specific number of years. A life annuity is paid from a certain age until death.

annulment The process establishing that a marriage is not legally valid, as opposed to *divorce, which ends a valid marriage. An invalid marriage is considered void, never to have existed. A marriage is usually void if there is a serious defect, for example if the husband or wife is insane, too young, or already married. In less serious cases, for example when the husband or wife is unable or unwilling to consummate the marriage, the marriage may be declared void if either partner wishes it.

Annunciation In the Bible, the announcement by the angel Gabriel to the Virgin Mary of her conception of Christ (Luke 1.26–38). The feast, in full called the Annunciation of the Blessed Virgin Mary, or Lady Day, is celebrated on Mar 25.

anoa A rare black hoofed mammal, *Anoa depressicornis*, standing 40 in (1 m) high at the shoulder. Anoas occur in thick tropical forests of Sulawesi (Indonesia) and nearby islands and are hunted for their hides, horns, and meat. Family: *Bovidae*.

anode The positive electrode of an electrolytic cell, valve, etc. It is the electrode by which the electrons leave the system. *Compare* cathode.

anodizing A process in which a light metal or alloy, usually aluminum, is covered with a protective layer by oxidation in an electrolytic cell. Usually the cell contains chromic acid; the metal treated is the anode of the cell. A porous layer of oxide is formed, which can be dyed to give a colored finish.

anole A small arboreal New World lizard belonging to the genus *Anolis* (165 species). 5–18 in (12–45 cm) long, anoles have a triangular head and pads on their fingers and toes covered with minute hooks for grip. Their skin changes color from brown to green in response to changes in temperature, light, or danger. Males have an expansible red or yellow throat fan (dewlap). Family: *Iguanidae*.

anomie A condition of a society or of individuals in which social standards or goals are unclear, in conflict, or absent. Anomic individuals reject or are unable to find meaningful social norms by which to interpret or organize their lives. Losing their sense of social belonging, they may turn to crime, the selfish pursuit of power, or even suicide. The term was first introduced into sociology in a systematic form by *Durkheim in his *Suicide* (1897).

Anopheles A widespread genus of *mosquitoes (about 350 species), the females of which are important as vectors of the malarial parasite *Plasmodium*. The best-known malaria carrier is *A. maculipennis*. Some species transmit filariasis and encephalitis. Unlike other mosquitoes the larvae lack a siphon and lie flat on the surface of the water.

anorexia nervosa A psychological illness in which the patient, usually an adolescent girl, refuses food over a long period. It often starts with dieting to lose weight, which becomes obsessional: the patient becomes emaciated and may—without treatment—starve to death. The psychological causes are complex, often involving disturbances in family relationships. Hospitalization may be required for the treatment, which involves intensive nursing, sedation, and *psychotherapy.

Anouilh, Jean (1910–87) French dramatist. His commitment to the theater was early and total; his first play, *The Ermine*, was performed in 1932. He achieved his first success in 1937 with *Traveller without Luggage*. His plays include reworkings of Greek myths (*Antigone*, 1944), social comedies (*Ring Round the Moon*, 1950), and historical dramas (*Becket*, 1962). A skilled craftsman, he exploits the most basic dramatic conventions, such as coincidences and flashbacks. His work, although often considered old-fashioned, remains popular both in France and abroad.

Anschluss (German: union; 1938) The union of Austria with Germany. Following the forced resignation of the Austrian chancellor *Schuschnigg, Nazi forces entered Austria and Schuschnigg was imprisoned. *Anschluss* was declared and ratified by a plebiscite.

Anselm of Canterbury, St (c. 1033–1109) Italian theologian and philosopher, Archbishop of Canterbury, and Doctor of the Church. Appointed to the see of Canterbury in 1093, Anselm defended church rights against William II Rufus until he went into exile to Rome in 1097. Recalled by *Henry I in 1100, he eventually reached an uneasy compromise with him. He is the leading early scholastic philosopher and is perhaps best known for his formulation of the ontological argument for the existence of God. Feast day: Apr 21. Emblem: a ship.

Ansermet, Ernest (1883–1969) Swiss conductor. Briefly a mathematics teacher, he studied composition with *Bloch and conducting with *Nikisch. After touring with *Diaghilev's ballet company he founded the Suisse Romande Orchestra in 1918, remaining its director until 1967. He was famous for his interpretations of *Stravinsky and other 20th-century composers.

Anshan (*or* An-shan) 41 05N 122 58E A city in NE China, in Liaoning province. Its steel complex, the largest in China, was developed under Japanese occupation (1931–45), when its population grew rapidly. It also has engineering, chemical, and cement industries. Population (1990): 1,203,986.

ant An insect belonging to the family *Formicidae* (over 10,000 species). Ants occur in almost all terrestrial habitats, are .02–10 in (0.05–25 cm) long, and show a high degree of social organization. A colony consists of wingless sterile female workers and a smaller number of fertile males and females that are generally the progeny of a single queen. The young males and females fly from the nest to mate, after which the males die and the young queens found new colonies. Ant societies range from simple groups of a few individuals to large complex nests comprising millions of ants and sometimes involving a second species taken as slaves to work in the colony (*see* slave-making ant).

Some ants have stings; others secrete burning acids (such as formic acid) as a defense. Feeding habits vary from rapacious predators (*see* army ant) to harmless scavengers; others milk honeydew from aphids and certain species cultivate fungi as a food supply within the nest. Order: **Hymenoptera.* □insect.

Antakya. *See* Antioch.

Antalya 36 53N 30 42E A city in SW Turkey, on the Gulf of Antalya. Founded in the 2nd century BC, it flourished particularly under the Seljuqs in the 13th century, and it is now an important coastal resort. Nearby are two Roman amphitheaters and the ruins of Perga. Population (1990): 378,208.

Antananarivo (former name: Tananarive) 18 52S 47 30E The capital of Madagascar. It was occupied by the French in 1895. A cultural center, it has a university (1961) and two cathedrals. Industries include tobacco and leather goods. Population (1990 est): 802,000.

Antar (6th century AD) Arab poet and warrior, celebrated in the 10th-century *Romance of Antar* as the model of desert chivalry. The son of a Bedouin chieftain and a slave girl, Antar was said to have proved his courage in numerous battles and adventures before being allowed to marry his beloved Abla.

Antarctica The most southerly continent, surrounding the South Pole. Almost circular in shape, it is indented by the Weddell and Ross Seas. It consists chiefly of a vast, ice-covered plateau and contains about 90% of the world's ice. Calculations suggest that should this ice melt sea levels would rise by about 200 ft (60 m). The continent's climate is the severest in the world; in 1960 the world's lowest recorded temperature—of −126°F (−87.8°C)—was made at the Russian station of Vostok. Although lacking in vegetation it has abundant wildlife including whales, seals, and penguins. Scientific stations were established during the International Geophysical Year (1957–58). Some nations (*see* Australian Antarctic Territory; British Antarctic Territory; Norwegian Antarctic Territory; Ross Dependency; Terre Adélie) have political claims to territory in Antarctica. Argentina and Chile have also laid claims, as yet unrecognized, to portions of British Antarctic Territory (*see also* Antarctic Treaty). *History*: in his voyage of 1772–75 Capt. James Cook reached 71°10″S. Many discoveries and explorations took place during the 19th century culminating in the famous race for the South Pole. This was reached first by Roald *Amundsen of the Norwegian Antarctic Expedition on Dec 14, 1911, and a month later by *Scott of the British Antarctic Terra Nova Expedition. Scott and his team perished on the return journey. Area: about 5,500,000 sq mi (14,200,000 sq km).

Antarctic Ocean The sections of the S Atlantic, Pacific, and Indian Oceans around Antarctica. Except in the height of summer (late Feb to early Mar), it is covered by drifting pack ice.

Antarctic Peninsula A peninsula extending 1200 mi (1930 km) N from Antarctica toward South America, claimed by the UK. The first part of Antarctica to be sighted (1820), it has volcanic mountains in the S.

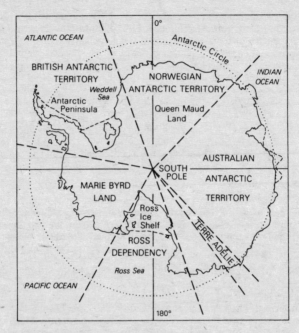

ANTARCTICA *Under the Antarctic Treaty all political claims were halted and freedom of scientific research in the continent was ensured.*

Antarctic Treaty (1959) An agreement, signed by Argentina, Australia, Belgium, Chile, France, Japan, New Zealand, Norway, South Africa, the Soviet Union, the UK, and the US, to maintain the Antarctic as a demilitarized zone for 30 years. An additional treaty (1991) prohibited mining for 50 years.

Antares An immense remote yet conspicuous red supergiant, apparent magnitude 0.94 and about 400 light years distant, that is the brightest star in the constellation Scorpius. It is a visual *binary star.

ant bear. *See* aardvark.

antbird A passerine bird belonging to a large family (*Formicariidae*; 223 species) occurring in the forest undergrowth of Central and South America. About 3–14 in (8–35 cm) long, antbirds have shrill voices and hooked bills and feed chiefly on insects (although the larger species may eat small lizards, snakes, and young birds). The female is dull brown but the male usually has a brightly patterned plumage.

anteater A long-tailed animal belonging to a family (*Myrmecophagidae*; 3 species) occurring in tropical South America. It is toothless and has a narrow snout with a long sticky tongue used to pick up ants and termites after tearing open their nests with its powerful claws. The giant anteater (*Myrmecophaga tridactyla*) reaches 6 ft (1.8 m) in length and has gray and black fur and a bushy tail (□mammal). The other species are smaller arboreal animals with prehensile tails (*see* tamandua). Order: *Edentata*.

The name anteater is given to several other unrelated animals that feed on ants or termites: the *pangolins (scaly anteaters), *echidnas (spiny anteaters), and *aardvark.

Antelami, Benedetto (active 1177–1233) Italian sculptor. The most famous Italian sculptor of the medieval period, Antelami developed a style that marked the transition between the *Romanésque and the *Gothic. His best-known works are the reliefs on the doors of the baptistry at Parma, of which he was probably also the architect.

antelope A hoofed mammal belonging to the family *Bovidae* and occurring chiefly in Africa but occasionally in Asia. Antelopes are typically fast-running and graceful, grazing or browsing in large herds on open grasslands, although some are more solitary and live in bush and woodland. The shoulder height varies from 10 in (25 cm) in the *royal antelope to 71 in (180 cm) in the *eland. All male antelopes and some females have horns. *See also* dik-dik; duiker; gazelle; gnu; kudu; waterbuck.

antenna (*or* aerial) An electrical conductor that transmits and receives radio or other electromagnetic waves. An oscillating *electromagnetic field, caused by waves from a distant source, induces an oscillating current in the receiving antenna. A transmitting antenna works by the same process in reverse, creating waves from an electrical signal. A modern antenna for UHF (ultra-high frequency) and VHF (very high frequency) consists of a dipole formed from two metal rods, each approximately one-quarter of the operating wavelength. In the Yagi antenna a reflector rod is set behind the dipole and several director rods are placed in front of it. This provides a considerably more directional array than the simple dipole and is widely used as both a receiving and transmitting antenna for television.

antenna (zoology) The sensory feeler of insects, crustaceans, and many other arthropods, one or two pairs of which are attached to the head. They are usually jointed threadlike structures containing receptors of sound, smell, touch, and temperature.

Antenor (late 6th century BC) Athenian sculptor. His signature appears on the base of a marble *kore on the Athenian Acropolis. He sculpted the Harmodios and Aristogeiton group, looted by Xerxes (480 BC) and restored after Alexander the Great's Persian expedition.

Antheil, George (1900–59) US composer. He studied with Ernest *Bloch and in 1922 moved to Europe, where his avant-garde work, *Le Ballet méchanique* (1924) for bells, motor horns, airplane propellers, etc., caused a furor. His later works are more traditional in style and include several film scores.

anthelminthics Drugs used to treat infections of the intestines caused by parasitic worms. Piperazine is commonly used to expel roundworms and threadworms. Tapeworm infections are treated with niclosamide or dichlorophen.

anther. *See* stamen.

antheridium The reproductive organ producing the male cells (gametes) in ferns, mosses, algae, and fungi. It is usually a club-shaped structure, the rounded head containing the gametes.

Anthony, Susan B(rownell) (1820–1906) US reformer and suffragette. A lifelong advocate of equal rights for women, she was instrumental in the passage, 14 years after her death, of the 19th Amendment to the Constitution, which granted full voting rights to women. She worked for the American Anti-slavery Society (1856–61) and the National Woman Suffrage Association (1869–90), led the National American Woman Suffrage Association (1890–1906), and was a co-author of the 4-volume *History of Woman Suffrage* (1881–1900).

Anthony of Egypt, St (c. 251–356 AD) Egyptian hermit and founder of Christian monasticism. An ascetic from the age of 20, he withdrew until 305 into complete isolation, emerging to organize followers into a monastic community living according to a rule. When he was about a hundred years old, he preached against *Arianism. His combat with temptation in the desert is described in Athanasius' *Life of Saint Anthony*; it became a frequent subject in Christian art. Feast day: Jan 17. Emblem: a pig and a bell.

Anthony of Padua, St (1195–1231) Portuguese friar and Doctor of the Church. Famous for his preaching, he devoted his efforts to converting heretics in N Italy and the Albigenses in S France until his appointment as professor of theology to the Franciscan Order in 1223. He is often invoked as a finder of lost property. Feast day: June 13.

anthracene ($C_{14}H_{10}$) A colorless crystalline *aromatic compound. It is obtained from coal tar and is used in making dyes.

anthracite. *See* coal.

anthrax A contagious disease of many animals, including farm livestock, that can be transmitted to man. Caused by the bacterium *Bacillus anthracis*, it is usually contracted by eating contaminated food. Onset is often sudden with a rise in body temperature, staggering, respiratory distress, convulsions, and death. In horses and pigs a subacute form may occur, with progressive swelling of the throat and neck resulting in labored breathing and choking. In many countries the authorities must be notified of any outbreaks. Treatment is with antibiotics and prevention is by vaccination of herds in areas where the disease is endemic. Man may develop localized swellings after handling infected carcasses or acquire a pneumonia from inhaling the bacterial spores.

anthropoid ape A tailless *primate belonging to the family *Pongidae*, includes the gibbons, chimpanzees, orangutans, and gorillas. *See* ape.

anthropology The scientific study of man in his physical and social aspects. In the widest meaning of the term it includes *archeology, *linguistics, cultural or social anthropology, and physical anthropology. It is particularly concerned with the systematic and comparative study of human diversity. Physical anthropology is concerned with the origins and evolution of man through the examination of his fossil remains, and the study and classification of the races of man through comparison of anatomical and physiological characteristics (*see also* anthropometry). Cultural anthropology is concerned with the evolution of human society and culture, including language, and with the systematic comparison of social, linguistic, technical, and behavioral diversity. Social anthropology has a more restricted meaning and is the comparative study of social behavior, social organization, social forms and institutions, custom, culture, and belief, and has traditionally confined itself to the study of "primitive" societies.

anthropometry The science concerned with the measurement of the human body, particularly with respect to the variation that exists between different populations and races. Anthropometry ranges from the measurement of structural characteristics, such as height, cranial capacity, etc., to the analysis of chemical constituents of the body, such as blood groups. By comparing fossil and present-day measurements anthropometry has also helped to reveal the sequence of events that has occurred during the evolution of man.

anthropomorphism Mankind's tendency to ascribe to nonhuman creatures the motives, feelings, etc., of human beings. This is particularly evident in the concept of God. The anthropomorphism of ancient Greek religion was ridiculed by *Xenophanes of Colophon (6th century BC) but Christian discussions of the divine personality, will, etc., have still not escaped from an implicit anthropomorphism. Religious art can scarcely avoid being anthropomorphic.

Anthurium A genus of tropical American plants (550 species), some of which are cultivated as greenhouse or pot plants for their ornamental flowers or foliage. The flower heads consist of a cylindrical cluster (spadix) of tiny flowers surrounded by a large, petal-like part (spathe), which is often brightly colored (e.g. in *A. scherzerianum* it is red). Family: *Araceae* (arum family).

anti-aircraft gun Any gun capable of rapid fire, high elevation, and speedy adjustment. Calibers are 0.8 in to 5.5 in (20–140 mm) but most common pieces are 3–4 in (87–100 mm). Upper range limit is about 40,000 ft (12,000 m) and targets may be engaged at a few hundred feet. Guns are aimed visually or electronically so that the aircraft flies into the round or shellburst. The role of anti-aircraft guns has largely been replaced by ground-to-air guided missiles.

antiballistic missiles High-speed nuclear weapons used to attack hostile *ballistic missiles. Operated by ground-based radar and computers, they rely for their final attack on their own guidance systems, destroying the target by radiation from their warheads. Short-range versions with low-yield warheads (e.g. US *Sprint*) are designed to seek and destroy targets within the earth's atmosphere; long-range missiles with high-yield warheads operate in space (e.g. US *Spartan*).

Antibes 43 35N 7 07E A city in France, in the Alpes-Maritimes department. A tourist resort and a port for pleasure craft on the Côte d'Azur, it produces flowers, perfumes, and chocolates. Population (1975): 56,309.

antibiotics Drugs derived from microorganisms and used to treat infections caused by bacteria or fungi. Synthetic drugs with similar properties are also known as antibiotics. Bactericidal antibiotics, such as *penicillin, actually kill bacteria, whereas bacteriostatic antibiotics, such as *tetracycline and *chloramphenicol, simply halt their growth. Examples of antifungal antibiotics are nystatin and griseofulvin. Possible adverse effects of antibiotic treatment include allergic reactions and the development of resistant strains of bacteria, which may set up a secondary infection. In spite of side effects, however, the widespread use of antibiotics since World War II has virtually eliminated the scourge of bacterial and fungal infectious diseases.

antibody A protein produced by certain white blood cells (lymphocytes) that reacts specifically with and neutralizes a foreign protein (e.g. a bacterium), which is known as the **antigen**. Antibody production is stimulated by contact with the antigen: subsequent exposure to the antigen produces a greater antibody response, which provides the basis of *immunity. Antibodies contribute to the body's resistance to infection and are responsible for the rejection of foreign tissue or organ transplants.

Antichrist In the New Testament, a person or institution opposed to Christ, whose appearance will precede His second coming (John 2.18–22). Some Christians believed *Nero to be the Antichrist; many reformers, for example Wycliffe and Luther, saw the pope or the papacy in this role.

anticline An arch-shaped *fold or upfold in folded rock strata, the oldest rocks occurring at the core. In areas of complex folding an upfold may have its youngest rocks at the core, the resulting structure being termed an antiform. *Compare* syncline.

anticoagulants Drugs, such as heparin and warfarin, that interfere with blood clotting. They are used when there has been, or there is a risk of, clots forming in the blood vessels, as after *thrombosis of the leg veins.

Anti-Comintern Pact An agreement among the Axis powers in opposition to the Comintern (*or* Third *International). Germany and Japan signed the Pact in 1936 to protect themselves against communism and they were later joined by Italy (1937) and Spain (1939).

Anti-Corn Law League A British organization formed in 1839 to work for the repeal of the *Corn Laws. Under the able leadership of Richard *Cobden and John *Bright, the League gained widespread support from manufacturers as well as workers and achieved its objective in 1846.

anticyclone (*or* high) An area of atmospheric pressure higher than the surrounding air with one or more isobars of approximately circular form around its center. Winds, generally light, circulate around the high pressure center in a clockwise direction in the N hemisphere and anticlockwise in the S hemisphere. Calm, settled weather is usually synonymous with anticyclones in temperate latitudes.

antidepressants A class of drugs used to relieve depression. The most widely used are the tricyclic antidepressants, which include amitriptyline and imipramine, and the tetracyclic antidepressants. They provide a wide range of drugs to treat a variety of depressive symptoms. The MAO inhibitors prevent the action of the enzyme monoamine oxidase in breaking down adrenaline and related compounds that affect mood. Some antidepressants may have serious side effects and are therefore restricted to the treatment of severe psychological disorders.

Antietam, Battle of (September 17, 1862) A decisive engagement in the US *Civil War, which prevented the Confederate capture of Washington, DC. In the last of a series of battles, the advance of the Confederate general Robert E. *Lee, was checked at Antietam by the Union general George B. *McClellan. The South lost about 10,000 men but McClellan allowed Lee to withdraw into Virginia.

Anti-Federalist Party US political party, advocating states' rights. Under the leadership of Thomas Jefferson and James Madison, a coalition formed to oppose the ratification of the US Constitution (1787–88). The addition of the Bill of Rights to the Constitution was largely an appeasement for the Anti-Federalists, who felt that a central government would wield too much authority. By 1793 the party was absorbed into the Jeffersonian Republican Party, which became the Democratic-Republican Party and then the Democratic Party.

antiferromagnetism The magnetic property of a material that has its microscopic magnetic *moments lined up in domains, as in *ferromagnetism, except that in these materials the antiparallel arrays oppose each other. The lower the temperature, the greater this alignment; up to a certain temperature, known as the Néel temperature, the relative magnetic *permeability is slightly greater than one and increases with temperature. Above this temperature the material is paramagnetic (*see* paramagnetism).

antifreeze A substance added to water in cooling systems to lower the freezing point and thus prevent damage in cold weather from freezing. Glycols and methanol, together with a corrosion inhibitor, are commonly used.

antigen. *See* antibody.

Antigone In Greek mythology, the daughter of *Oedipus and Jocasta, whose story forms the basis of Sophocles' tragedy *Antigone*. When her father was banished from Thebes she accompanied him into exile in Colonus. Her brothers Eteocles and *Polyneices had agreed to reign alternately in Thebes, but Eteocles' refusal to yield the crown led to their killing each other in single combat. Despite the Theban senate's decree prohibiting the burial of Polyneices, Antigone performed the funeral rites for her brother. She was consequently ordered to be buried alive by Creon, ruler of Thebes, and hanged herself.

Antigonus I (c. 382–301 BC) Macedonian general, nicknamed Monophthalmus or Cyclops (One-eye). After the death of his patron *Antipater, Antigonus became ruler of Asia Minor. He declared himself king in 306 but his ambition to rule a reunited Macedonian empire was opposed. His rivals combined forces, after Antigonus' successes against them individually, and defeated and killed him in battle at Ipsus.

Antigonus II Gonatas (c. 320–239 BC) King of Macedon (276–239), who reestablished Macedonian hegemony in Greece. He defeated Athens and Sparta in the Chremonidean War (c. 267–c. 262) and Ptolemy II of Egypt in the naval battle of Cos. During his reign the Macedonian court became a center of culture.

Antigua and Barbuda A West Indian country in the E Caribbean Sea, comprising the islands of Antigua, Barbuda, and Redonda (uninhabited). Tourism is the chief source of revenue, sugar and cotton production are also important. *History*: Antigua was discovered by Columbus (1493) and colonized by British settlers in 1632. It formed an associated state within the British Commonwealth from 1967 until gaining independence in 1981. It is a member of CARICOM. Area: 170 sq mi (440 sq km). Population (1990): 64,000. Capital: St John's.

antihistamines Drugs that interfere with the action of *histamine, a chemical produced by the body that is responsible for the symptoms of an allergic reaction. Antihistamines are therefore used to treat hay fever, nettle rash, and other allergies. Some antihistamines (e.g. dramamine) are used to prevent travel sickness and others are effective sedatives (drowsiness is a common side effect of many antihistamines).

Anti-Lebanon Mountains A mountain range running NE–SW for 93 mi (150 km) along the Lebanese-Syrian border and rising to 9232 ft (2814 m) at Mount Hermon.

Antilles The islands of the West Indies, excluding the Bahamas. The group is divided into the *Greater Antilles and the *Lesser Antilles.

Anti-Masonic Party A minority US political party that arose after the disappearance of a former freemason in 1826. The widely held belief that the man had been murdered by freemasons for revealing their secrets led to the formation of the party to oppose Masonic candidates for office in the New York Assembly. Effective on the state level, the party held the first national nominating convention in US politics (1831), a system later adopted by the major parties. The Anti-Masons merged with the Whigs (who opposed the policies of Andrew Jackson) in 1838.

antimatter Hypothetical matter in which the constituent atoms consist of antiparticles. For every elementary particle (*see* particle physics) there exists an antiparticle that is identical except for certain of its properties, such as electric charge and isospin number, which are of equal magnitude but opposite in sign. The photon and the neutral pion are their own antiparticles. An atom of antimatter would contain a nucleus of antiprotons and antineutrons surrounded by positrons (antielectrons). If matter were to meet antimatter, they would annihilate each other in a burst of radiation. *See also* annihilation.

antimony (Sb) A metallic element, probably known in antiquity. It occurs in nature as the element and more commonly in the sulfide *stibnite (Sb_2S_3). The element exists in two forms: the normal metallic form, which is brittle bluish-white and flaky, and an amorphous, gray form. Antimony is a poor conductor of heat and electricity. It forms the oxide (Sb_2O_3) by burning in air and the volatile hydride, stibine (SbH_3), which like many antimony compounds is toxic. Pure antimony is used in making *semiconductors; other uses include addition to lead to increase its hardness in battery plates, in type metal, and as oxides or sulfides in paints, glasses, and ceramics. At no 51; at wt 121.75; mp 382°F (630.7°C); bp 1003°F (1750°C).

anti-novel. *See* nouveau roman.

Antioch (modern Turkish name: Antakya) 36 12N 36 10E A city in central S Turkey, near the coast and the Syrian border. Founded in 301 BC, it had a large early Christian community, and there are notable Roman mosaics in the Archeological Museum. Population (1990): 123,871.

Antiochus I Soter (324–261 BC) King of Syria (281–261) of the Seleucid dynasty. Antiochus lost some Seleucid territory to Egypt but achieved peace with Macedon (278) and repulsed a Gallic invasion, which earned him the title Soter (Saviour). He founded many cities.

Antiochus II (c. 287–246 BC) King of Syria (261–246) of the Seleucid dynasty. Little is known of his reign apart from his reconquest (260–253) of some of the territory in Asia Minor lost by his father *Antiochus I Soter and his political marriage (252) to the Egyptian princess Berenice.

Antiochus (III) the Great (c. 242–187 BC) King of Syria (223–187) of the Seleucid dynasty. After crushing separatist revolts at home, Antiochus initiated a policy of expansion. His incursions on Egyptian territory were temporarily halted by his defeat at Raphia (217) but his great campaign (212–206) through Armenia, Parthia, and Bactria to the Indus River paralleled that of Alexander the Great. He finally defeated the Egyptians in 198. Antiochus then became involved in hostile diplomacy with Rome and in 192 invaded Greece. Driven out by the Romans (190), his defeat destroyed Seleucid power in the Mediterranean.

Antiochus IV Epiphanes (c. 215–163 BC) King of Syria (175–163) of the Seleucid dynasty. Antiochus maintained the empire, campaigning successfully against the Egyptians until forced by the Romans to withdraw (168). He promoted Greek culture throughout the empire but met with resistance from the *Maccabees (167–160) when he ruthlessly imposed Greek religion on the Jews.

Antiochus VII Sidetes (c. 159–129 BC) The last Seleucid King of Syria (139–129). Following early military successes, including the reconquest of Jerusalem (134), he attempted to postpone the Parthian conquest of the Seleucid empire and died in battle.

anti-oxidants Substances that inhibit oxidation of such products as foods, paints, plastics, fuels, etc. Natural anti-oxidants include ascorbic acid (vitamin C). Additives are usually phenol derivatives.

antiparticle. *See* antimatter.

Antipater (397–319 BC) Macedonian general. Antipater was chief military and diplomatic aide to Philip of Macedon and then to Alexander the Great, becoming regent after Alexander's departure for the East. To maintain this position after Alexander's death, he suppressed internal rebellions and crushed the imperial ambitions of Alexander's second-in-command Perdiccas (d. 321). After Antipater's death Alexander's empire began to disintegrate.

Antipater (d. 4 BC) The son of *Herod the Great. Disowned in infancy, but restored to favor in about 17 BC, he struggled ruthlessly to succeed his father. He had his half-brothers executed in about 7 BC but was himself executed shortly before Herod's own death.

Antipater the Idumaean (d. 43 BC) Procurator (governor) of Judea (47–43). His adroit manipulation of successive Roman backers, including *Caesar, who appointed him procurator, brought privileges for Judea and financial advantages for himself. He was assassinated and his son *Herod the Great subsequently succeeded to his position.

Antiphon (c. 480–411 BC) Athenian orator, important in the development of a vigorous and precise Greek prose style. Antiphon conspired to establish oligarchic rule at Athens (411) but a more moderate democratic government prevailed and he was tried and executed despite a brilliant self-defense.

Antipodes Islands 49 42S 178 50E A small group of rocky uninhabited islands in the S Pacific Ocean, belonging to New Zealand. Their fur seal population has been greatly reduced by hunting. Area: 24 sq mi (62 sq km).

antipope Those raised to the papacy in opposition to a lawfully elected pope. There have been about 40 antipopes. The first, Hippolitus, was created in the early 3rd century. During the later Roman Empire and during the Middle Ages most antipopes represented rival factions supporting different political or doctrinal claims. In the 11th and 12th centuries some 14 antipopes were chosen by the Holy Roman Emperors, who had had until 1059 a considerable voice in papal elections and who resented the Church's growing independence from lay control. From 1378 another group of antipopes was elected following the *Great Schism, when a group of cardinals left Avignon (*see* Avignon papacy) to return to Rome; the popes remaining at Avignon and under French control were styled antipopes thereafter. The Council of Pisa (1409) elected a new pope to end the Schism, but he too was regarded as an antipope until unity was restored at the Council of *Constance (1515). There have been no antipopes since the mid-14th century.

antique An artifact of aesthetic and historical or sociological significance, now not in general use or manufacture. The term does not include painting and sculpture. Until recently an antique was required to predate about 1830, when factory production increased, but today import and export laws of most countries require an age of a hundred years for antiques. Antique collecting was a pastime of the wealthy until the 20th century, when its increasing popularity has widened the scope of collectable objects to include all kinds of domestic items.

Antirrhinum A genus of chiefly Mediterranean and W North American herbaceous plants (about 40 species). The most widely cultivated species is the ornamental snapdragon (*A. majus*), 12–31 in (30–80 cm) high with brightly colored, two-lipped, tubular flowers adapted to pollination by large bees. It grows naturally as a perennial but is usually treated as an annual and grown from seed. Family: *Scrophulariaceae*.

Anti-Saloon League (1895–1950) US temperance organization. The league worked for the prohibition of liquor in the US prior to the ratification of the 18th (Prohibition) Amendment in 1919 and afterwards for enforcement of the amendment. In 1950 it became part of the National Temperance League.

anti-Semitism Hostility toward the *Jews, which has characterized their existence since the *Diaspora (6th century BC). Its origins perhaps go back to the distrust invariably felt for a coherent minority held together by strong religious and cultural ties, which are themselves strengthened as the hostility intensifies.

The early history of the Jews did nothing to dispel this inherent mistrust: represented as God's chosen people in the Old Testament and the betrayers of Christ in the New Testament, their unpopularity in medieval Europe was reflected in totally unfounded beliefs that they used Christian children as human sacrifices. Encouraged and, in some cases, forced to become moneylenders (an activity forbidden to Christians by canon law; *see* usury), they were by the 13th century persecuted throughout Europe. Expulsion (England, 1290; France, 1306; Spain, 1492), massacre (Germany, 1348; Spain, 1391), the Inquisition (1478), and papal bull (1555) deprived medieval Europe of large numbers of its Jews, many of whom enriched the Muslim countries of N Africa and Turkey. It was not until the 18th-century *Enlightenment had introduced a degree of religious freedom that they came back in any numbers. However, in the 19th century anti-Semitism gained new impetus from nationalist sentiments, especially in Germany. In France, it became public in the *Dreyfus affair. In Russia, government-tolerated (and sometimes government-inspired) *pogroms were common in the late 19th and early 20th centuries but anti-Semitism reached its peak in Hitler's "final solution," which cost the Jews between five and six million lives (*see* holocaust). In the postwar years, after the establishment of the state of Israel, anti-Semitism was to some extent replaced by Arab anti-Zionism, but it continued to be active in E Europe, especially the Soviet Union. Social discrimination, such as the exclusion of Jews from private clubs, still exists in even apparently tolerant western countries that have legislation against racial discrimination.

antiseptic A substance that kills bacteria and other dangerous microorganisms and can be applied to the skin (to cleanse wounds, before surgery, etc.) or taken internally. Antiseptics are generally distinguished from *disinfectants, which are too toxic to be used on or within the body.

Antisthenes (c. 445–c. 360 BC) Greek philosopher and disciple of *Socrates. Antisthenes was a critic of society and is regarded as a formative influence on cynicism (*see* Cynics). Principally a moral philosopher, he argued for a simple and virtuous way of life that would lead to happiness.

antitank gun Any flat-trajectory *gun using ammunition suitable for destroying *tanks. Guns in tanks themselves are the most common examples. Artillery weapons are light, low-silhouette, easily deployed pieces. Short-range specialized missiles are replacing the lighter antitank guns.

antitoxin An *antibody produced against a toxin. Antitoxins can be isolated from inoculated healthy animals and used to treat or prevent specific infections; for example, an antitoxin against tetanus is obtained from the plasma of animals inoculated against tetanus.

antitrust acts Federal and state legislation to protect trade and commerce from unlawful restraints, price discrimination, price fixing, and monopolies. In the 19th century some businessmen fixed prices and destroyed rival businesses by manipulating raw materials and access to transport. The Sherman Antitrust Act (1890), the first of several measures, prohibited contracts "in restraint of trade." Interpreted narrowly at first, these laws were strengthened by successive legislation (including the Clayton Act 1914, Federal Trade Commission Act 1914, and the Robinson-Patman Act 1936).

antlers The paired bony structures growing from the heads of deer, generally confined to males. In temperate regions the antlers begin to grow in early summer: they are at first covered with velvety skin, which is later shed. Used for fighting and display, the antlers are shed each year at the end of the mating season. Deer grow their first set of antlers, which are usually straight spikes, at the age of 1–2 years. The number of points is increased in successive years.

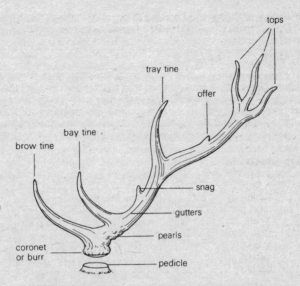

ANTLERS *The number of branches increases with the age of the stag. This antler has 6 branches; a stag with a head of 12 branches is called a royal.*

antlion An insect belonging to a family (*Myrmeleontidae*) in which the adults resemble dragonflies and live only long enough to mate and lay eggs. The predatory larva lives 1–3 years, generally at the bottom of a conical pit in loose sand: any insect that falls into the pit is snapped up with its large jaws, which protrude from the sand. Order: **Neuroptera*.

Antofagasta 21 51S 102 18W A city in NW Chile, a port on the Pacific Ocean. It is a commercial and industrial center. The chief industries are metal refining and founding; exports include nitrates and copper. The University of the North was established here in 1956. Population (1991 est): 221,000.

Antonello da Messina (c. 1430–1479) Italian painter, born in Messina (Sicily). He trained in Naples, where he probably learned the Flemish technique of oil painting; this he introduced to Venice during a visit in 1475. The realism of Flemish art also deeply influenced his style, particularly in *St Jerome in His Study* and *Portrait of a Man* (both National Gallery, London).

Antonescu, Ion (1882–1946) Romanian general and politician. A pro-Nazi, he became prime minister (1940), replacing *Carol II's government with a totalitarian regime. In 1941 he commanded the army in Bessarabia. He was executed for war crimes.

Antoninus Plus (86–161 AD) Roman emperor (138–61). Antoninus was admitted by Emperor Hadrian to his advisory council and adopted as his successor in 138. His reign was peaceful and generally prosperous. Only minor campaigns were fought abroad and noted legal reforms were introduced; the *Antonine Wall was built during his reign. He was deified after his death.

Antonioni, Michelangelo (1912–   ) Italian film maker. Born into a bourgeois provincial family and interested in film making as a student, in 1939 he moved to Rome to work for the magazine *Cinema*. His first films were *Gente del*

Po (1943–47) and *Cronaca di un amore* (1950). Later films include *L'avventura* (1959), *La notte* (1961), *Blow-Up* (1966), *Zabriskie Point* (1970), and *The Passenger* (1975).

Antony, Mark. *See* Mark Antony.

Antrim A former county in NE Northern Ireland, bordering on the Atlantic Ocean and the Irish Sea. It consists mainly of a basalt plateau sloping inland to lough Neagh in the SW. On the N coast is the famous *Giant's Causeway. The county is predominantly agricultural producing oats, potatoes, flax, and livestock. Industry includes the manufacture of man-made fibers, which has largely replaced traditional linen production. Area: 1200 sq mi (3100 sq km). Chief city: Belfast.

An-tung. *See* Andong.

Antwerp (Flemish name: Antwerpen; French name: Anvers) 51 13N 4 25E A city in Belgium, on the Scheldt River. Antwerp is one of the largest seaports in the world and has important shipbuilding and ship-repairing industries. Other industries include oil refining, diamond cutting, textiles, and electronics. It possesses many fine buildings, including the 14th-century Gothic cathedral, the printer Christopher Plantin's house (now a museum), and the 16th-century Butchers' Hall. It is the birthplace of Rubens and Van Dyck and some of their paintings form part of a fine collection housed in the Royal Gallery of Fine Arts. There is a large Flemish-speaking population. *History*: it was the leading commercial center of western Europe in the 16th century but religious strife and its sacking by Spaniards (1576) led to its decline, further hastened by the closure of the Scheldt River (1648). The revival of its economy began when Belgium purchased the shipping rights of the river from the Netherlands. Antwerp was occupied and damaged in both World Wars. Population (1991): 467,518.

Anu The Mesopotamian god of the heavens and father of all the gods. He represented the infinite and all-embracing sky and was worshiped as the source of all order and rule.

Anubis Egyptian god of the dead, usually represented as a crouching jackal or a jackal-headed man. He supervised the weighing of the souls of the dead, and also the embalming of the body. He was reputed to have invented this process to preserve the body of *Osiris.

Anura An order of amphibians (over 2000 species) comprising the *frogs and *toads. Anurans are specialized for jumping, having a short backbone, no tail, and large muscular hind legs. The eggs hatch into tadpoles, which undergo *metamorphosis into adults. This order is also called the *Salientia*.

Anuradhapura 8 20N 80 25E A city in Sri Lanka. The ancient capital of the island (5th century BC to 8th century AD), it is the site of the sacred bo tree descended from the original at *Buddh Gaya and the first Buddhist temple in Sri Lanka. Population (1981): 36,248.

anus. *See* intestine.

Anvers. *See* Antwerp.

Anville, Jean-Baptiste Bourguignon d' (1697–1782) French geographer and cartographer, specializing chiefly in ancient and medieval geography. As geographer to the French king from 1719, he greatly improved the accuracy of maps of Italy, Asia, and Africa.

anxiety Generalized pervasive fear. Anxiety is partly the feeling of apprehension, partly the behavior of avoiding frightening situations, and partly the associated bodily changes, such as sweating, a fast pulse, and tense muscles. It is normal to feel anxiety when some danger is present or expected. However, when severe anxiety is out of all proportion to any real threats it can be a sign of mental illness. Tranquilizing drugs, *psychotherapy, *behavior therapy, and *autosuggestion are used as treatments. *See also* neurosis; phobia.

Anyang 36 04N 114 20E A city in E China, in Henan province. It was the last capital (1384–1111 BC) of the Shang dynasty and splendid archeological remains have been unearthed here. Industries include cotton and steel. Population (1990): 420,332.

ANZAC The Australian and New Zealand Army Corps, which served in World War I in Europe and the Middle East. On ANZAC Day, Apr 25 (the day of the ANZAC landing in Gallipoli in 1915), in Australia and New Zealand the dead of both World Wars are remembered.

Anzengruber, Ludwig (1839–89) Austrian dramatist and novelist. Originally an actor, he wrote a successful series of realistic plays about rural life, many of them in local dialect. They include the tragedy *Der Meineidbauer* (1871) and the comedy *Die Kreuzelschreiber* (1872). He also wrote short stories and two novels.

Anzio 41 27N 12 38E A seaport and resort in Italy, in Lazio on the Tyrrhenian Sea. It is the birthplace of Nero. During World War II it was the scene of Allied landings in Italy. There is an important fishing industry. Population: 22,927.

ANZUS A security treaty concluded in 1951 by Australia, New Zealand, and the US, requiring members to provide mutual aid in the event of aggression by foreign powers.

Aomori 40 50N 140 43E A city in Japan, in N Honshu on Mutsu Bay. One of Japan's major ports, it exports rice, fish, and timber. Population (1990): 287,808.

aorta. *See* artery; heart.

Aosta 45 43N 7 19E A city in Italy, capital of Valle d'Aosta on the Dora Baltea River. Situated amid impressive mountain scenery, it has important Roman remains and a cathedral (12th–19th centuries). Tourism and steel are the main industries. Population: 36,906.

aoudad A tawny-colored sheep, *Ammotragus lervia*, also called Barbary sheep, that is the only wild sheep in Africa. Aoudads live in dry, rocky northern regions and obtain water mainly from vegetation and dew. They stand 41 in (102 cm) at the shoulder and have outward-curving horns and a long fringe of hair hanging from the neck and chest.

Apache A North American Indian people inhabiting areas of Arizona, New Mexico, and Oklahoma. Their main divisions are the Jicarillos, Mescaleros, Chiricahuas, Western Apache, Lipan, and Kiowa-Apache and their language is of the *Athabascan type. The Apaches migrated from the Northwest to their present area of settlement around 1000 AD and preserved a semi-nomadic way of life. In addition to hunting, some groups practiced farming and handicrafts. Their raids on the villages of the Pueblo Indians and the Spanish settlements of the Southwest earned the Apaches a warlike reputation. Although the various Apache groups were usually independent, they sometimes formed alliances under the leadership of national chiefs such as *Cochise and *Geronimo, who led Apache warriors in continuing warfare against the US Army until 1886.

Apache Wars (1860–86) US frontier battles between the Apache Indians and the US Army in the Southwest. The refusal of the Apache and other Indian tribes to give up their lands to the whites led to a series of fierce battles, mainly in Arizona, New Mexico, Texas, and Oklahoma. Apache chief Cochise made peace in 1872, but renegade chief Geronimo resisted until 1886, when he and his followers were settled at Fort Sill, Okla.

apartheid (Afrikaans: apartness) The policy of separate development of the white and non-white populations in South Africa. Apartheid, which was introduced by the Afrikaner National Party in 1948, aimed to divide South Africa into separate regions for whites and blacks. The white minority that governs South Africa has been criticized for this policy and in 1961 South Africa was forced to withdraw from the British Commonwealth. The main apartheid regulations were repealed in 1991.

apatite The most common phosphorous mineral, whose composition is $Ca_5(PO_4)_3(OH,F, Cl)$. It is found as an accessory mineral in many igneous rocks, especially pegmatites, as well as metamorphosed limestones. It is used in the production of fertilizers. The enamel of teeth is composed almost entirely of apatite (*see also* fluoridation) and the chief inorganic constituent of bone is hydroxyapatite, $Ca_{10}(PO_4)_6(OH)_2$.

Apatosaurus *See* Brontosaurus.

ape A highly intelligent tailless *primate belonging to the family *Pongidae* (11 species), found in central Africa and S Asia. There are two subfamilies: the arboreal *Hylobatinae* (*see* gibbons; siamang) and the ground-dwelling *Ponginae* (*see* chimpanzees; orangutans; gorillas), also called great apes. Forest apes are often solitary but ground-dwelling apes live in complex societies and all have highly developed means of communication.

Some tailless primates of other families are also called apes.

Apeldoorn 52 13N 5 57E A city in the E central Netherlands, in Gelderland province. The 17th-century Castle Loo, a royal summer residence, is nearby. Its industries include blanket, cloth, and paper production. Population (1990 est): 148,200.

Apelles (4th century BC) The court painter of Alexander the Great. He seems to have specialized in portraits and allegories aiming, like many contemporary artists, at *trompe l'oeil* realism. His most famous pictures included *Aphrodite Rising from the Waves* and *Alexander as Zeus*. His style of portraiture influenced fashions in painting for more than two centuries.

Apennines (Italian name: Appènnino) A mountain range in Italy. It extends about 652 mi (1050 km) down the Italian peninsula from the Maritime Alps in the NW to the Strait of Messina in the S. The range is not generally very high but it affords few easy crossing points; the highest peak is Monte Corno at 9560 ft (2914 m). The Apennines are volcanic in the S (*see* Vesuvius).

aphelion The point in the orbit of a body around the sun at which the body is furthest from the sun. The earth is at aphelion on about July 3. *Compare* perihelion.

aphid An □insect, also called a plant louse, belonging to a family (*Aphidae*) of important plant pests. Small, soft, and often wingless, aphids have long, thin antennae and weak legs and are usually green (greenfly), red, or brown. There are two thin tubes projecting from the abdomen from which honeydew is secreted. Aphids feed on plant sap, piercing plant tissues with sharp beaklike mouthparts, causing leaf curl, retardation of growth, and often forming galls. The aphid's great fecundity and the ability of the female to reproduce by *parthenogenesis results in frequent outbreaks of the pest. Order: *Hemiptera*.

Aphraates (4th century AD) The first Father of the Syrian Church. He lived a monastic life and may also have been a bishop. He wrote numerous tractates summarizing the Christian faith.

aphrodisiac A drug that increases sexual desire or sexual performance. No true aphrodisiac has yet been discovered and most preparations act (if at all) by suggestion. Some drugs (such as *alcohol and *morphine) produce a general euphoria and reduce inhibitions but usually have an adverse effect on sexual performance. Local irritants, such as cantharides (Spanish fly), can prolong an erection at the cost of considerable discomfort.

Aphrodite In Greek mythology, the goddess of love, called *Venus by the Romans. According to Homer she was the daughter of Dione and Zeus; Hesiod says that she was born from the foam after *Uranus had been castrated and his genitals thrown into the sea. She was said to have emerged from the sea at Paphos in Cyprus or at the island of Cythera. She was the wife of Hephaestus but was unfaithful to him and had an affair with Ares. She is portrayed by later writers as the mother of Eros. Paris' choice of her as the most beautiful of the three goddesses at the wedding feast of Peleus and Thetis (the others were Hera and Athena) caused the *Trojan War. She was revered throughout Greece as the personification of spiritual love but she also embodied sensual lust.

Apia 13 48S 171 45W The capital and chief port of Western Samoa, in N Upolu on the S Pacific Ocean. The head of state's residence was formerly the home of Robert Louis Stevenson. Copra, bananas, and cocoa are exported. Population (1991): 32,859.

Apis The Egyptian bull god. Originally a minor fertility god, he became associated with *Ptah and later *Osiris, at which point he became known as Serapis. A bull sacred to him was kept until another with appropriate markings was found; it was then ritually drowned in the Nile and its body mummified in the Serapeum vault at Saqqarah.

apocalypse (Greek: revelation) In the New Testament, the Revelation of St John the Divine. The term is also used of various noncanonical writings, such as the *Book of Enoch*, and of parts of the Old Testament books of *Isaiah, Ezekiel*, and *Daniel*. These are all examples of "apocalyptic literature." Full of symbolism and imagery, they describe visions of a great new era that will suddenly supersede the present age of suffering.

Apocrypha (Greek: hidden things) Twelve books taken over by the early Christian Church from the Greek version of the Old Testament but not forming part of the Hebrew Bible. They originated in the Hellenistic Judaism of Alexandria but were not accepted as canonical by orthodox Jews and were treated in various ways in Christian Bibles. In the *Vulgate, most of them are printed with the Old Testament but they are omitted or printed as a separate section in Protestant versions of the Bible. They are: I Esdras, Tobit, Judith, the Rest of Esther, the Wisdom of Solomon, Ecclesiasticus, Baruch with the Epistle of Jeremy, the Song of the Three Holy Children, the History of Susanna, Bel and the Dragon, the Prayer of Manasses, and I and II Maccabees.

apogee The point in the orbit of the moon or of an artificial satellite around the earth at which the body is furthest from the earth. *Compare* perigee.

Apollinaire, Guillaume (Wilhelm de Kostrowitzky; 1880–1918) French poet. Born in Italy, he settled in Paris in 1900. A champion of *cubism and other avant-garde movements, he blended lyricism with experiment in his poetry, first collected in *Alcools* (1913). While recovering from a head wound sustained in World War I, he wrote a surrealist play, *Les Mamelles de Tirésias* (1917), and a modernist manifesto, *L'Esprit nouveau et les poètes*. The poems in *Calligrammes* (1918) included daring typographical experiments. He died in the 1918 flu epidemic.

APIS *The sacred bull of Memphis was associated with the solar cult and was often depicted with its emblem, the sun disc, between its horns.*

Apollo A Greek god of many aspects, symbol of light, of reason, and of male beauty. He is also associated with medicine, prophecy, music and poetry, the care of animals and crops, morality, and the maintenance of society. He and his sister *Artemis were the children of *Zeus by *Leda. He established his oracle at Delphi after killing Python, its dragon guardian.

Apollo moon program The US program to land men on the moon by 1970, announced by President Kennedy in 1961. The program was directed by *NASA. The preliminary manned Mercury (1961–63) and Gemini (1965–66) projects provided valuable information and experience. The method selected for the landing was for a Saturn V rocket to launch the Apollo spacecraft toward the moon and, once the craft was in lunar orbit, for a capsule—the lunar module—to descend to the moon's surface carrying two astronauts. The third astronaut remained in the orbiting craft. At the end of the surface mission the lunar module's descent stage was left on the moon while its ascent stage was shot into lunar orbit and docked with the orbiting craft. Following the transfer of the two astronauts, the ascent stage was jettisoned and the spacecraft put in a flight path toward earth. The astronauts traveled to and from the moon in the command module, the rocket engines for in-flight maneuvers, fuel cells, etc., being carried in the separate service module. The latter was jettisoned prior to re-entering the earth's atmosphere; the command module finally splashed down in the ocean.

APOLLO MOON PROGRAM

craft	astronauts	launch date	comments
Apollo 7	W. Schirra W. Cunningham D. Eisele	October 11, 1968	first manned flight of Apollo spacecraft
Apollo 8	F. Borman J. Lovell W. Anders	December 21, 1968	first manned flight around moon
Apollo 9	J. McDivitt D. Scott R. Schweickart	March 3, 1969	complete Apollo craft tested in earth orbit
Apollo 10	T. Stafford J. Young E. Cernan	May 18, 1969	rehearsal of moon landing
Apollo 11	N. Armstrong E. Aldrin M. Collins	July 16, 1969	first manned moon landing July 20
Apollo 12	C. Conrad A. Bean R. Gordon	November 14, 1969	second moon landing

APOLLO MOON PROGRAM

craft	astronauts	launch date	comments
Apollo 13	J. Lovell F. Haise J. Swigert	April 11, 1970	mission aborted after in-flight explosion in service module
Apollo 14	A. Shepard E. Mitchell S. Roosa	January 31, 1971	third moon landing
Apollo 15	D. Scott J. Irwin A. Worden	July 26, 1971	fourth moon landing
Apollo 16	J. Young C. Duke T. Mattingly	April 16, 1972	fifth moon landing
Apollo 17	E. Cernan H. Schmitt R. Evans	December 7, 1972	last moon landing

The first six Apollo missions were unmanned test flights, the next four being manned. Apollo 11 made the first manned lunar landing in July, 1969. Of the six ensuing missions, all, except Apollo 13, were highly successful, the scientific content of the information obtained increasing with each lunar landing.

Apollonius (2nd century AD) Greek grammarian, nicknamed Dyskolos (Badtempered). Of his 29 works on grammar, four survive. He introduced critical methods into grammar, seeking explanations rather than descriptions of sentence structure.

Apollonius of Perga (c. 261–c. 190 BC) Greek mathematician, who studied under *Archimedes. In a series of eight books, he described a family of curves known as *conic sections, comprising the circle, ellipse, parabola, and hyperbola.

Apollonius of Rhodes (3rd century BC) Greek epic poet. He was sometime head of the Library of Alexandria and was the chief rival of the poet *Callimachus. His four-volume *Argonautica*, in the style of *Homer, tells the story of the quest for the *Golden Fleece and is notable for its treatment of Medea's love for Jason, showing a sympathy to the woman's viewpoint unusual at this time. He also wrote epigrams, and commentaries on other Greek poets.

Apollonius of Tyana (1st century AD) Pythagorean philosopher and reputed miracle worker, from Tyana in Cappadocia. He was the subject of a biography by the Roman Flavius Philostratus in about 200 AD, possibly commissioned as anti-Christian propaganda by the empress Julia Domna.

apologetics In Christianity, the defense of the faith by theologians using intellectual and philosophical arguments. The name apologists refers especially to 2nd-century writers, such as *Justin Martyr and *Tertullian, who argued for Christianity against paganism. Later apologists defended orthodox Christian doctrines against heretical ones. In the 20th century one of the main apologetic tasks has been to explain how orthodox Christian belief is still reasonable in a scientific age.

apomixis The formation and development of an embryo without the fusion of male and female sex cells. This can occur in both plants and animals. The embryo is usually formed from the unfertilized egg (*see* parthenogenesis). In certain cases apomixis is triggered by a male sex cell that enters the egg but does not fuse with it.

apoplexy. *See* stroke.

Apostles In the New Testament, the 12 men chosen by Jesus as his disciples who, after his death, were to spread his teaching throughout the Roman world. Originally they were: Andrew, Bartholomew (*or* Nathaniel), James son of Alphaeus, James son of Zebedee, John, Jude (*or* Thaddeus), Judas Iscariot, Matthew (*or* Levi), Philip, Simon Peter, Simon the Zealot, and Thomas. After his suicide, Judas Iscariot was replaced by Matthias. St Paul is also included among the Apostles because of his claim to having seen Jesus after the resurrection. *See also* Acts of the Apostles.

Apostles' Creed A Christian profession of faith in three sections concerning God the Father, Jesus Christ, and the Holy Spirit. Widely used in the Western Churches, it is of uncertain date but its present title first occurs in a letter of St Ambrose of about 390 AD.

Apostolic Constitutions A collection of Christian ecclesiastical administrative regulations and instructions for worship. Although its full title is "Ordinances of the Holy Apostles through Clement," and it ends with the 85 "Apostolic Canons," it probably originated in late 4th-century Syria and not from the

Apostles. Its eight books contain much that is derived from the 3rd-century *Didascalia Apostolorum* and the 2nd-century *Didache*, which are significant sources of information about the early Church.

apostolic succession A Christian doctrine held by the Roman Catholic and Orthodox Churches and by some Anglicans. Its upholders claim that the Apostles appointed the first bishops and that there is thus a continuous line of succession from the Apostles to the present ministries of these Churches along which the power and authority given by Christ to the former have passed to the latter.

Appalachian Mountains A mountain range that extends NE-SW from the Mohawk River to Alabama, separating the Mississippi-Missouri lowlands from the Atlantic coastal plain. It consists of a series of mountain ranges and plateaus, including the *Allegheny Mountains, the *Catskill Mountains, and the White Mountains of New Hampshire. Its highest point is Mount Mitchell, at 6684 ft (2038 m). Coalmining is important, providing anthracite and bitumen; iron ore is also extracted. Poor communications and lack of employment have contributed to the establishment of a regional assistance program within the area. It also contains the **Appalachian Trail**, the longest continuous footpath in the world.

Appaloosa An American breed of spotted riding horse with a wispy mane and tail. The white Appaloosa is completely white with dark spots over the whole body but other types may be of any color as long as the hindquarters are white with spots of the color of the rest of the coat. Height $14\frac{1}{2}$–$15\frac{1}{3}$ hands (1.47–1.60 m).

appeal In law, the review of a court decision by a higher court, usually at the request of one of the parties to the case. The decisions of some administrative or professional bodies may also be appealed against in the courts. Appeals in *common law systems are usually based on alleged errors of law in the original trial, but may sometimes also be based on errors of fact. *See also* courts of law.

appeasement The policy implemented by the British prime minister, Neville *Chamberlain, of giving way to the demands of Hitler and Mussolini in the hope of maintaining peace. It culminated in the *Munich Agreement (1938) and was finally shown to be futile in March, 1939, when Hitler seized Czechoslovakia.

appendicitis Inflammation of the *appendix. Appendicitis is most common in childhood and adolescence. It usually starts with a vague pain around the navel that becomes localized in the right lower region of the abdomen. Diarrhea may also occur. Surgical removal to prevent rupture of the appendix and subsequent *peritonitis is usually required.

appendix (*or* vermiform appendix) A thin, blind-ended tube, 3–4 in (7–10 cm) long, that opens from the end of the large intestine. It has no known function in man and is prone to infection (*see* appendicitis). In herbivorous animals (e.g. rabbits and cows) the appendix is large and plays an important part in the digestion of vegetable matter.

Appert, Nicolas (1750–1841) French inventor, who discovered that food can be preserved by boiling it in sealed containers. In 1812 he opened the world's first commercial canning factory.

Appian Way The road, built about 312 BC by the statesman Appius Claudius, between Rome and Capua. It was the first in the strategic network of Roman roads. A short stretch is still visible near Rome.

apple A deciduous tree or shrub of the genus *Malus* (about 35 species), native to N temperate regions and widely cultivated for their rounded fleshy □fruits (pomes). Several species have been cultivated, especially *M. pumila* of W Asia, with the development of numerous varieties of dessert, cooking, and *cider apples. Shoots of the required variety are grafted onto selected rootstocks. Some varieties are ornamental. Apples are also used for soft drinks and as a source of pectin. Family: *Rosaceae*. *See also* crab apple.

Appleseed, Johnny (John Chapman; 1774–1845) US nurseryman and folk hero. He acquired the name of Johnny Appleseed and became a legend in his own time by walking throughout the Midwest, planting, selling, or giving away apple seeds to the settlers. His eccentricity and bizarre appearance and his pious gentleness with people and animals contributed to the myth.

Appleton layer. *See* ionosphere.

Appomattox 37 21N 78 51W A town in central Virginia. The Confederate leader, Robert E. Lee, surrendered here to Ulysses Grant on Apr 9, 1865, effectively ending the US Civil War.

Appomattox River A river rising near Appomattox in central Virginia and flowing E to its junction with the James River at Hopewell. Length: 137 mi (221 km).

apricot A tree, *Prunus armenica*, native to China and widely grown in warm temperate countries, especially Spain, for its fruits. It is 20–30 ft (6–9 m) tall and has white, five-petaled flowers and toothed, heart-shaped leaves. The hairy-skinned, orange-yellow fruits have sweet flesh and smooth stones. Family: *Rosaceae*.

April Fourth month of the year. Derivations of the name vary; it may be from *aperire* (Latin: to open), *aper* (Latin: wild boar), *aphros* (Greek: Aphrodite), or *áparas* (Vedic: following). It has 30 days. The zodiac signs for April are Aries and Taurus; the flowers are sweet pea and daisy, and the birthstone is the diamond.

April Theses The *Bolshevik party program devised by *Lenin during the *Russian Revolution (1917). Its demands included the cessation of Bolshevik support for the Provisional Government, Russia's withdrawal from World War I, and the redistribution of land among the peasants.

a priori knowledge Any kind of knowledge that is in no way derived from sense experience, observation, or experiment. Many philosophers therefore hold that a priori knowledge is impossible. However, those attracted to *intuitionism have defended its possibility, especially with regard to theological problems. Kant insisted on the reality of a priori knowledge in the form of the necessary conditions of our having any experience at all, e.g. the notions of causality, space, and time.

apse A semicircular or polygonal eastern end of a church, characteristic of the *basilica and *Romanesque and *Norman architecture. Seats for the clergy ran around the apse walls behind the centrally placed altar.

Apuleius, Lucius (2nd century AD) Roman writer and rhetorician. Educated at Carthage and Athens, he traveled in the East before returning to Africa to marry Pudentilla, a rich widow. His *Apologia* is his defense against a charge that he had won her by magic. *The Golden Ass*, the only surviving complete Latin novel, describes the misadventures of one Lucius, who is accidentally turned into an ass; he is finally restored to human form by Isis.

Apulia (*or* Puglia) A region in SE Italy, on the Adriatic Sea. It consists of lowlands in the N and S (the "heel" of Italy) and a hilly central area. Wheat is the main agricultural crop; tobacco, vegetables, olives, figs, vines, and almonds are also produced. Manufacturing industry is mainly related to agriculture although modern industries are being developed, particularly at Taranto. Area: 7470 sq mi (19,347 sq km). Population (1991): 3,970,525.

Aqaba 29 32N 35 00E A port in Jordan, on the **Gulf of Aqaba**, a narrow inlet at the NE end of the Red Sea. Aqaba was the Roman stronghold of Aelana. Being Jordan's only port, it has been considerably expanded, despite difficult navigation and an exposed site, to handle the export of phosphates. Population: 10,000.

aquamarine A pale blue or green variety of *beryl. Many fine specimens of this gemstone come from Brazil, Madagascar, and California.

aqua regia A fuming, yellow, corrosive mixture of one part *nitric acid to three or four parts *hydrochloric acid. It dissolves all metals, even gold, and is used in *metallurgy.

aquarium A receptacle containing fresh or salt water for maintaining aquatic plants or animals (particularly fish) or a building in which such receptacles are kept or displayed. To duplicate natural conditions, modifications including the use of a water heater (for tropical species), aerator, and filter may be necessary. The first public aquarium was opened at the London Zoo in Regent's Park, London, in 1853.

Aquarius (Latin: Water Bearer) A large constellation in the S sky, lying on the *zodiac between Pisces and Capricornus.

aquatint An etching technique that produces a tonal effect similar to that of wash drawing. A satisfactory method was invented in the 1760s by a Frenchman, Jean Baptiste Le Prince (1733–81). Sharply defined areas of tone are employed, usually in conjunction with etched lines. A printing plate is sprinkled with powdered asphaltum or resin, which is then fixed to the plate by heating. Stopping-out varnish is used to mask different areas as the plate is immersed for varying lengths of time in an acid bath. *Goya, *Picasso and *Miró have used the technique with outstanding effect.

aquavit A *spirit distilled from grains and flavored with caraway seeds. It is best served ice cold. Aquavit is drunk predominantly in Scandinavia.

Aquaviva, Claudio (1543–1615) Italian churchman, the fifth general of the Society of Jesus, elected in 1581. The son of a nobleman, he saw Jesuit numbers increase from 5000 to 13,000 during his office and laid down definitive educational guidelines for the order in *Ratio studiorum* (1599).

aqueduct A narrow bridge, channel, or conduit designed to enable water to flow at a steady rate over an irregular, natural terrain, such as a valley. Aqueducts were built by the Greeks, but the technique was developed to its highest level of sophistication by the Romans. Impressive Roman examples still survive at Nîmes, Segovia, and Rome. Much the same principles are still used in modern irrigation systems throughout the world.

Aquila (Latin: eagle) An equatorial constellation lying in the Milky Way near Cygnus. The brightest star is *Altair.

Aquilegia A genus of perennial herbaceous plants (100 species) of temperate regions, commonly known as columbines. Their showy flowers have petals with long honey-secreting spurs. A favorite garden flower, aquilegias have been cultivated since the 16th century. Many modern garden hybrids, which have large, long-spurred flowers, are derived from the European columbine (*A. vulgaris*), 16–40 in (40–100 cm) high with purple to white flowers. Family: *Ranunculaceae*.

Aquilèia 45 47N 13 22E A town in N Italy, at the head of the Adriatic Sea. Founded by the Romans in 181 BC, it was of great strategic and military importance but failed to regain its former prominence following its destruction by Attila in 452 AD.

AQUEDUCT *The Pont du Gard built by the Romans in 19 BC across the River Gard in Provence (France).*

Aquinas, St Thomas (c. 1225–74) Italian Dominican theologian, scholastic philosopher, and Doctor of the Church, known as *Doctor Angelicus*. Born near Naples, the son of Count Landulf of Aquino, he was educated at the Benedictine school at Monte Cassino and at the University of Naples. Joining the Dominican Order in 1244 in spite of parental opposition, he became a pupil of *Albertus Magnus in Paris (1245) and followed him to Cologne in 1248. He returned to Paris as a lecturer in 1252, becoming a leading defender of the Dominicans against their critics at the University of Paris. He was a lecturer and theological adviser to the papal Curia between 1259 and 1269 and then taught at Paris until 1272, when he was appointed a professor at Naples. He died at Fossanova on his way to the Council of Lyons and was canonized in 1323. His prolific writings include commentaries on the Scriptures, on Aristotle and other philosophers, and academic disputations. His two most influential works are the *Summa contra gentiles* (1259–64), written for the use of missionaries, and the uncompleted *Summa theologica* (1266–73), the first systematic work on Latin theology. In opposition to the Averroists (*see* Averroes) and Augustinians he attempted to reconcile Christian faith and human reason. His arguments to prove the existence of God have been very influential in Roman Catholic theology. Feast day: Mar 7.

Aquino, Corazon (1933–), president of the Philippines (1986–92). The widow of Benigno Aquino, a political opponent of Pres. Ferdinand Marcos who was murdered in 1983, she opposed Marcos in the 1986 presidential election. Although Marcos declared himself the election winner, widespread fraud charges and popular demonstrations forced him to step down. Aquino became president, facing the problem of winning the support of the country's military. With US support, she survived a 1989 coup attempt. She declined to run for re-election in 1992.

Aquitaine (Latin name: Aquitania) A planning region in SW France, bordering on the Bay of Biscay. Formerly an administrative region in Roman Gaul, it extended from the Pyrenees N to the River Loire. It became an independent duchy under the Merovingians (7th century). The marriages of Eleanor of Aquitaine to Louis VII of France and then to Henry II of England resulted in rival French-English claims to the territory (*see* Hundred Years' War). Area: 15,984 sq mi (41,408 sq km). Population (1991 est): 2,812,000.

Arab horse An ancient breed of horse originally bred by the Bedouins in Arabia. It is usually gray, chestnut, or bay with a long silky mane and tail, a wedge-shaped head, and an arched neck. The Arab is prized as a riding horse because of its speed, hardiness, and docile temperament. Height: 14–15 hands (1.42–1.52 m).

Arabia A peninsula in the Middle East, forming the SW tip of Asia and bordered by the Red Sea, the Gulf of Aden, the Gulf of Oman, and the Persian Gulf. It consists of Saudi Arabia, Yemen, Oman, the United Arab Emirates, Qatar, Bahrain, and Kuwait. Mountains in the W (most fertile in the S) slope downward to steppe and desert in the E. Agriculture is still the main occupation, despite flourishing modern oil industries. *History*: as remains of irrigation systems show, S Arabia was the site of technologically advanced ancient civilizations. Arabia was often conquered in part, but its total conquest was long prevented by its deserts. It was conquered briefly by the Persians in 575 AD and later unified from Mecca by Islam in the 7th century, when the previously warring Arab tribes turned their attention to the conquest of N Africa, SW Asia, and S Europe. Arabia quickly became disunited again, however. From the 16th century until World War I the Ottoman Turks held nominal control over much of the peninsula, challenged chiefly by the *Wahhabiyah, a Muslim sect that was led by the Saud family, which conquered Arabia (except for the SW) and finally established Saudi Arabia (1932).

Arabian Desert 1. A desert chiefly in Saudi Arabia, covering most of *Arabia. Area: about 887,844 sq mi (2,300,000 sq km) **2.** A desert in E Egypt between the River Nile and the Red Sea.

Arabian Sea A section of the NW Indian Ocean between Arabia and India. Connected to the Mediterranean Sea by the Red Sea and the Suez Canal, it forms a major shipping route.

Arabic A member of the *Semitic group of languages. It is written from right to left. Arabic is the mother-tongue of some 110 million people inhabiting SW Asia (the Middle East) and the countries of N Africa. Arabic can be roughly classified into three parts: (a) Classical Arabic, the language of the *Koran and the great Arab writers and poets; (b) Modern Literary, or Standard, Arabic, the language of the press and broadcasting; and (c) the colloquial dialects (vernaculars), which differ in a greater or lesser degree from country to country. Categories (a) and (b) are known as "Written Arabic," the vernaculars are almost entirely spoken forms.

Arabic literature The literature of the Arabic-speaking peoples, the majority of whom live in N Africa and the Middle East. Most Arabic writing is scholarly, consisting of works on religion, philosophy, grammar, history, translations from the Greek, etc. Literature strictly speaking may be divided into two periods, the classical (6th–16th centuries) and the modern literary revival in the Middle East, which started in the 19th century and reflected a heavy indebtedness to the West. The earliest example of classical literature was a pre-Islamic poetic form, the *qasidah* (6th century), which continued to dominate Arabic verse for generations. An ode of 60 to 100 lines, it was written in praise of the poet himself, his tribe, or his patron. Its main interest for modern readers lies in the dramatic descriptions of early Bedouin desert life; the most important collection is the *Mu'allaqat* (8th century). During the Umayyad period (661–750) there arose a second important poetic genre, the *ghazal*, a short love poem. The golden age of classical Arabic literature developed during the 'Abbasid period (750–1055) with the assimilation of many Greek and Roman authors and the growth of a cosmopolitan urban culture, of which *Abu Nuwas was the outstanding poet. The traditional verse continued to flourish, however, its most famous practitioner being al-*Mutanabbi, who brought a new rhetorical sophistication to the *qasidah*. Sufi mysticism influenced some Arabic writers in the 11th–12th centuries, but its main effect was on Persian and Turkish writers. Literary prose also developed during the 'Abbasid period; among the most influential writers were the essayist al-Jahiz (d. 869) and the critic and philologist Ibn Qutaybah (d. 899). Because of the authority of the Koran, Arabic was maintained as the language of religion and scholarship, but declined as a literary medium under the *Mamelukes (1250–1517) and in the Ottoman Empire (16th–19th centuries). Nationalist movements especially in Egypt and Syria beginning in the late 19th century largely account for the modern literary renaissance in these countries, where writers have adopted such western forms as the novel and drama.

Arabic numerals The number symbols 0, 1, 2, 3, 4, 5, 6, 7, 8, 9. They are believed to have originated in India and were introduced into Europe by the Arabs in about the 10th century AD. *Compare* Roman numerals.

Arab-Israeli Wars. *See* Israel, State of.

Arab League An organization formed to promote unity and cooperation among Arab nations. Formed in Cairo in 1945, it consisted of those Arab countries that were then independent; others joined on attaining independence. The current members are Algeria, Bahrain, Democratic Republic of Yemen, Djibouti, Egypt, Iraq, Jordan, Kuwait, Lebanon, Libya, Mauritania, Morocco, Oman, Qatar, Saudi Arabia, Somalia, Sudan, Syria, Tunisia, United Arab Emirates, and Yemen. The League has had some success in the economic, scientific, and cultural fields, but in political affairs, unified action has been hindered by ideological conflicts between its moderate and radical members. In 1975 the Arab League recognized the *Palestine Liberation Organization as the official representative of the Palestinian people and admitted it to full membership in the League. Following the Egyptian-Israeli peace treaty in 1979, Egypt was temporarily expelled from the organization and the headquarters of the Arab League was transferred to Tunis.

arable farming The cultivation of plants for food, fibers, vegetable oils, etc., especially on a field scale. Fruit and vegetable production is usually considered as a specialized farming activity (*see* horticulture). The methods employed in arable farming depend on the crop being grown, the climate and soil type of the region, farming traditions, and the economic state of the farmer and his market. Arable farming is often carried out in conjunction with livestock farming, enabling the farmer to grow his own animal feeds and to make use of animal manures as *fertilizers. Grass is the chief feed for *ruminant livestock and a major arable crop. Special seed mixtures are sown to produce either permanent pasture or a temporary grass meadow lasting only a few years, often as part of a system of *crop rotation. Apart from grazing, grass is cut and conserved for winter food as either hay (dried grass) or *silage.

Cereal crops are a principal source of food for man and are important animal feed. The major cereals are wheat, barley, rice, and corn with oats, millet, sorghum, and rye cultivated to a lesser extent. Wheat may be sown either in autumn or spring, according to the variety, and is harvested in late summer when the grain is hard, yielding between 0.6 and 1.5 tons of grain per acre. Cereals are harvested using a *combine harvester and the grain is often dried to ensure safe storage.

Beans are grown as a major source of vegetable protein, the most important being soybeans, produced chiefly in China and the US. They are harvested mechanically using a specially adapted combine harvester that separates the beans from the rest of the crop. Harvesting root crops, such as potatoes and sugar beets, requires specialized machines that excavate the crop and remove soil. Turnips and rutabagas are root crops grown mainly for animal fodder. Crops grown for their oil content include sunflower, peanut, linseed, cottonseed, and rape; cotton, flax, and jute are important sources of textile fibers. Many other crops, including tea, coffee, and tobacco, are of major economic importance and each requires specialized husbandry techniques to give maximum yields. Modern scientific investigation of arable crops (*see* agronomy) and their requirements, together with innovations in mechanization, fertilizers, pesticides, *irrigation, and plant breeding, have resulted in dramatic increases in crop yields and productivity, bringing about a Green Revolution in western countries and, more recently, in developing countries.

Arabs A Semitic people originally inhabiting the Arabian peninsula. They are roughly divided into two cultural groups: the nomadic *Bedouin tribes and the settled communities of the towns and oases. Wealth from oil has recently led to industrialization and westernization in the towns, but Islam remains a strong conservative force in social customs, particularly in the restrictions it places upon women's role in society. The Arabs were known in antiquity to the Greeks, Romans, and Jews and are mentioned by name in the later Old Testament books. They appeared as a power in world history early in the 7th century AD, with the rise of Islam, and they carried their language (*see* Arabic), religion, and culture as far as Spain in the W and Indonesia in the E. In modern usage "Arab" designates Arabic-speaking peoples of SW Asia, Egypt, N Africa, and parts of sub-Saharan Africa, whether or not they are of Arab descent.

Aracajú 10 54S 37 07W A city and port in NE Brazil, the capital of Sergipe state near the mouth of the Rio Continguiba. It is a commercial and industrial center; the chief industries are sugar refining, cotton milling, and tanning. Its university was founded in 1967. Population (1980): 293,485.

Arachne In Greek mythology, a girl from Lydia who defeated Athena in a tapestry-weaving contest. The jealous goddess destroyed all Arachne's work; she attempted to hang herself, but Athena changed her into a spider.

arachnid An invertebrate animal belonging to an order (*Arachnida*; 65,000 species) of chiefly terrestrial *arthropods, including the *spiders, *scorpions, *harvestmen (daddy-longlegs), *ticks, and *mites. An arachnid's body is divided into two parts: a combined head and thorax (cephalothorax) and an abdomen. The cephalothorax bears four pairs of legs and two pairs of head appendages, one of which consists of strong pincer-like claws. Arachnids are mostly carnivorous, feeding on the body juices of insects and other small animals; many secrete poison from specialized glands to kill prey or enemies. Others are parasites, some of which are carriers of disease. Arachnids usually lay eggs, which hatch into immature adults.

Arad 46 10N 21 19E An industrial city in W Romania, on the Mures River. It was Austro-Hungarian until 1919 and has a large Hungarian community. Population (1985 est): 185,900.

Arafat, Yasser (1929–   ) Palestinian leader. Committed to military confrontation with *Israel as a means of restoring the territory and rights of the Palestinians, Arafat was one of the founders of al-Fatah, also known as the Palestinian National Liberation Movement, which began guerrilla warfare and terrorism against Israel in the late 1950s. Arafat became the president in 1968 of the *Palestine Liberation Organization, which was recognized in 1974 by the *Arab League as the sole legitimate representative of the Palestinian people. Arafat's flamboyant style and personal charisma helped the PLO to survive expulsion from Jordan in 1970, evacuation from Beirut in 1982, and divisiveness among Palestinian factions in the late 1980s and early 1990s. In 1993 he took part in agreements with Israel.

Arafura Sea A shallow section of the W Pacific Ocean between Australia and New Guinea. It contains uncharted rocks, which make navigation dangerous.

Arago, (Dominique) François (Jean) (1786–1853) French astronomer and physicist, who was professor of physics at the École Polytechnique in Paris. He did important work in astronomy, electricity, magnetism, meteorology, and optics (particularly polarized light). He was an advocate of the wave theory of light and worked with *Fresnel to obtain experimental evidence to support it.

Aragon A region and medieval kingdom in NE Spain, of which Ramoir I (d. 1063) was the first king (1035–63). A series of conquests during the 11th and 12th centuries brought the Aragonese rule over much of N Spain. Union with Catalonia was secured by marriage in 1140. Later expansion gave the Aragonese Sicily (1282) and Sardinia (1320) and culminated in the conquest by *Alfonso the Magnanimous of the kingdom of Naples (1442). In 1469 *Ferdinand the Catholic, heir to the Aragonese throne, married *Isabella the Catholic of Castile, and on his accession in 1479 the two kingdoms were united.

Aragon, Louis (1897–1982) French poet, novelist, and journalist. In 1919 he and André *Breton founded the surrealist journal *Littérature*; his first books of poetry, *Feu de joie* (1920) and *Le Mouvement perpétuel* (1925), and his novel, *Le Paysan de Paris* (1926), are vigorously surrealist. He committed himself to communism and turned to Marxist-oriented social realism, especially in novels, such as *Holy Week* (1958) and the series entitled *Le Monde reél* (1933–51). He was editor of the left-wing weekly *Les Lettres françaises*.

aragonite A white or grayish mineral consisting of calcium carbonate, usually with sharp orthorhombic crystals that are often twinned. With age, heat, or pressure aragonite changes into calcite and is therefore generally found in relatively young rocks. Many shells consist of aragonite.

Arakan A state in W Myanmar, extending along the Bay of Bengal and flanked by the Arakan Yoma, a mountain range rising over 1000 ft (3000 m). The principal economic activity is the cultivation of rice. The majority of the inhabitants are of Burmese descent but there is a large minority of Bengali Muslims in the N. *History*: a powerful kingdom in the 15th century, it was absorbed into Burma (1783) before passing to Britain (1826–1948). The activities of secessionist movements led to its change of status (from a division to a state) in 1975. Area: 14,191 sq mi (36,762 sq km). Population (1985): 2,046,000. Capital: Sittwe.

Arakcheev, Aleksei Andreevich, Count (1769–1834) Russian soldier and statesman. From 1796 to 1798 Arakcheev reorganized the Russian army but his brutality led to his dismissal. He was recalled by Alexander I in 1808 and became war minister. After Napoleon's defeat (1815) he served as minister of internal affairs, establishing many military-agricultural communities, in which Russia's army lived in times of peace. On the accession of Nicholas I in 1826 he resigned.

Aral Sea The fourth largest lake in the world, in Kazakhstan and Uzbekistan. It receives the Amu Darya and Syr Darya Rivers and has no outlets. Its maximum depth varies by 10%. Area: about 25,477 sq mi (66,000 sq km).

Aramaic A western branch of the Semitic group of languages. Its 22-character alphabet is the ancestor of both Hebrew and Arabic alphabets. Aramaic became extensively used during the late Babylonian empire and was the official language of the Persian Empire under *Darius I. It replaced Hebrew as the language of the Jews from about the time of the Exile in 605 BC until after the rise of Islam.

Aran Islands (Irish name: Arainn) A group of islands in Galway Bay, off the W coast of the Republic of Ireland, comprising Inishmore (the largest), Inishmaan, and Inisheer. Their harsh environment was portrayed in J. M. Synge's *Riders to the Sea*. Area: 18 sq mi (46 sq km). Chief town: Kilronan.

Aranjuez 40 02N 3 37W A city in central Spain, in New Castile on the Tagus River. Its fine palace (1778) was used by the Spanish court until 1890. It is a tourist resort and market town. Population (1970): 29,548.

Arany, János (1817–82) Hungarian poet. Born into a poor peasant family, he became a teacher, editor, and notary. His poem *Toldi* (1847), the adventures of a peasant youth at the 14th-century Hungarian court, was acclaimed as a national epic; he added two sequels, the romantic *Toldi szerelme* (1848) and the comic *Toldi estége* (1854). His powerful but melancholy ballads are perhaps his finest works.

Arapaho Group of North American Indians, of the Algonquian language. They were found in the Red River Valley in N Minnesota. Migration to the plains split up the group; the Northern Arapaho lived in Wyoming and the Southern Arapaho were found in Colorado. The Atsina or Gros Ventre Indians were also part of the Arapaho group. Closely related to the *Cheyenne and *Blackfoot Indians, the Arapaho's main ceremony was the sun dance. Presently, the Northern Arapaho are found on the Wind River Reservation, Wyo., the Southern in Oklahoma; and the Atsina on Fort Belknap Reservation in Montana.

Ararat, Mount (Turkish name: Ağrı Dağı) 39 44N 44 15E A mountain in E Turkey, near the Iranian border. It is volcanic in origin and isolated but for a secondary peak 7 mi (12 km) away. Traditionally, Noah's ark came to rest here after the flood (Genesis 8.4). Height: 16,946 ft (5165 m).

Araucanians Indians of central Chile, divided into three major groups, the Picunche, Mapuche, and Huilliche. They were farmers and herders of llamas, living in small autonomous hamlets of patrilineal kin. They could build in stone but lacked the elaborate culture of other Andean peoples, such as the *Inca. The Mapuche resisted Chilean rule until late in the 19th century. There are now about 200,000 living on reservations. The Araucanian language has been comparatively resistant to Spanish influence.

Araucaria A genus of coniferous trees (about 15 species), native to Australasia and South America (it is named for a district of Chile). They have whorled, horizontal branches covered with scale leaves, and male and female flowers usually grow on separate trees. The genus includes the ornamental *monkey puzzle and several trees yielding useful timber, including the Norfolk Island pine (*A. heterophylla*); the hoop pine (*A. cunninghamii*) and the bunya bunya (*A. bidwillii*), both from E Australia; and the parana pine (*A. angustifolia*), of Brazil. Family: *Araucariaceae*.

Arawak Indians of the Greater Antilles and northern and western areas of the Amazon basin. Their languages are the most widespread of the South American

Indian languages and include Goajiro in Colombia, Campa and Machiguenga in Peru, and Mojo and Bauré in Bolivia. They are sedentary farmers growing manioc and corn. Prior to the Spanish conquests they were divided into numerous hereditary chiefdoms. They were never a warlike people and in the Caribbean area *Carib tribes frequently raided Arawak groups and enslaved Arawak women. Their religion involved belief in personal guardian spirits. The tribal gods were the spirits of chiefs represented by a hierarchy of idols called zemis, which were housed in temples.

Arbil. *See* Irbil.

arbitration 1. A method of settling a commercial dispute in which each party presents his case to a disinterested third party (arbitrator). The disinterested third party is chosen by the disputing parties. The disputing parties agree beforehand to abide by the third party's decision. This method of settling disputes is widely used in commerce because it is quicker and cheaper than litigation. **2.** An attempt to settle an industrial dispute by submitting the case to an arbitrator, such as a government conciliation service. In this case the award is usually accepted as morally binding on both sides, but usually it is an issue, such as wage rates, that cannot be settled by law.

arborvitae A coniferous tree of the genus *Thuja* (6 species), native to North America and E Asia. They have scalelike leaves, which densely cover the flattened stems, and small scaly cones, 0.4–0.7 in (1–1.8 cm) long. The Chinese arborvitae or cedar (*T. orientalis*), which grows to a height of 98 ft (30 m), is a popular ornamental tree; the giant arborvitae, or western red cedar (*T. plicata*), of W North America, grows to a height of 130 ft (40 m) and yields a valuable timber. Family: *Cupressaceae*.

Arbutus A genus of evergreen trees and shrubs (about 20 species) distributed in Central and North America and W Europe. The small white or pinkish flowers are borne in terminal clusters and the berries are fleshy and reddish. The leaves are tough, dark green, toothed, and shiny above. The strawberry tree (*A. unedo*) of SW Europe is widely grown as an ornamental, reaching a height of 30 ft (9 m) Family: *Ericaceae*.

Arcadia A mountainous region of ancient Greece, in the central Pelopponesus, that was identified in the literature of Greece, Rome, and the Renaissance (e.g. in Sidney's *Arcadia*) as an earthly paradise. It is a modern department.

Arc de Triomphe A ceremonial arch standing at the center of the Étoile at the top of the Champs Elysées in Paris. It was commissioned to celebrate the victories of *Napoleon I and built between 1806 and 1836 to the designs of Jean Chalgrin (1739–1811).

arch In architecture, a structure spanning a horizontal space. The development of the arch was one of the greatest Roman contributions to building technology. By using interlocking and mutually supporting pieces of stone, it is possible to span greater distances than can be achieved with single megaliths; also, arches can be employed to provide a more even distribution of pressure throughout the building. The basic forms of arch are the pointed, or Gothic, arch and the rounded, or classical, arch.

Archangel (Russian name: Arkhangelsk) 64 32N 40 40E A port in NW Russia on the Dvina River, 30 mi (50 km) from the White Sea. Founded in 1584, it was Russia's leading port until the early 18th century. Russia's largest timber-exporting port, it has timber-processing and shipbuilding industries and also supports a fishing fleet. Population (1991 est): 428,000.

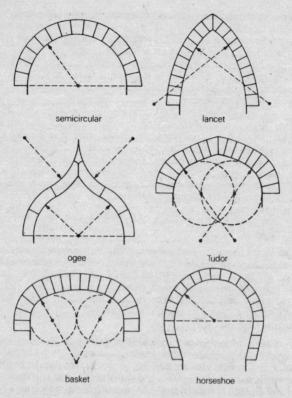

semicircular   lancet

ogee   Tudor

basket   horseshoe

ARCH *The semicircular arch characterized Roman, Romanesque, and Norman architecture; the lancet, ogee, Tudor, and basket arches were Gothic and later medieval developments; the horseshoe arch is typical of Islamic architecture.*

archangels In Christian belief, supernatural beings ranked immediately above *angels in the celestial hierarchy. Michael is the only archangel mentioned in the New Testament (Jude); in Revelation 12 he is the leader of the angels who cast out the dragon from heaven. Gabriel, as the angel of the annunciation, is traditionally included among the archangels, as is Raphael, the helper of Tobias in the apocryphal Book of Tobit. Another archangel, Uriel, is named in II Esdras.

archbishop A chief bishop who has some jurisdiction over the other bishops in an ecclesiastical province, i.e. a group of dioceses, as well as having authority in his own diocese. Until the 8th or 9th century such men were called "metropolitans," a title still used by Orthodox Christians whose archbishops are of lower rank. Some Roman Catholic archbishops have no provincial authority, their titles being merely honorary. The Church of England has only the Archbishops of Canterbury and of York.

archegonium The reproductive organ producing the female cells (gametes) in ferns, mosses, algae, fungi, and some gymnosperms. It is flask-shaped, the swollen base containing the egg cell and the neck providing an entrance for the male gametes.

archeology The scientific study that is concerned with the recovery and interpretation of the material remains of man's past. Archeology may be supplemented by written records, where they exist, but its techniques are principally concerned with nonliterary evidence for man's social and cultural development. Modern archeology has numerous specialized branches—classical, industrial, underwater, etc. Before the 19th century, digging was carried out to plunder precious objects from ruins. Scientific excavation followed the realization that often more could be learned from the surroundings in which objects are discovered than from the objects themselves. Essential techniques include stratigraphy, based on the principle that in any sequence of deposits the uppermost is latest and the lowest earliest, and typology, the study of changes in forms (e.g. of pottery). New methods of dating constantly evolve: *radiometric dating, *paleomagnetism, *thermoluminescence, *varve dating, and *dendrochronology are all valuable with different types of material.

Archeopteryx A genus of extinct primitive birds, fossils of which date from the Jurassic period (160–120 million years ago). It had many reptilian features, such as numerous teeth, a long, bony tail, and claws on the hand, but was fully feathered and is believed to be the ancestor of modern birds. *Archeopteryx* lived in dense forests, climbing trees using its claws and gliding down in search of food.

archer fish A small fish of the genus *Toxotes*, especially *T. jaculatrix*, which occurs in coastal and estuarine waters of SE Asia and Australia. Up to 7 in (18 cm) long, archer fish capture flying insects by firing a stream of water droplets through the mouth and are able to shoot down prey over distances of more than 40 in (1 m). Family: *Toxotidae*.

archery A sport in which generally a specified number of arrows are shot at a target over a prescribed distance. The modern bow developed from the medieval longbow, but the skill of shooting arrows from a bow dates back 30 millenniums. **Target archery** consists of shooting at a target of standard size marked with five or ten scoring zones. Different competitions require different permutations of distances and numbers of arrows. **Field archery** consists of shooting at large animal figures with superimposed scoring rings. In **clout shooting** arrows are shot into the air to fall on a target marked on the ground, while in **flight shooting** the purpose is to achieve the maximum distance. Archery is an amateur sport, governed internationally by the Fédération internationale de Tir à l'Arc (founded 1931).

Arches National Park A national park in SE Utah. Established as a national monument in 1929 and as a national park in 1971, it features wind-eroded rock formations of giant arches. Area: 130 sq mi (336 sq km).

Archilochus (c. 680–c. 640 BC) Greek poet. Probably the bastard son of an aristocrat of Paros and a slave woman, he was forbidden to marry Neobule by her father Lycambes, who became the target of viciously satirical poems. Archilochus became a mercenary soldier and probably died in battle. His poems, only fragments of which survive, range from the lyrical to the biting, and are frequently colloquial in style.

Archimedes (c. 287–c. 212 BC) Greek mathematician and inventor, regarded as the greatest scientist of classical times. Archimedes was born in Syracuse, Sicily, and studied in Alexandria, afterward returning to Syracuse, where he remained for the rest of his life. He is best known for his discovery of *Archimedes' principle, supposedly in response to the King of Syracuse asking him to determine whether a gold crown had been adulterated with silver. Legend has it

ARCHEOLOGY

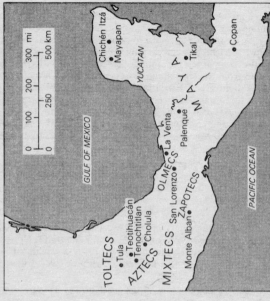

Pre-Columbian Mesoamerica *The principal ancient Mesoamerican peoples and the sites of their towns (c. 1000 BC–1500 AD).*

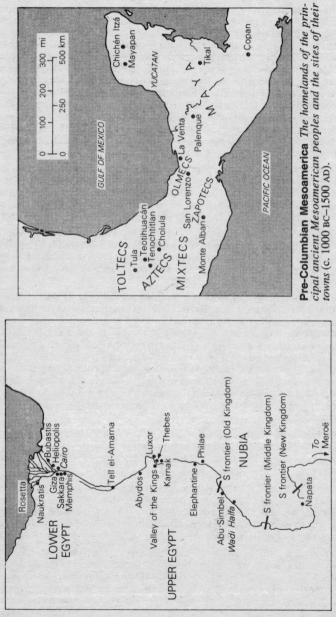

Ancient Egypt *Civilization grew up in the narrow fertile strip along the banks of the Nile (c. 4500–343 BC).*

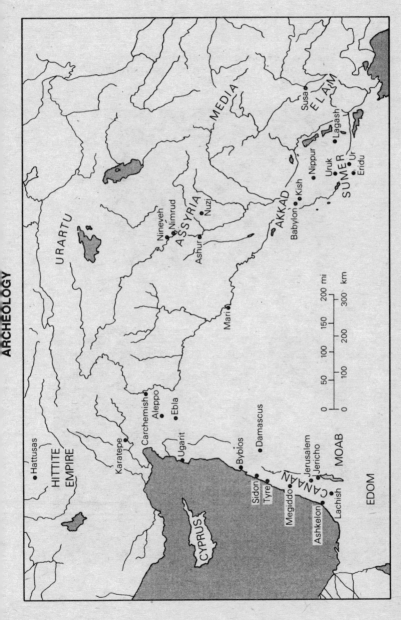

Mesopotamia and the Levant *Kingdoms and towns* (c. 2000–700 BC).

ARCHEOLOGY

The discovery and subsequent restoration of an Early Bronze Age jar, which was excavated at Myrtos (Crete) in 1968 (see below).

ARCHEOLOGY

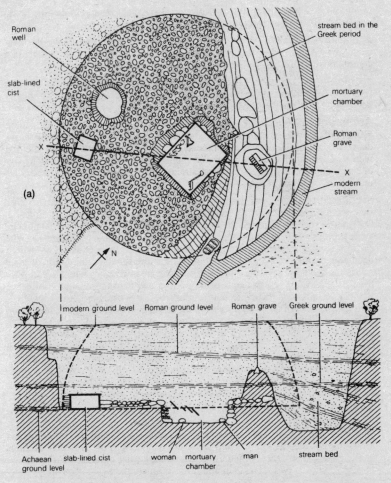

(a) *A plan of an ancient Greek burial mound showing the relative positions of the original mortuary chamber and other burials in the mound.*
(b) *A stratigraphic section (through XX) of the same mound showing the comparative levels of the ground at various periods.*

that he made his discovery while taking a bath and ran through the streets of Syracuse shouting "Eureka!" He is also credited with the invention of *Archimedes' screw, although the device was probably already known to the Egyptians. He was killed by a soldier during the Roman invasion of Syracuse.

Archimedes' principle The principle that when a body is partly or wholly immersed in a fluid its apparent loss of weight is equal to the weight of the liquid displaced. Named for *Archimedes.

Archimedes' screw A device for raising water, reputed to have been invented by *Archimedes. It consists of an inclined helical screw rotated about a central axis in a trough of water.

archipelago A group of islands within close proximity to each other. The term was formerly used for the sea in which the islands are scattered, originally being applied to the Aegean Sea.

Archipenko, Alexander (1887–1964) Russian-born sculptor and painter. From 1908 he worked in Paris, where he was associated with *cubism. He introduced the use of the hole as an elemental part of sculpture and created the first works of art combining sculpture and painting. His sculptures of moving figures, which were abstracted into geometrical shapes, declined in quality after his move to New York (1923).

architecture The art of designing and constructing buildings that are both functionally and aesthetically satisfying. Factors principally influencing an architect are: the use to which the building will be put; the materials obtainable; the resources available in money and labor; and contemporary artistic taste. The earliest civilizations built on a monumental scale for their gods or the deified dead (*see* pyramids; ziggurat). Secular architecture reflected the needs of local rulers for security, comfort, and—very important—display. The Greeks were the first to develop the concepts of proportion and harmony that still influence western architectural theory. Roman engineers greatly extended flexibility of design by their use of arches and domes. Medieval European architecture reached its zenith in the Gothic *cathedral but the Renaissance brought a resurgence of interest in all types of building; the rediscovered principles of classical architecture dominated theory and practice until the *Gothic revival at the beginning of the 19th century. In the 20th century technical advances in the use of prestressed concrete opened the way to modern architecture; while the necessities of engineering increasingly determine a building's appearance, the best modern architects demonstrate that architecture can still survive as an art form.

archons The supreme magistrates in most ancient Greek city states. At Athens there were nine archons, including an eponymous archon, who was the chief archon and gave his name to the year, a king-archon (responsible for religion), and a polemarch (responsible for military affairs). In origin the Athenian archons were a ruling aristocracy, which had replaced the earlier monarchy. After 487 BC they were chosen by lot and their authority declined, their role becoming chiefly judicial.

Archytas (early 4th century BC) Greek mathematician, from Tarentum (S Italy). Famous in antiquity as an innovator in many fields of mathematics, he distinguished between geometrical, arithmetical, and harmonic progressions, worked out the numerical relations between notes of different musical scales, and found a geometrical construction to double the cube.

Arcimboldo, Giuseppe (1527–93) Mannerist painter, born in Milan. He moved to Prague in 1562, becoming painter and designer of court pageants to successive Hapsburg emperors. Contemporaries praised his ingenious symbol-

ARCHITECTURE

Sagrada Familia (1903–26; Barcelona) *By Antonio Gaudi y Cornet.*

The Seagram Building (1956–58; New York) *By Mies van der Rohe and Philip Johnson.*

Guggenheim Museum (1956–59; New York) *By Frank Lloyd Wright.*

154

ARCHITECTURE

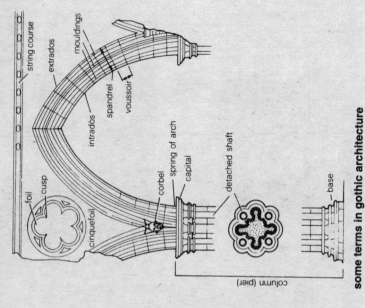

some terms in classical architecture

some terms in gothic architecture

ARCHITECTURE

base | shaft | capital | entablature

Doric   Tuscan   Ionic   Corinthian   Composite

plan

the orders of classical architecture

Chapel Notre-Dame-du-Haut (1950–55; Ronchamp)
By Le Corbusier.

Georges Pompidous Center
(1972–77; Paris) *By Richard
Rogers and Renzo Piano.*

Sydney Opera House (1957–73)
By Joern Utzon.

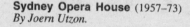

ARCHITECTURE *The early 20th century, just before World War I, saw the birth
of the modern movement in architecture. The use of steel and the introduction of
reinforced concrete (first used in France), together with the extensive use of glass,
enabled new architectural concepts, such as the skyscraper, to be developed.
Modern architecture has been characterized by a functional approach and a
greater freedom in design.*

ism and he is remembered for his grotesque portraits, such as the head of a cook composed of pots and pans, fish and meat.

Arctic Circle The area around the North Pole enclosed by the parallel of latitude 66°32"N. It includes parts of Greenland, the Soviet Union, the US, Canada, and Scandinavia and extensive areas of ice-covered ocean, notably the Arctic Ocean. Within the Arctic Circle the sun remains below the level of the horizon for a period of time in winter and remains above it in summer; the length of time for which this occurs increases poleward. The population consists mainly of Eskimos, who live by hunting. *History*: during the 16th century exploration of the Arctic by the Dutch and English began in the search for a Northeast or Northwest Passage to the Far East. In 1725–42 the Russian Imperial Navy carried out exploration under the direction of Peter the Great and Russia became the most active of the Arctic explorers. In 1879 a US expedition under G. W. De Long (1844–81) became trapped in the ice while attempting to reach the North Pole and its ship was crushed. Wreckage found off the coast of Greenland having drifted across the Arctic Ocean suggested that a sea route through the ice was possible. The Norwegian Fridtjof *Nansen in the *Fram* drifted for nearly two years (1893–95) through the ice and proved that the North Pole was within an ice-covered sea. Robert E. *Peary was the first to reach the North Pole (1909). Since then extensive exploration has been carried out with mapping and geological and meteorological studies; the Soviet Union was particularly active and, like the US, established several drifting scientific stations.

Arctic fox A small fox, *Alopex lagopus*, found throughout tundra regions. It feeds on birds and small □mammals, especially lemmings and Arctic hares, and grows a dense woolly coat of fur in winter. There are two color varieties; the white fox, which has a white winter coat and a brown summer coat; and the blue fox, which is dark gray in summer and pale gray in winter. Arctic foxes have been farmed commercially for their fur.

Arctic Ocean The world's smallest ocean, almost completely enclosed by North America, Eurasia, and Greenland. Explored since the 17th century, it is covered by ice.

Arctic tern A slender, red-billed *tern, *Sterna paradisaea*, up to 15 in (38 cm) long and having a white plumage with gray wings and a black crown. It breeds in coastal regions from N Britain to the Arctic and migrates to Antarctic seas in winter.

Arcturus A conspicuous, *red giant in the constellation Boötes that is the brightest star in the N sky. It has an apparent magnitude of −0.05 and is 36 light years distant. The three stars in the handle of the *Plow curve in its direction.

Ardashir I Shah of Persia (224–41 AD), who founded the Sasanian dynasty. In 224 Ardashir defeated and killed the last Parthian ruler at the battle of Hormizdagan. He made *Zoroastrianism the state religion and is honored in Zoroastrian tradition.

Ardebil 38 15N 48 18E A city in NW Iran, close to the Caspian Sea. It has a carpet- and rug-making industry. Population (1986): 281,973.

Ardennes A chain of hills in W Europe. It extends through N Luxembourg, S Belgium, and NE France at an average height of about 1640 ft (500 m), forming the watershed between the Meuse and Moselle Rivers. Chiefly wooded, agriculture is limited to pastoralism. There was heavy fighting here in both World Wars.

are (a) A unit of area in the *metric system equal to 100 square meters. The *hectare is more frequently used than the are.

Areca. *See* betel.

Arendt, Hannah (1906–75) US political theorist and author; born in Germany. She fled Nazi Germany and came to the United States in 1941. After *The Origins of Totalitarianism* (1951) was published, she taught at several universities. Her works include *The Human Condition* (1958), *Eichmann in Jerusalem* (1963), *Crises of the Republic* (1972), and the unfinished 3-volume *The Life of the Mind* (1978).

Areopagus A hill in Athens, Greece, NW of the Acropolis and the name of the ancient Athenian court that met there. Originally an aristocratic council, the Areopagus became primarily a homicide court after about 462 BC, when its political authority was transferred to the democratic assembly.

Arequipa 16 25S 71 32W A city in S Peru. Originally an Inca city, it was refounded by the Spanish (1540). Notable buildings include the cathedral (1612) and two universities. It is an important commercial center and the wool-processing center of Peru. Population (1990 est): 622,000.

Ares The Greek god of war, identified by the Romans with *Mars. Son of Zeus and Hera, his popularity never rivaled that of the other Olympian gods. He loved *Aphrodite, by whom he had three offspring, Deimos, Phobos, and Hàrmonia.

Aretino, Pietro (1492–1556) Italian satirist. Son of a shoemaker, he claimed to be the bastard son of a nobleman. He lived in Rome (1517–27), patronized by Pope Leo X and becoming famous for his vicious satires and bawdy lyrics. He then settled in Venice, where he made a fortune by writing scurrilous satires on people or by being bribed not to do so. His letters, published in six volumes (1537–57), provide a vivid portrait both of Aretino and of his times. The earthy *Ragionamenti* (1534–36) portrayed the underworld of prostitutes. He also wrote five comedies.

Arezzo 43 28N 11 53E A city in central Italy, in Tuscany. Originally an Etruscan settlement, it has many fine medieval buildings. Petrarch was born here. A market town, it has various industries. Population (1990 est): 92,000.

argali A race of mountain-dwelling sheep, *Ovis ammon*, of central Asia. Argalis are the largest Eurasian wild sheep, reaching a weight of 375 lbs (170 kg) and having massive deeply ridged, curved horns. They live in herds and graze at very high altitudes during the summer.

Argenteuil 48 52N 2 20E A city in France, a NW suburb of Paris on the Seine River. An industrial center, it developed around the 7th-century convent of which Héloïse was abbess. Population (1982): 96,045.

Argentina, Republic of The second largest country in South America, occupying almost all the land S of the Tropic of Capricorn and E of the Andes. It includes the E part of the island of Tierra del Fuego and has claims to the *Falkland Islands and their dependencies in the Antarctic. It consists chiefly of subtropical plains and forests (the Gran Chaco) in the N, the fertile temperate pampas in the center, the Andes in the W, and the semidesert Patagonian plateau in the S. The inhabitants are almost entirely European in origin, mainly Italian and Spanish, with a very small and dwindling Indian population. *Economy*: chiefly agricultural with stock rearing, especially cattle, having overwhelming importance. The main industries have traditionally been meat processing and packing but there has been recent growth in a variety of areas, including oil refining, plastics, textiles, and chemicals. Natural-gas deposits have been intensively explored and developed and Argentina is practically self-sufficient in oil, the most notable oilfields being around Comodoro Rivadavia. There are plans to increase the use of hydroelectric power and nuclear energy is also being developed. Main exports include meat and meat products (badly affected by the EEC ban on meat imports in 1974), wool, cereals, minerals, and metals. *History*: colonized by the Spanish from 1515 onward. During this period the native Indian inhabitants, who had previously had to defend themselves against the Incas, put up a fierce resistance but by the 19th century they had almost been wiped out. The country gained its independence in 1816, under José de San Martín, and a new constitution in 1853 marked the end of a period of civil war and unrest. Since the late 19th century Argentina has been ruled for most of the time by a series of military dictatorships. Most prominent among the rulers since World War II has been Lt. Gen. Juán *Perón, who came to power in 1946. Following the death (1952) of his very popular wife, Eva, his power was weakened and in 1955 he was overthrown in a military revolution. The Perónist movement, however, continued to attract strong popular support and in 1973, following the election of one of his supporters, Dr. Hector Campóra, he returned to power but died the following year. He was succeeded by his second wife, Isabel, but as the economic situation continued to deteriorate and political violence and industrial unrest increased, many allegations of corruption were made against her government. In 1976 Lt. Gen. Jorge Rafael Videla came to power at the head of a three-man junta and strong measures were introduced to combat the violence and unrest and to steady the economy. Lt. Gen. Roberto Viola succeeded Videla as president in 1981 but was later removed from office by the military junta, led by Gen. Leopoldo Galtieri, who subsequently became president in December, 1981. On Apr 2, 1982, Argentina launched an invasion of the Falkland Islands (which it calls the Islas Malvinas) but following armed conflict with a task force sent by the UK was forced to surrender on June 14, 1982. This defeat forced Galtieri's resignation and he was succeeded as president by Reynaldo Bignone. In 1983 the junta under Bignone was forced to call a popular election. After eight years of military rule, which was characterized by "death squads," left-wing terrorist reprisals, and a ruined economy, Raul Alfonsín was elected president in an unexpected victory over the Perónist Party candidate. Pledging to bring democratic government to Argentina and to the right-wing Perónist labor party, Alfonsín brought exiled Isabel Perón back into political life in an attempt to unify the country.

In the 1980s Argentina faced the worst economic crisis of its history. Staggering international debt that threatened to precipitate a world banking crisis brought demands for economic austerity measures from the International Monetary Fund, one of its chief lending agents. This, combined with an inflation rate over 600%, all-time high prices, and ongoing general strikes, placed the country in a severe economic and social position. Perónist Carlos Saul Menem was elected president in 1989. He initiated programs to stabilize the economy, unite the country, and improve foreign relations, but his administration was charged with widespread corruption. Despite a renewal of full diplomatic relations with Britain in 1992, the Falkland Islands sovereignty issue continued to be debated. Official language: Spanish. Official religion: Roman Catholic. Official currency: new peso of 100 centavos. Area: 1,072,515 sq mi (2,777,815 sq km). Population (1990 est): 32,290,000. Capital and main port: Buenos Aires.

argentite An important ore of silver, sometimes called silver glance. It is a sulfide of silver, found in association with other sulfide ores, such as lead, zinc, and copper.

argon (Ar) A noble gas that occurs in the atmosphere (0.94%). Although previously observed in the solar spectrum, it was first isolated in 1894 by Rayleigh and Ramsay, by the distillation of liquid air. Because it is chemically inert, it is used to fill fluorescent lamps and as an inert gas blanket for welding reactive metals. At no 18; at wt 39.948; mp −308.6°F (−189.2°C); bp −302.3°F (−185.7°C).

Argonauts In Greek mythology, the 50-man crew of *Jason's ship *Argo*, on the quest of the *Golden Fleece. Accounts of its composition vary, but all agree that it included the shipbuilder Argo, the tireless helmsman Tiphys, the keen-sighted Lynceus, *Heracles and his follower Hylas, and even *Orpheus and the Dioscuri, *Castor and Pollux. During the voyage the Argonauts encountered such perils as the *Sirens, the *Harpies, the Symplegades (moving rocks that crushed ships) and the bronze giant Talos.

Argonne A hilly forested area in NE France. It was the scene of heavy fighting during both World Wars.

Argos 37 38N 22 43E A town in the NE Peloponnese (S Greece). Belonging in Homeric times to a follower of *Agamemnon, Argos gave its name to the surrounding district (the Argolid). Eclipsed by nearby Sparta after the 6th century BC, Argos remained neutral or the ineffective ally of Athens during the 5th-century struggles between Sparta and Athens. Considerable remains of the city survive.

Århus (*or* Aarhus) 56 10N 10 13E A seaport in Denmark, in E Jutland. One of the oldest Danish cities, it has a Gothic cathedral, a university (1928); and oil re-fining, machinery, and textile industries. Population (1987 est): 255,000.

aria (Italian: air) A solo song with instrumental accompaniment, usually in an opera or oratorio. The name was originally also used for separate instrumental pieces but its meaning became restricted with the development of the three part *aria da capo* in the works of Monteverdi, Scarlatti, and Handel. Attacked as un-dramatic by reformers, such as Gluck and Wagner, the aria form is little used in modern opera.

Ariadne In Greek legend, the daughter of *Minos, King of Crete, and Pasiphaë. She helped *Theseus to kill the Minotaur and escape from its labyrinth. He abandoned her on the island of Naxos, where she was found by *Dionysus, who married her.

Arianism A Christian heresy started by *Arius, which held that the Son of God, Jesus Christ, was not truly divine. In 325 AD the Council of Nicaea ban-ished the Arians, who included some influential bishops, and affirmed that the Father and the Son were coequal, coeternal, and "of one substance." Although the Arians were soon restored and a version of the heresy was accepted for a time, Arianism was finally defeated at the Council of Constantinople in 381 AD.

Arica 18 30S 70 20W An oasis city and port in N Chile, on the Pacific Ocean. A railroad line connects it with La Paz in Bolivia and it handles about half of Bolivia's trade. Population (1989 est): 175,000.

Aries (Latin: Ram) A constellation in the N sky, lying on the *zodiac between Taurus and Pisces. The brightest star, Hamal, is of 2nd magnitude.

Arias Sanchez, Oscar (1941–) Costa Rican president (1986–90). He was elected president from the National Liberation Party. Educated in England, he had served in several government posts from 1972. He favored Costa Rican neu-trality and was instrumental in promoting a peace plan for Central American countries, for which he received the Nobel Peace prize in 1987.

Arikara An Indian people of North America who lived along the Missouri River in what are now North and South Dakota. They were related to the *Pawnee in their language, and culture. They were expert corn growers and their farming villages were often trade centers visited by the nomadic hunting tribes. They practiced the sun-dance cult involving self-torture. There are today ap-proximately 700 living on the Fort Berthold Reservation.

Ariosto, Ludovico (1474–1533) Italian poet. He spent most of his life in the active service of the Este family. He is best known for his long epic poem. *Orlando furioso* (1516). One of the greatest works of the Italian Renaissance, it recounts the adventures of the paladin Roland (*see* Charlemagne) and the wars between the Franks and Saracens. It was published in its final revised form in 1532. Its precursor was the *Orlando innamorato* (1483) of *Boiardo.

Aristaeus In Greek legend, the son of *Apollo and the nymph Cyrene. He was the patron of bee keepers, and was credited with the introduction of the vine and the olive. According to Virgil, he caused the death of *Eurydice.

Aristagoras (5th century BC) Tyrant of *Miletus (Asia Minor). Aristagoras persuaded the Greek cities of *Ionia to rebel against Persian rule (499) but despite Athenian assistance the rebellion failed (494). He died fighting in Thrace.

Aristarchus of Samos (c. 310–230 BC) Greek astronomer, who maintained that the earth rotates upon its axis and orbits the sun. He made the first attempts to estimate trigonometrically the size and distance from the earth of the sun and the moon.

Aristarchus of Samothrace (c. 217–145 BC) Greek critic and grammarian. He was head of the great Library of Alexandria from about 180 to 145, and later retired to Cyprus. He edited important editions of *Homer and wrote commentaries on *Aeschylus, *Sophocles, *Herodotus, and many other writers.

Aristides the Just (c. 520–c. 468 BC) Athenian statesman and noted commander in the *Greek-Persian Wars. Ostracized (c. 485) because of his opposition to Themistocles' naval policy, Aristides returned in 480 and offered his services against the Persians, commanding land forces at Salamis. In 477 he was chosen to assess the tribute required from each member of the *Delian League.

Aristippus (c. 435–c. 356 BC) Greek philosopher and a pupil of *Socrates. Aristippus founded the Cyrenaic school of *hedonism and was exclusively concerned with practical morality (*see* Cyrenaics). He equated the highest good with pleasure, virtue he equated with the rationally controlled pursuit of enjoyment.

Aristophanes (c. 450–c. 385 BC) Greek comic dramatist. He wrote about 40 plays, of which 11 survive: *The Acharnians* (425), *The Knights* (424), *The Clouds* (423), *The Wasps* (422), *The Peace* (421), *The Birds* (414), *Lysistrata* (411), *Thesmosphoriazusae* (410), *The Frogs* (405), *Women in Parliament* (393), and *Plutus* (388). His plots were satirical fantasies on contemporary topics, such as literature, *Socrates, social manners, and militaristic Athenian foreign policy; this led to his unsuccessful prosecution by the politician *Cleon.

Aristotelianism Tendencies in philosophical thought that originated with *Aristotle. Interpretations of his work appeared until the eclipse of ancient philosophy in the 6th century AD. Texts were preserved by Arab scholars, their work culminating in the 12th-century commentaries of *Averroes. *Aquinas in the 13th century made Aristotle the metaphysical basis of Christian theology but the Latin Averroists produced their own conflicting theories, holding, for instance, that a proposition can be philosophically true although theologically false. In the Renaissance the term Aristotelianism became synonymous with obscurantist opposition to new learning and science.

Aristotle (384–322 BC) Greek philosopher and scientist. His father was court physician in Macedonia. Aristotle joined *Plato's Academy at Athens (367–347) but, failing to become head of the Academy at Plato's death, he accepted the protection of Hermeias, ruler of Atarneus in Asia Minor, and married his patron's niece. About 343 *Philip of Macedon appointed Aristotle tutor to his son *Alexander, then aged 13. After Alexander's accession in 336, Aristotle founded, with generous assistance from Alexander, a research community complete with library and museum at Athens (the *Lyceum). There *Theophrastus studied botany and Aristoxenus (born c. 370) music, and Aristotle, among other projects, organized a comparative study of 158 constitutions of Greek states. When Alexander died in 323 BC, anti-Macedonian reaction at Athens forced Aristotle to withdraw to *Chalcis, where he died. Aristotle wrote over 400 books on every branch of learning, including logic, ethics, politics, metaphysics, biology, physics, psychology, poetry, and rhetoric. Ironically, those that survive (about one-quarter), edited by Andronicus of Rhodes about 40 BC, are apparently memoranda for his students' use, not intended for general publication. *See also* Aristotelianism.

arithmetic The branch of mathematics that deals with elementary theories of numbers, measurement, and computation. The fundamental operations of arithmetic are addition, subtraction, multiplication, and division. Addition and multiplication are assumed to obey the *associative law, the *commutative law, and the *distributive law. Other operations in arithmetic include extracting roots, raising a number to a power, and taking *logarithms. Arithmetic is also concerned with fractions and the various number systems, such as the *decimal system and the *binary system.

arithmetic progression (*or* arithmetic sequence) A sequence of numbers in which successive terms have a constant difference, for example, 1, 4, 7, 10, 13. . . .

Arius (c. 250–336) Libyan theologian, who initiated the heresy *Arianism. He was a priest at Alexandria until excommunicated for his views in 321. However, by enlisting the support of such prominent churchmen as *Eusebius, Arius developed his cause into a major controversy. At the first Council of *Nicaea (325) he was condemned through the influence of *Athanasius. Recalled from exile (c. 334), he died a few days before he was to be received back into the Church.

Arizona A state in the SW US. Utah lies to the N, New Mexico to the E, where the Colorado River forms the border; Mexico lies to the S and California and Nevada to the SW and NW. It falls into two natural regions: in the NE lies part of the Colorado Plateau, an area of dry plains and escarpments, and in the S and W is an area of desert basins and gentle valleys, drained by the Gila and Salt Rivers. The Colorado River flows through the Grand Canyon in the NW of the state. In such an arid region inadequate water supplies have long been a problem and a number of major irrigation projects have been built since the beginning of the 20th century. Most of the population lives in urban settlements in the S and W. Manufacturing (electrical, communications, aeronautical, and aluminum products) is the major industry. The state produces over half of the US's copper as well as gold, silver, oil, and timber. Tourism is an important source of revenue. The main crops are cotton, vegetables, and citrus fruits; livestock is also important. It is traditionally a center for Indian folk arts and crafts, having the largest Indian population in the US; the main tribes are the Navajo, Hopi, and Apache. *History*: inhabited by Indians as early as 25,000 BC, the area was explored by the Spanish in the 16th century. Following the Mexican War, Arizona, then part of New Mexico, was ceded to the US (1848). Prospectors heading for California during the 1849 gold rush discovered copper in Arizona. Within 20 years the industry was flourishing; Arizona became known as the Copper State. Arizona was part of the Confederacy during the Civil War. When Confederate troops were routed, many of the settlers fled the state leaving an almost entirely Indian population. Legislation such as the Homestead Act, giving land to settlers with the requirement that they worked it, encouraged resettlement. It was in Tombstone, famous for its lawlessness, that Wyatt Earp participated in the notorious gunfight at the O.K. Corral. Intermittent warfare with the Apaches made ranching and cattle raising precarious. The defeat of Geronimo, the Apache chief, in 1886, freed Arizona from the Indian threat, and ranching prospered. When Arizona received statehood in 1912, it was still a rugged and undeveloped territory. The Roosevelt Dam and subsequent federal irrigation projects marked the beginnings of its transformation into a thriving state. A desert region, with low precipitation, Arizona has had continual problems with the threat of water shortage. The water problem took another form in 1983 when early melting snows led to overflowing dams and a water release that caused the most severe flooding of the Colorado River in the state's history. In 1991, the Central Arizona Project, bringing water from the Colorado River to southern Arizona, was completed. Area: 113,909 sq mi (295,023 sq km). Population (1990): 3,665,228. Capital: Phoenix.

Arkansas A S central state of the US, lying W of the Mississippi River. Missouri lies to the N, Tennessee and Mississippi to the E, with the Mississippi River forming the E border; Louisiana lies to the S and Texas and Oklahoma to the W. It consists chiefly of the largely forested uplands of the N and W, descending to the Mississippi alluvial plain in the E and the West Gulf coastal plain in the S. The Arkansas River bisects the state from W to E. The state is no longer primarily agricultural although the Mississippi Plain provides rich fertile agricultural land; soybeans and rice have replaced cotton as the major crop. Oil production began in 1921; there are major lumbering, petroleum, and gas developments around Smackover and El Dorado and coal deposits in the Arkansas River Valley. The state produces 90% of US bauxite from an area to the S and SW of Little Rock. Manufacturing is chiefly of consumer goods. Arkansas remains, however, one of the poorest US states. *History*: explored by the Spanish and French in the 16th and 17th centuries, it formed part of the *Louisiana Purchase by the US in 1803. It became a state in 1836, seceded from the Union in 1861. The cotton-based economy suffered after the break-up of the plantation holdings, and a shift to sharecropping followed the Civil War. Arkansas farmers were subject to severe control by money and transportation interests. The Democratic Party, which has dominated the state since Reconstruction, gradually adopted legislative reforms that favored agriculture. However, the subsistence farming, poverty, and poor education that characterized the farmers of the Ozark Mountains has remained little changed. Their unique culture has been romanticized in American song and literature. Racial issues have often been central in Arkansas' history. Gov. Orville Faubus brought worldwide attention to Little Rock in 1957, when he called in the National Guard to prevent integration of the public schools, thereby defying a federal court order to integrate. Federal troops were sent to Little Rock to enforce the integration order. In 1983, West Memphis voters elected the first African-American mayor of a major Arkansas city. Former governor Bill *Clinton became the first president from Arkansas in 1993. Area: 153,104 sq mi (137,539 sq km). Population (1990): 2,350,725. Capital: Little Rock.

Arkansas River A river in the S central US, rising in central Colorado and flowing E and SE to join the Mississippi in Arkansas. Length: 1450 mi (2335 km).

Ark of the Covenant In the Old Testament, the sacred chest of the Israelites that contained the tablets of the law (*see* Ten Commandments) and was symbolic of God's presence and the *covenant made between God and Israel. Made of acacia wood, inlaid, and covered with gold, it was eventually placed in the Temple of Jerusalem. It probably disappeared during the *Babylonian exile. The shrine in a synagogue where the encased scrolls of the *Torah are kept is also called an ark or "holy ark" (*aron kodesh*).

ark shell A *bivalve mollusk belonging to a chiefly tropical family (*Arcidae*). Ark shells are boat-shaped and are attached to rocks by means of strong threads. The Noah's ark shell (*Arca tetragona*) occurs in rock crevices along the S coast of Britain and is about 1.8 in (4.5 cm) long.

Arkwright, Sir Richard (1732–92) British inventor and industrialist, who invented a spinning frame powered by water, the so-called water frame (patented in 1769). Arkwright subsequently mechanized other spinning processes and his mills were vandalized by spinners put out of work by the incipient factory system.

Arlberg Pass A mountain pass in W Austria, in the Alps, linking Vorarlberg with the Tirol by road. A railroad tunnel (completed 1884) cuts through the mountain for a distance of over 6 mi (10 km). Height: 5910 ft (1802 m).

Arles 43 41N 4 38E A town in SE France, in the Bouches-du-Rhône department on the Rhône delta. An important Roman settlement, it became the capital of Gaul in the 4th century AD and the capital of the kingdom of Arles (formed from the kingdoms of Burgundy and Provence) in the 10th century. It has many Roman remains, including an amphitheater. Other notable buildings include the 11th-century cathedral and the museum of arts and crafts founded by the poet Mistral. Several painters have lived and worked here, including Van Gogh and Gauguin. An agricultural market, it manufactures chemicals, machinery, and food products. Population (1982): 50,772.

Arlington National Cemetery The largest cemetery in the US, comprising 420 acres (170 hectares). Since 1864 it has been the burial ground of Americans killed in action and of eminent public servants.

arm In human anatomy, the upper limb, which extends from the shoulder to the wrist. The bone of the upper arm (the humerus) is connected by a ball-and-socket joint to the shoulder bone, permitting a wide range of movements. It forms a hinge joint at the elbow with the bones of the forearm (the ulna and radius), permitting movement in one plane only. The radius can be twisted across the ulna, enabling the palm of the hand to be turned upward.

Armada, Spanish The fleet of 130 ships sent by Philip II of Spain in 1588 to invade England. After indecisive encounters with the English fleet the Armada anchored off Calais only to be dispersed by English fireships during the night of July 28. A major engagement off Gravelines followed, in which the Armada was defeated. It suffered further losses in storms as it escaped around Scotland and Ireland, arriving in Spain with 86 ships. The defeat was a major psychological blow to Spain, which had claimed divine authority for its crusade against Protestant England.

armadillo A mammal belonging to the family *Dasypodidae* (12 species), widespread in open country in the southern US and South America. Armadillos have a covering of jointed bands or horny plates that enables them to roll themselves into a ball for protection. They have long-clawed toes for burrowing, simple, peglike teeth, and feed on insects and other invertebrates. Armadillos range in size from the giant armadillo (*Priodontes giganteus*), about 48 in (120 cm) long, to the rare pink fairy armadillo (*Chlamyphorus truncatus*), 5 in (12 cm) long. Order: *Edentata*.

Armageddon. *See* Megiddo.

Armagh An inland county in S Northern Ireland, bordering on the Republic of Ireland. It consists of lowlands in the N adjoining lough Neagh and low hills in the S. It is predominantly agricultural; produce includes potatoes, flax, and apples. There are few industries, the manufacture of linen having declined in importance. Area: 512 sq mi (1326 sq km). County town: Armagh.

Armenia Independent nation in SE Europe, formerly the Armenian SSR, a constituent republic of the Soviet Union. It is a densely populated and mountainous region, with no navigable rivers. Industry is developing rapidly and includes food processing, metallurgy, and chemicals. The rich mineral deposits include copper, lead, and zinc. The raising of livestock is the chief agricultural activity. *History*: the region formed the E part of the historic area inhabited by the *Armenians. It was acquired by Russia in 1828. The Russian province declared its independence in 1918 but it subsequently formed part of the Transcaucasian Soviet Federated Republic (*see* Transcaucasia). It became a separate republic in 1936. An earthquake in Dec 1988, destroyed much of the region around Kumayry (formerly Leninakan). The Armenian National Movement was formed in late 1989, leading to independence and membership in the *Commonwealth of Independent Nations (CIS) in 1991. Armenia joined the UN in 1992. Disputes with Azerbaijan led to fighting in 1993. Area: 11,490 sq mi (29,800 sq km). Population (1987 est): 3,412,000. Capital: Yerevan.

Armenian Church The Church founded by St Gregory the Illuminator (c. 240–332) about 300 AD. Armenia was the first nation to adopt Christianity as a state religion. Its Church is the second largest of the Eastern Christian Churches and has much in common with the others as regards dogma and liturgy, although it has also absorbed some Western influences. The head of the Church is the Patriarch of Etchmiadzin, called the Catholicos. There are Armenian churches in several parts of the world.

Armenians A people of NE Turkey and SW Russia speaking an Indo-European language. Approximately 1.5 million live in Turkey, Europe, and America and 4 million in the country of Armenia with smaller numbers in Georgia and Azerbaijan. Their culture is ancient and highly developed, with a literature written in an alphabet derived from Greek and Syriac script. Their language is the only representative of a distinct branch of the Indo-European family. Herodotus claimed they were related to the ancient Phrygians. They call themselves Hay and their land Hayastan. They are mainly Monophysite Christians and belong to the *Armenian Church. During the 19th and 20th centuries they suffered massacres at the hands of the Ottoman Turks, their rulers since the 16th century, who feared the growing influence of nationalism among them.

Arminius (c. 18 BC–17 AD) Leader of the Germanic tribe of the Cherusci, famous as a master of the surprise attack. He organized a revolt against the Romans (9 AD), destroying three Roman legions. Defeated (16 AD) by Germanicus, Arminius nevertheless thwarted the Roman conquest of Germany. He was killed by a pro-Roman German tribesman.

Arminius, Jacobus (1560–1609) Dutch Protestant theologian and reformer. A pupil of *Beza, he was a professor of theology at Leiden. Current Calvinist theology taught that God preordained some men to salvation and others to destruction. Arminius, however, emphasized God's grace and man's freedom to accept or reject salvation. This doctrine was later known as Arminianism.

armor Defensive equipment used as protection in warfare. Body armor (helmet, breastplate, greaves) was used in Bronze Age Greece. The Romans evolved heavier armor for both men and horses. In the early Middle Ages *chain mail was widely used but after about 1300 plate armor, often sumptuously decorated and encasing the whole body, was worn by knights on horseback. Gunpowder gradually rendered body armor obsolete, although in World War I metal helmets were revived as a protection from shrapnel.

Armor is also used to protect modern war vehicles and their occupants against projectiles or fragments. Armor plate includes hardened metal alloys cast in varying thicknesses and designed to be mounted with sloping surfaces to give protection against armor-piercing projectiles. Its considerable weight prompted the development of armor made from light alloys and plastics, using multiple skins to inhibit projectile penetration.

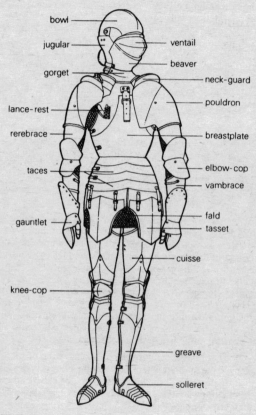

bowl
jugular
ventail
beaver
gorget
neck-guard
lance-rest
pouldron
rerebrace
breastplate
taces
elbow-cop
vambrace
gauntlet
fald
tasset
cuisse
knee-cop
greave
solleret

ARMOR *The skill of the European armorer reached its height in the late 15th and early 16th centuries when suits of plate armor were made to cover the entire body.*

armored car A wheeled armored patrol vehicle, first used in combat in Libya (1912). Early types were commercial vehicles and converted trucks with inadequate protection, armament, and cross-country performance. They now have independent suspension, all-wheel drive, better armor, carry machine guns or a light gun, and may be amphibious. They use speed, concealment, and skillful tactical handling to perform their role.

Armory show The first exhibition of European avant-garde art organized in the US. It was held by a group of New York artists in the 69th Regiment Armory in New York in 1913. *Picasso, *Braque, *Matisse, and the entire cubist school were given great prominence.

Armstrong, Edwin Howard (1890–1954) US electrical engineer, who in 1939 introduced frequency *modulation as a method of broadcasting radio signals to eliminate much of the static associated with amplitude modulation. He had earlier invented the *superheterodyne receiver, which made radio reception much better and greatly increased the popularity of radio sets. A contentious and litigious man, he committed suicide.

Armstrong, Louis (1900–71) US jazz trumpeter and singer, known as "Satchmo." Born in New Orleans, he learned to play the cornet in his youth. His career took him to Chicago, where he made many recordings (some of them with Earl Hines), which earned him a worldwide reputation. He played with several large orchestras as a soloist but most frequently led his own group. His gravelly singing voice and superb trumpet playing were featured in many films. His infectious enthusiasm made many jazz converts and generated good will on several world tours, during some of which he represented the US for the government.

LOUIS ARMSTRONG

Armstrong, Neil Alden (1930–) US astronaut, the first man to walk on the moon. A Navy pilot during the Korean War, he began working for the National Aeronautics and Space Administration (NASA) (1955–71) and became an astronaut in 1962. He flew Gemini 7 (1966) and was commander of Apollo 11 (1969). As he stepped onto the moon he said "That's one small step for a man, one giant leap for mankind."

army An organized force of soldiers, which may be composed of full-time professionals, *militia reserves, conscripts, or mercenaries or of a combination of these. Armies exist for combat and to enhance a nation's prestige; they may also exert domestic political power and provide manpower for such activities as road-building and land development.

Armies were raised throughout the ancient world, where mercenaries were usually relied upon to supplement a militia (as in the Greek city states) or a standing army (as in Rome). The medieval armies of Europe depended upon the mounted feudal knight, who was obliged to undertake short-term military service for his lord. As campaigns became longer, mercenaries were increasingly relied upon and with the introduction of firearms in the 15th century the foot soldier became important. Early modern standing armies reached their zenith with those of the 17th- and 18th-century absolute monarchs, especially Louis XIV of France and Frederick the Great of Prussia. By comparison the standing army maintained since 1661 in England was small, Cromwell's *New Model Army having left a lasting distrust of militarism. The 19th century saw a growing emphasis on the mass armies that resulted from *conscription—a measure widely adopted in Continental Europe. During World Wars I and II nations relied heavily on conscription and trained reserve troops to meet manpower needs. Postwar trends have included the combination of national armies into allied forces, such as those of NATO and the Warsaw Pact states, and the growing specialization of armies in response to technological advances.

army ant A New World *ant of the genus *Eciton* or related genera that does not build a permanent nest but has alternating nomadic and static phases synchronized to the egg-laying of the wingless queen. The wasplike males are large and winged and the soldier ants have large hooked jaws and hunt in vast "armies," killing other insects, young birds, reptiles, and small mammals. Subfamily: *Dorylinae. See also* driver ant.

Army, Department of US government military department within the Department of *Defense. Directed by the Secretary of Defense and the Secretary of the Army, it is charged with organizing, training, and equipping active duty and reserve forces. It also administers environmental improvement programs. Originally the Department of War (1789–1947), it became the Department of the Army by the passage of the *National Security Act of 1947.

Army, United States Ground forces of the military. Its programs ensure the readiness of land forces, both active duty and reserve troops. It also administers environmental protection, waterway navigation, flood and beach erosion control, and water resource development programs. The Army provides assistance at all levels in times of natural disaster. Established as the American Continental Army in 1775, the US Army has fought in all major conflicts since the War of 1812. The draft has been implemented from time to time, but since 1973 it has been a volunteer army with a 1980 stipulation that all men between 18 and 20 must register for the draft. The US Military Academy at West Point, administered by the Army, educates and trains men and women to be Army officers.

army worm The *caterpillar of a widely distributed moth, *Leucania unipunctata*. Army worms periodically swarm in large numbers, eating crops in their path and causing severe damage, especially in North America.

Arnauld, Antoine (1612–94) French theologian, philosopher, and logician; member of a prominent Jansenist family closely connected with the Abbey of Port-Royal. His attacks on the Jesuits, especially *De la fréquente communion* (1643), eventually forced him into exile in Brussels. He presented important objections to *Descartes' *Meditations* and, in collaboration with *Pascal and Pierre Nicole (1625–95), wrote the influential *La Logique ou l'art de penser* (1662), known as the *Port-Royal Logic*.

Arnhem 52 00N 5 53E A city in the E Netherlands, the capital of Gelderland province. In World War II a large airborne landing of British troops attempted to secure a bridgehead over the Rhine River here to facilitate an Allied invasion of Germany. The attempt failed with heavy casualties (September 1944). A railroad junction, its industries include engineering and pharmaceuticals. Population (1991 est): 131,703.

Arnhem Land A plateau in Australia, in N Northern Territory. It is primarily an Aboriginal reserve. Bauxite deposits are worked at Gove. Area: about 60,000 sq mi (150,000 sq km).

Arno River A river in central Italy. Rising in the Apennines, it flows mainly W through Florence and Pisa to the Ligurian Sea. It burst its banks in 1966 causing disastrous floods in Florence. Length: 150 mi (240 km).

Arnold, Benedict (1741–1801) American general in the American Revolution. Brilliant but erratic, he served with distinction at Fort Ticonderoga and Quebec (1775), commanded a fleet on Lake Champlain (1776), and fought in Connecticut, the Mohawk Valley, and Saratoga (1777). In 1780 he treacherously planned to surrender the vital West Point position. The plot miscarried and he fled to the British for whom he led raids in Virginia and Connecticut. From 1781 he lived in England.

Arnold, Henry Harley ("Hap"; 1886–1950) US Air Force general. A West Point graduate (1907) who trained for flying under the *Wright brothers, he served in World War I as head of an air squadron and, afterwards, as department air service officer (1919–22). He commanded the US Army Air Forces (1942–46) and became the first five-star general in the Air Force (1949).

Arnold, Matthew (1822–88) British poet and critic, son of Thomas Arnold. He worked as a government inspector of schools from 1851 to 1886. His critical works include *Essays in Criticism* (1865; 1888) and *Culture and Anarchy* (1869), in which he asserted literary and cultural values as an antidote to the progressive materialism of Victorian society. His moral beliefs and doubts were given more personal expression in his poetry, which included "Dover Beach" (1867) and the narrative poems "The Scholar Gypsy" (1853) and "Sohrab and Rustum" (1853).

Arnold of Brescia (d. 1155) Italian religious reformer. He studied at Paris, perhaps under *Abelard, and became an Augustinian canon after returning to Italy, where he immediately condemned the worldliness prevalent in the Church. He argued, among other things, that the papacy should not have secular power. He was excommunicated in 1148 and was eventually captured by Emperor Frederick Barbarossa, condemned, and hanged at Rome.

Arnold, Thomas (1795–1842) British educator. Appointed headmaster of Rugby (1828), Arnold reformed the school and instituted the form and prefectorial systems, which came to characterize English public schools. Arnold's piety was infectious, and Rugby became noted for "muscular Christianity." *Tom Brown's Schooldays* (*see* Hughes, Thomas) provides a eulogistic record of Arnold's achievement.

aromatic compound A type of cyclic organic chemical compound that includes *benzene and its derivatives. On conventional theories of valence these compounds appear to be unsaturated (i.e. contain double bonds). However, benzene and similar compounds are much less reactive than the *alkenes, tending to undergo substitution reactions rather than addition reactions. The explanation for the stability of the benzene ring lies in a model in which the carbon atoms are joined by single bonds and the extra six valence electrons are free to move around the ring in a delocalized orbital. The phenomenon also occurs in some other compounds having an unsaturated ring, for example ferrocene $(Fe(C_5H_5)_2)$. Aromatic compounds were originally distinguished from *aliphatic compounds because of the distinctive properties of benzene compounds, many of which have a fragrant odor.

The conventional formula of benzene devised by F. A. Kekulé von Stradonitz (1829–96). With alternating double bonds it would be unsaturated and have properties similar to the *alkenes.

In the benzene molecule the bonds are actually intermediate between single and double bonds. This is often represented as a resonance hybrid between the two conventional structures.

often represented as

The modern explanation of the bonding involves a delocalized orbital above and below the ring. The six valence electrons (one from each carbon atom) are free to move in this orbital. This explains the properties of benzene and the fact that all C-C bonds are equal.

AROMATIC COMPOUND

Aroostook River A river rising in N central Maine and flowing NE into Canada to join the St John River in New Brunswick. A boundary dispute in 1839, which was settled by the Webster-Ashburton Treaty (1842) which set Maine's boundaries, was known as the Aroostook War. Length: 140 mi (226 km).

Aroostook War (1839) US-British border dispute in Maine and New Brunswick, Canada. When Maine became a state in 1820, the boundaries were never officially charted. The Aroostook River Valley area was claimed by both countries and skirmishes over the land resulted. A preliminary boundary agreement was effected in 1839 and fighting was averted, but it was not until 1842 that the Webster-Ashburton Treaty fixed the boundaries.

Arp, Jean (Hans) (1887–1966) French sculptor and poet. He was one of the founders of the *dada movement (1916) and later associated with the surrealist movement in Paris. Arp experimented with collages of torn colored papers, designed according to chance, and produced numerous painted wood reliefs. In about 1930 he began his abstract sculptures suggesting organic rather than geometric forms. His wife and occasional collaborator was the artist Sophie Tauber (1889–1943).

Árpád (died c. 907 AD) Magyar chieftain. In 875 Árpád led the Magyars from the Caucasus region into present-day Hungary in search of a new homeland after their defeat by the Pechenegs. He founded the first Hungarian royal dynasty, the Árpád, which ruled Hungary until 1301.

arquebus. *See* musket.

Arrabal, Fernando (1932–   ) Spanish playwright and novelist, who writes in French and lives in France. His plays, which have some of the characteristics of the *Theater of the Absurd, deal chiefly with themes of terror and violence; they include *Le Cimitière des voitures* (1958), *Le Grand Cérémonial* (1966), and *And They Put Handcuffs on the Flowers* (1973).

Arras 50 17N 2 46E A city in N France, the capital of the Pas-de-Calais department on the Scarpe River. The former capital of Artois, it passed to France in 1640. It had a famous medieval tapestry trade and the tapestry called "arras" is named for it. Robespierre was born here. The 18th-century cathedral and fine 16th-century town hall were badly damaged during World War I. An agricultural market, its industries include agricultural machinery and hosiery. Population (1982): 45,364.

Arrau, Claudio (1903–91) Chilean pianist. He gave his first recital at the age of five and studied in Berlin under Martin Krause (1853–1918), a pupil of Liszt. He returned to Chile in 1940 to found a piano school. He is famous particularly for his interpretations of Beethoven and Brahms.

arrest The forcible detention of a person to compel obedience to the law. A person is taken into custody for the purpose of holding or detaining him to answer a criminal or civil charge. Arrest involves the authority to arrest, the assertion of that authority, and the restraint of that person to be arrested. In theory any citizen can make an arrest and is bound to do so if a felony or breach of the peace is committed in his presence, but in practice most valid arrests are made by the police or other law-enforcement officers, who are empowered to make arrests without warrants.

Arrhenius, Svante August (1859–1927) Swedish physicist and chemist, who became professor of the University of Stockholm in 1895. He won the 1903 Nobel Prize for Chemistry for his theory of electrolytic dissociation. He later worked on the application of physical chemistry to living processes. His theory of universal life-diffusion involved "spores" emitted by habitable worlds and driven by light-pressure across space.

arrhythmia An abnormal rhythm of the heart beat. Sometimes this may produce symptoms, such as palpitation, breathlessness, and chest pain. Arrhythmias may be associated with heart disease but may occur without any obvious cause.

Arrian (Flavius Arrianus; 2nd century AD) Roman historian. As governor of *Cappadocia, he defeated a barbarian invasion (134 AD). He wrote several works on Asian history; his *Anabasis* is our most important source of information about *Alexander the Great.

arrow-poison frog A small, generally brightly colored, terrestrial frog belonging to a family (*Dendrobatidae*) occurring in Central and South American forests. Poisons produced by skin glands protect the frogs from predators and were used by Indians to poison arrow tips. In many species the young are incubated on the back of the male. Chief genera: *Dendrobates, Phyllobates*.

arrowroot A herbaceous perennial plant, *Maranta arundinacea*, native to Guyana but widely cultivated in the West Indies for the edible and very pure fine starch that is extracted from its underground fleshy tubers and used in cooking. The plant is about 5 ft (1.5 m) high and has short-stalked, white flowers and broad-bladed leaves with long, narrow sheaths. Several other species yield a similar starch. Family: *Marantaceae*.

Arrowsmith (1925) Novel about early 20th-century American medicine by Sinclair *Lewis; winner of a Pulitzer Prize (declined by Lewis) in 1926. It tells of Dr. Martin Arrowsmith and his experiences in rural and urban medicine and in research. It also shows his efforts to avoid the commercialism that had crept into American medicine.

Arrow War. *See* Opium Wars.

arrow worm A small planktonic invertebrate animal belonging to a phylum (*Chaetognatha*; 50 species) occurring chiefly in tropical seas. Arrow worms have an elongated, arrow-shaped body divided into a head, trunk, and tail, with fins on the sides and tail. They feed on crustaceans, larvae, etc.

ars antiqua (Latin: old art) A style of European music of the 13th century. It was particularly associated with composers of the Parisian school, such as *Pérotin and Léonin (late 12th century), and characterized by the use of complex forms of *organum. It was succeeded by *ars nova*.

arsenic (As) A brittle semimetal that occurs in nature in a variety of forms: native, as the sulfides realgar (As_2S_2) and orpiment (As_2S_3), as sulfarsenides, such as arsenopyrite ($FeSAs$), and as arsenates. The element occurs in several forms and was known to the ancients. Pure arsenic has important uses as a dopant in the semiconductor industry. Arsenic and its common compounds are extremely poisonous; tests for its presence need to be accurate and reliable. Compounds include the white oxide (As_2O_3), the gaseous hydride arsine (AsH_3), and arsenates, some of which are used as insecticides. At no 33; at wt 74.9216; mp 485°F (817°C) 28 atm; sublimes 372°F (613°C).

arsine (*or* hydrogen arsenide; AsH_3) A colorless poisonous gas that smells like garlic. It is an unstable compound and decomposes into *arsenic and hydrogen.

Arsinoe II (c. 316–270 BC) The daughter of *Ptolemy I Soter of Egypt. After two dynastic marriages she became the wife of and coruler with her brother *Ptolemy II Philadelphus (c. 276). Ambitious, forceful, and capable, she was an active participant in war, politics, and administration.

Arsinoe III (c. 235–c.204 BC) The sister and wife of Ptolemy IV Philopator (reigned 221–203 BC) of Egypt. She participated energetically in the power politics surrounding her lethargic husband. News of her murder, suppressed until Ptolemy's death, caused rioting, which overthrew her former rivals.

ars nova (Latin: new art) A style of European music of the 14th century, which succeeded *ars antiqua*. The name was taken from the title of a treatise by Philippe de Vitry (1291–1361), which set out new principles for the composition of *motets and for the notation of complex rhythms. Its greatest French exponents were *Machaut and *Dufay.

arson In common law, maliciously setting fire to something, originally someone else's house. This definition, however, has been broadened by state statutes and criminal codes. In several states, this crime is divided into arson in the first, second, and third degrees. The first degree includes the burning of an inhabited dwelling-house in the nighttime; the second degree, the burning (at night) of a building other than a dwelling-house, but so situated with reference to a dwelling house to endanger it; the third degree, the burning of any building or structure not the subject of arson in the first or second degree, or the burning of property with intent to defraud or prejudice an insurer.

Artaud, Antonin (1896–1948) French actor, poet, producer, and theoretician of the theater. In the 1920s he was involved with *surrealism and cofounded, with the poet and playwright Roger Vitrac (1899–1952), the Théâtre Alfred Jarry, where surrealist-inspired plays were produced that were forerunners of the

*Theater of the Absurd. Impressed by the symbolism, gesture, and other nonlinguistic elements of oriental theater, he developed the theory of a *Theater of Cruelty in essays later collected in *Le Théâtre et son double* (1938).

Artaxerxes II (c. 436–358 BC) King of Persia (404–358). He defended his position against his brother *Cyrus the Younger, who was defeated and killed at *Cunaxa (401), and against a revolt of the provincial governors, the Satraps (366–358). Persia nevertheless declined under his rule.

Art Deco The style of design predominant in the decorative arts of the 1920s and 1930s. The name derives from the 1925 Exposition Internationale des Arts Décoratifs et Industriels Modernes in Paris. In deliberate contrast to *Art Nouveau, Art Deco was characterized by emphatic geometrical lines and shapes, vibrant color schemes, and the use of modern man-made substances, such as plastic. Influenced by the *Bauhaus, Art Deco included among its practitioners *Lalique and *Erté. It was debased by shoddy mass production, but interest in it rekindled late in the 1960s.

Artemis In Greek mythology, the daughter of Zeus and Leto and twin sister of Apollo. Settled in *Arcadia, she and her band of Oceanids and nymphs spent their time hunting. Love was banned, and Artemis rigorously punished all transgressors. *Actaeon was killed for watching her bathe and *Orion for touching her. Despite this severity, her help was invoked during childbirth, and she was protectress of both animal and human young. Ephesus was the most famous center of her worship. She was associated with the moon and identified by the Romans with *Diana. *Compare* Hecate.

Artemis, Temple of One of the Seven Wonders of the World, built at *Ephesus in 356 BC. The deity worshiped here was the many-breasted fertility goddess called Diana of the Ephesians in Acts 19.28, rather than the classical *Artemis.

Artemisia (5th century BC) Queen of Halicarnassus. She accompanied Xerxes I on his invasion of Greece, despite her prophecy that the mission would fail, and fought bravely at Salamis (480).

Artemisia (died c. 350 BC) Queen of Caria (c. 353–c. 350), who succeeded her brother and husband Mausolus. Artemisia initiated the construction of his famous tomb, the *Mausoleum. In 350 she subjugated Rhodes and nearby islands.

arteriosclerosis The loss of elasticity in the walls of arteries. This somewhat vague term is used to cover various conditions of the arteries and arterioles (small arteries) associated with the aging process. It is also used loosely as a synonym for *atherosclerosis.

artery A thick-walled blood vessel that carries oxygen-rich blood away from the *heart to supply all the tissues and organs of the body. The largest is the aorta, which leads directly from the heart and descends into the abdomen, giving rise to all the other arteries. In middle age the lining of the arteries commonly becomes thickened by *atherosclerosis, which may lead to various diseases caused by obstruction of blood flow (e.g. strokes, heart attacks). *See also* blood pressure.

artesian well A well sunk into an aquifer (a water-saturated rock stratum) that is confined between two layers of impermeable rock and through which water flows upward under pressure. The aquifer reaches the surface and receives rainfall where the water table is higher than the place at which the well is sunk, resulting in a head of pressure.

Artevelde, Jacob van (c. 1290–1345) Flemish statesman. In the 1330s he established the alliance of Flemish towns with those of Brabant, Hainault, and Holland to protect the Low Countries from the economic repercussions of the war between France and England. His dictatorial policies in Ghent, his home town, led to his assassination in 1345.

arthritis Inflammation of one or more joints, causing pain, swelling, and restriction of movement. Many different diseases can cause arthritis, the most important of which are *osteoarthritis, rheumatoid arthritis, and *gout. **Rheumatoid arthritis**, which is more common in women, usually affects the hands and feet and often also the hips, knees, and shoulders. The synovial membrane lining the joint becomes inflamed, resulting in damage to the cartilage over the joint with consequent pain and deformity. Rheumatoid arthritis is an autoimmune disease (*see* autoimmunity) and is diagnosed by a blood test (the blood contains the characteristic rheumatoid factor) and X-rays. Treatment is usually based on drugs to reduce the pain and inflammation (*see* analgesic); some patients benefit from treatment with gold salts and steroids, while severe cases may require surgical replacement of the affected joint(s).

arthropod An invertebrate animal belonging to the largest and most diverse phylum (*Arthropoda*) of the animal kingdom, containing about a million species (i.e. 75% of all known species). There are about 12 classes, the most important of which are the *arachnids, *crustaceans, *insects, *centipedes, and *millipedes. An arthropod has a segmented body with a hard outer skeleton (cuticle) made of *chitin, which is shed periodically to allow the body to grow. Jointed appendages are modified for swimming, walking, feeding, respiration, reproduction, etc. Young arthropods are often very different from the adults and go through a series of changes (*see* metamorphosis) to reach the adult form. Arthropods are found in fresh and salt water, air, and land and have exploited every food source. Many are harmful—as pests, parasites, or vectors of disease—but others are beneficial to man, as pollinators, food sources, predators of pests, and decomposers of organic wastes.

Arthur, Chester Alan (1830–86) US political leader; 21st President of the United States (1881–85). Born in Vermont and educated at Union College, Arthur became a lawyer active in the Abolition movement before the Civil War. During the war he served in the Union army and was appointed quartermaster general of New York. In 1871 President Grant named him collector of customs at the Post of New York. Throughout his career, Arthur was an active member of the Republican Party and he was elected as the party's candidate for vice president in 1880. Following the assassination of Pres. James *Garfield in 1881, Arthur succeeded to the presidency himself. The most notable achievement of his single term in office was a reform of the government bureaucracy through the Pendleton Civil Service Act of 1883. Because of political differences with the leaders of the Republican Party, Arthur was denied renomination for president in 1884. After leaving office, he returned to private life and died in New York City in 1886.

Arthurian legend The body of medieval *romances concerning the legendary British king Arthur and his knights; also known as the Matter of Britain. Arthur first emerges as a figure of romance in the *Historia Regum Britanniae* of *Geoffrey of Monmouth, although a 6th-century military leader of the Welsh may have been a historical model. In the legend, he is the son of Uther Pendragon, was born at Tintagel in Cornwall, became king of Britain at 15, and won a number of famous victories. He married Guinevere and held court at Caerleon in Wales (or, in some versions, at Camelot, which may have been near South Cadbury, Somerset). Involved in a war at Rome, he left his kingdom in the charge of his nephew Modred, who betrayed him and abducted Guinevere. Arthur returned to Britain and defeated Modred but was himself mortally wounded. He was taken away to the Isle of Avalon (the Celtic paradise, associated with Glastonbury) to be healed. Succeeding writers added a wealth of detail to this story, developing new characters, themes, and episodes. *Wace introduced the knightly fellowship of the Round Table and also mentioned the ancient tradition that one day Arthur would return from Avalon to rule Britain again. *Layamon added magical elements to the story, and French and other writers from the 12th century onward, starting with *Chrétien de Troyes, took up the exploits of individual knights, such as Lancelot, Perceval, Gawain, and Galahad. Arthur himself gradually became a background figure, interest centering on the quest of the *Holy Grail, the adulterous affair of Guinevere and Lancelot, and other episodes. Other well-known characters were the magician Merlin and the sorceress Morgan le Fay (Arthur's sister). Sir Thomas *Malory's *Morte d'Arthur* (c. 1470) was the culmination of the medieval tradition, although the material has continued to inspire such versions as Tennyson's *Idylls of the King* (from 1842) and T. H. White's *The Once and Future King* (1958).

artichoke A perennial, thistle-like, herbaceous plant, *Cynara scolemus*, also known as globe artichoke, native to central and W Mediterranean regions and widely grown in warm temperate areas for its nutty-tasting immature flower heads, which are considered a great delicacy. The hairy indented straplike leaves, 40 in (1 m) long, arise each year from the base of the short annual stems, which carry branched flower stalks bearing purplish flowers. Family: *Compositae*. *See also* Jerusalem artichoke.

Articles of Confederation The first national constitution of the United States. First proposed by Richard Henry *Lee of Virginia in 1776 and formulated by a committee headed by John *Dickinson of Delaware, the Articles of Confederation granted each of the states one vote in Congress and apportioned federal taxes according to the value of the surveyed land in each state. By its terms, Congress could wage war and borrow and issue money. After considerable debate in the *Continental Congress, the Articles were passed in 1777, but it was not until 1781 that they were ratified by all the states. The most serious weakness of the federal system under the Articles of Confederation was the inability of Congress to compel the states to obey federal laws, to levy new taxes, and to regulate interstate trade. Because of these shortcomings, a stronger federal system was needed and in 1789 the Articles of Confederation were replaced by the US *Constitution.

artificial insemination The artificial introduction of semen into the vagina of a female at a stage in the menstrual or estrous cycle when the chances of conception are high (i.e. at ovulation). Although practiced as early as the 14th century by Arab horse breeders, the techniques of artificial insemination used in the livestock industry were developed largely in the Soviet Union during the early 20th century. Semen collected from a single well-bred male can be stored at low temperatures for months before being used to fertilize many females. This has resulted in dramatic breed improvements and the control of venereal disease. Artificial insemination is occasionally used in human medicine. In cases when the husband is infertile semen is obtained from an anonymous donor (artificial insemination donor—AID). Semen may be provided by the husband in cases of impotence (artificial insemination husband—AIH). *See also* test-tube baby.

artificial kidney. *See* dialysis.

artificial respiration The restoration of the flow of air into and out of the lungs when the patient's own breathing movements have ceased, for example after drowning, poisoning, etc. Mouth-to-mouth respiration—the "kiss of life"—involves a person breathing out into the patient's mouth: carbon dioxide in this exhaled air acts as a stimulus for the natural breathing reflexes. In hospitals artificial respiration is provided by a *respirator, which may be required during surgery, severe pneumonias, and after head injuries.

Artigas, José Gervasio (1764–1850) The national hero of Uruguay. He fought for the independence of his country from Argentina until he was driven into exile in Paraguay in 1820.

artillery *Firearms with a caliber in excess of 20 mm, used to bombard enemy positions, disrupt communications, destroy enemy artillery, and provide cover and support for friendly troop deployments. Early guns were classed by projectile weight, e.g. 12-pounder. Modern weapons are identified by caliber: light (below 120 mm), medium (121–160 mm), heavy (161–210 mm), and super or very heavy (above 211 mm). *Gun projectiles have flat trajectories, while *mortars and *howitzers have high trajectories, with correspondingly short ranges. Artillery rockets (excluding antitank missiles) deliver more explosive further, without needing heavy launchers. Some artillery projectiles have nuclear warheads, but most are high explosive. Modern electronic equipment enables artillery fire to score a direct hit with near certainty on any visible target; as this also applies to the guns themselves (as targets) the tendency is now for artillery to be fired by remote control.

Artiodactyla An order of hoofed mammals (150 species), distributed worldwide except for Australasia and Antarctica. Artiodactyls are terrestrial herbivores having two or four toes on each foot and often bearing horns. They range in size from the smallest *chevrotains to the *giraffe. The group is divided into three suborders: *Suiformes* (pigs, peccaries, and hippopotamuses); *Tylopoda* (camels and llamas); and *Ruminantia* (*see* ruminant), which comprises deer, cattle, antelopes, giraffes, pronghorns, and chevrotains. *Compare* Perissodactyla.

Art Nouveau A decorative style pervading all visual art forms in Britain, France, Germany (*see* Jugendstil), Austria (Sezessionstil), Belgium, Spain, and the US in the 1890s and early 1900s. It is characterized by designs of naturalistic foliage and biomorphic shapes linked by undulating lines. In Britain it is associated with the *Arts and Crafts movement of William *Morris, the architectural and interior designs of C. R. *Mackintosh, and the graphic work of Aubrey *Beardsley. Louis Comfort Tiffany (1848–1933), influenced by the arts and crafts movement, popularized Art Nouveau in the US with his interior designs and glass creations. On the Continent leading examples of Art Nouveau are the Parisian metro designs of Hector Guimard (1867–1942), the extravagant Barcelona flats and hotels designed by Antonio *Gaudí, and the Belgian stores and houses of Victor *Horta, all of which use sinuous lines and exposed ironwork. A parallel effect in glassware of tinted glass and lead solder was achieved by René *Lalique and Emile *Gallé.

Artois A former province of NW France approximating to the present-day Pas-de-Calais. It belonged from the 9th century until 1180 to the Counts of *Flanders, after which it passed to *Philip II Augustus of France. It was acquired from the French crown by the Counts of *Burgundy in 1329, passing to the *Hapsburgs in 1500 until regained by France during the *Thirty Years' War (1618–48).

Arts and Crafts movement An English 19th-century aesthetic movement derived from William *Morris and his Pre-Raphaelite associates, whose firm was founded (1861) to produce handmade furnishings. In opposing contemporary mass production the movement revived the principles of medieval craftsmanship and respect for materials; it also promoted the ideal of the artist as craftsman-designer. It culminated in the establishment of the Century Guild for

Craftsmen (1882) and the Arts and Crafts Exhibition Society (1888). The preference for curvilinear patterns helped to create the emerging *Art Nouveau style.

Aruba 12 30N 70 00W A West Indian island, in the Netherlands Antilles. Oil refining is important. Area: 75 sq mi (193 sq km). Chief town: Oranjestad.

arum (*or* arum lily) A plant of the tropical African genus *Zantedeschia* (8 species), especially *Z. aethiopica*, widely grown as an ornamental. It has arrow-shaped leaves and the flower head consists of a cylindrical cluster of tiny, yellow flowers surrounded by a white, funnel-shaped bract (spathe), resembling a petal. Family: *Araceae*.

The European genus *Arum*, of the same family, contains the *cuckoopint. The related bog arum, or wild calla (*Calla palustris*), grows in swamps of N temperate and subarctic regions. It has heart-shaped leaves and small flowers enveloped in a white spathe.

Arunachal Pradesh (name until 1972: North-East Frontier Agency) A state in NE India, stretching N from the Brahmaputra Valley to the Himalayas. There it shares a disputed border with Tibet, from which Chinese troops have twice invaded since 1945. Mostly rainforest, Arunachal Pradesh is inhabited by hill tribes. Area: 31,430 sq mi (81,426 sq km). Population (1991): 858,392. Capital: Ziro.

Arundel 50 51N 0 34W A market town in SE England, in West Sussex on the River Arun. Its 11th-century castle (mainly rebuilt in the 19th century) is the seat of the Dukes of Norfolk. Other notable buildings include the 19th-century Roman Catholic cathedral. Population (1981): 2235.

Arval Brethren (Latin: *Fratres Arvales*, Brothers of the Field) In ancient Rome, a college of 12 priests, who organized a festival every May dedicated to the corn goddess Dea Dia. The priests were chosen from high-ranking officials and included the emperor.

Aryans Peoples speaking *Indo-European, *Indo-Iranian, or *Indo-Aryan languages. It has been claimed that all the Indo-European peoples originated from an Aryan people who dispersed from a common homeland into Europe and N India. Indo-Aryan-speaking peoples certainly invaded and settled in N India in the second millennium BC. They were tribal herdsmen who later became farmers. The earliest literature of India, the Vedas, written in *Sanskrit, contains hymns, spells, and details of the ritual practices of the Aryans.

Arya Samaj A controversial Hindu theosophical movement, founded in 1875 at Bombay by Swami Dayananda Saraswali (1824–83). It denounced popular idolatry and advocated a return to the oldest Vedic authorities. It also supported the emancipation of women and untouchables, because the old authorities neither justified nor assumed their lower status. Unlike many contemporary movements, Arya Samaj made no attempt to convert non-Indians.

ASA rating The American Standards Association measure of the sensitivity or speed of photographic *film. A film rated at 200 is twice as fast (i.e. needs half the exposure time) as 100 ASA film. General-purpose films have speeds between 50 and 160 ASA. High-speed films for indoor photography and poor light are rated between 200 and 500 ASA.

asbestos A fibrous form of certain silicate minerals, particularly the *amphiboles anthophyllite, tremolite, riebeckite, and actinolite, or a fibrous form of *serpentine, called chrysotile. Blue asbestos is crocidolite, a fibrous riebeckite. Asbestos is heat-resistant, chemically inert, and has a high electrical resistance; it has, therefore, a wide industrial application. The fibers are spun and woven or made into blocks. The main producers are Canada and Brazil. *See also* asbestosis.

asbestosis A lung disease caused by the inhalation of asbestos fibers. It is an occupational disease to which those exposed to large amounts of the mineral are particularly prone: tighter factory health controls have greatly reduced its incidence. It affects the air sacs of the lungs, which become thickened and scarred, causing breathlessness: patients are liable to develop lung cancer.

Ascaris A genus of *nematode worms with a worldwide distribution, important as parasites of livestocks and man. Adult worms are smooth and cylindrical, 6–12 in (15–30 cm) in length, and can live in the intestines of their hosts for up to a year. After mating, eggs pass out in the host's feces and infection occurs when food contaminated with eggs is eaten.

Ascension 7 57S 14 22W A British island in the S Atlantic Ocean, a dependency of St Helena. It is rocky, has little vegetation, and was uninhabited until 1815. A British telecommunications center, it is also a US air base and space research station. Area: 35 sq mi (88 sq km). Chief settlement: Georgetown.

Ascension In the Christian calendar, the day on which it is believed Christ ascended into Heaven (*see* Acts 1.4–11). Since the 4th century it has been celebrated 40 days after Easter.

asceticism Systematic self-discipline for spiritual ends, usually involving fasting, vigils, sexual abstinence, and renunciation of worldly goods and pleasures. *Stoicism advocated ascetic practices in order to subdue unruly passions. Christian asceticism is based on the theory of identifying with Christ's sufferings and is viewed not as an end in itself but as a means to contemplation of and spiritual union with the divine. It became an important element in certain monastic orders and in Christian *mysticism. In Islam, asceticism is particularly associated with *sufism and there is also a strong tradition of asceticism in Buddhism and Hinduism (*see* fakir).

Asch, Sholem (1880–1957) Jewish novelist, born in Poland, who wrote chiefly in Yiddish. He traveled in Europe, Israel, and the US, becoming a US citizen in 1920. In his controversial later novels, which include *The Nazarene* (1929) and *The Apostle* (1943), he expressed his belief in the essential unity of Judaism and Christianity.

Asclepius In Greek mythology, a son of *Apollo and the god of medicine. He was instructed by the centaur *Chiron in hunting and medicine and learned to effect many miraculous cures. When he restored *Hippolytus to life as a favor to Artemis, Zeus became angry and struck him dead with a thunderbolt. It was believed that those suffering from illness or disease could be cured by sleeping all night in one of his temples.

Ascomycetes A large class of fungi (about 15,000 species), known as sac fungi because their spores are formed in a saclike structure (called an ascus). The nonreproductive part of these fungi is often a microscopic meshwork of cells. The group includes *truffles, *yeasts, *Penicillium, and *Aspergillus.

ascorbic acid. *See* vitamin C.

Ascot 51 25N 0 41W A village in S England, in Berkshire. The construction of its famous racetrack was ordered by Queen Anne in 1711. Traditionally the sovereign opens the Royal Ascot meeting in June.

ASEAN. *See* Association of South-East Asian Nations.

asepsis The condition in which material is uncontaminated by bacteria, fungi, and other disease-causing microorganisms. Surgical operations, the packaging of surgical supplies, and the preparation of intravenous drugs are carried out under aseptic conditions, which are produced by using *antiseptics, heat, or radiation.

Asgard In Norse mythology, the home of the gods and of heroes killed in battle, comprising over 12 kingdoms, and palaces, as well as *Valhalla. From earth it was reached by the bridge Bifrost (the rainbow).

ash A tree of the genus *Fraxinus* (about 50 species), native to the N hemisphere. Many species yield a pale-yellow wood of commercial importance and others are widely grown as ornamentals. Reaching a height of 98 ft (30 m), ashes have compound leaves made up of pairs of oval or lance-shaped leaflets, small, inconspicuous flowers, and winged fruits ("ash keys"). Most species are deciduous, including the European ash (*F. excelsior*). Family: *Oleaceae* (olive family). *See also* mountain ash.

Ashanti A people of the S part of Ghana, who speak the Twi language. They are an agricultural people producing crops for local markets and cocoa for export. Their social organization is based upon matrilineal kin groups living in villages governed by headmen. The Ashanti established an empire in S Ghana during the 18th and 19th centuries, ruled by a paramount chief with military and religious functions. They worship a pantheon of gods and practice an ancestor cult.

Ashanti A former kingdom in West Africa, now comprising S Ghana. During the 18th century it was active in the slave trade, supplying slaves to British and Dutch traders. Following several wars it became a British colony in 1902. The modern region of Ashanti now occupies part of its area.

Ashcan School A group of early 20th century artists who portrayed life in New York City realistically. Known as "The Eight," their paintings depicted everyday, common living conditions, complete with the ashcans and garbage cans on streets and in backyards. The group included Robert Henri (1865–1929), William Glackens (1870–1938), George Luks (1867–1933), and Maurice Prendergast (1861–1923).

Ashdod 31 48N 34 38S A city in central Israel, on the Mediterranean coast. It was an important city in the ancient Philistine Empire, and an artificial harbor (started 1961) has now made it into one of Israel's major ports. There is also textile manufacturing. Population (1982): 65,000.

Ashe, Arthur (Robert) (1943–93) US tennis player, the first African-American player to win the US singles title (1968) and winner of the 1975 singles title at Wimbledon. South Africa's refusal to allow him to play there in 1970 led to its exclusion from the *Davis Cup. In 1979 he retired from tournament play following heart surgery, but subsequently served as the captain of the US Davis Cup team. In 1992 he announced that he had contracted the AIDS virus through blood transfusions.

Asher, tribe of One of the 12 *tribes of Israel. It claimed descent from Asher, the son of Jacob and Jacob's concubine Zilpah. Its original territory was to the W and NW of the Sea of Galilee, adjoining Phoenicia.

Ashkelon (*or* Ashqelon) 31 40N 34 35E A seaport 12 mi (19 km) N of Gaza (Israel), known from the biblical story of Samson as a *Philistine stronghold. In Hellenistic times it was a cultural center. The Arabs captured it in 636 AD. During the Crusades it changed hands several times before being destroyed by Sultan *Baybars (1270). The modern Israeli settlement was established in 1948.

Ashkenazim Jews of German or Eastern European origin, as opposed to *Sephardim. They have a distinct tradition of pronouncing Hebrew, as well as other customs, and until this century they mostly spoke *Yiddish. The first Ashkenazy synagogue in London was founded in 1690. Ashkenazim now form some 85% of world Jewry.

Ashkenazy, Vladimir (1937–   ) Russian pianist and conductor, famous for his interpretations of Mozart and Chopin, among others. He won the 1955 Warsaw Chopin Competition and was joint winner of the 1962 Tchaikovsky Competition. In 1973 he settled in Iceland.

Ashkhabad 37 58N 58 24E The capital city of Turkmenistan. It is near the Iranian border in an oasis in the *Kara Kum desert. Although virtually destroyed in 1948 by an earthquake, it has been rebuilt and is now an administrative, industrial, and transportation center, producing food, carpets, glass, and machinery. Population (1987): 382,000.

Ashley Cooper, Anthony. *See* Shaftesbury, Anthony Ashley Cooper, 1st Earl of.

Ashmolean Museum A museum in Oxford, England, housing paintings and archeological collections. The collection was donated to Oxford University in 1675 by Elias Ashmole (1617–92) and put on public display in 1683. Its highlights include Italian Renaissance paintings and English 19th-century works.

ashrama In *Brahmanism, the *ashramas* are the four ideal stages of life through which Hindus of the upper three castes should pass. First comes the celibate student of religion, then the married householder, the forest hermit, and finally the wandering ascetic. Only in later life, therefore, can spiritual release be sought.

Ashton, Sir Frederick (William Mallandaine) (1904–88) British ballet dancer and choreographer, born in Ecuador. He joined the Sadler's Wells ballet in 1935, became an associate director in 1952, and was director of Britain's Royal Ballet from 1963 to 1970. His works include *Cinderella* (1948), *Ondine* (1958), *La Fille mal gardée*, and many ballets choreographed for Margot Fonteyn.

Ashur The oldest Assyrian capital (modern Qalat Sharqat) on the Tigris River 60 mi (96 km) S of Mosul in Iraq. Ashur was already an important trading city in the heyday of *Sumer and *Akkad. Named for its guardian sun-god, Ashur became capital of the rising *Assyrian empire (14th century BC) to which it gave its name. With its later cocapitals *Nimrud and *Nineveh it was destroyed in 612 BC. First excavated in 1903, Ashur's ruins include major temples and a *ziggurat.

Ashurbanipal King of Assyria (668–627? BC), son of Esarhaddon. He suppressed two serious revolts during his reign and conquered the city of Tyre, but is best known as the founder of a remarkable library at Nineveh, some of the items in which are now in the British Museum.

Ashurnasirpal II King of Assyria (883–859 BC), who continued the restoration of the *Assyrian Empire by efficient administration, an invincible army, and brutality in punishing rebellion. He used deported captives to rebuild Kalhu (now *Nimrud, Iraq).

Ashwander v. Tennessee Valley Authority (1936) US Supreme Court case that ruled that the government may dispose of its property as it wishes. The Tennessee Valley Authority (TVA) contracted to sell excess power to private companies. The suit filed in federal court maintained that the TVA had acted unconstitutionally and, therefore, the government contracts were invalid. The Supreme Court ruled in the government's favor.

Ash Wednesday In the Christian calendar, the first day of *Lent, which is so named from the custom, probably dating from the 8th century, of marking the foreheads of the congregation with ashes as a sign of penitence.

Asia The largest continent in the world, it occupies about one-third of the dry land in the world. Asia is generally accepted as extending W to the Ural Mountains of Russia, although physically Europe is a peninsula of Asia. It is separated from the continent of Africa by the Red Sea and bounded on the N by the Arctic Ocean. Its S and E limits are less distinct and it includes the islands of Indonesia, Japan, the Philippines, and Taiwan. Asia is a continent of great diversity. Topographically it is the highest of the continents and has the greatest relief. It contains the world's highest point (Mount *Everest) and also its lowest (the *Dead Sea). Its great central mass of mountains and plateaus, which include the Himalayas, has historically formed a major barrier between N and S Asia. Vast alluvial plains border the major rivers, including the Ganges, Mekong, and Ob and the Yangtze and Yellow Rivers. Containing about half of the world's total population, it is the most populous continent, the highest concentrations being in the SE (China, India, and Japan). There are three main population groups: Negroid (in the Philippines), Mongoloid (including the Chinese, Japanese, and Koreans), and Caucasoid (including the Arabs, Afghans, and Pakistanis). Other groups, including the Malays, are a mixture of these main races. All the world's major religions originated in Asia, only Christianity spreading W to any great extent. Others include Hinduism (with the largest following), Buddhism, Islam, Confucianism (in China), and Shintoism (in Japan). Agriculture is the chief occupation, employing about two-thirds of the total population. Asia also has important mineral resources, notably the oil and natural-gas deposits of the Arab states. Area: 17,139,445 sq mi (44,391,162 sq km). Population (1991 est): 3,050,000,000.

Asia Minor (*or* Anatolia) The westernmost part of Asia between the Black Sea in the N, the Mediterranean Sea in the S, and the Aegean Sea in the W; it approximates present-day Turkey in Asia. For much of the second millennium BC, Asia Minor was the center of the *Hittite empire. After the Hittites' collapse (12th century BC) central and W Asia Minor were dominated by *Phrygia, which reached its zenith in the 8th century, when the Assyrian Empire conquered SE Asia Minor. Phrygia fell to *Lydia in the 6th century but in 546 Cyrus the Great established Achaemenian control over Asia Minor. In 333 it was conquered by Alexander the Great of Macedon and after his death, during the *Hellenistic age, the S was contested by the *Seleucids and the *Ptolemies, while small kingdoms, such as *Pergamum, *Cappadocia, *Bithynia, and *Pontus, established themselves elsewhere. Asia Minor came under Roman control in the 2nd and 1st centuries BC, forming part of the *Roman Empire and then the *Eastern Roman (subsequently Byzantine) Empire. Conquered by the Seljuq Turks in the 11th century AD and overrun by the Mongols in the 13th, Asia Minor was incorporated in the Ottoman Empire during the 14th and 15th centuries.

Asian Games An athletics meeting for all Asian countries affiliated with the International Amateur Athletic Federation. Quadrennial from 1954, they were first held in New Delhi in 1951.

asiento de negros A contract between the Spanish Crown and a private contractor, in which the Crown sold the exclusive rights to import slaves into its American colonies. The *asiento* began in 1595 and was held successively by Portuguese, Genoese, French, English, and Spanish contractors before it was suppressed in 1778.

Asimov, Isaac (1920–92) US science-fiction writer and biochemist, born in Russia. He began writing science-fiction stories in 1939, and his many books include the *Foundation* Trilogy (1951–53; sequel 1982) and collections of short stories, notably *I, Robot* (1950) and *Nightfall* (1969). His books popularizing scientific topics include *Inside the Atom* (1956), *The Human Brain* (1964), and *The Stars in their Courses* (1971).

Aske, Robert *See* Pilgrimage of Grace.

Asmara (*or* Asmera) 15 20N 38 49E The capital city of Eritrea. The population long included many Italians, Eritrea having been an Italian colony from 1890 until Allied occupation (1941). Notable buildings include the cathedral (1922) and Grand Mosque (1937); it has a university (1958). Industries include meat processing, distilling, and clothes manufacture. Population (1984): 275,400.

Aso, Mount 32 55N 131 02E A volcano in Japan, on central Kyushu. It has five cones, one with the longest active crater in the world, 71 mi (114 km) in circumference. Height: 5223 ft (1592 m).

Asoka (died c. 232 BC) Emperor of India (c. 270–c. 232 BC) of the Maurya dynasty (c. 321–c. 185 BC). His dominion extended over the whole of N India and most of the S. After his conquests he adopted the Buddhist faith and had his edicts carved on rock and stone pillars throughout the empire, telling the story of his conversion and issuing orders to comply with the morality of the new faith.

asp An aggressive European *viper, Vipera aspis*, that lives in dry habitats. About 24 in (60 cm) long, it is gray-brown to coppery brown with dark bars or zigzags, gray, yellowish, or blackish underparts, and a yellow patch under the tail tip. The snout is upturned into a small spike.

The asp that killed Cleopatra was probably the Egyptian cobra (*Naja haje*).

Asparagus A genus of herbaceous plants (about 300 species), with creeping underground stems (rhizomes), found throughout the Old World. *A. officinalis* is widely cultivated in temperate and subtropical regions for its young, edible shoots, which are considered a delicacy. Several African species are ornamental: *A. plumosus*, known as **asparagus fern**, produces attractive feathery sprays of branchlets. Family: *Liliaceae*.

Aspen 39 11N 106 49W A city, 7800 ft (2378 m) above sea level in the Rocky Mountains, in W central Colorado. Chiefly a resort, Aspen began as a silver mine camp in 1879 and flourished until 1893, when silver was devalued. Population (1990): 5049.

aspen One of several *poplar trees having slender, flattened leafstalks, so that the leaves tremble in the faintest breeze. The European aspen (*Populus tremula*), which grows to a height of 80 ft (25 m) has rounded, toothed leaves. Its soft, white wood is used for matches and paper pulp.

Aspergillus A genus of fungi that includes many common molds, often found on rotting food. Some species, especially *A. fumigatus*, can cause disease in humans (aspergillosis), the most severe form of which affects the lungs producing tuberculosis-like symptoms. *A. flavus*, a mold that infects peanuts, produces the poison aflatoxin, which may be responsible for certain cancers. Class: *Ascomycetes*.

asphalt A black highly viscous or solid hydrocarbon compound, used in road construction and the manufacture of roofing materials. It is obtained from the distillation of certain crude oils and from surface deposits (asphalt lakes), which occur naturally after the lighter fractions of a crude oil reservoir have evaporated.

asphodel A white- or yellow-flowered, lily-like plant of the mostly Mediterranean genera *Asphodelus* and *Asphodeline*. In Greek mythology, the asphodel associated with the dead and said to grow in the Elysian fields was *Asphodeline lutea*, which has yellow flowers. The asphodel of the early English and French poets was probably the daffodil. The bog asphodel (*Narthecium ossifragum*), of

NW Europe, grows in swampy regions. It grows to a height of 12 in (30 cm) and has a head of small yellow flowers. Family: *Liliaceae*.

asphyxia Suffocation: obstruction to the supply of oxygen to the tissues. This is a life-threatening condition since the brain cannot survive for longer than about four minutes without oxygen. It can result from any condition that prevents air from reaching the lungs, including drowning and choking. Breathing poisonous gas (e.g. carbon monoxide) also causes asphyxia.

Aspidistra A genus of herbaceous plants (8 species) native to E Asia. *A. elatior* is commonly grown as a hardy pot plant in western countries for its ornamental leaves, which are long, stiff, dark green (sometimes striped), and grow in sheaves from the reduced stem. It may occasionally produce small, purple bell-shaped flowers. Family: *Liliaceae*.

aspirin Acetylsalicylic acid: a drug widely used in the form of tablets to treat mild pain, such as headache and toothache. It also relieves inflammation and is therefore helpful in the treatment of rheumatoid arthritis, and it reduces fever. In some people aspirin may cause bleeding from the stomach. *See also* analgesics.

Asquith, Herbert Henry, 1st Earl of Oxford and (1852–1928) British statesman and Liberal prime minister (1908–16). Asquith's government introduced important social reforms, including noncontributory, old-age pensions (1908) and the National Insurance Act (1911); it ended the veto power of the House of Lords with the 1911 Parliament Act. After the outbreak of World War I, Asquith headed a Liberal-Conservative coalition government (1915–16). He remained leader of the Liberal Party until 1926. His second wife **Margot Asquith** (1865–1945) wrote an outspoken *Autobiography* (1922).

ass A small, fast-running mammal belonging to the genus *Equus* (horses), native to Africa and Asia. Asses are about 80 in (200 cm) long, weighing up to 55 lb (250 kg), and have characteristically long ears. The Asiatic wild ass (*E. hemionus*) has a gray or tan hide, a dark bristly mane, and a dark stripe along the back. The African wild ass (*E. asinus*) is the ancestor of the domestic donkey. Asses have long been used as pack animals. *See also* mule.

Assad, Hafiz al- (1928–   ) Syrian statesman; president (1971–   ). In 1966, following the coup in Syria by the radical Ba'athists, he became minister of defense. In 1970 he led a coup by the military wing of the *Ba'ath party and was elected president the following year. He was reelected in 1978, 1985, and 1992.

Assam A state in NE India, mostly in the Brahmaputra Valley beyond Bangladesh. High rainfall supports tea, Assam's economic mainstay. Rice, jute, sugar cane, and cotton are also grown. Other than forest products and crafts there is little manufacturing. Assam produces half of India's oil, as well as coal. *History*: a flourishing region by 1000 BC, Assam received later migrants from China and Burma (now Myanmar). Burmese invasions led Britain to assume control (1826). In World War II Assam played a strategic role in the Allied advance into Burma. Area: 30,310 sq mi (78,523 sq km). Population (1991): 22,300,000. Capital: Dispur.

assassin bug An insect belonging to a widely distributed family (*Reduviidae*; 4000 species), usually black or brown with a long beak used to pierce the skin and suck blood or body fluids from its prey. Assassin bugs generally prey on other insects but some attack mammals, including man. As well as inflicting a painful bite, they may transmit diseases, such as kala-azar and Chagas' disease. Suborder: *Heteroptera*; order: *Hemiptera*.

Assassins (Arabic: hashish eaters) A sect of the Ismaili. In Persia and Syria in the 12th and 13th centuries they were notorious for their practice of stabbing opponents to further their political and religious aims. It was commonly believed that the stabbings were carried out while they were under the influence of hashish, hence their name. They killed mainly Muslims, but also some Crusaders.

Assateague Island 38 05N 75 10W An island, separating Chincoteague Bay from the Atlantic Ocean, off the coasts of and part of Maryland and Virginia. The home of wild ponies and a Coast Guard station, Assateague became a National Seashore preserve in 1965. Length: 32 mi (52 km).

assault and battery In law, battery is the unlawful use of any physical force on someone else. Assault is an attempt to commit a battery or any other unlawful act that makes someone reasonably fear battery, whether or not there is any real intention to harm him. The offender is likely to face criminal charges and may also be sued for damages by his victim. Some "aggravated" assaults, as for example with a deadly weapon, carry higher penalties.

assemblage A work of art in which random objects and materials are integrated on a panel or in a free-standing construction, often to produce a satirical or surrealist effect. Early examples, from around 1915, include the *ready-mades of *Duchamp and the collages of Picasso. More recent assemblages are those of the *pop art movement, using everyday objects, such as clothing, furniture, and household utensils.

assembler A computer *program that makes up part of the *software of a computer. It converts instructions in a programming language into a form that the machine can follow directly.

assignats Paper money issued (1789–96) during the *French Revolution in order to pay off the government's debts. Initially they stimulated the economy and solved the problem of money shortage but ultimately they caused inflation, which reached a peak in 1795, when assignats with a face value of 45,500 million francs but virtually no real value were in circulation.

Assiniboine River A river in W Canada, rising in SE Saskatchewan and flowing generally SE through wheat-growing country to join the Red River at Winnipeg. Length: 590 mi (950 km).

Assisi 43 04N 12 37E A city in central Italy, in Umbria. It is the birthplace of St *Francis of Assisi, who founded the Franciscan Order in 1209, and is the site of a Franciscan convent, which has two Gothic churches containing frescoes by Giotto. Population: 24,002.

Associated Press. *See* news agency.

association In psychology, the linking of one idea to another. Similarity of meaning, physical similarity, and contrast can all cause an idea to call forth several others. When two mental events occur together an association forms between them: this is the basis of one kind of learning. According to the associationist school of psychology, the association of ideas is the basic process underlying human behavior. **Free association** is the chief method of *psychoanalysis: a patient speaks aloud his stream of consciousness, from which the analyst obtains clues to the underlying unconscious thought processes.

Association of South-East Asian Nations (ASEAN) An international organization, founded in 1967, to assist the cultural, economic, and social development of its member states (Brunei, Indonesia, Malaysia, the Philippines, Singapore, and Thailand). It aims to eliminate trade barriers, promote cultural exchanges, facilitate communications between members, and improve technology, commerce, and industry.

associative law The mathematical rule, obeyed by addition and multiplication in ordinary *arithmetic, that the order in which successive identical operations are performed does not affect the results: for addition $a + (b + c) = (a + b) + c$; for multiplication $a(bc) = (ab)c$.

Assyrian Empire An ancient kingdom on the Upper Tigris (now N Iraq), where the Assyrians (named for their god Ashur) settled in about 2500 BC, forming a dependency of Babylon. Ashur-uballit I (c. 1365–c. 1330) laid the foundations of the Empire, which after a period of decline was extended by *Tiglath-pileser I (1120–1074), who conquered the city of Babylon. A new era of aggressive expansion was initiated by *Ashurnasirpal II (883–859). The Assyrian domain was extended to Syria and Palestine under Shalmaneser III (858–824) and Assyrian ascendancy reached its zenith under *Tiglath-pileser III (745–727). *Sargon II (722–705), *Sennacherib (704–681), and *Esarhaddon (680–669) maintained the Empire but *Nineveh, the capital, fell to Media and Babylon in 612. The Assyrians built magnificent palaces with friezes that reflected their warlike character.

Astaire, Fred (Frederick Austerlitz; 1899–1987) US dancer and film star. He began his career as a music-hall dancer with his sister, Adele, a frequent partner. His best-known films are the 1930s musicals in which he was teamed with Ginger Rogers. These include *Top Hat* (1935), *Follow the Fleet* (1936), and *Shall We Dance* (1937). His later costars included Judy Garland, Leslie Caron, and Audrey Hepburn.

Astarte The Phoenician goddess of love and fertility, equivalent to the Babylonian *Ishtar and sometimes regarded as the counterpart of *Aphrodite. She was associated with the moon and often represented by a crescent.

astatine (At) A short-lived radioactive *halogen. Its longest-lived isotope, ^{210}At, has a half-life of 8.3 hours. Small amounts exist in nature as a result of uranium and thorium decay. At no 85; at wt 210; mp 200°F (302°C); bp 219°F (337°C).

Aster A genus of perennial herbaceous plants (about 500 species), many species of which are commonly known as Michaelmas daisies. Native to N temperate regions, they are widely grown as garden plants. Usually 24–40 in (60–100 cm) tall, they have flowers with blue, red, or white rays and a central yellow disc. *A. amellus* and *A. aeris* are common ornamental species. Family: *Compositae.

asteroid A small nonluminous rocky body that orbits a star. Over 100,000 orbit the sun, mostly (probably 95%) in a main belt between the orbits of Mars and Jupiter, 2.17–3.3 astronomical units from the sun. Of the remainder, some, such as *Icarus, have highly elliptical orbits that bring them close to the sun while others, including the *Trojan group, lie far beyond the main belt. The smallest asteroids are less than 0.6 mi (1 km) across with only about 200 exceeding 60 mi (100 km): the largest is *Ceres (623 mi, 1003 km). They are probably debris from collisions of bodies that formed between Mars and Jupiter. In turn, most meteorites (*see* meteor) are considered fragments of asteroids.

asthma A disorder in which breathlessness and wheezing are aggravated by certain stimuli, which cause the bronchi (which conduct air to the lungs) to become constricted. Bronchial asthma may be stimulated by a wide range of conditions and substances: it may be an allergic reaction (*see* allergy), it may occur secondarily to respiratory infection, or it may be brought on by exertion, certain drugs, or strong emotion. Treatment is by means of drugs that dilate the bronchi and—in the case of allergic asthma—by removing the allergen or by *desensitization. Severe asthmatic attacks require injections of corticosteroids. Cardiac asthma is associated with some forms of heart disease and requires a different treatment.

Asti 44 54N 8 13E A town in NW Italy, in Piedmont. It is famous for its sparkling wine (Asti Spumante). Population: 76,048.

astigmatism A form of *aberration that can occur in mirrors and lenses (including the eye). It results when the curvature is different in two mutually perpendicular planes; rays in one plane may then be in focus while rays in the other are out of focus. It is corrected in the eye by the use of cylindrical lenses.

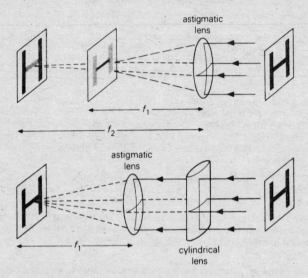

ASTIGMATISM *An astigmatic lens cannot focus vertical and horizontal lines at the same time. Here the vertical focal length f_1 is shorter than the horizontal focal length f_2. In the human eye this would be corrected by glasses with cylindrical lenses, reducing the overall focal length in the horizontal plane only, so that both vertical and horizontal lines are in sharp focus at distance f_1.*

Astilbe A genus of perennial, herbaceous, flowering plants (about 25 species), native to E Asia and North America and commonly cultivated for ornament in temperate regions. The flowers (usually pink or red) grow in branching, plumelike clusters; the plants may reach a height of 5 ft (1.5 m). Family: *Saxifragaceae.*

Aston, Francis William (1877–1945) British chemist, who developed the mass spectrometer for separating ions according to their atomic weight. His discovery of the isotopes of many nonradioactive elements, and of the whole number rule governing their masses, won him the 1922 Nobel Prize for Chemistry.

Astor, John Jacob (1763–1848) American businessman and financier. Born in Germany, Astor arrived in New York in 1783 and became active in the fur trade. With the opening of the American West, he quickly expanded his business to include shipping to the Far East and international agreements with Canadian traders and merchants. In 1811 he established his first Northwestern outpost, called Astoria, at the mouth of the Columbia River, and in later years he established many more fur trading stations throughout the Far West. In addition to amassing vast wealth through shipping and the fur trade, Astor also invested heavily in New York real estate. At the time of his death, he was reportedly one of the wealthiest men in America, leaving an estate estimated at more than $20,000,000.

Astoria 46 11N 123 50W A city and port in NW Oregon, near the mouth of the Columbia River. It was first explored by Meriwether Lewis and William Clark in 1805–06, and John Jacob Astor established the Pacific Fur Company here in 1811. Population (1990): 10,069.

Astrakhan 46 22N 48 04E A port in SE Russia on the Volga River. The city was an important trading center with the East until the Russian Revolution, after which its importance declined. Astrakhan fur, from the Karakul lamb of central Asia, was first brought to Russia by Astrakhan traders. More than half the population is employed in fishing or allied occupations. Population (1987): 509,000.

astrolabe An instrument for observing the altitude of celestial bodies and for solving other astronomical problems. Dating back to antiquity, it was used by mariners to determine latitude from the 15th century until the invention of the *sextant. The simple medieval astrolabe consisted of a graduated brass disc suspended in a vertical plane, with a movable sighting arm (the alidade) pivoted at its center. The modern prismatic astrolabe is used to measure the time taken for a celestial body to reach a predetermined altitude. It consists of an artificial horizon, such as a pool of mercury, and a prism placed in front of a telescope. Starlight enters the telescope directly by reflection from the prism and also indirectly after reflection by the artificial horizon. The two images thus formed move diagonally across the field of view of the telescope as a result of diurnal motion. At the altitude defined by the angle of the prism (usually 60°) the two images coincide.

astrology The study of the movements and positions of the heavenly bodies in relation to their presumed influence upon human affairs. Astrology originated in *Babylonia and then passed to Greece, India, China, and the Islamic lands. In medieval Europe astrologers had a respected role in public and personal life. Astrology is based upon an elaborate system of putative correspondences between celestial and mundane phenomena: each "house" (*see* zodiac), for instance, imparts a particular character to those born under its influence and the sun, moon, and principal planets in various positions relative to the houses and to each other predispose people to good or ill. The two branches of astrology are "natural" (concerned mainly with observations and theory) and "judicial" (foretelling events in individual lives by means of a horoscope). *See also* birthstone.

astronomical unit (AU) A unit of length equal to the mean distance between the earth and the sun 92.9 × 10^6 miles (1.495 × 10^{11} meters).

astronomy The study of celestial bodies and the universe of which they form part. One of the most ancient of the sciences, naked-eye astronomy flourished in China, Babylonia, Egypt, and classical Greece (*see* Aristarchus of Samos; Hipparchus; Ptolemaic system). After the decline of ancient Greek culture, interest in astronomy was the preserve of the Arabs for many centuries and it was they who developed the *astrolabe. European interest in the heavens, transmitted from the Arabs through Spain, reawakened in the 16th century with the work of *Copernicus and Tycho *Brahe, who were able to separate the science of astronomy from *astrology. But it was not until 1609 that Galileo's refracting *telescope (invented in Holland in 1608) enabled the sky to be investigated in any detail; in 1671 Newton devised the more effective reflecting telescope. These devices provided the means for the development of **descriptive astronomy, astronometry** (the measurement of the position of celestial bodies), and *celestial mechanics. In the 19th century, the use of spectroscopy (*see* spectrum) to study the physical and chemical composition of the universe provided the basis for the new sciences of *astrophysics and astrochemistry.

Until the 1940s all observations of the heavens were made by observing the light that passed through the "optical window" in the atmosphere. *Jansky's discovery (1932) that radio waves are emitted by celestial bodies, enabled the "radio window" in the atmosphere to be opened; with *radio astronomy a whole new dimension was added to the investigation of the universe.

With the use of rockets, artificial satellites, space probes, and space observatories all restrictions on observation imposed by the atmosphere were removed, enabling investigations to be made over the whole electromagnetic spectrum. But dependence on electromagnetic radiation as the source of information for astronomical investigations ended with the first moon landings and the unmanned *planetary probes.

This gradual evolution of astronomical instruments has been parallelled by far-reaching changes in *cosmology.

astrophysics The study of the physical and chemical processes and characteristics associated with celestial objects. It is based on theories developed in astronomy, physics, and chemistry and on observations of the radiation emitted by the objects. Originally only studies at optical and then at radio and infrared wavelengths were made, but with the recent advent of rockets and artificial satellites, sources of X-rays, gamma rays, and ultraviolet radiation can also be observed. *See also* cosmology.

Asturias A coastal region in NW Spain corresponding to the present-day province of Oviedo. When the Muslims invaded Spain in 718, the Visigoths withdrew to Asturias, where, protected by the Cantabrian Mountains in the S, they established a new kingdom, preserving Visigothic and Christian traditions. During the next two centuries, Asturias, the sole surviving Christian Spanish kingdom and the center of resistance to the Muslim advance, expanded into León and Galicia, especially under Alfonso III (reigned 866–c. 910). After his death the kingdom was divided between León, Castile, and Navarre.

Asturias, Miguel Ángel (1899–1974) Guatemalan novelist and poet. His novel *El Señor Presidente* (1946) is a study of political dictatorship; many of his other works, such as *Hombres de Maíz* (1949) and *Mulata de tal* (1960), reflect his interest in Mayan mythology and culture. He was awarded the Nobel Prize in 1967.

Asunción 25 15S 57 40W The capital of Paraguay, an important port in the S on the Paraguay River. Founded in 1536, it was for a time the center of the Spanish settlements in the area. The National University was founded in 1890 and the Catholic University in 1960. Industries, include flour milling, food processing, and textiles. Population (1990 est): 608,000.

Aswan (*or* Assuan; Greek name: Syene) 24 05N 32 56E A city in S Egypt, on the Nile River. Some ruins of the ancient city of Syene remain. The city is a popular tourist center and winter resort. Nearby quarries supplied granite for many Egyptian monuments. The *Aswan High Dam and earlier Aswan Dam are also nearby and have stimulated growth within the city. Population (1976): 144,000.

Aswan High Dam A major dam in Egypt, on the Nile River near Aswan. Begun in 1960 and financed by the Soviet Union, it was completed in 1970. It is about 3 mi (5 km) long and 328 ft (100 m) high; its reservoir, **Lake Nasser**, extends for about 350 mi (560 km) behind the dam. Since its construction the famous annual Nile floods have been controlled and water is available for irrigation, for domestic and industrial purposes, and for hydroelectric power. Ancient Nubian monuments (notably the *Abu Simbel and □Philae temples) that were threatened with permanent flooding were moved to new sites. About 4 mi (7 km) downstream is the earlier **Aswan Dam** (completed 1902); 1.2 mi (2 km) long and 177 ft (54 m) high, this provides irrigation water.

asymptote A straight line that a two-dimensional curve approaches but never meets as the curve is extended infinitely.

Asyut (*or* Assiut; ancient name: Lycopolis) 27 14N 31 07S The largest city in Upper Egypt, on the Nile River. It is an important commercial center and is renowned for its handicrafts, such as ivory carvings and tulle shawls, and its textile industries. Below the city the Asyut barrage provides water for irrigation. It has a university (1957). Population (1986): 273,191.

Atacama Desert (Spanish name: Desierto de Atacama) A cool arid area in N central Chile, extending for about 700 mi (1100 km) S from the Peruvian border. It consists chiefly of a series of salt basins and is one of the driest areas in the world; in some parts no rain has ever been recorded. There are valuable deposits of copper and it is a major source of nitrates. Area: about 31,000 sq mi (80,290 sq km).

Atahuallpa (*or* Atahualpa; d. 1533) The last King of the Inca Empire (1532–33). On the death of his father, Huayna Capac (1525), the Empire was divided between Atahuallpa and his brother Huascar. Atahuallpa overthrew his brother and declared himself king but was then captured by the Spanish conquistador Pizarro and, in spite of agreeing to the payment of a ransom, was executed.

Atalanta A swift-footed huntress of Greek mythology. Hippomenes (or Meilanion), on her promise to marry any man who could outrun her, raced with her. Furnished with three of the Hesperides' golden apples by *Aphrodite, which he dropped to distract her, he won the race and married her.

Atatürk, Kemal (Mustafa Kemal; 1881–1938) Turkish statesman, who was the chief founder of modern Turkey; president (1922–38). Born in Salonika, he entered the army and distinguished himself in World War I. After the war he opposed the humiliating Treaty of *Versailles and as president of the provisional government organized the defeat of the Greek invasion of Asia Minor (1920). In 1922 the Ottoman sultan was deposed and Mustafa Kemal became the first president of Turkey. From then until his death he worked to make Turkey a modern secular state. He took the surname Atatürk (Father of the Turks) in 1934.

ataxia Loss of muscular coordination, often caused by disease of the part of the brain (the cerebellum) that controls movement. Ataxia may accompany severe vitamin B_{12} and folic acid deficiencies or follow a brain hemorrhage.

Atget, (Jean) Eugène (Auguste) (1856–1927) French photographer. He turned to photography in 1898 after a career first at sea and later on the stage. He specialized in scenes of Parisian life, including a notable series on brothels (commissioned 1921). Apart from Man *Ray's interest in the surrealist effect of his shop-window series, he received recognition only after his death.

Athabasca, Lake A lake in W Canada, in NW Saskatchewan and NE Alberta, drained by the Slave River. Uranium ores were discovered on the N shore (1950s). Area: 3120 sq mi (8080 sq km).

KEMAL ATATÜRK *In the center, photographed in 1922.*

Athabascan A group of North American Indian languages spoken by tribes living to the west of Hudson Bay in Alaska and Canada, and by some tribes of the SW US. The northern group includes Koyukon, Tanana, *Chippewa, Slave, and Yellowknife, and the southern group includes *Apache and *Navajo.

Athabasca River A river in W Canada, in N Alberta flowing from the Rocky Mountains to Lake Athabasca through tar sands estimated to contain half the world's known oil reserves. Length: 765 mi (1230 km).

Athanasian Creed A Christian profession of faith traditionally attributed to St *Athanasius but probably dating from the 5th century. Its central statements concern the doctrines of the *Trinity and of the *Incarnation. Once popular in the Western Churches, it is now little used.

Athanasius, St (296–373 AD) Egyptian churchman, Bishop of Alexandria. After attending the Council of *Nicaea in 325, he was appointed Bishop of Alexandria in 328 and remained primate of Egypt for 43 years. During this time he led the opposition to the powerful *Arianism that flourished in the East under the emperors Constantine and Constantius. He was expelled from his see four times, but his orthodox teaching regarding the divinity of Jesus Christ was ultimately affirmed by the Council of Constantinople (381). Feast day: May 2.

atheism The denial of the existence of God (or gods). Historically atheism has taken many different forms. In theocratic societies charges of atheism were frequently made against individuals or groups suspected of antisocial behavior or of dissent from the prevailing orthodoxy. Philosophical materialists, such as *Hobbes, were also attacked as atheists but the spread of *rationalism in the 18th century created a climate sympathetic to atheism. In the 19th century, scientific advances challenged the old arguments for the existence of God, making atheism respectable philosophically, if not socially. Today rigorous atheists hold either that the concept of God, being untestable, is simply meaningless (*see* logical positivism) or that all we know by scientific means about the universe suggests that God is a false notion (*see* humanism). *Compare* agnosticism.

Athelstan (d. 939) King of England (925–39), succeeding his father Edward the Elder; he was crowned King of Mercia in 924. He defeated a Scottish invasion force in 937 and is also known for six extant legal codes.

Athena (*or* Pallas Athena) The Greek goddess of war and of wisdom, the protectress of Athens. Born from the head of Zeus, fully armed with a javelin, she was his favorite child. In the Trojan War she constantly aided the Greeks. She also helped Heracles in his labors and guided Perseus on his expedition against the Gorgons. Odysseus voyaged home from Troy under her protection. A virgin goddess, in peacetime she was a patroness of the arts and industry. Athens is named for her, and the Parthenon was the center of her worship. She is identified with the Roman *Minerva.

Athenagoras (2nd century AD) Greek Christian apologist, who taught in Athens and Alexandria. His *Apology* or *Legatio pro Christianis* (177) addressed to *Marcus Aurelius, defended Christianity against charges of cannibalism and licentiousness arising from misunderstandings of the doctrines of the Eucharist and universal love.

Athens 33 57N 83 23W A city in NE Georgia, on the Oconee River. The University of Georgia was established here in 1801. Industries include textiles, lumber, dairy products, and electrical appliances. Population (1990): 45,734.

ATHENS *The Parthenon.*

Athens (Modern Greek name: Athínai) 37 59N 23 42E The capital of Greece, situated on a plain in the SE of the country near the Saronic Gulf. It is the administrative, cultural, and economic center of the country and is administratively joined to its port and main industrial sector, *Piraeus. Tourism is an important source of revenue. Athens is a city that combines the ancient and the modern, with only one or two small Byzantine and neo-Byzantine churches surviving to testify to the period between Roman times and the early 19th century. The many remains of ancient Athens are focused on the Acropolis. Crowned by the *Parthenon, it contains the Ionic Erechtheum, the Propylaea (a gateway), and the tiny temple of Athena Nike. To the NW, the recently restored Agora (market), contains the Theseum (5th century BC), probably the best-preserved ancient temple. To the N and E lies modern Athens, which includes the university, founded in 1837. *History*: there is evidence of settlements dating back to the 3rd millennium BC. Athens probably enjoyed its first rise to fame under Pisistratus and his sons in the 6th century BC. Around the year 506 Cleisthenes established a democracy for the free men of Athens. During the following century it became the leading Greek city state, defeating the Persians with the aid of its powerful navy (*see* Greek-Persian Wars). The Long Walls, connecting the city to Piraeus, and the Parthenon date from this period. Under Pericles, it reached a peak of intellectual brilliance with the philosophy of Socrates and the drama of Aeschylus, Sophocles, and Euripides. Defeated by Sparta in the *Peloponnesian War (431–404), it recovered slowly, regaining its intellectual supremacy with such figures as Plato, Aristotle, and Aristophanes. Its role as a major political power, however, was finally lost when defeated by Philip of Macedon in 338 BC, and in the 2nd century BC it came under the rule of Rome. Owing to the influence of Hellenic culture on the Romans it continued to prosper and, despite being overrun by Germanic tribes in the 4th century AD, maintained its academic standing until the closure of the schools of philosophy by Justinian in 529. The city fell to the Crusaders in 1204 and was under Turkish occupation from 1456 until 1833, when it became the capital of the newly independent kingdom of Greece. Since then it has grown from almost nothing to a busy modern city. It has been the scene of frequent revolts and civil wars and was occupied by the Germans in World War II. Population (1991): 748,110.

atherosclerosis (*or* atheroma) Patchy thickening of the lining of arteries caused by the deposition of fatty material and fibrous tissue. This tends to obstruct the blood flow and predisposes to *thrombosis, which may lead to a heart attack or a stroke. In the western world atherosclerosis is common in adults: its underlying cause remains a controversial issue but is believed to be associated with a diet high in animal fats (*see* cholesterol) and refined sugar, cigarette smoking, and obesity. Its incidence increases with age and it is exacerbated by high blood pressure. The extent of the condition can be reduced by treatment of any underlying illness.

athlete's foot. *See* ringworm.

athletics Sports that involve running, walking, throwing, and jumping competitions. They are divided into track and field events. At international level the track events include races over 100 m, 200 m, 400 m, 800 m, 1500 m, 5000 m, and 10,000 m; the 110 m and 400 m hurdles (*see* hurdling); the 4 × 100 and 4 × 400 m relay races; the 3000 m steeplechase; the *marathon; and the 20 km walk (*see* walking). The standard field events are *high jump, *long jump, *triple jump, *pole vault, *shot put, *discus throw, *hammer throw, and *javelin throw. In addition there are the *decathlon (for men), the modern pentathlon, and the *pentathlon (for women). The governing body is the International Amateur Athletic Federation.

Athos, Mount 1. 40 10N 24 19E A mountain in NE Greece, at the end of Aktí, the easternmost of the three promontories of Chalcidice. Height: 6670 ft (2033 m). **2.** An autonomous Greek Orthodox monastic republic occupying the mountain. Area: 31 sq mi (80 sq km).

Atlanta 33 45N 84 23W The capital of Georgia, situated at the foot of the Appalachian Mountains. Founded in 1837 and partly destroyed by Gen Sherman in 1864, it is now the industrial, administrative, transportation, and cultural center of the whole of the SE of the US. Its major industries include aircraft, machinery, cottonseed oil, textiles, clothing, and chemicals. In 1991 it was chosen as the site for the 1996 Summer Olympics. Population (1990): 394,017.

Atlantic, Battle of the. *See* World War II.

Atlantic Charter (1941) An agreement between Pres. Franklin D. Roosevelt and British prime minister Winston Churchill that stated common national policies. Freedom of choice of government, improved worldwide economic and social conditions, freedom of the seas, and freedom from unwanted territorial takeovers and changes were some of the main points, as well as an end to Nazism and the use of force.

Atlantic City 39 23N 74 27W A city in the US, in New Jersey on Absecon Beach (an island on the Atlantic coast). A major pleasure resort, it has five piers and a multitude of amusements, shops, hotels, and parks; gambling casinos were introduced in the late 1970s. A popular conference center, it is the site of the annual Miss America Pageant (first held in 1921). Its industries, aside from gambling, include glassware, china, and confectionery. Population (1990): 37,986.

Atlantic Intracoastal Waterway A shipping route along the Atlantic coast. It serves the ports between Cape Cod and Florida Bay. Length: 1550 mi (2495 km).

Atlantic Ocean The world's second largest ocean, extending between Antarctica, America, Europe, and Africa. It is the world's most heavily traveled seaway, although floating ice is a hazard. Its major currents include the *Gulf Stream crossing it W–E. Its floor is rich in minerals, oil and gas now being exploited. The Mid-Atlantic Ridge has peaks rising above sea level as islands, such as the Azores. The youngest of the oceans, the Atlantic was formed when the continents now surrounding it first split apart about 200 million years ago.

Atlantic Wall The extensive fortifications built by the Germans in *World War II along the Atlantic coast. They failed to prevent *D-day Normandy landings by US and British troops (June 6, 1944).

Atlantis In Greek legend, a large island civilization in the Atlantic beyond the Pillars of Hercules (Straits of Gibraltar), which, according to Plato's dialogues the *Timaeus* and *Critias*, was destroyed by earthquake. The story, transmitted to the Greeks by the Egyptians, may refer to a cataclysmic volcanic eruption (c. 1450 BC) on the island of *Thera in the Cyclades N of Crete.

Atlas In Greek mythology, the brother of Prometheus and son of the Titan Iapetus and the nymph Clymene. As a punishment for his part in the revolt of the Titans against the Olympians he was forced to hold up the pillars separating heaven from earth. From the 16th century this was commonly depicted in the frontispieces of books of maps, which thus came to be called atlases.

Atlas Mountains A mountain system in NW Africa, extending generally NE from the Atlantic coast of Morocco to Tunisia. It consists of several mountain chains and plateaus and rises to 13,664 ft (4165 m) at Mount Toubkal in the Moroccan Great Atlas range.

atman (Sanskrit: breath, soul) A fundamental concept of Hinduism, signifying the individual soul or the eternal essential self. When the body dies the *atman* is continuously reincarnated until final spiritual release is achieved. In the later *Upanishads, and in the Hindu philosophical schools of Samkhya and orthodox Vedanta, the function of *atman* and its relation to *Brahman is the central issue. Some thinkers regard these two as analogous principles only; for others they are essentially identical.

atmosphere (meteorology) The gaseous envelope surrounding the earth or any other celestial body. The earth's atmosphere is composed of nitrogen (78.08%), oxygen (20.95%), argon (0.93%), and carbon dioxide (0.03%), together with small proportions of other gases and variable amounts of water vapor. In the lowest layer of the earth's atmosphere, the **troposphere**, air temperature decreases as height increases. The thickness of this layer varies from about 4.5 mi (7 km) to about 10 mi (16 km) at the equator. It is here that most meteorological phenomena occur. In the **stratosphere**, which goes up to about 31 mi (50 km), temperature is fairly constant because the sun's radiation counteracts the effect of decreasing density. Above the stratosphere lies the **mesosphere**, extending up to about 50 mi (80 km), in which temperatures decrease with height, and the **thermosphere**, in which temperatures increase with height; these fall within the *ionosphere. The outermost layer, from about 248 mi (400 km), is called the **exosphere**. From 62 mi (100 km) upward the oxygen dissociates into atoms. There is little nitrogen above 93 mi (150 km). The atmosphere protects the earth from excessive radiation and cosmic particles and is important in maintaining the heat balance of the earth. *See also* ozone.

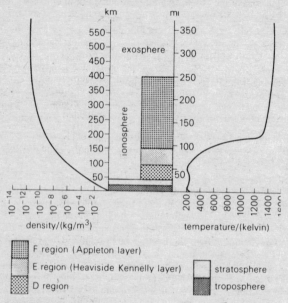

ATMOSPHERE *The density of the atmosphere falls off sharply with height above the earth's surface. The more complicated temperature variation is shown in the graph, which also illustrates the regions of the ionosphere.*

atmosphere (unit) A unit of pressure equal to 101,325 pascals or 760 millimeters of mercury.

atmospheric pressure The pressure exerted by the atmosphere. It decreases with altitude and, at ground level, varies around 760 millimeters of mercury, 101,325 pascals, or 1013.25 millibars.

atom. *See* atomic theory.

atomic bomb. *See* nuclear weapons.

atomic clock A highly accurate clock based on the frequency at which certain atoms or molecules vibrate between two states. For example, the nitrogen atom in the ammonia molecule vibrates through the plane of the three hydrogen atoms and back again with a frequency of 23,870 hertz. In the ammonia clock, a quartz-crystal oscillator feeds energy into ammonia gas at this frequency. The ammonia only absorbs energy at this frequency, enabling a feedback circuit to control the frequency of the oscillator. *See also* cesium clock.

atomic energy. *See* nuclear energy.

Atomic Energy Commission *See* Nuclear Regulatory Commission.

atomic mass unit (amu) A unit of mass equal to one-twelfth of the mass of an atom of carbon-12 ($1.660,33 \times 10^{-27}$ kg). Atomic weights (relative atomic masses) are based on this unit. The unit is also called the dalton (after John *Dalton).

atomic number (Z) The number of protons in a nucleus of an atom. It determines the position of the element in the *periodic table and, in a neutral atom, is equal to the number of electrons surrounding the nucleus. It is also known as proton number.

atomic theory The theory that an atom is the smallest particle of an element that can take part in a chemical reaction. *Democritus is credited with first conceiving the idea, which was, however, vigorously attacked by *Aristotle since Democritus's atoms existed in a vacuum, an idea repugnant to Aristotle. The atomic concept fell from favor until the early 19th century, when John *Dalton used the idea to explain the fact that elements combined together in simple proportions. The structure of the atom was first investigated by Lord *Rutherford, who discovered that it consisted of a heavy positively charged core (the *nucleus) surrounded by *electrons. Niels Bohr elaborated on this model (*see* Bohr atom) but the modern concept of the atom was not finally elucidated until the advent of Schrödinger's *wave mechanics.

Almost all of the atom's mass is concentrated in the nucleus, which consists of positively charged *protons and neutral *neutrons of almost equal mass (the mass of the electron is only 1/1836 that of the proton). The number of electrons in a neutral atom is equal to the number of protons in the nucleus, as the charge on the proton is equal but opposite to that of the electron. The electrons can be thought of as existing in a series of shells around the nucleus, each shell corresponding to a particular energy level. According to the *Pauli exclusion principle each shell may only hold a certain number of electrons. The chemical behavior of an atom is largely determined by the number of electrons in its outermost shell, as atoms are most stable when they have no partly filled shells, a state often achieved by chemical combination. In combining, atoms may either share electrons to form covalent bonds or gain (or lose) electrons to form electrovalent (ionic) bonds (*see* chemical bond).

All the nuclei of an element contain the same number of protons (p) but not always the same number of neutrons (n). Atoms with the same value of p but a different value of n are called isotopes of that element. The value of (n + p) is called the mass number. Isotopes are referred to in several ways, e.g. uranium-235, U-235, ^{235}U, $^{235}_{92}$U (the subscript in this case being the *atomic number, the value 235 being the mass number of a particular uranium isotope). *See also* particle physics.

atomic weight The ratio of the average mass of the atoms in a given sample to one-twelfth the mass of a carbon-12 atom. The modern, more correct, name is relative atomic mass.

atomism The philosophical attitude that seeks irreducible elements, whether of matter or thought, to account for the (compound) phenomena that we actually experience. The Greek *Democritus believed that the world is composed of qualitatively similar atoms of different shapes. In this view, atoms may be either

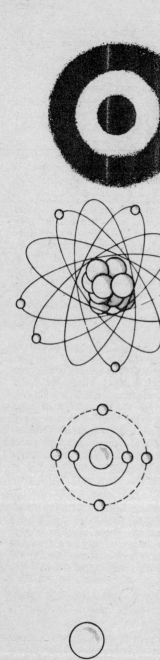

By the 19th century, it was regarded as a minute solid billiard ball.

With the work of Rutherford between 1906 and 1914 and Bohr in 1913, it was depicted as a miniature solar system with a central nucleus and orbiting electron.

Sommerfeld's refinements of quantum theory in 1916 led to a model with precessing elliptical orbits and spinning electrons.

By 1926, Schrödinger's wave mechanics had been published, based on de Broglie's dual wave-particle concept of electrons. The atom is now regarded as a nucleus surrounded by a "haze" of probabilities that electrons will occur in certain positions.

ATOMIC THEORY

The main characteristic of an atom, as the smallest particle of matter, is not what our models of it look like but the way it absorbs and emits energy.

When an atom absorbs energy (e.g. when light of the right wavelength falls on it), its electrons jump to a higher energy level.

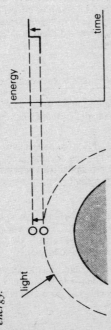

When these electrons fall back to their original (ground) state they emit energy (as light, ultraviolet, etc.).

All matter and therefore all atoms, according to modern physics, consists of two kinds of particles: leptons and quarks. Electrons are leptons; the particles of the nucleus (protons and neutrons) are each made up of different arrangements of three quarks.

The simplest atomic nucleus is the hydrogen nucleus consisting of one proton.

An isotope of hydrogen, deuterium, has a nucleus consisting of one proton and one neutron.

All other nuclei consist of arrangements of protons and neutrons. The carbon nucleus consists of six protons and six neutrons.

ATOMIC THEORY

completely independent of one another or related in contingent or necessary ways. *Lucretius was an influential proponent of atomism, and *Gassendi, *Boyle, and *Locke revived it in the 17th century. Logical atomism, held temporarily by both *Russell and *Wittgenstein, assumed that there were unanalyzable specks of meaning that could be articulated in atomic propositions, from which no subordinate proposition could be derived.

Aton In Egyptian religion, the one supreme god proclaimed by *Akhenaton and symbolized by a solar disk with arms.

atonality The use in music of all 12 notes of the scale in such a way as to avoid *tonality. Atonality arose from the increasing *chromaticism of the music of the late 19th century. Schoenberg's second string quartet (1907–08), for example, begins in the key of F sharp minor but has an atonal final movement. *See also* serialism.

atonement In religious belief, the idea of reconciliation between God and man or, literally, at-one-ment with God. The idea implies that the relationship between God and mankind has been interrupted or damaged by human failing or sin. In Judaism, *Yom Kippur or the Day of Atonement is the holiest day of the year. In Christianity, the crucifixion of Christ is traditionally interpreted as a sacrifice for men's sins that effects a reconciliation with God and brings to an end the estrangement started by Adam's sin.

Atonement, Day of. *See* Yom Kippur.

ATP (adenosine triphosphate) An energy-rich compound (a nucleotide) with an important role in the metabolism of living organisms. On its formation from ADP (adenosine diphosphate) in the mitochondria of cells, ATP incorporates a large amount of energy that, on release, is used by cells to manufacture proteins, carbohydrates, fats, etc., and to provide the energy for muscle contraction and other dynamic processes.

Atreus In Greek mythology, King of Mycenae, the son of Pelops and father of Agamemnon and Menelaus. His house was cursed as a result of a feud between him and his brother Thyestes over the throne of Mycenae. After Thyestes had seduced his wife, Atreus killed Thyestes' sons and served them at a feast. Another son of Thyestes, Aegisthus, later killed Atreus.

atrium (anatomy). *See* heart.

atrium (architecture) **1.** Originally an important part of a Roman house, a central, partly covered court, frequently colonnaded, which often contained the shrine to the household god. Around it were the entrances to the main rooms. Later it became the main reception room of the house. **2.** An open area or courtyard in front of early Christian churches.

atropine An alkaloid, extracted from deadly nightshade, that acts on certain nerves of the autonomic nervous system. It is used during anesthesia to decrease secretions of the lungs, which lowers the risk of postoperative chest infections. It also dilates the pupil of the eye and speeds up the heart rate.

Atropos. *See* Fates.

Attalus I Soter (269–197 BC) Ruler of *Pergamum (241–197), who took the title of king after a victory over the Galatians (before 230). By his conquests in Asia Minor and his support of Roman opposition to Philip V of Macedon (237–179; reigned 220–179), he made Pergamum a significant power.

attar of roses (otto of rose *or* essence of rose) A fragrant, colorless or pale-yellow oil distilled from fresh rose petals. It is produced in Bulgaria, S France, Morocco, and Turkey. About 1 gram of attar is extracted from 10 lbs (4 kg) of roses. Rosewater is a by-product of the distillation. It is used to make perfumes and in flavorings.

Attenborough, Sir Richard (1923–   ) British film actor, director, and producer. After numerous appearances in British war films and comedies he developed into a versatile character actor in such films as *Loot* (1969) and *10 Rillington Place* (1971). As director, his films include *Young Winston* (1974), *A Bridge Too Far* (1977), *Gandhi* (1982), and *Cry Freedom* (1987).

attenuation The reduction in amplitude of an electromagnetic wave or an electric current during transmission. In electric circuits attenuation is often introduced to reduce unwanted components of a signal. Broadcast electromagnetic radiation is attenuated as it passes through buildings, etc., and to a lesser extent by its passage through the atmosphere. In space, however, the attenuation is negligible.

Attica A region of ancient E central Greece. According to Greek legend the 12 towns of Attica were united by Theseus into a single state, which was dominated by Athens by the 5th century BC.

Attila (c. 406–53) King of the Huns (434–53), known as the Scourge of God. After murdering his brother and coruler, Bleda, he extended his possessions in central Europe and attacked (441–43) the eastern frontier of the Roman Empire. In 451 he invaded Gaul and suffered his only defeat, at the battle of the *Catalaunian Plains. His campaigns in Italy (452) caused much destruction. The pope paid him to spare Rome and Attila died shortly afterward.

Attlee, Clement (Richard), 1st Earl (1883–1967) British statesman; Labour Prime Minister (1945–51). A lawyer by profession, Attlee taught at the London School of Economics (1913–23). He was elected to Parliament in 1922 and was leader of the Labour Party (1935–55). As the first postwar prime minister he presided over the establishment of the welfare state, nationalizing major industries and introducing the National Health Service. His government also granted independence within the Commonwealth to India.

attorney general Chief law officer of the US, appointed by the President and a member of the cabinet. The attorney general administers the Department of *Justice, directs the penal system, advises the President and executive department heads on legal issues, oversees US marshals and represents the country in legal matters. The Judiciary Act of 1789 provided for the office of attorney general. Each state also has an attorney general, who is that state's chief law officer and who fulfills most of the above duties at the state level.

Attucks, Crispus (?1723–70) US African-American slave and sailor, the first American victim of the American Revolution. An escaped slave, Attucks was a merchant seaman for twenty years. While in Boston in 1770, he was part of a group of protesters against excessive colonial taxation that was fired upon by the British and was the first to die.

Aube River A river in N central France, rising on the Plateau de Langres and flowing NW to the Seine River. Length: 140 mi (225 km).

Auber, Daniel François Esprit (1782–1871) French composer. He is remembered for his 48 operas, chiefly light works to librettos by the playwright A. E. Scribe (1791–1861), written for the Paris Opéra-Comique. Of these only *La Muette de Portici* (1828) and *Fra Diavolo* (1830) are performed with any frequency.

aubergine A spiny herbaceous plant, *Solanum melongena*, native to S Asia and also known as eggplant. It is commonly grown in warmer regions for its fruit, a large white, yellow, or purple berry that is eaten as a vegetable. The plant grows to a height of 24–40 in (60–100 cm). Family: *Solanaceae*.

Aubrietia (*or* Aubrieta) A genus of trailing herbaceous perennial flowering plants (about 15 species), native to mountainous areas of E Europe and W Asia. *A. deltoidea* is commonly grown in rock gardens, bearing small purple, red, or pink flowers. Family: *Cruciferae*.

Auburn 32 36N 85 29W A city in E Alabama. The site of Auburn University (1856), it also has textile and lumber mills. Population (1990): 33,830.

Aubusson 45 58N 2 10E A town in central France, in the Creuse department on the Creuse River. It has been renowned for its carpets and tapestries since the 16th century. Population (1982): 6500.

Aubusson, Pierre d' (1423–1503) French cardinal and grand master of the Knights *Hospitallers. Remembered chiefly for his defense of Rhodes against the Turks in 1480, he secured a long-term truce in 1481 by agreeing to imprison the Ottoman sultan's enemy and brother.

Auckland 36 55S 174 47E The largest city and port in New Zealand, on North Island occupying an isthmus between Waitemata Harbor and Manukau Harbor. Founded in 1840, it was the capital of New Zealand until 1865. The University of Auckland was established in 1882 and there are two cathedrals (Roman Catholic and Anglican). The city is connected with the mainly residential North Shore by the Auckland Harbor Bridge (1959). Auckland is a major industrial center with engineering, food processing, ship building, and chemical industries. The chief exports are iron and steel, dairy products, and meat. Population (1991): 953,058.

Auckland Islands 50 35S 166 00E A group of six uninhabited islands in the S Pacific Ocean, belonging to New Zealand. An attempt to introduce cattle and sheep was unsuccessful (1852). Area: 234 sq mi (611 sq km).

auction A method of selling goods publicly, in which many prospective buyers compete with each other, the sale being made to the highest bidder. If bidding does not reach a reserve price specified by the vendor, then the auctioneer withdraws the goods. Rules vary from trade to trade, but the auctioneer usually acts as the seller's agent, charging a commission on goods sold. Antiques, works of art, houses, and some commercial commodities are sold by auction. In a **Dutch auction**, the sale is offered first at an unrealistically high price, which is lowered gradually until a bid is made.

Auden, W(ystan) H(ugh) (1907–73) British-American poet. His early volumes, beginning with *Poems* (1930) and *Look, Stranger!* (1936), established him as the leading figure of a group of left-wing poets of the 1930s, that included Stephen *Spender, Louis *MacNeice, and C. *Day Lewis. He also wrote verse dramas in collaboration with Christopher *Isherwood, with whom he went to the US in 1939. He became a US citizen in 1946. He wrote several opera libretti, notably for Stravinsky's *The Rake's Progress* (1951), and his later poetry was characterized by a form of Christian existentialism that replaced his earlier Marxism.

Audenarde. *See* Oudenaarde.

audio frequency A frequency in the range 20 to 20,000 hertz, i.e. the range of frequencies to which the human ear is sensitive.

audiovisual education Education carried out with the help of audio (sound) or visual techniques. There are a whole range of audiovisual aids, including television, tape and video recorders, teaching machines, and overhead projectors and the long-established wallcharts and blackboards. Although audiovisual education has been used throughout history, its systematic application developed in the 20th century. Research into the method has shown that, when properly used, it increases both the student's interest in and recall of the material presented. Since 1958 the US Congress has provided aid for educational broadcasting.

auditing. *See* accountancy.

Audubon, John James (1785–1851) US naturalist and artist noted for his lifelike drawings and paintings of birds. Educated in France, Audubon emigrated to the US, where he developed an interest in bird migration and began painting birds and other animals. *The Birds of America* (4 vols, 1827–38) established his reputation as an illustrator. The National Audubon Society, founded in his honor in 1886, is dedicated to the conservation of birds throughout the US.

Auger effect The spontaneous ejection of an electron from an excited, singly charged, positive ion to form a doubly charged ion. The ion may be excited by a gamma ray from its nucleus or by bombarding it with particles, such as photons or electrons. It is named for the French physicist Pierre Auger.

Augsburg 48 21N 10 54E A city in S Germany, in Bavaria at the confluence of the Wertach and Lech Rivers. It is a major industrial center; its manufactures include textiles, chemicals, cars, aircraft, and printing machinery. Many of its historic buildings, including the 10th-century cathedral, survived the bombardment of World War II. *History*: founded by the Romans in 15 BC, it became an important banking and commercial center in the 15th and 16th centuries mainly with the aid of the Fugger and Welsen merchant families. An imperial free city from 1276, it was the seat of the notable diets of 1530 (*see* Augsburg Confession) and 1555 (*see* Augsburg, Peace of). It is the birthplace of Holbein and Brecht. Population (1991 est): 257,000.

Augsburg, League of (1686) An alliance originally consisting of the Holy Roman Empire, Spain, Sweden, and several German states. In 1689 they were joined by England, Holland, and Savoy, thus forming the *Grand Alliance, which waged war on Louis XIV of France from 1689 to 1697.

Augsburg, Peace of (1555) A religious compromise issued by an imperial diet at Augsburg, over which the future Emperor *Ferdinand I presided, which established the coexistence of Roman Catholicism and Lutheranism in Germany. Each prince was to determine the denomination of his territory, which was to be either Catholicism or Lutheranism. In order to safeguard Catholic property, any prince who became a Protestant was to renounce his land and revenues. The settlement gave Germany 50 years of peace.

Augsburg Confession The main and distinctive confession of faith of the Lutheran Churches. Drawn up in its original form by Melancthon and approved by Luther, it was presented to the imperial diet that Emperor Charles V had summoned at Augsburg in 1530 to judge Luther's controversial preaching.

augury Ritual divination practiced in ancient Rome by augurs, priests skilled in the auspices, or interpretation of certain natural occurrences. The word "auspice" derives from the Latin for "bird" + "observation"; the commonest means of augury were the flight and song of birds, but thunder, lightning, movements of animals, and the appetites of tame chickens were also studied. Signs on the augur's left were propitious, those on his right unpropitious. Augury accompanied every major undertaking, to ascertain through the auspices whether the gods were favorably inclined.

August Eighth month of the year. Its name is derived from *Augustus* in honor of Augustus Caesar, the first Roman emperor. It has 31 days. August's zodiac signs are Leo and Virgo; its flower is the poppy, and its birthstones are the sardonyx and the peridot.

Augusta 33 29N 82 00W A town in Georgia on the Savannah River. It is a medical and service center for the many government installations nearby. Population (1990): 44,639.

Augusta 44 17N 69 50W The capital of Maine, on the Kennebec River. Established as a trading post in 1628, it has a large timber industry. Population (1990): 21,325.

Augustine of Hippo, St (354–430 AD) North African theologian; Father and Doctor of the Church, born at Tagaste. His mother was a Christian but, after studying at Carthage, he became a Manichaean. He taught rhetoric in Rome and in Milan, where he was attracted to *Neoplatonism. However, under the influence of St *Ambrose, Bishop of Milan, he was finally converted to Christianity in 386. On his return to Africa, he lived as a monk until he was ordained at Hippo in 391. He became Bishop of Hippo in 396 and died there during a Vandal siege. His works are the most important and influential of those written by the early Fathers, especially *The City of God*, a defense of Christianity in 22 books, and his spiritual autobiography, *The Confessions*. His other writings include commentaries on the scriptures, sermons, letters, and treatises against the heresies *Manichaeism, Donatism (*see* Donatists), and Pelagianism (*see* Pelagius). He was most actively involved in the Pelagian controversy, in which he upheld the doctrines of original sin and divine grace. Feast day: Aug 28.

Augustinians A term sometimes used generally to refer to all the Roman Catholic religious orders that follow the Rule of St Augustine, a program for the religious life drawn up by *Augustine of Hippo. More specifically it refers to the orders of the Augustinian (*or* Austin) Canons, founded in the 11th century, and the Augustinian Hermits (*or* Austin Friars), founded in the 13th century, both of which have corresponding orders for women.

Augustus (*or* Octavian; 63 BC–14 AD) The first Roman emperor, who restored the greatness of the Roman world following the disintegration of the Republic. Augustus, who was born Gaius Octavius, was the great-nephew and adopted son of Julius Caesar. After Caesar's assassination in 44, Augustus (now Gaius Julius Caesar Octavianus; *or* Octavian) came to an agreement with *Mark Antony and in 43 they formed the second *Triumvirate with *Lepidus. Lepidus was forced to retire in 36 and Augustus' relations with Mark Antony failed to withstand Antony's abandonment of his wife Octavia (Augustus' sister) for *Cleopatra. Antony's defeat at Actium in 31 allowed Augustus to establish his personal supremacy at the head of an autocratic government known as the principate. In 27 he was proclaimed Augustus (sacred).

Augustus was an outstanding administrator and consolidated the so-called Pax Romana (Roman Peace) that he had established with a durable administrative and financial system. The patronage of his close adviser, *Maecenas, fostered a literary renaissance and with the military assistance of *Agrippa, and later of his own stepson,*Tiberius, he secured and then expanded the Empire. In 4 AD he named Tiberius, the son of his third wife *Livia Drusilla, his heir. Augustus was deified after his death.

Augustus I (1526–86) Elector of Saxony (1553–86). A moderate Protestant, he was a follower of Lutheranism and a harsh opponent of Calvinism. His economic, administrative, and social reforms made Saxony one of the most prosperous German states.

AUGUSTUS *During his reign the coinage was restored to the control of the Senate and coins were marked S.C. (senatus consulto, by decree of the Senate); the emperor's head is shown on the obverse.*

Augustus (II) the Strong (1670–1733) King of Poland (1697–1706, 1710–33). Augustus' invasion of Livonia (1700) began the Great *Northern War, in which he was defeated by Charles XII of Sweden (1702). Augustus was deposed by the Polish diet (1704), formally abdicating in 1706, but was restored by Russia in 1710. His malgovernment precipitated Poland's decline.

auk A stout-bodied seabird belonging to a family (*Alcidae*; 22 species) occurring in the N hemisphere and having a black and white plumage and short, pointed wings. The family includes *puffins, *razorbills, *guillemots, the little auk (*Plautus alle*), and the extinct flightless great auk (*Pinguinus impennis*). Order: *Charadriiformes* (gulls, plovers, etc.).

Aung San (c. 1914–47) Burmese statesman; leader of the independence movement. Committed to radical politics from his student days at Rangoon University, Aung San founded the Anti-Fascist People's Freedom League in 1944. He played a crucial role in the negotiations that led to Burmese independence from Britain but was assassinated before it was fully attained.

Aung San Suu Kyu (1945–   ) Human rights activist in Myanmar (formerly Burma), who was put under house arrest by the military government in 1989 for her efforts to force democratic reforms. The daughter of Burma's independence leader, Aung San, she was raised and lived abroad until 1988, when she returned to her homeland and became involved in politics. Her campaign for democracy was recognized in 1991 when she was awarded the Nobel Prize for peace.

Aurangzeb (1618–1707) The last Mogul emperor of India (1658–1707); the youngest son of *Shah Jahan. When Shah Jahan fell ill in 1657 Aurangzeb fought a war of succession against his older brother Dara Shikoh. Easily winning, he ascended the throne of Delhi with the title Alamgir ("world-seizer"). A ruthless ruler, he augmented the empire to its greatest extent but in his fervent Muslim orthodoxy he made enemies of his Hindu subjects and in effect weakened Mogul power.

Aurelian(us), Lucius Domitius (c. 215–275 AD) Roman emperor (270–75). Aurelian was of humble birth and owed his accession to the army. He restored imperial unity by his victories over the Vandals, *Zenobia of Palmyra, and the Gallic Empire at Châlons. He was murdered near Byzantium.

Auriga (Latin: charioteer) A conspicuous constellation in the N sky near Orion, lying in the Milky Way. The brightest star is *Capella.

Aurignacian A culture of the Upper *Paleolithic marked by the use of thick scrapers and heavy blades of stone and flint, flat bone points, and polished bone or antler pins. First recognized at Aurignac (SW France) in 1860 the industry dates back to about 34,000 BC. Since it differs, especially in bonework, from earlier and later (*Gravettian) toolkits, Aurignacian culture may have come from outside Europe. These people hunted mammoth and horse; they also engraved symbols and pictures on rocks (*see* Lascaux).

auroch An extinct European wild ox, *Bos primigenius*, that survived in Poland until the early 17th century. Standing 6 ft (1.8 m) at the shoulder, aurochs were black with long, curved horns and are believed to be ancestors of modern domestic cattle.

Aurora In Roman mythology, the goddess of the dawn. She was called Eos by the Greeks.

aurora A display of diffuse, changing, colored light seen high in the earth's atmosphere, often taking the form of streamers or drapery and usually green or red. Aurorae occur predominantly in polar regions when energetic charged particles from the sun become trapped in the earth's magnetic field. The rapidly moving particles interact with atoms and molecules in the upper atmosphere and cause them to emit light.

Auschwitz. *See* Oświęcim.

auscultation The use of a *stethoscope to listen to sounds produced within the body, which forms an essential part of a medical examination. Auscultation of lungs, heart, and intestines are the most useful for reaching a diagnosis.

Austen, Jane (1775–1817) British novelist. She was the daughter of a clergyman and lived an outwardly uneventful life with her family in the south of England, settling in Chawton in Hampshire in 1809. Her six major novels are *Sense and Sensibility* (1811), *Pride and Prejudice* (1813), *Mansfield Park* (1814), *Emma* (1815–16), *Northanger Abbey* (1818), and *Persuasion* (1818). Their heroines are drawn from the rural landed gentry, and their plots trace the development of relationships that generally culminate in marriage. Her novels are distinguished by her delicate and often ironic wit and her sensitive insight into personal and social tensions.

austenite A form of *steel that exists when the metal is heated to about 587°F (1000°C), in which the carbon exists as a solid solution in the iron. Austenitic steels retain this structure at room temperature because of the presence of an alloying element, such as manganese. Austenite is nonmagnetic and has a high ductility. Named for Sir William C. Roberts-Austen (1843–1902).

Austerlitz, Battle of (Dec 2, 1805) The battle in which Napoleon's 68,000-strong army outmaneuvered and defeated almost 90,000 Russians and Austrians led by *Kutuzov. It took place near Austerlitz (near Brno, Czech Republic). Napoleon's great victory forced the Austrians to make peace with France by the Treaty of Pressburg and the Russian army to return to Russia.

Austin 30 18N 97 47W A city in the US, the capital of Texas on the Colorado River. The site of the University of Texas (1883), its industries include food processing and electronics. Population (1990): 465,622.

Austin, Stephen F(uller) (1793–1836) US settler leader in Texas. In 1821 he paved the way for an Anglo-American colony in then-Spanish Texas on a land grant left to him by his father. He negotiated with Mexican President Santa Anna and when he saw no future for Texas as a part of Mexico, fought valiantly for Texas's independence (1836). He served briefly, before his death, as the first secretary of state for Texas.

JANE AUSTEN *The only portrait of her from life, which was done by her sister Cassandra.*

Australasia A term applied loosely to encompass the islands of the S Pacific: Australia, New Zealand, New Guinea, and their associated islands. The Malay Archipelago and the Philippines are also sometimes included. *See also* Oceania.

Australia, Commonwealth of A country in the S Pacific comprising the smallest continent. The nation of Australia is a federation of states (including Tasmania, an offshore island state to the SE). There are five mainland states (Queensland, New South Wales, Victoria, South Australia, and Western Australia) and two territories (the Northern Territory and the Australian Capital Territory, an enclave within New South Wales where Canberra, the federal capital, is located). External territories include *Norfolk Island, *Christmas Island, the *Cocos (Keeling) Islands, and the *Australian Antarctic Territories. Much of the country has a hot dry climate and a large part of the vast central plains, the Australian Shield, is desert or semidesert. The Great Barrier Reef, the world's most extensive coral reef, lies off the tropical NE coast, and the highest mountains, reaching 7,000 ft (2,000 m), are in the Great Dividing Range, which runs parallel to the E coast. The Murray River and its tributaries form the main river system. The inhabitants are very largely of European, especially British, origin, but there are about 125,000 Aborigines (45,000 of pure stock and 80,000 of mixed stock). Constituting the native people, the Aborigines were detribalized and placed on reservations with the arrival of the whites in the 18th and 19th centuries. Most have now been assimilated into rural and urban areas, but race relations remain a problem. Efforts have been made toward equalization of treatment of the Aborigines, including the enfranchisement of Aborigines of pure stock in 1962, but economic and social barriers persist.

Australia is noted for its unique flora and fauna, including the koala bear, the kangaroo, the wallaby, the dingo, and the distinctive gum tree, or eucalyptus. Since World War II the population has increased dramatically, largely as a result of immigration. *Economy*: agriculture continues to make a substantial contribution to the economy, the main crops being wheat and other cereals, sugar cane, and fruit. Livestock, particularly sheep and cattle, is also important. Since the 1960s, however, growth in the industrial sector has been especially marked, the leading manufactures being iron and steel products, transportation equipment, and machinery. Mining is now of vital importance, especially the extraction of coal, iron, bauxite, uranium, copper, lead, and zinc. There have been significant discoveries of oil and natural gas and about 70% of oil for home consumption is now produced in Australia. The main exports are wool, meat, cereals, sugar, iron ore, and nonferrous ores. *History*: the country was inhabited by the Aborigines, immigrants from SE Asia, for approximately 20,000 years before the arrival of the Europeans, beginning with the Portuguese in the 16th century and the Dutch in the early 17th century. In 1770 Captain Cook claimed the fertile E coast for Britain and the area, known as New South Wales, was at first used mainly as a penal colony. The introduction of the merino sheep, however, encouraged expansion of civilian settlements, and Australia gradually became a British dependency. The discovery of gold in Victoria in 1851 attracted large numbers of immigrants, and from this period the colonies struggled for greater independence, developing broadly similar structures and policies. In 1901 the six colonies were federated to form the Commonwealth, becoming an independent dominion of the British Empire. In 1911 the site for the federal capital, under the title of the Australian Capital Territory, and the Northern Territory were added to the Commonwealth. Strong measures were introduced in the late 19th century to prevent immigration by non-whites and these had a continuing influence on immigration policy. In 1974, however, Gough *Whitlam abolished the "white Australia" policy and a new immigration scheme was introduced in 1979, which was aimed at extending the country's nondiscriminatory image. Australia played a significant part in both World Wars, taking an important role in the Gallipoli campaign in World War I and cooperating closely with the US in World War II. Since the war, closer ties have been developed with Asia, especially with Japan, a major trade partner. In 1978 the Northern Territory achieved self-government. In 1988 the country celebrated the bicentennial of settlement. The Australian Labor Party was expected to lose the 1993 general election, but Prime Minister Keating led the party to an upset victory and then received high ratings in popularity polls. Australia is a member of the British Commonwealth. Prime Minister: Paul Keating. Official language: English. Official currency: Australian dollar of 100 cents. Area: 2,967,283 sq mi (7,686,884 sq km). Population (1992 est): 17,568,700.

Australian Alps A mountain range in SE Australia. Part of the *Great Dividing Range, it extends from E Victoria into SE New South Wales and contains the *Snowy Mountains and Mount *Kosciusko, Australia's highest mountain. It is a popular winter-sports area.

Australian Antarctic Territory The area of Antarctica claimed by Australia. It includes all the land lying S of latitude 60°S and between longitudes 45°E and 160°E, excluding *Terre Adélie. Several research stations are sited here.

Australian Capital Territory An administrative division of SE Australia. It was created in 1911 from the Limestone Plains region of New South Wales as a site for *Canberra, the capital of Australia. Jervis Bay was transferred to the territory in 1915 for development as a seaport. It is the site of several important institutions, including the Australian Academy of Science, the Royal Military College, and the Royal Australian Naval College (at Jervis Bay). Area: 939 sq mi (2432 sq km). Population (1992 est): 295,500.

Australopithecus A genus of fossil manlike, higher primates of the late Pliocene and Pleistocene eras of S and E Africa. Although small in brain size, their cranial and skeletal structures were more like those of modern man than of apes. They walked erect and probably hunted and used primitive tools. They may have been the direct ancestors of modern man, but opinion differs on this. The question is complicated by the fact that there were two basic types of australopithecine, a more robust apelike form called *Paranthropus* and the more manlike form of *Australopithecus*. One branch of the latter may have evolved into *Homo erectus* (□*Homo*). The creature discovered by Louis *Leakey at *Olduvai in 1959 and given by him the generic name of *Zinjanthropus* has now been included with the other australopithecines as *Australopithecus boisei*.

Austrasia The eastern Frankish kingdom created together with *Neustria by the partition in 511 A.D. of the Merovingian kingdom by *Clovis. Occupying an area that is now NE France and W Germany, its capital from 629 AD was at Metz. Austrasia was increasingly dominated by the mayors of the palace (viceroys), the last of which, *Pepin the Short, deposed the Merovingians in 751 AD and reunited the Frankish territories into what became the Carolingian empire. *See also* Franks.

Austria, Republic of (German name: Österreich) A country in central Europe, on the N side of the Alps. A large part of the country is mountainous but the E area consists of lower hills and plains, with the Danube River flowing through the NE. Most of the inhabitants are German but there are minorities of Croats, Slovenes, and others. *Economy*: although agriculture and forestry are important, there is considerable heavy industry, based particularly on iron and steel. Hydroelectric power is a valuable source of energy. Tourism has grown in recent years, both summer and winter. Main exports include iron and steel, machinery, paper and paper products, wood, and textiles. *History*: Austria has a long history of human habitation, going back to the Celtic settlements of the early Iron Age. The area was part of the Roman Empire from 15 BC until the 5th century AD when it was overrun by Germanic tribes. In succeeding centuries it was occupied in turn by Slavs and Magyars from whom it was taken in 955 by the Holy Roman Emperor *Otto I. He conferred it upon Leopold of Babenberg, who founded the first Austrian dynasty. In 1282 the *Hapsburgs acquired Austria, which was to become the core of their vast empire. In 1526 Bohemia and Hungary were united under the Austrian crown. The Austrian Empire continued to hold a predominant position in Europe until the middle of the 19th century when its power was lessened by successive defeats, especially in the *Austro-Prussian War. In 1867 the Hapsburgs were forced to acknowledge the nationalist aspirations of Hungary and formed the Dual Monarchy of *Austria-Hungary, under the Emperor *Francis Joseph. During his reign there was considerable unrest, especially among the Slav peoples of the very diverse Empire; the assassination of the Archduke Francis Ferdinand by Serbian nationalists in 1914 was the immediate cause of World War I. In 1918 Austria became a republic. In spite of efforts on the part of the chancellor *Schuschnigg to maintain independence, it was annexed by Nazi Germany in 1938 (*see* Anschluss). After World War II it was occupied jointly by the Allies, regaining its independence as a republic in 1955. Chancellor Bruno *Kreisky came to power in 1970 as head of Austria's first all-socialist government. In the 1983 elections, in which debate focused on economic issues, the Social Democrats (Kreisky's party), lost their absolute majority in the legislature (held since 1971) to the Christian Democrats. A coalition cabinet composed of Social Democrats and members of the Freedom party was formed. During 1986, former UN secretary general (1972–82) and presidential candidate Kurt Waldheim was implicated in World War II Nazi war crimes. This revelation led to Austria's diplomatic isolation until Waldheim announced that he would not run in the 1992 election. Official language: German. Currency: schilling of 100 groschen. Area: 32,375 sq mi (85,853 sq km). Population (1990 est): 7,595,000.

Austria-Hungary, Dual Monarchy of The Habsburg monarchy from 1867 to 1918. It was established by the *Ausgleich* (compromise) in response to the militant demands of Hungarian nationalism. The empire of Austria and the kingdom of Hungary each had its own laws, parliament, and ministries but were united by the monarch (Emperors *Francis Joseph and then *Charles), minister for foreign affairs and minister for war, and by the biannual meetings of delegations of representatives of each parliament. The Dual Monarchy was weakened by resurgent nationalism in the early 20th century and disappeared in 1918 with the proclamation of an Austrian republic.

Austrian Succession, War of the (1740–48) The war between Austria and Prussia, in which Britain supported Austria and France and Spain were allied to Prussia. It was brought about by the disputed succession of *Maria Theresa to the Austrian lands. Hostilities were begun by *Frederick the Great of Prussia, who annexed the Austrian province of Silesia in 1740. Unstable alliances were formed between European powers on the Continent and hostilities overseas, especially between France and Britain, were exacerbated. The war was ended by the Treaty of *Aix-la-Chapelle, at which Prussia obtained the greater share of Silesia.

Austro-Asiatic languages A family of about 150 languages and dialects spoken in SE Asia. They include Vietnamese, *Khmer, Nicobarese in the Nicobar Islands, and the *Munda languages of India. In fact there is little superficial resemblance among languages of the family, and their common ancestors and date of separation are difficult to establish. There have, accordingly, been attempts to link them to other language families, as was done in the Austro-Tai hypothesis (first proposed in 1906), which postulated a super-family to include the Austro-Asiatic languages, the *Austronesian languages, and certain languages of Indochina.

Austronesian languages A large language family, also called Malayo-Polynesian, spoken in the Malay peninsula, Taiwan, Madagascar, and the islands of the Pacific Ocean. There are two subgroups: the Western branch, which has up to 200 member languages and includes Malay, Indonesian, Malagasy, Javanese, and Tagalog; and the Eastern or Oceanic branch, which has up to 300 members and includes the languages of the islands in the S and central Pacific, such as Samoa, Tahiti, Tonga, Fiji, New Guinea, and Hawaii. There is some doubt as to whether the languages of Taiwan form a separate group or are part of the Western branch.

Austro-Prussian War (*or* Seven Weeks' War; 1866) A war between German states led respectively by Austria and Prussia. The Prussian victory was an important landmark in Bismarck's strategy for uniting Germany under Prussian leadership.

auteur theory In film criticism, emphasis on the dominant role of the director. It was developed in the 1950s by several writers for the French magazine *Cahiers du Cinéma* who later became directors themselves, notably Truffaut, Godard, Rohmer, and Chabrol. Their method of evaluation, which was based on a consideration of the director's technique, intentions, and personal style, influenced several British and US film critics during the 1960s.

autism A rare and severe mental illness that starts in early childhood. Autistic children are aloof and do not form normal personal relationships but they can become emotionally attached to things. They do not communicate normally, often cannot form abstract concepts, and they are very upset by tiny changes in their familiar surroundings. Most, but not all, are mentally retarded. Autism can be caused by brain damage and can also be inherited. Lengthy specialized education is usually necessary for autistic children.

auto-da-fé (Portuguese: act of faith) The public ceremony at which persons convicted of crimes by the *Inquisition in Portugal, Spain, and their colonies were sentenced. Punishment of victims, including the burning of heretics, was the responsibility of the secular authorities. The first *auto-da-fé* was held in Seville in 1481 and the last, in Mexico in 1815.

autogiro An aircraft with large horizontal freely rotating blades to obtain lift. It differs from the *helicopter in that a propeller provides forward motion, which in turn causes the rotation of the unmotorized horizontal blades.

autoimmunity A condition in which the body produces antibodies (called autoantibodies) that damage or destroy its own tissues. This produces symptoms of various **autoimmune diseases**, the majority of which are poorly understood. Rheumatoid *arthritis is caused by the production of autoantibodies against joint tissue; the disease can be diagnosed by the detection of these antibodies in the serum. A more general production of autoantibodies causes systemic *lupus erythematosis, which can affect most tissues in the body.

automatic pilot A device utilizing a gyroscope for keeping an aircraft on a given course. When the aircraft goes off course, the gyro axis rotates, operating electrical contacts, which make the necessary adjustments to the control surfaces.

automation The use of electronic devices controlled by a computer in mechanical processes that would otherwise be controlled by human operators. It has made considerable impact on production engineering in such fields as steel and chemical manufacture. Telecommunications (automatic telephone exchanges), transport (navigation, railroad signals), and mining also employ automated systems.

automobile A self-propelled road vehicle. The search for a means of replacing the horse as a means of transport began seriously at the beginning of the 18th century, when *Newcomen and *Watt had shown that steam could be harnessed to produce power. Joseph Cugnot (1725–1804) in 1770 used a steam engine to drive a gun tractor and in 1808 Richard *Trevithick built a working steam carriage. But neither these vehicles nor the many other steam carriages of the first half of the 19th century were more than cumbersome novelties. An effective horseless carriage needed a smaller, more efficient power source. This was eventually provided by two German engineers, Nikolaus *Otto and Gottlieb *Daimler, who in 1876 patented the Otto-cycle *internal-combustion engine. In 1885, another German, Karl *Benz, used a 3 hp version of this engine to power a tricycle capable of 15 mph (20 km per hour). By 1890 both Daimler and Benz were selling the motorized dog carts that were the forerunners of the modern car. In France, during the closing decade of the 19th century, Panhard, Comte Albert de Dion, Georges Bouton, and Peugeot were all producing and selling cars. In the US, Henry Ford built his car in 1896. In the UK, Henry *Royce, dissatisfied with the quality of foreign cars decided to build his own. In partnership with C. S. *Rolls, he sold his first Rolls-Royce Silver Ghost in 1907.

By the start of World War I, automobiles were in common use; by this time they were much the same in basic shape and design as they are today. Propeller shafts had replaced chains and belts, pneumatic tires had ousted solid tires, and open carriage bodies had given way to closed sedans. Although World War I was the last of the "horse" wars, by 1918 more and more motorized vehicles (including *tanks) were in military use. Nevertheless, motoring was still the preserve of the affluent. It was not until 1925, when Ford brought the price of his Model T down to $290 that motoring became accessible to ordinary people. During the 1930s the price of cars steadily declined, but the real mass market did not develop until after World War II. Before the war it was rare for a model to sell a million vehicles, now a popular car has to do so to be a commercial success.

The future of the private car is uncertain: diminishing world reserves of oil make fuel increasingly expensive, the cost of the cars themselves has risen sharply, and the pollution and noise they create makes them the enemy of conservationists and urban planners. It may be that the gasoline supplies will hold out until an economic alternative is found (*see* electric car) or it may be that once again the private car will become the privilege of the rich. .

automobile racing Racing in cars, from stockcars to highly specialized Grand Prix vehicles, one of the most popular US spectator sports. Early races, such as the 1895 race from Paris to Bordeaux and back, were held on public roads, but since the early 1900s they have usually been held on closed-circuit courses. The most prestigious form of racing is Grand Prix (Formula One) racing, for which specially built single-seater vehicles are raced by professional drivers for manufacturers or private owners. The Drivers World Championship (instituted in 1950) is awarded according to points won in certain Formula One races. Formulas Two and Three function largely as training grounds for Formula One drivers. The most famous race is the Indianapolis 500, held annually in Indianapolis, Ind. **Sports-car racing** is for production-type modified sports cars; the most famous sports-car race is the Le Mans 24 Hours. *See also* drag racing; karting; rally; stock-car racing.

autopsy (necropsy *or* postmortem) The dissection and examination of a dead body. An autopsy is performed when the cause of death is uncertain: it may provide further information on a poorly understood disease or evidence of criminal involvement. Except for sudden death or death due to obscure causes, permission for autopsy must be granted by the relatives.

autoradiography The use of photography to examine the distribution of a *radioisotope in a thin specimen. The specimen is placed on a photographic plate, which after development shows the distribution of the radioisotope.

autosuggestion A way of changing one's behavior by firmly repeating ideas to oneself. It can be used to control undesirable habits or to cope with anxiety and is sometimes taught to psychiatric patients. *See also* hypnosis.

autumnal equinox. *See* equinox.

autumn crocus A herbaceous perennial European plant, *Colchicum autumnale*, also called meadow saffron. It has narrow, strap-shaped leaves, up to 12 in (30 cm) long, and a single purple-blue, crocus-like flower, which appears in autumn after the leaves have died. The drug colchicine, extracted from the corms, is used in the treatment of gout and in genetic research. Some plants of the genus are cultivated for ornament. Family: *Liliaceae. Compare* Crocus.

Autun 46 58N 4 18E A city in central France, in the Saône-et-Loire department on the Arroux River. Famous for its school of rhetoric during Roman times, it has several Roman remains. Its manufactures include furniture and leather. Population (1975): 22,949.

AUTOMOBILE

Benz 8hp *1600 of these "horseless carriages" were sold between 1898 and 1900. Described as the first reliable car offered to the public, its twin-cylinder 1570 cc engine gave it a top speed of 18 mph (29 km/hr).*

Rolls-Royce Silver Ghost *First built in 1907 (and continuing in production until 1927) it quickly established itself as "the best car in the world." Its 7-liter 6-cylinder engine gave it a top speed of 65 mph (105 km/hr).*

Ford Model T *15 million of this first mass-produced car (nicknamed the "Tin Lizzie") were made between 1908 and 1927. Its 4-cylinder, 2898 cc engine gave it a top speed of 40 mph (64 km/hr).*

Volkswagen *Nicknamed "the Beetle," this 1937 German design by Ferdinand Porsche sold well into the 1970s, making it the best selling car ever made. Its air-cooled slow-revving rear engine increased from 1131 to 1600 cc over the years.*

Bugatti Royale *Made to compete with the Rolls-Royce, this magnificent 13-liter 8 cylinder automobile cost about $25,000 in 1927—a price even outside the range of its intended customers—the crowned heads of Europe. Seven were sold.*

AUTOMOBILE

MG TC *This post-war British sports car (1946–55) was little changed from the TA model first built in 1937. The TC had a 1250 cc engine.*

Buick *This 1949 US car represented a release from wartime restrictions and set the trend for a generation of large American cars.*

Mini *The best selling British car ever made. Designed by Alec Issigonis, the Mini was introduced in 1959. Its front-wheel drive, transverse engine, and 10-inch wheels make it an extremely roomy car for its size.*

Citroën GS *This 1970 French car featured Citroën's highly successful self-leveling hydropneumatic suspension. Its 1-liter engine drove the front wheels.*

Auvergne A planning region and former province in S central France. Its name derives from the Averni, who strongly resisted Roman control of the area. Crossed by the volcanic Auvergne Mountains that rise to over 6000 ft (1800 m), it has many mineral springs and some level fertile districts. It is predominantly agricultural and is noted for the growing of wheat and grapes and the rearing of cattle; cheese and wine are also produced. Area: 10,032 sq mi (25,988 sq km). Population (1991 est): 1,322,000.

Auxerre 47 48N 3 35W A city in central France, the captial of the Yonne department on the Yonne River. Its Gothic cathedral has exceptional 13th-century stained glass windows. Wine and metal goods are produced here. Population (1975): 39,955.

auxin An organic substance, produced within a plant, that stimulates, inhibits, or modifies growth of the plant. Auxins are sometimes known as plant hormones. The main auxin is indoleacetic acid (IAA). Auxins are responsible for a variety of effects, for example shoot curvature, leaf fall, and fruit growth. Synthetic auxins, such as 2,4-dichlorophenoxyacetic acid (2,4-D), are used as weedkillers for broad-leaved weeds (see herbicide).

avadavat A small plump songbird, *Estrilda amandava*, also called red munia. Occurring in meadows and marshes of Asia, it is the only *waxbill found outside Africa. In the breeding season the male plumage is bright red with mottled brown patches and white speckling.

avalanche A rapid movement of snow and ice, and sometimes rock debris, down steep slopes. They may occur in winter, when fresh snow slides off an older compacted snow surface, and in spring, when thaws cause the mass to slip. Avalanches can cause severe damage with loss of life and property and in populous mountain areas, steel avalanche-sheds are used to protect roads and railroads.

Avalon The paradise of Celtic mythology to which King Arthur (*see* Arthurian legend) was taken after his final battle. It was ruled by *Morgan le Fay, famous for her magical powers, and has been identified with Glastonbury, England.

Avebury 51 27N 1 51W A village in S England, in Wiltshire, on the site of a large complex of Neolithic and early Bronze Age stone circles, banks, and ditches. The principal circle, with its ditch and outer bank, encloses over 30 acres (12 hectares); within it are two smaller ones. Nearby is *Silbury Hill.

Aveiro 40 38N 8 40W A port in NW Portugal, on an inlet of the Atlantic Ocean. Its museum contains medieval art treasures. It has agricultural industries. Population: 51,709.

Avellaneda 34 40S 58 20W A city in Argentina, a suburb of Buenos Aires on the Río de la Plata. It is highly industrialized with meat processing, oil refining, and tanning. Population (1991): 346,620.

avens A perennial herbaceous plant of the genus *Geum* (about 40 species), native to temperate and Arctic regions. Most species rarely exceed 24 in (60 cm) in height. Their flowers, 8–12 in (2–3 cm) long, are white, yellow, orange, or red, either solitary or in clusters. *G. coccineum* is a common ornamental. Family: *Rosaceae*.

average 1. (mathematics) A representative or middle value of a set of quantities. The arithmetical average (*or* arithmetical mean) is found by adding the quantities in a set and dividing the total by the number of quantities: the arithmetical average of 7, 8, 13, and 20 is 12 (48 divided by 4). The geometric average (*or* geometric mean) is found by multiplying together the numbers in a set and extracting a root equal to the number of quantities: the geometric average of

2, 9, and 12 is 6 ($\sqrt[3]{}$ 216). **2.** (insurance) Loss or damage to property. In *marine insurance it refers to a partial loss. A **particular average** affects only one interest, whereas a **general average** is shared among all the parties concerned (e.g. if a deck cargo has to be jettisoned to save a ship in a storm, all the cargo owners have to contribute to the loss). In fire insurance, average is used to combat underinsurance. For example, if an insurer has only insured his goods for a proportion of their total value, he will only be paid that proportion of any claim for a partial loss.

AVENS *Water avens* (Geum rivale) *is widely distributed in damp shady places of the N hemisphere. Its flowers have purple sepals and orange-pink petals.*

Avernus, Lake A small crater lake near Naples and Cumae (the earliest Greek colony in Italy). In ancient times it was believed to be the entrance to the infernal regions, and *Avernus* was often used by writers as a synonym for the underworld. In Virgil's *Aeneid*, Aeneas descends to the underworld through a cave near the lake.

Averroes (Ibn Rushd; 1126–98) Muslim philosopher and a judge in Córdoba and Seville. Averroes' main works were his commentaries on Aristotle, which greatly influenced the philosophy of medieval Christianity. He defended philosophy as the highest form of inquiry, holding that faith and reason are not necessarily in conflict but are separate ways of arriving at the truth.

aversion therapy A form of *conditioning used to treat some kinds of undesirable behavior, such as sexual deviation, alcoholism, and drug addiction. An unpleasant stimulus (e.g. an electric shock) is associated with a stimulus related to the problem behavior (e.g. the taste of alcohol). *See also* behavior therapy.

Avesta The sacred scriptures of *Zoroastrianism. Written in Old Iranian, the five books of the *Avesta* contain prayers (probably by Zoroaster himself) hymns, ritual and liturgical instruction, and the main body of Zoroastrian law. Its surviving form dates from about the 6th century AD.

Avicenna (980–1037) Persian philosopher and physician. Avicenna received extensive education in science and philosophy and served various rulers during his life, as government official and physician. His encyclopedia of philosophy, *Ash-Shifa* (*The Recovery*), encompasses logic, psychology, metaphysics, and natural sciences and parts were subsequently translated into Latin. Avicenna's *Canon of Medicine*, based on Roman and Arabic medicine and his own medical knowledge, became a popular text throughout the Middle East and Europe.

Avignon 43 56N 4 48E A city in SE France, the capital of the Vaucluse department on the Rhône River. The papacy, under French control, was removed to Avignon (1309–77; *see* Avignon papacy) and there were subsequently rival popes at Rome and Avignon until 1417 (*see* Great Schism). Famous landmarks include the 14th-century papal palace and the 12th-century bridge, of which only four arches remain. A popular tourist center, Avignon trades in wine and has chemical, soap, and cement industries. Population (1975): 93,024.

Avignon papacy (1309–77) The period during which the popes resided in Avignon (France) rather than Rome. It is sometimes called the Babylonian Captivity (in reference to the *Babylonian exile in Jewish history). The papal court was established in Avignon, a papal fief, by *Clement V, who, like his six successors in Avignon, was French. English and German criticism of French dominance over the papacy eventually forced its return to Rome under Gregory XI. Shortly afterward the division in the Church known as the *Great Schism occurred, largely in response to the increased power acquired by the cardinals during the Avignon papacy.

Avignon school A school of painting established when Clement V moved the papal court from Rome to Avignon in 1309 and imported Italian 14th-century masters, notably Simone *Martini, to decorate the papal palace. After the pope's return to Rome (1377) painters remaining in Avignon developed a unique style, fusing Italian and Flemish influences. The artists of the school include Nicholas Froment (active 1450–90) and its most celebrated work is the anonymous *Ville-neuve Pietà* (c. 1460; Louvre).

Avila 40 39N 4 42W A city in central Spain, in Old Castile on the Adaja River. A popular tourist center, the old part of the town is enclosed by 12th-century walls and has a notable Gothic cathedral (11th–15th centuries). St Teresa was born here. Population: 30,983.

avocado A tree, *Persia americana*, up to 59 ft (18 m) tall, native to Mexico and Central America but now extensively cultivated in Florida, California, and South Africa for its fruit. These fruits—**avocado pears**—may reach a weight of 4 lb (2 kg): they have a green to dark-purple skin, a fatty flesh rich in fat, protein, and vitamins A and B, and a single hard seed.

avocet A wading bird of the genus *Recurvirostra*, having long, slender legs and a long, thin, upcurved bill used to skim the surface of mud or water in search of small invertebrates. The Eurasian avocet (*R. avosetta*), 20 in (50 cm) long, has a black-and-white plumage and gray-blue legs and is protected in Britain. Family: *Recurvirostridae*; order: *Charadriiformes* (gulls, plovers, etc.)

Avogadro, Amedeo, Conte di Quaregna e Ceretto (1776–1856) Italian physicist, who became professor of physics at the University of Turin. He developed *Gay-Lussac's hypothesis that equal volumes of gases contain equal numbers of particles, establishing the difference between atoms and molecules. Because he made this vital distinction the theory is now known as Avogadro's hypothesis. His name is also commemorated in **Avogadro's number** (*or* the

Avogadro constant), the number of molecules in one mole of substance (it has the value $6.022,52 \times 10^{23}$). Avogadro's work was largely neglected during his life and was not acknowledged until *Cannizzaro brought it to public notice in 1854.

Avon, 1st Earl of. *See* Eden, Anthony.

Avon River The name of several rivers in the UK, including: **1.** A river in central England, flowing SW from Northamptonshire to the Severn River at Tewkesbury. Length: 96 mi (154 km). **2.** A river in SW England, flowing S and W from Gloucestershire to the Severn estuary at Avonmouth. Length: 75 mi (120 km). **3.** A river in S England, flowing S from Wiltshire to the English Channel. Length: 60 mi (96 km).

axiology The theory of values in ethics and aesthetics, particularly the search for the good and its nature. Axiology investigates basic principles governing moral judgment, types of value, and the place of values (or norms) within the frameworks of philosophical systems. *Plato, for instance, held to an absolute theory of the Idea of the Good, while *Hume and others believed that values were relative, depending on degrees of approval felt by persons making value judgments. *Kant found the source of value in practical reason, while in *utilitarianism it lay in the principle of the greatest happiness for the greatest number.

axiom An assumption or principle, used to prove a theorem, that is itself accepted as true without proof. Some mathematicians reserve the term for an assumption in logic, using postulate for an assumption made in other fields.

axis deer A slender deer, *Axis axis*, also called chital, that usually lives in small herds near rivers in India and Sri Lanka. Axis deer measure up to 40 in (100 cm) at the shoulder and are reddish with white spots and pale underparts.

Axis Powers The coalition of Germany, Italy, and Japan that opposed the *Allied Powers in *World War II. It originated in agreements going back to 1936 and it culminated in the Tripartite Pact (1940).

axolotl A salamander, *Ambystoma mexicanum*, occurring in Mexican lakes. It reaches a length of 10 in (25 cm), has a long tail and weak limbs, and is typically dark brown. Axolotls retain their larval characteristics permanently, reproducing in this state, although under certain conditions they may develop into adults. Family: *Ambystomatidae*.

axon. *See* neuron.

Axum. *See* Aksum.

Ayacucho 13 10S 74 15W A city in S central Peru. The battle of Ayacucho (1824) was fought nearby, resulting in Peru gaining independence from Spain. An agricultural center, tourism is also important. It has a university (founded in 1677 and reopened in 1957). Population (1990 est): 102,000.

Ayatollah Ruholla Khomeini. *See* Khomeini, Ayatollah Ruholla.

aye-aye A rare arboreal *prosimian primate, *Daubentonia madagascariensis*, occurring only in the coastal forests of N Madagascar. It is 34–46 in (86–104 cm) long including the tail (20–24 in [50–60 cm]) and has dark, shaggy fur and large ears used to detect wood-boring insects, extracting them with its incisor teeth and narrow elongated third finger. The aye-aye is the only member of its family (*Daubentoniidae*).

Ayer, Sir Alfred (Jules) (1910–89) British philosopher. Ayer's major contribution to British philosophy was his bringing to England the teachings of the *Vienna Circle, in particular the doctrine of *logical positivism. This he expounded in *Language, Truth and Logic* (1936). His later books include *The

Foundations of Empirical Knowledge (1940), *The Problem of Knowledge* (1956), and an autobiography *Part of My Life* (1977).

Ayers Rock The largest monolith in the world, in Australia, in SW Northern Territory. It consists of a vast red rock rising 1099 ft (335 m) above the surrounding plain with a circumference of 6.25 mi (10 km). Its color varies according to atmospheric changes and the position of the sun.

AYERS ROCK

Ayesha (c. 613–78) The third and favorite wife of *Mohammed and daughter of *Abu Bakr. She married at the age of nine. She led a revolt against *Ali but was defeated (656) and ended her life in exile in Medina. She is known as "the mother of believers."

Aymara A people of the Peruvian and Bolivian highlands. They grow potatoes and other crops and herd llamas and alpacas. Their costume is characterized by the woolen poncho and conical headwear with earflaps. They live in small, extended-family settlements in which elders, who are also ritual shamans (*see* shamanism), have authority. In the 15th century the Aymara were incorporated into the Inca empire under Viracocha. Later Spanish influence made them nominally Catholic but earlier beliefs persist. Today there are approximately 1,360,000 Aymaras and their language, Aymaran, is one of the strongest surviving native Indian languages.

Ayrshire cattle A breed of red or brown and white cattle originating in Ayrshire, SW Scotland. A hardy breed, Ayrshires are primarily producers of good quality milk, used especially in cheese making. Many herds have been replaced by the higher yielding *Friesians.

Ayub Khan, Mohammad (1907–74) Pakistani statesman; president (1958–69). After a distinguished military career he became defense minister in 1954. Following Pres. Iskander Mirza's coup d'état in 1958, Ayub Khan became chief martial law administrator and then ousted Mirza to become president. He negotiated (1966) the ceasefire agreement with *Shastri following the India-Pakistan war of 1965. He was forced to resign following civil unrest in East Pakistan.

azalea A deciduous shrub of the genus *Rhododendron*. (Most horticulturalists prefer to restrict the term rhododendron to the large evergreen species.) Growing to a height of up to 6.5 ft (2 m), azaleas are all native to the uplands of North America and S Asia but are now widely cultivated as ornamentals. The attractive flowers are large, fragrant, and funnel-shaped (about 2.4 in [6 cm] in diameter) and of various colors. Family: *Ericaceae*.

Azaña, Manuel (1880–1940) Spanish statesman, who was prominent in the Second Republic (1931–39). His premiership (1931–33) introduced internal reforms but was unpopular for its repression of opposition. He was president (1936–39) during the Spanish Civil War and fled to France after Gen. Franco's Nationalist victory.

Azande An African people speaking a Sudanic language who live in areas of the Sudan, Zaïre, and the Central African Republic. They are an ethnically mixed people, who practice agriculture, hunting, and various crafts, including ironwork. They were traditionally divided into a number of warring kingdoms. They live in scattered homesteads and are organized into a number of dispersed patrilineal clans. Their religion takes the form of an ancestor cult. Belief in witchcraft is a central aspect of their lives, most misfortunes being attributed to it.

Azerbaijan, Republic of Independent nation in SE Europe, formerly the Azerbaijan SSR, a constituent republic in the Soviet Union, on the Caspian Sea. It consists mainly of the hot dry plain of the Kura and Araks Rivers, surrounded by the Caucasus Mountains. The Azerbaijani, who comprise most of the population, are a Turkic-speaking Shiite Muslim people renowned for their carpet weaving. The region was acquired by Russia from Persia in the early 19th century, proclaimed its independence in 1918, but subsequently formed part of the Transcaucasian Soviet Federated Socialist Republic (*see* Transcaucasia), becoming a separate republic in 1936. Independence came in 1991 with the collapse of the USSR. In 1992, Azerbaijan became a member of the UN. Disputes with Armenia led to fighting in 1993. Azerbaijan is one of the oldest oil-producing areas of the world, and its most important industries are oil and gas, with a developing chemical industry. Agriculture is diversified. The main crops are cotton, tobacco, and fruit, including grapes for wine. Area: 33,430 sq mi (86,600 sq km). Population (1987): 6,810,000.

Azhar, al- A mosque and center of traditional Muslim studies in Cairo. Inaugurated in 972 AD following the Fatimid conquest of Egypt, al-Azhar was originally controlled by the *Ismaili. It became a *Sunnite institution under Saladin but it was not until after the Ottoman conquest (1517) that it gained its present preeminence. It is now regarded as the most authoritative center of Islam and receives students from the whole Muslim world. In Egypt it has university status.

azimuth. *See* altitude.

azo dyes A class of synthetic dyes containing the **azo group** ($-N = N-$). First produced in 1858, they now outsell all other dyes combined. This success is due to exceptional color-fastness and versatility in application, including the ability to dye natural and synthetic fibers direct, i.e. without a mordant. Virtually any color may be obtained; examples are methyl orange, Bismarck brown, and Congo red.

Azores (Portuguese name: Açôres) 38 30N 28 00W Three groups of volcanic islands in the N Atlantic Ocean, in Portugal. The chief islands include São Miguel, Terceira, Faial, and Flores. Settled by the Portuguese in the 15th century, they were previously uninhabited. Naval fighting between the English and Spanish took place here in the 16th and 17th centuries. The site of US air bases, they produce fruit, tobacco, and wine. Area: 888 sq mi (2300 sq km). Population (1991): 236,700. Capital: Ponta Delgada, on São Miguel.

Azorín (José Martinéz Ruíz; 1874–1967) Spanish novelist, essayist, and critic. His works include the autobiographical novels *La voluntad* (1902) and *Antonio*

Azorín (1903), as well as the collection of essays *Los pueblos* (1905), inspired by the history and landscape of Castile.

Azov, Sea of A NE arm of the Black Sea, to the main body of which it is connected by the narrow Kerch Strait. Area: 14,668 sq mi (38,000 sq km).

Aztecs A *Nahuatl-speaking people who ruled an empire in central and S Mexico before their defeat by Hernán Cortés in the 16th century. They had an advanced, elaborate, and rich civilization centered in their capital Tenochtitlán and other cities. They were expert builders and constructed large palaces and temples in which they worshiped many gods, especially Huitzilopochtli to whom they sacrificed human victims, captives of warfare, by ripping out their hearts while they still lived. Their social organization was hierarchical with authority and influence vested in a class of chiefs and priests and in the kings, the last of whom was *Montezuma.

AZTECS *The calendar stone in the National Museum of Anthropology, Mexico City. The inner circle contains the 20 day signs of the Aztec calendar, while the central panel depicts the day on which the Aztecs believed the world would be destroyed by earthquake.*

Aztec-Tanoan languages An American Indian language group, spoken in the SW US and central America. It has two branches: Uto-Aztecan and Kiowa-Tanoan. Uto-Aztecan is the larger; its most widely used language, Nahua, is spoken by the *Nahuatl people of central and W Mexico. Other Uto-Aztecan languages include those of the Paiute Indians in California and Utah, the *Hopi in Arizona, and the *Comanche in Texas. The Kiowa-Tanoan branch has only four members and is spoken in New Mexico and by the *Kiowa of Oklahoma.

Azuela, Mariano (1873–1952) Mexican novelist. He practiced medicine in Mexico City before joining Pancho Villa's forces during the Mexican revolution. *The Underdogs* (1916) described the suffering it caused. Later novels, such as *Los caciques* (1917) and the posthumous *Esa sangre*, express disgust with Mexican society both before and after the revolution.

B

Baal An ancient fertility god worshiped throughout the Near East, especially in Canaan. As champion of the divine order against chaos he defeated the sea god Yamm. The myth of his conflict with Mot, god of death and sterility, is closely linked to the natural processes of vegetation: his defeat and descent into the underworld represents famine and drought, and his resurrection and victory over Mot symbolizes rain and fertility.

Baalbek 34 00N 36 12E A town in E Lebanon, originally commanding Phoenician trade routes. The Roman colony here, called Heliopolis, has left extensive and imposing remains, including temples dedicated to Jupiter and Venus (1st–3rd centuries AD).

Ba'al Shem Tov (Israel ben Eliezer; c. 1700–60) Charismatic Jewish leader and mystic, the founder of *Hasidism. He lived in Podolia (then part of Poland) and attracted an enormous following by his powerful personality and his teaching, a blend of popular pietism and mystical Judaism. He is the subject of many colorful legends. His name means "Master of the Good Name."

Ba'ath Party An Arab political party, influential in many Middle Eastern countries, notably Syria and Iraq, that urges the creation of a united socialist Arab nation. The Ba'athists supported the formation of the *United Arab Republic (1958–61) and rose to power in Iraq and Syria in 1963.

Babbage, Charles (1792–1871) British mathematician and inventor. In an attempt to produce more accurate mathematical tables, Babbage conceived the idea of a mechanical computer that could store information. Although never completed, it was the forerunner of the modern computer.

Babbitt, Irving (1865–1933) US scholar and critic. While professor of French at Harvard (1894–1935), he wrote extensive works on literature and social questions, including *Rousseau and Romanticism* (1919) and *Democracy and Leadership* (1924). He was a leader of the "neohumanist" thinkers, who opposed Romanticism and advocated the classical values of restraint and moderation.

Babbitt, Milton (1916–) US composer. He taught music and mathematics at Princeton University. His compositions employ *serialism, which uses all 12 tones of the chromatic scale equally, and include music for synthesizers. His works include *Philomel* (1963–64) and *A Solo Requiem* (1976–77).

babbler A small songbird belonging to a family (*Timaliidae*; 280 species) occurring in Old World regions, particularly in SE Asia. Babblers have short rounded wings, a long tail, strong legs and bill, and a noisy babbling cry. The plumage is often brightly colored, although some species are plain brown. Babblers live in wooded regions, searching the undergrowth in groups for insects and berries.

Babel, Isaac Emmanuilovich (1894–1941) Russian short-story writer. Of Jewish descent, he served in the imperial army, but fought for the Bolsheviks in 1917. His *Odessa Tales* were published in 1916 in a journal edited by *Gorki. *Red Cavalry* (1926) was a series of sketches based on his experience in the war against Poland. He died in a Siberian prison camp, a victim of Stalin's purges, but was posthumously rehabilitated in the 1950s.

Babel, Tower of In the Bible (Genesis 2.1–9), a tower intended to reach heaven. Angered by the presumption of the building, Jehovah caused the builders to speak different languages, so that they were incomprehensible to each other and were forced in confusion to abandon the work. The legend attempts to account for the diversification of languages. It also probably alludes to the Babylonian ziggurats, which for the Israelites were examples of Gentile pride.

Bab el-Mandeb A strait between Africa and the SW Arabian Peninsula, connecting the Red Sea with the Gulf of Aden. It is 20 mi (32 km) wide and at one point is divided by Perim Island.

Babeuf, François-Noël (1760–97) French revolutionary. Propagator of extreme egalitarian ideas, he plotted to overthrow the *Directory. His "conspiracy of equals" was exposed and Babeuf was executed. Secret societies perpetuated his doctrines, known as Babouvism.

Babi faith A religion founded in 1844 by Mirza 'Ali Mohammed (1819–50), who became known as the Bab (the Gate). He proclaimed himself the 12th and last imam of certain *Shiite sects, which had prophesied his reappearance. He was imprisoned and later shot on government orders, and his followers were subsequently persecuted. Babism centered on the belief that God reveals himself to man through prophets who would continue to appear until the end of the world. It was the immediate precursor of the *Baha'i faith.

babirusa A hairless wild pig, *Babyrousa babyrussa*, of Sulawesi (Indonesia). About 40 in (100 cm) long, babirusas live in damp forests and are good swimmers, feeding on water plants, fruit, and tubers. Males have two pairs of curved tusks; the tuskless females have only one pair of teats.

baboon A large *Old World monkey belonging to the genus *Papio* (5 species), of African and Asian grassland. Baboons are 37–73 in (95–185 cm) long including the tail (18–28 in [45–70 cm]) and have a shaggy mane and a long doglike face with large teeth. They feed on insects, small vertebrates, and vegetable matter. They live in well-organized troops containing 40–150 individuals arranged in a social hierarchy according to age and sex. *See also* hamadryas. □mammal.

Babur (Baber *or* Babar; 1483–1530) Emperor of India (1526–30), who founded the *Mogul dynasty. Descended from Genghis Khan and Timur, Zahiruddin-Muhammad (nicknamed Babur) became ruler of Fergana (1495) in Uzbekistan but failed to reconquer his ancestors' kingdom of Samarkand. Capturing Kabul, he invaded India from Afghanistan in 1525. In 1526 he defeated and killed Ibrahim Lodhi, Sultan of Delhi (1517–26), and rapidly subjugated all of N India. His story is related in his famous memoirs, the *Babur-Nameh*.

Babylon The capital of ancient Babylonia, strategically positioned on the *Euphrates River S of modern Baghdad. Its first period of prominence was about 2150 to 1740 BC, under a dynasty of which *Hammurabi was the most illustrious member. Subsequently, rising *Assyrian power threatened Babylonian independence, although some Babylonians, such as Nebuchadnezzar I (reigned c. 1146–1123), temporarily reversed the trend. Sacked by *Sennacherib (689 BC), Babylon was rebuilt from 625 BC onward, especially during the reign (c. 605–562) of *Nebuchadnezzar II. It was the remains of this city that were excavated by *Koldewey and from which the famous Ishtar Gate was recovered. In 539 BC Babylon surrendered to *Cyrus the Great of Persia. By 275 BC it was virtually depopulated. *See also* Babel, Tower of; Hanging Gardens; ziggurat.

Babylonia The area of *Mesopotamia on the alluvial plain along the lower reaches of the Euphrates River, which was controlled by ancient *Babylon. Before about 2000 BC approximately the same area was known as *Sumer. The Babylonians were a blend of Semitic peoples, like their rivals, the *Assyrians, to the NW. Apart from Babylon, the former Sumerian capital of *Ur and the port of *Eridu were major cities.

Babylonian exile The period from the destruction of the Jerusalem *Temple by *Nebuchadnezzar (586 BC) to the Jews' return under *Cyrus the Great (538 BC), during which time most of the Jews lived in exile in *Babylonia. It was here that parts of the Hebrew Bible were written, and that certain characteristic Jewish attitudes and institutions (e.g. the *synagogue) developed. This exile established the beginnings of the *diaspora; many Jews remained in Babylonia, and in late antiquity and the middle ages it had one of the largest and most important Jewish communities in the world.

Bacău 46 32N 26 59E A city in E Romania, on the Bistrilă River. An important road and rail junction, its industries include oil refining, textiles, and paper manufacture. Population (1979): 141,981.

baccarat games Various related card games, the object of which is to hold cards totaling nine, counting only the final digit of a total of ten or over (thus 10 equals 0). **Chemin de fer** was formerly popular in casinos. In this game the players take turns to be banker, against whom the other players make their bets. The banker then deals two cards to another player and two to himself. If the cards of either total nine, or failing that eight, this total wins and bets are settled accordingly. Otherwise a third card is taken or refused as necessary (taken if the total is four or under, refused if six or over). The highest total wins. **Punto banco** is identical to chemin de fer except that bets are placed against the casino on either the banker or his opponent.

Bacchanalia The Roman form of the Hellenistic mystery rites in honor of Bacchus (*see* Dionysus). The cult reached Rome from S Italy in the 2nd century BC. Originally involving only women, Bacchic worship included ecstatic rituals and secret orgies. In 186 BC a decree of the Senate prohibited Bacchanalia in Rome.

Bacchus. *See* Dionysus.

Bacchylides (c. 516–c. 450 BC) Greek lyric poet, nephew of Simonides and a rival of Pindar. Born on the island of Ceos, he lived at the court of Syracuse until the death of his patron Hiero in 467. Egyptian papyrus fragments discovered in 1896 contain parts of 14 odes and 6 dithyrambs (choral songs).

Bach, Johann Sebastian (1685–1750) German composer and keyboard player, the greatest member of a large musical family. An orphan from the age of nine, he was brought up and taught by his brother Johann Christoph Bach (1671–1721). He subsequently became a chorister in Lüneburg and in 1703 a violinist at the Weimar court. In 1707 he married his cousin Maria Barbara Bach (1684–1720); after her death he married Anna Magdalena Wilcken (1701–60). In 1708 he rejoined the Weimar court as organist, remaining there for nine years. He became kapellmeister at the court of Prince Leopold of Anhalt at Köthen in 1717 and finally cantor of St Thomas's Church, Leipzig, in 1723. During his lifetime Bach achieved greater recognition as an organist than as a composer; he composed much organ music and was a skilled improviser on keyboard instruments. Among his greatest works are the *St John Passion* (1723), the *St Matthew Passion* (1729), and the *Mass in B minor* (1733–38), as well as over 200 cantatas. His compositions for orchestra include violin and harpsichord concertos and the *Brandenburg Concertos* (1721). For the harpsichord and clavichord he composed a collection of 48 preludes and fugues entitled the *Well-Tempered Clavier* (Part I, 1722; Part II, 1744) and the *Goldberg Variations* (1742); he also wrote music for the violin, cello, and lute. Bach's music did not become widely known until Mendelssohn revived it, giving the first performance of the *St Matthew Passion* since Bach's time in 1829.

Of Bach's 20 children, 3 sons became famous musicians. His eldest son **Wilhelm Friedemann Bach** (1710–84) studied in Leipzig and became church organist in Dresden (1733–46) and subsequently in Halle (1746–64). He ended his life in poverty, leaving cantatas, concertos, and symphonies.

His third son **Karl Philipp Emanuel Bach** (1714–88) studied law and philosophy but later turned to music, becoming musician to Frederick the Great in Berlin and subsequently becoming director of the principal church in Hamburg in succession to Telemann. In his works, which were highly regarded by Haydn and Mozart, he developed a new monophonic style of composition that became the basis of the classical style. His works include symphonies, concertos, and much keyboard music.

J. S. Bach's 11th son **Johann Christian Bach** (1735–82), called the English (or London) Bach, studied in Berlin and after holding posts in Italy became music master to the British royal family. He composed 13 operas, as well as concertos, church music, and piano pieces.

JOHANN SEBASTIAN BACH

bacillus Any rod-shaped bacterium. The term is used specifically for bacteria of the genus *Bacillus*: spore-forming species including parasites of plants and animals. *B. anthracis* was first shown to cause anthrax in livestock by Robert *Koch.

backgammon A board game for two players that was known in ancient Mesopotamia, Greece, and Rome and in medieval England (as "the tables"). Each player has 15 pieces, which are moved around the 24 chevrons (points) marked on the board, the number of points moved being indicated by the throws of two dice. From their prescribed starting positions the players move in opposite directions. Each tries to bring all his pieces into the last quarter (his home board or inner table), after which he can remove them from the board (bear them off). Simultaneously he must block his opponent's moves. A chevron is occupied (point is made) when a player has two or more pieces on it, i.e. his opponent cannot land on it. A single piece on a point is a blot, i.e. vulnerable to the opponent's taking it and forcing it to travel around the board again.

background radiation Low-intensity radiation naturally present on the earth. It results either from the bombardment of the earth by *cosmic rays or from naturally occurring radioactive substances in the earth's crust.

backswimmer A *water bug, belonging to the worldwide family *Notonectidae* (nearly 200 species), that swims on its back, using a pair of oarlike legs for propulsion. Backswimmers can fly but are normally found in fresh water, preying voraciously on insects, tadpoles, and small fish. They must return to the surface periodically to replenish their air store.

Bacolod 10 38N 122 58E A port in the central Philippines, in NW Negros. It is a sugar-refining center serving the Philippines' most important sugar-growing area. Population (1980): 266,604.

Bacon, Francis (1909–92) British painter. He was self-taught and began painting in the 1930s. His mature style is evident in his *Three Studies* (of figures for the base of a *Crucifixion* [1945]). Another of his well-known paintings is *Study After Velázquez* (1951), a version of Velázquez's portrait of Pope Innocent X. His paintings are characterized by strong rich colors, a sinister blurring or erasure of human features, and an often violent dramatic quality.

Bacon, Francis, 1st Baron Verulam, Viscount St Albans (1561–1626) English lawyer and philosopher. He became a lawyer in 1582 and was elected to Parliament in 1584. During the 1590s, in the hope of political advancement, he cultivated the friendship of the 2nd Earl of *Essex but in 1601 assisted the prosecution for treason of his former patron. Under James I (reigned 1603–25) Bacon's career advanced more smoothly: he became a commissioner for the union of Scotland and England (1604), attorney general (1613), and Lord Chancellor (1618). In 1621, found guilty of bribery and corruption he was fined and banished from office and parliament.

Bacon's fame rests more securely on his philosophical and literary output and his influence on scientific thought in the later 17th century was considerable. In 1597 he published his first group of *Essays* on truth, death, friendship, etc. *The Advancement of Learning* (1605) presented a new classification of sciences and was expanded in the *De augmentis scientiarum* of 1623. In *Novum organum scientiarum* (1620) he argued that knowledge can be derived only from experience, advocating the scientific method of *induction. His other works include a *History of Henry VII* (1622) and the *New Atlantis* (1626), which describes his ideal state.

Bacon, Roger (c. 1214–c. 1292) English monk, scholar, and scientist, called Doctor Mirabilis for his diverse skills and learning. In three books written for Pope Clement IV he attempted to systematize the current state of knowledge; other works prophesied airplanes, microscopes, around-the-world voyages, steam engines, and telescopes. His astronomical knowledge enabled him to detect errors in the Julian *calendar. He has also been credited with the invention of *gunpowder and of the magnifying glass.

Bacon's Rebellion (1676) An uprising in Virginia that protested excessive taxation on tobacco crops and lack of defense against Indian raids. Nathaniel Bacon (1647–76), asked by the colonists to lead an army against the Indians, received little support from Virginia Gov. William *Berkeley. Bacon, with a large following, drove the governor out of Jamestown, burned the city, and asked the people of Virginia to make an oath of allegiance to him. Even after his death from a fever shortly thereafter, Bacon's Rebellion continued under new leadership until it was subdued by the governor.

bacteria Microscopic single-celled organisms found wherever life is possible. Generally 0.000004–0.0002 in (0.0001–0.005 mm) long, they may be spherical (*see* coccus), rodlike (*see* bacillus), or spiral-shaped (spirillum) and often occur in chains or clusters of cells. The so-called true bacteria have a rigid cell wall, which may be surrounded by a slimy capsule, and they often have long whiplike flagella for locomotion and short hairlike pili used in a form of sexual reproduction. A few bacteria are autotrophic, i.e. they can grow on simple inorganic substrates using carbon dioxide gas from the atmosphere to manufacture their own nutrients, but the majority are heterotrophic, requiring a source of organic carbon and a variety of other nutrients for growth. A single bacterium reproduces by dividing into two new cells; some species can do so every 15 minutes leading to rapid population growth. Some form resistant spores, which can survive for several years in adverse conditions.

The most important role of bacteria is in decomposing dead plant and animal tissues and releasing their constituents to the soil (*see* carbon cycle). Nitrogen-fixing bacteria in the soil or sea convert atmospheric nitrogen gas to nitrites and nitrates, which can then be used by plants (*see* nitrogen cycle). Many industrial processes are dependent on bacteria, including cheese making and *fermentation reactions. Bacteria inhabit the digestive systems of animals and play an important part in digestion, especially in *ruminants. However, certain (pathogenic) species may infect body tissues and cause disease while others, such as *Salmonella*, can cause *food poisoning.

bacteriophage (*or* phage) A *virus that infects a bacterium; 25–800 nanometers in size, phages may be spherical, filamentous, or tadpole-shaped with a head and tail. They consist of a protein coat surrounding a core of nucleic acid (either DNA or RNA) that is inserted into the bacterium. The viral genes then use the protein-synthesis apparatus of the bacterium to produce new phages, which are released from the cell, usually causing its destruction.

Bactria An ancient region of central Asia, SE of the Aral Sea. An Achemenian province from about 600 BC, it was conquered, despite fierce resistance, by Alexander the Great and subsequently passed to the Seleucids. In the mid-3rd century BC Diodotus I (died c. 239) established an independent Bactrian-Greek kingdom that later encompassed Soviet Central Asia (and its successor republics), Afghanistan, and Pakistan. From the 1st century AD the nomadic Kushan tribe occupied Bactria, introducing Buddhism and artistic styles influenced by Buddhist, Iranian, and Greek-Roman sources. Until about 600 AD Bactria was the hub of overland trade between east and west and a center for the interchange of religious and artistic ideas.

Badajoz 38 53N 6 58W A city in SW Spain, in Estremadura on the Guadiana River. Attacked on numerous occasions, it was pillaged by Wellington's troops (1812) during the Peninsular War. It has a 13th-century cathedral. Population (1986): 126,000.

Badalona 41 27N 2 15E A port in NE Spain, in Catalonia, forming an industrial suburb of Barcelona. Industries include glass, ship building, and textiles. Population (1986): 223,444.

Baden 47 28N 8 19E A spa city in N Switzerland. The diet (assembly) of the Swiss Confederation met here (1424–1712). Its hot sulfur springs have been visited since Roman times. Population (1981): 23,140.

Baden-Baden 48 45N 8 15E A spa in SW Germany, in Baden-Württemberg in the Black Forest. The hot springs have been used since Roman times. Population (1984): 49,000.

Baden-Powell, Robert Stephenson Smyth, 1st Baron (1857–1941) British general and founder of the Boy Scouts. After service in India and various parts of Africa, he achieved fame through his defense of Mafeking in the *Boer

War (1899–1900). Utilizing the experience of character training he had gained overseas, he founded the Boy Scouts in 1908 and, with his sister Agnes, the Girl Guides in 1910. *See also* Scouting.

Baden-Württemberg A *Land* in SW Germany, bordering on France and Switzerland, formed by an amalgamation of three former *Länder* (1952). It contains the Black Forest, several spas, and fertile agricultural land. Its population and economy have expanded greatly since World War II, when many refugees from further E settled here. A large proportion of Germany's watches, jewelry, and musical and medical instruments are made in Baden-Württemberg and there are also textile, chemical, and car industries. Area: 13,800 sq mi (35,751 sq km). Population (1988): 9,390,000.

badger A nocturnal burrowing mammal of the *weasel family (*Mustelidae*). The largest of the eight species is the gregarious Eurasian badger (*Meles meles*), about 3 ft (90 cm) long, with short strong legs, long coarse grayish hair on the body, and a black and white striped head. It lives in a complex of burrows (a set) and feeds on insects, rodents, worms, berries, etc. The American badger (*Taxidea taxus*) is smaller and lives alone when not breeding. The remaining badgers are found in S and SE Asia and include the smallest species—the ferret badgers (genus *Melogale*), about 2 ft (60 cm) long.

Bad Godesberg. *See* Godesberg.

badlands An elevated area dissected by gullies and deep valleys. This type of landscape is typical of arid and semiarid areas, where rainfall is intermittent and an adequate vegetation cover is prevented from forming or is destroyed through, for example, overgrazing; severe soil erosion may occur. The name was originally applied to the Badlands of South Dakota.

badminton An indoor court game for two or four players, played with rackets and a shuttlecock or bird of nylon or cork and feathers. It originated in India and is the national sport of several Asian countries. Badminton was introduced in England and the US in the 1870s. It is a volleying game (the shuttles do not bounce) and points are scored only by the serving side. If the serving side fails to make a good return the service changes (in doubles games both partners serve before their opponents). A game is usually played to 15 points (women's singles go to 11 points).

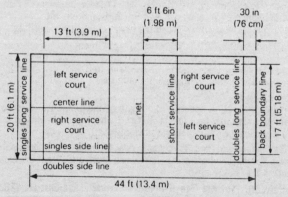

BADMINTON *The dimensions of the court. The top of the net at the center is 5 ft (1.5 m) above the floor.*

Badoglio, Pietro (1871–1956) Italian general, who rose to prominence during World War I. He directed Mussolini's conquest of Ethiopia (1935–36) but in 1940 resigned during the disastrous Italian campaign in Greece. After Mussolini's fall (1943), he became prime minister and negotiated the armistice with the Allies. He resigned in 1944.

Baeck, Leo (1873–1956) German Jewish theologian. Under the *Nazis, he became the spiritual leader of German Jewry, continuing to teach in Theresienstadt concentration camp (1943–45). After the war he settled in London. In his major work, *The Essence of Judaism* (1905), Baeck argued for the superiority of Judaism to Christianity.

Baedeker, Karl (1801–59) German publisher of guidebooks. His first guide, to Coblenz (1829), was followed by a series that became internationally famous.

Baekeland, Leo Hendrik (1863–1944) US industrial chemist, born in Belgium. He invented Bakelite (*see* urea-formaldehyde resins), the first synthetic thermosetting plastic. The discovery was made while Baekeland was searching for a synthetic substitute for *shellac.

Baer, Karl Ernest von (1792–1876) Russian embryologist. He showed that mammalian eggs were not the follicles of the ovary but microscopic particles inside the follicles. He described the development of the embryo from layers of tissue, which he called *germ layers*, and demonstrated similarities in the embryos of different species of vertebrates.

Baeyer, (Johann Friedrich Wilhelm) Adolf von (1835–1917) German chemist, who became professor at the University of Strasbourg and then at Munich. He discovered barbituric acid (1865), synthesized indigo (1878), and developed several organic dyes. Baeyer also calculated the angles between the carbon atoms in organic compounds, showing (1885) how strained bonds affect chemical reactivity in closed carbon chains. He was awarded the 1905 Nobel Prize for his synthesis of indigo.

Baez, Joan (1941–   ) US folksinger, whose performance at the 1959 Newport Festival led to a series of successful recordings of folksongs and later of contemporary protest songs. An active pacifist, she opposed the Vietnam War and worked to relieve suffering and famine in Cambodia.

Baffin, William (c. 1584–1622) English navigator. In two voyages (1615, 1616) with Capt Robert Bylot he attempted in the *Discovery* to find the *Northwest Passage. He eventually despaired of its existence but explored the Hudson Strait, giving his name to Baffin Bay and Baffin Island.

Baffin Island The largest island of the Canadian Arctic, in Franklin district lying N of Hudson Strait. It is separated from Greenland by a Strait forming **Baffin Bay** (in the N) and Davis Strait. Mountainous with many glaciers and snowfields, its sparse population is concentrated in Frobisher Bay. Area: 183,810 sq mi (476,068 sq km).

Bagehot, Walter (1826–77) British economist, political theorist, literary critic, and journalist. He first worked as a banker, his interest in banking theories being reflected in his *Lombard Street* (1873). While editor of the *Economist* magazine (1860–77), he wrote his major political works, *The English Constitution* (1867), which analyzes the comparative powers of the British organs of government, and *Physics and Politics* (1872), applying Darwin's principles of natural selection to political society.

Baghdad 33 20N 44 26E The capital of Iraq, on the Tigris River near the center of the country. Built by the caliph (Islamic leader) Mansur in the 8th century, it was a center of commerce, learning, and religion until sacked by the Mongols in 1258. Modern Baghdad grew after becoming the capital of independent Iraq (1927) and is now an important administrative, communications, and manufacturing center with three universities (1947, 1957, and 1963). Population (1985 est): 3,840,000.

Baghdad Pact A treaty between Turkey, Iraq, Pakistan, and the UK. Signed in 1955, its goals were military, economic, and social cooperation in the Middle East. When Iraq withdrew from it in 1959, its headquarters moved to Ankara from Baghdad and it was renamed the *Central Treaty Organization.

Baghdad Railroad A rail link between Europe and Asia Minor, running from Turkey to Iraq. Its construction, begun in the late 19th century with German finance, was seen by the British as a threat to their position in India and it was a point of contention in World War I.

Baglioni A family that dominated Perugia (Italy) from 1425 until 1534. Its leading members were **Malatesta Baglioni** (1389–1437), who established the family's position in Perugia; **Giampaolo Baglioni** (c. 1470–1520), who came to power in 1500 following a family feud that resulted in the assassination of many of his relatives; and **Malatesta Baglioni** (1491–1531) a *condottiere who served both Venice and Florence, betraying the latter to the pope in 1530. The Baglioni were banished from Perugia in 1534.

bagpipes A reed-pipe instrument of ancient origin, found in many countries. Air is forced into a windbag either by the mouth (Scottish bagpipes) or by a bellows (Northumbrian pipes). By pressing the bag under his arm the player pushes air into the sounding pipes, which consist of one to three drones and a single chanter pipe. Drone pipes each sound one continuous note. The chanter pipe is fitted with holes, which are covered by the player's fingers. Bagpipes are regarded as the national instrument of Scotland, having been introduced to the British Isles in the 13th century.

Baguio 16 25N 120 37E A city in the N Philippines, in W Luzon. It is a popular summer resort and the site of the national military academy. Gold and copper are mined. Population (1990 est): 183,000.

bagworm moth A moth belonging to the widely distributed family *Psychidae* (800 species). The larvae live in cases made of silk covered with leaves, twigs, grass, etc., with only the head and forelegs projecting. Males emerge after pupation, flying in search of the wingless females, which remain in their cases.

Baha'i faith A religion founded in Persia in 1863 by Mirza Husain 'Ali (1817–92), who was known as Baha' Allah (Glory of God). He proclaimed himself to be the Promised One whose coming was foretold by the Bab (*see* Babi faith). His eldest son and then his great-grandson led the Baha'is after his death until 1957. Since 1963 the faith has been governed by the Universal House of Justice, a council at Haifa, Israel, elected by national spiritual assemblies. The basis tenet of the faith is that God reveals himself to man through prophets who appear at various stages in history and the most recent of these is Baha' Allah. Baha'is advocate a universal faith, world peace, an international language, the equality of men and women, and the abolition of all prejudices. During the 20th century the faith has spread to the West.

Bahamas, Commonwealth of the A state consisting of about 700 islands and innumerable cays in the West Indies, off the SE coast of Florida. The principal islands, which are mainly low lying, include New Providence (with the capital Nassau), Grand Bahama, Abaco, Eleuthera, Andros, and Watling Island (San Salvador). The majority of the population is of African descent. *Economy*: with its mild subtropical climate and beautiful beaches, the main industry of the Bahamas is tourism, which accounts for over 50% of revenue and employment. Efforts are now being made to develop agriculture and fisheries, finance, and industry (especially oil refining). Foreign investment is encouraged by the tax position, 90% of companies being foreign-owned. Main exports include cement, petroleum and petroleum products, chemicals, and fish. *History*: in 1492 Columbus made his first landing in the W hemisphere on the island of San Salvador. The first European occupation comprised an English religious settlement in the mid-17th century, and the islands became a British crown colony in 1717. From 1964 the country had increasing control over its own affairs and in 1973 it attained full independence within the Commonwealth. In the 1980s high unemployment and its effects on the populace brought concern that standards of service in tourism were declining. An increase in crime, drugs, and unrest among the youth was also seen as related to unemployment, which in 1983 had reached 25%. Bahamian disaffection with the US government over provisions of the Caribbean Basin initiative requiring the Bahamas to divulge banking secrets, became public. Prime Minister Pindling also claimed unequal tax treatment by the US, regarding business tourism as compared with other Caribbean nations. In 1992, Pindling, attacked for corruption, was voted out of office. The Bahamas is a member of CARICOM. Prime Minister: Hubert Ingraham. Official language: English. Official currency: Bahamian dollar of 100 cents. Area: 5353 sq mi (13,864 sq km). Population (1990 est): 250,000. Capital and main port: Nassau.

Bahia. *See* Salvador.

Bahía Blanca 38 45S 62 15W A port in Argentina. It is a major distribution center; exports include grain, meat, and wool. The National University of the South was founded here in 1956. Population (1980): 233,126.

Bahrain, State of An independent sheikdom in the Arabian Gulf, occupying a low-lying archipelago between Saudi Arabia and the Qatar Peninsula. The two main islands, Bahrain and Al-Muharraq, are connected by a causeway and there are also plans for a causeway to Saudi Arabia. The inhabitants are mainly Arabs. *Economy*: almost totally dependent upon oil. A large refinery on Bahrain Island processes not only the relatively small amounts of local oil, first discovered in 1931, but also much larger amounts coming from Saudi Arabia by pipeline. Efforts are being made to develop other industry with some success. An aluminum smelter on Bahrain is the largest non-oil industrial plant in the Gulf. The formerly important pearl-fishing industry is now in decline. Bahrain is important as a transport center in the Gulf and the modern harbor of Mina Salman has extensive shipping facilities and a free transport area. In 1975 the government licensed the setting up of Offshore Banking Units, a move that increased Bahrain's commercial importance. By the early 1980s Bahrain had become the most important money center between Europe and Singapore. *History*: the islands were under Portuguese rule from 1521 until 1602, and during parts of the 17th century Iran had control, eventually being expelled by the Khalifa family, who have ruled the area for most of the time since. It was a British protected state from 1861 until 1971 when full independence was declared by the emir, Sheik Isa ibn Sulman al-Khalifa. In 1975 political unrest led to the dissolution of the National Assembly. Bahrain became a member of OPEC in 1970. The majority of the population are Arab Muslims, equally divided between Sunni and Shiah sects. Differences between the two groups have created political and social tensions. In 1981 plans for a coup by Shiah Muslims who were part of an Iranian-backed underground group, were exposed. Causing widespread disruption in the government, the fomenting of the plot underscored the rift between Sunni and Shiah, which some observers had thought was healing. Bahrain was a founding member of the Gulf Cooperation Council (GCC) in 1981. In 1991, the country joined the UN-led allied troops against Iraq in the Persian Gulf War. Official language: Arabic; English is also widely spoken. Official religion: Islam. Official currency: Bahrain dinar of 1000 fils. Area: 255 sq mi (660 sq km). Population (1990 est): 512,000. Capital and main port: Manama.

Baikal, Lake A lake in SE central Russia, in the Buryat Republic. It is the largest freshwater lake in Asia and at 5316 ft (1620 m) the deepest in the world. It is fed by over 300 streams but drained by only one, the Angara River. Area: 12,160 sq mi (31,500 sq km).

bail The release by a court of an imprisoned person, usually while awaiting trial, into the keeping of people who agree to ensure his reappearance at a particular date and time. If these people, called "sureties," then fail to produce him, they forfeit whatever sum of money the court has set for bail. The person bailed must also stand as surety for himself; if thought trustworthy, he may be bailed without other sureties, "in his own recognizance." Judges have wide discretion as to whether bail should be granted and for what amount.

Bailey bridge A type of military bridge invented by Britain's Sir Donald Bailey during World War II. Consisting of light strong standardized interlocking truss sections, it can be easily assembled in the field. Pontoons can be provided for longer spans, the longest of which was that of the 4000 ft (1200 m) bridge built across the Maas River in Holland.

Baja California. *See* Lower California.

Bakelite. *See* urea-formaldehyde resins.

Baker, Howard (Henry, Jr.) (1925–) US politician. A Republican from Tennessee, he served in the US Senate (1966–85). He headed the Senate committee that probed the Watergate scandal (1973) and was Senate minority (1977–81) and majority leader (1981–85). He ran unsuccessfully for the Republican presidential nomination in 1980 and did not seek reelection to the Senate in 1984.

Baker, Josephine (1906–75) US singer and dancer. She danced in *La Revue Nègre* (1925) in Paris and then went on to a leading role in the *Folies-Bergère*. A blues singer, she spent most of her life in France, entertaining and running her own nightclub there and touring internationally; eventually, she became a French citizen (1937). She was awarded the French Legion of Honor for her World War II work in the resistance; she supported the US civil rights movement during the 1960s and worked closely with international adoption agencies.

Bakhtyari A major tribe of W Iran of some 400,000 members speaking the Luri dialect of Persian. About one-third are still nomadic herdsmen living in tents. They make an annual grueling migration of 150 miles (240 km) from their winter pastures on the plains to the summer pastures in the mountains. Authority is vested in hereditary chiefs, who have often played an influential role in Iranian politics. The Bakhtyari are of the Islamic faith, but their women have a greater degree of freedom than is usual among Muslims.

baking powder A mixture, usually of *sodium bicarbonate and *tartaric acid or *cream of tartar, used in baking. It generates carbon dioxide on heating or wetting, thus making the dough rise.

Bakst, Léon (Lev Samoilovich Rosenberg; 1866–1924) Russian artist, who modernized theater design. He was born in St Petersburg, where he trained in the Imperial Academy of Arts and became court painter, before turning to scenery design in 1900. His greatest achievements were for ballets produced by Sergei *Diaghilev in Paris, where he later settled.

Baku 40 22N 49 53E A port in and the capital of Azerbaijan, on the Caspian Sea. The old town is a maze of narrow streets and ancient buildings, including mosques and a 17th-century palace. It is the region's oldest center of oil production, and oil is still the basis of its economy. Population (1987 est): 1,741,000.

Bakunin, Mikhail Aleksandrovich (1814–76) Russian anarchist. An interest in dialectics led Bakunin to study German philosophy at Berlin University, where he became exposed to socialist philosophy. He participated in the Revolutions of 1848 and in 1849 he was arrested in Dresden, handed over to Russian officials, and exiled to Siberia. In 1861 he escaped to London. He participated in the First *International but came into conflict with Marx and was expelled. He had many followers in Italy, Spain, Russia, and elsewhere.

Bakwanga. *See* Mbuji-Mayi.

Balaclava, Battle of (October 25, 1854) An indecisive battle between Russian and British-Turkish forces in the *Crimean War. It is notorious for the heavy British casualties caused by misunderstanding between Lord *Raglan, the British commander in chief, and Lord Lucan (1800–88), the cavalry commander. The courageous Light Brigade charged Russian artillery at the end of a narrow valley and of its 673 men, 113 were killed and 134 wounded.

Balakirev, Mili Alekseevich (1837–1910) Russian composer, one of the *Five. He was the founder of the Free School of Music in St Petersburg (1862). His works, such as the tone poem *Tamara* (1867–82) and the piano fantasy *Islamey* (1869), reflect his romanticism and Russian musical nationalism.

balalaika A Russian plucked instrument of the guitar family, played singly or in a balalaika orchestra. It has a long fretted fingerboard, a triangular body, and three wire strings that are plucked with a plectrum. It is made in different sizes, the smaller being held like a guitar and the larger balanced on the floor like a double bass.

balance A sensitive device for comparing two masses, consisting of a beam pivoted at its center (usually on an agate knife edge) with pans hanging from each of its ends. The material of unknown mass is placed in one pan and standard weights are placed in the other. A pointer indicates when the beam is horizontal and the whole device is enclosed in a glass case to avoid drafts and temperature changes. The accuracy of a balance is increased by using a rider—a small weight hung on a calibrated scale on the balance arm itself. A standard balance will weigh to the nearest 0.0001 g, while extremely sensitive **microbalances** can be used to weigh objects with a mass of only 1 microgram. *See also* spring balance.

balance of payments The difference between a country's income and its expenditure abroad. It is usually divided into a current account and a capital account. The current account records the country's *balance-of-trade earnings or deficit on visible goods and its invisible earnings or deficit on such items as insurance, transport, tourism, and some kinds of government spending. The capital account records all long- and short-term capital flows, both in the public and private sectors. If the sum of the current and capital accounts shows a deficit there will be a net loss of foreign exchange, which the government must take steps to remedy. Measures include deflation by *monetary or *fiscal policy to reduce imports, the imposition of *tariffs or import *quotas, incentives to increase exports, the introduction of stringent *exchange control regulations, and ultimately *devaluation of the currency. If the balance of payments shows a persistent surplus a revaluation of the currency may be required.

balance of power The principle seeking to ensure that no nation or group of nations becomes too dominant. Practiced by Greek city states, which formed intercity alliances, the principle was adopted in Europe in the alliance system of 15th-century Italy. In 1815 at the Congress of *Vienna, Prussia, Russia, Britain,

France, and Austria realigned European frontiers to establish themselves as equal powers and to ensure peace. Tensions remained, however, and rival alliances led to further wars to prevent or restore national dominance. In the 20th century the League of Nations and the UN have both tried to establish international harmony, but the development of nuclear weapons acts as the greatest deterrent to any state sufficiently ambitious to threaten international equilibrium.

balance of trade The difference in money between the value of a country's imports and its exports. The balance of trade is sometimes known as the visibles account because it refers only to actual goods. Together with the invisibles account and capital transfers it makes up the *balance of payments. The invisibles account includes such earnings as selling insurance abroad and spending by foreign tourists. Thus the balance of trade can be in deficit without necessarily meaning that the balance of payments will also be in deficit.

Balanchine, George (Georgy Melitonovich Balanchivadze; 1904–83) US ballet dancer and choreographer, born in Russia. He worked for Diaghilev's Ballets Russes in Europe from 1924 and went to the US in 1933. In 1948 he became first artistic director of the New York City Ballet (1948–83). His ballets include *Firebird* (1950) and *Don Quixote* (1965), and he also choreographed for films and stage musicals.

Balaton, Lake A lake in W Hungary, the largest in central Europe. There are vineyards and holiday resorts on its shore and its outlet is a canal leading to a tributary of the Danube River. Area: 231 sq mi (598 sq km).

Balboa 8 57N 79 33W A port in the Panama Canal Zone, at the Pacific end of the Panama Canal. It was named for the explorer Vasco Núñez de *Balboa. It has extensive harbor facilities.

Balboa, Vasco Núñez de (c. 1475–1517) Spanish explorer. Having settled in Hispaniola, he became a stowaway on an expedition to present-day Colombia (1510), moved on to Panama, and founded a settlement at Darién (1511). In 1513 he set off across the Isthmus in search of gold. Sighting the Pacific, which he called the South Sea, after 25 grueling days, he claimed it for Spain. He was subsequently accused, unjustly, of treason and beheaded by the governor of Darién, Pedrarias (d. 1531).

bald eagle A large sea *eagle, *Haliaetus leukocephalus*, also called the American eagle; it is the national emblem of the US and an endangered species. It is dark brown with a white head and tail and has a prominent curved beak and unfeathered legs. It feeds on carrion and fish and has rough skin on the toes for grasping slippery prey.

Baldwin, James Arthur (1924–87) US novelist, essayist, and dramatist. His first novel, *Go Tell It on the Mountain* (1953), is based on his experience of poverty and religion in Harlem, New York City, where he was born. He lived in Paris from 1948 to 1957, when he returned to the US as an active civil-rights campaigner. He subsequently moved to France again. His works include novels, such as *Giovanni's Room* (1956) and *Tell Me How Long the Train's Been Gone* (1968), two plays, and several collections of essays, notably *Notes of a Native Son* (1955), *The Fire Next Time* (1963), and *Just Above My Head* (1979).

Baldwin, Stanley, 1st Earl (1867–1947) British statesman, who was Conservative prime minister (1923–24, 1924–29, 1935–37). As chancellor of the exchequer (1922–23), Baldwin negotiated the British World War I debt to the US. He dealt as prime minister with the *General Strike (1926). Baldwin was much criticized for condoning Italy's conquest of Ethiopia and his apparent reluctance to rearm in the face of Germany's military build-up. His management of the events leading to Edward VIII's abdication complied with public opinion.

Baldwin I (c. 1058–1118) King of Jerusalem (1100–18). Baldwin succeeded his brother Godfrey of Bouillon, whom he had accompanied on the first Crusade, taking Edessa in 1098. Baldwin considerably expanded the territory of Jerusalem.

Balearic Islands An archipelago in the W Mediterranean Sea comprising a Spanish province. It includes the chief islands of *Majorca, *Minorca, *Ibiza, and Formentera, together with several islets. The islands were taken by Aragon from the Moors in the 14th century. Area: 1936 sq mi (5014 sq km). Capital: Palma, on Majorca.

baleen (*or* whalebone) The horny material that forms the food-sieving plates in whalebone *whales. Baleen was formerly used to manufacture stays in corsets, but has now largely been replaced by synthetic materials.

Balenciaga, Cristóbal (1895–1972) Spanish fashion designer, who moved to Paris in 1937. He built up an elite clientele, which was attracted by his starkly elegant styles, especially his tailored suits.

Balfour, Arthur James, 1st Earl of (1848–1930) British statesman and Conservative prime minister (1902–05). His government passed an *Education Act (1902), the Irish Land Purchase Act (1903; *see* Land Acts, Irish), and concluded the Anglo-French entente (1904). In World War I Balfour, as foreign secretary (1916–19) issued his famous *Balfour Declaration.

Balfour Declaration (1917) The decision of the British government, made known in a letter of Nov 2 from the British foreign secretary, Arthur *Balfour, to the chairman of the British Zionist Federation, to support the establishment of a national Jewish home in Palestine. The letter promised British aid to Zionist efforts to establish such a home, providing that the interests of existing non-Jewish communities in Palestine be maintained as well as the rights and political status of Jews in any other country. Arab aspirations in Palestine, however, prevented the British government from fulfilling the promise of the Declaration, which was abandoned in 1939.

Bali An Indonesian island off E Java. Mountainous and volcanic, it has southern fertile plains that produce chiefly rice. The Balinese are famed for their arts and handicrafts, and it is a popular tourist resort. *History*: Hindu since the 7th century AD, Bali resisted the 16th–17th century spread of Islam through Indonesia and became an enclave of Hindu culture. Dutch rule became complete only in 1908, although trade began in the 17th century. In the 1965–67 Indonesian purge of communists 40,000 people were killed. Area: 2146 sq mi (5558 sq km). Population (1980): 2,469,930. Chief town: Denpasar.

Balikpapan 1 15S 116 50E A port in Indonesia, in SE Kalimantan on the Makassar Strait. Its refinery processes local and imported oil. Population (1980): 280,675.

Balkan Mountains (Bulgarian name: Stara Planina) A mountain range extending 311 mi (500 km) E–W for the entire width of central Bulgaria. It rises to 7795 ft (2376 m) at Botev Peak.

Balkans An area in SE Europe consisting of present-day Greece, Albania, Yugoslavia, Bosnia-Hercegovina, Croatia, Macedonia, Slovenia, Bulgaria, part of Romania, and the European part of Turkey. Part of the Roman empire from the 2nd century BC and of the Eastern Roman (Byzantine) Empire from the 5th century AD, the Balkans were ruled by the Ottoman Turks from the 15th to the 19th and 20th centuries, when independence was granted to Greece (1829), Serbia (1878), Romania (1878), Bulgaria (1908), and Albania (1912). The competition between European powers for control of the Balkans, coupled with integral rivalries, contributed to the outbreak of World War I, after which Yugoslavia was created out of Serbia. All the Balkan states, except Greece, became communist after *World War II until the 1990s.

Balkan Wars (1912–13) Two military confrontations that preceded World War I. In the first (1912–13) the Balkan League (Bulgaria, Serbia, Greece, and Montenegro) defeated Turkey. In the concluding Treaty of London, Turkey lost all its European possessions except E Thrace. In the second Balkan War (1913) the victors fought over their acquisitions in Macedonia, from most of which Bulgaria was excluded by the Treaty of *Bucharest; Turkey regained Thrace.

Balkhash, Lake A lake in E Kazakhstan. Since it has no outlet, it fluctuates in size, and it is generally shrinking. Area: about 20,000 sq km (7720 sq mi).

Balla, Giacomo (1871–1958) Italian futurist painter, born in Turin. He was influenced by *pointillism before he became associated with *futurism (1910) and painted many dynamic studies of light and movement, notably birds in flight, and the humorous *Dog on a Leash* (1912; Buffalo).

ballad A form of popular narrative poetry. Originally intended for singing or recitation, ballads have a simple basic stanza form (four lines rhyming *abcb*); repetition and direct speech are characteristic devices. Subject matter includes love, family feuds, war, magic, biblical tales, the deeds of Robin Hood and the knights of the Round Table (*see* Arthurian legend), the exploits of cowboys and outlaws. The ballad dates back many centuries. Some of the finest examples of the form were composed in the 15th century in N England and Scotland; debased versions were later printed on single sheets of paper (broadside ballads) for sale by peddlers. Later still a tradition of literary ballads grew up (e.g. Kipling's "Danny Deever"). Notable ballad collections are Bishop *Percy's *Reliques* (1765) and F. J. Child's *English and Scottish Popular Ballads* (1883–98).

ballade A form of medieval French lyric poetry or song. It consists of three stanzas and a final *envoi* (address); each stanza has the same rhyme scheme and final line, which serves as a refrain. It was used for formal and commemorative songs. Guillaume de *Machaut pioneered this form in the 14th century, and in the 15th century it was used by Charles d'*Orléans and François *Villon, among others.

ballet A dramatic art in which dancing and mime, accompanied by music, combine to tell a story or evoke a mood. Ballet originated in the formal dances of French court entertainments, notably under Louis XIV (*see* Lully). In the 18th century ballet established itself in the public theater but still as an adjunct to *opera or other forms of drama. Idolized ballerinas such as Sallé (1707–56) and Carmargo (1710–70) introduced less constricting dress and Jean-Georges Noverre (1727–1810) extended ballet's dramatic range. Dancing on the tips of the toes (*sur les pointes*) was introduced early in the 19th century, possibly by Taglioni (1804–84). This period saw the heyday of romantic ballet, epitomized by Coralli's *Giselle* (1841).

Modern ballet arose in the early 20th century when *Fokine and subsequently *Diaghilev (*see also* Ballets Russes) combined the polished technique of the imperial Russian dancers with the naturalism advocated by the American Isadora *Duncan. Their reforms gave scope to the talents of such dancers as *Nijinsky and *Pavlova, the composers *Stravinsky and *Ravel, the choreographers *Massine and *Balanchine, and the designer *Bakst. Independent ballet companies grew up all over Europe and the US during the 1930s. England had two such groups, one led by Marie *Rambert (now the Ballet Rambert) and the other by Ninette de *Valois and Frederick *Ashton (now the *Royal Ballet). Other notable companies are the *Bolshoi and *Kirov from the Soviet Union and George *Balanchine's New York City Ballet. Since World War II innovative choreographers such as *Cranko, *Béjart, Merce Cunningham, Alvin Ailey, and Twyla Tharpe have created new ballets inspired by folk dance, jazz, and even gymnastics.

Ballets Russes A Russian ballet company (1909–29) founded in Paris by *Diaghilev. It gave the West its first opportunity to see Russian imperial dancers and through its world tours brought ballet to a wider public. In attempting to fuse dance, mime, music, and scenery into a harmonious unity, it fostered the most avant-garde talents of the period and greatly influenced the subsequent development of ballet. Its choreographers included *Fokine, *Massine, *Balanchine, and *Nijinsky, who was also one of its principal dancers. *Ravel and *Stravinsky composed music for several of its ballets. Among its scene designers were *Bakst and the painters *Picasso, *Matisse, and *Miró.

Ballinger-Pinchot Controversy (1909–11) A disagreement over the public rights to western water lands. Richard Ballinger (1858–1922), Pres. William H. Taft's secretary of the interior, made public again lands that had been closed by the government. Gifford Pinchot (1865–1946), chief of the forestry division of the Department of Agriculture, accused Ballinger of catering to private enterprise. Ballinger was cleared by a congressional committee and Pinchot was fired by President Taft.

ballistic missiles Rocket-powered nuclear missiles without wings or other lift surfaces that are propelled to desired altitudes and velocities and then follow an unpowered trajectory similar to that of a projectile fired from a gun. Their accuracy requires careful thrust calculations and on-board preset or inertial guidance systems and is calculated as a probability (e.g. 45–60%) of landing within a stated radius about their target (Circular Error of Probability). Intercontinental ballistic missiles (ICBMs) are capable of reaching any point on the surface of the earth. Both the US and the components of the former Soviet Union possess large numbers of these, some of which (MIRVs—multiple independently targeted re-entry vehicles) have up to ten separate warheads. See also antiballistic missiles; V-2 rocket.

ballistics The study of projectiles and the extent to which their trajectories are affected by shape, propulsion systems, gravity, temperature, wind, etc. There are three branches: interior, dealing with all aspects of propulsion within a gun barrel or at launch; exterior, concerned with the trajectory of the projectile in flight; and terminal, relating to the effects of the missile on the target.

ball lightning A luminous moving sphere, several centimeters in diameter, occurring just above the ground on rare occasions during thunderstorms. It hisses, has a distinct odor, and may be either red, orange, or yellow. It lasts for only a few seconds and then either dies away or explodes. The phenomenon is not fully understood but one theory suggests that it consists of *plasma.

balloons Lighter-than-air craft, consisting of a bag of gas that displaces a volume of air of greater mass than the total mass of the balloon and its contents. The first successful balloon flight, indeed man's first aerial voyage, was made in 1783 by the *Montgolfier brothers' hot-air balloon; it flew 2 mi (9 km) across Paris. Two years later a *Charlière* hydrogen balloon (designed by J. A. C. Charles, the formulator of *Charles's Law) flew across the English Channel. In 1821 coal gas was used for the first time as a cheap alternative to hydrogen. This opened the way for many exploits by showmen, scientists, and explorers. Balloons must be tethered (for parachuting, scientific experiments, etc.) or they will fly where the wind blows them; *dirigible balloons first appeared in the middle of the 19th century. However, by the end of the century interest in flying was centered on heavier-than-air machines (*see* aircraft).

The use of balloons in war began with Napoleon's observation balloons in 1794, after which they continued to play a sporadic but largely ineffectual part, until their extensive use in both World Wars in the form of barrage balloons.

The sport of **ballooning** has enjoyed a revival in recent years, the preferred vehicle being a hot-air balloon carrying its own propane air heater. The height record for a manned balloon is 30,480 m (1957). A solo balloon crossing of the Atlantic Ocean was made in 1984.

balm A fragrant-leaved herbaceous plant of, or related to, the genus *Melissa*, native to the Old World. Lemon balm, or balm gentle (*M. officinalis*), is widely grown in temperate regions and used for flavoring foods or beverages and scenting perfumes. The European bastard balm (*Melittis melissophylum*) is more strongly scented. Others species include bee balm (*Monarda didyma*) and horse balm (*Collinsonia canadensis*). Family: **Labiatae*.

balsa An evergreen tree, *Ochroma pyramidale*, native to Central and South America, also called corkwood. About 40 ft (12 m) tall, it is the source of an extremely light pale-colored wood, which is widely used for corks, canoes, floats, etc. Although easily crushed, it is technically a hardwood. Family: *Bombacaceae*.

balsam An aromatic resinous substance of plant origin, used in medicine for its soothing and healing properties and in perfumery. Balsam of Peru is derived from the Central American leguminous tree *Myroxylon peneirae*, grown in El Salvador.

The name is also given to many plants of the family *Balsaminaceae*. The garden balsam (*Impatiens balsamina*), native to India, is widely cultivated for its showy red flowers, which have a tubular spur and five unequal petals. The balsam apple (*Momardica balsamina*) is an ornamental vine.

Baltic languages A group of Indo-European languages closely related to the Slavonic languages and spoken on the E shores of the Baltic Sea. **Lithuanian and **Latvian (Lettish) are still extant: Old Prussian has been extinct since the 17th century. Deriving from northern Proto-Indo-European, the Baltic, Slavonic, and Germanic languages share important morphological and word-formation features.

Baltic Sea A section of the Atlantic Ocean in N Europe, bounded by Denmark, Sweden, Finland, Russia, Poland, and Germany. To the W, it leads into the Little Belt, the Great Belt, and the Sound, and to the E, the Gulfs of Bothnia, Finland, and Riga. It has very low salinity since it receives rivers draining almost one-fifth of Europe, and it can freeze sufficiently to hinder navigation.

Baltic Shield. *See* shield.

Baltic states The territories on the SE coast of the Baltic Sea that comprise present-day Latvia, Lithuania, and Estonia. The Danes conquered N Estonia in the 13th century while S Estonia with Latvia (then comprising Livonia) fell to the Teutonic Knights. Lithuania formed an independent state until united with Poland in 1569 in the Union of **Lublin. The region came under Russian rule in the 18th century but briefly, between World Wars I and II, formed the independent states of Latvia, Lithuania, and Estonia. They regained independence and joined the UN in 1991.

Baltimore 39 25N 76 40W The largest city in Maryland, at the mouth of the Patapsco River. Established in 1729, it was named for the Barons Baltimore, the first of whom, George Calvert (c. 1580–1632), founded Maryland. It was the

BALLET

the five ballet positions

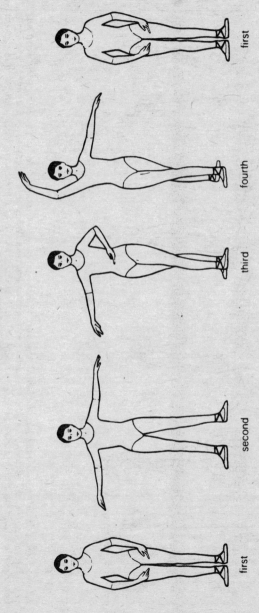

first   second   third   fourth   first

LABANOTATION *Since Rudolph Laban (1879–1958) published his system for recording dance movements in 1928 it has gained wide-spread acceptance. In this simple example, the initial positions of the legs and arms are indicated at (1). Subsequent positions (2–5) are seen by reading upwards from the bottom. The dancer, starting with feet together and arms at her sides, takes four even steps forward, beginning with the right foot, and moves her arms upwards and outwards (the different shadings representing low, middle, and high positions).* **LABANOTATION** *Since Rudolph Laban (1879–1958) published his system for recording dance movements in 1928 it has gained*

238

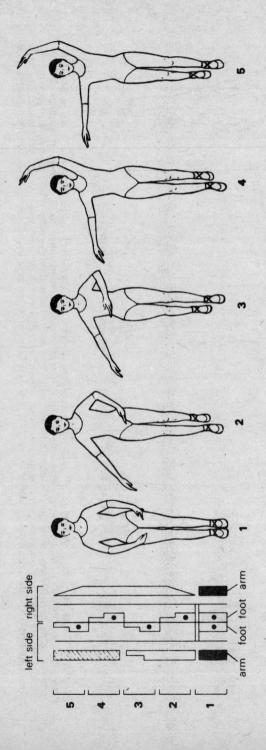

widespread acceptance. In this simple example, the initial positions of the legs and arms are indicated at (1). Subsequent positions (2–5) are seen by reading upwards from the bottom. The dancer, starting with feet together and arms at her sides, takes four even steps forward, beginning with the right foot, and moves her arms upwards and outwards (the different shadings representing low, middle, and high positions).

starting point of the first US railroad (1827). It is the site of many historical buildings, including the US's first Roman Catholic cathedral (1806–21) and the Edgar Allan Poe House (1830). Baltimore is a major educational and cultural center and contains a number of universities; in the 1980s considerable rebuilding around the port area has revitalized the city. It has been a busy seaport and shipbuilding center since the late 18th century (Baltimore clippers were renowned throughout the world); other important industries include the manufacture of steel, sugar and food processing, oil refining, and chemicals. Population (1990): 736,014.

Baltimore oriole An American *oriole, *Icterus galbula*, of North America, so named because the black and orange plumage of the male resembles the colors of the Barons Baltimore (*see* Baltimore). It feeds on insects, has an attractive song, and builds a woven pouchlike nest.

Baluchistan A province in W Pakistan, on the Arabian Sea and the Iranian and Afghani borders. Mostly rough arid highlands, it is inhabited by pastoral Pathans, Baluchs, and other peoples. The NW deserts are practically uninhabited but the coastal plain and E lowlands support wheat, barley, maize, and herbs. There is little industry other than crafts, textiles, and food processing. Baluchistan has extensive mineral resources. *History*: on the trade routes from India to the Middle East, Baluchistan has flourished since ancient times. Nominally part of larger empires, it usually enjoyed autonomy until Britain won control (19th century). In 1947 it became part of Pakistan. Area: 134,050 sq mi (347,190 sq km). Population (1985): 4,908,000. Capital: Quetta.

Baluchitherium An extinct hornless rhinoceros that lived in the Oligocene epoch (between 30 million and 20 million years ago). Fossilized remains found in central Asia show that it was over 16 ft (5 m) high, with a heavy giraffe-like body, and was probably the largest terrestrial mammal ever to have lived.

Balzac, Honoré de (1799–1850) French novelist. Educated at Vendôme, he became a lawyer's clerk in Paris. He wrote popular novels under pseudonyms, and then attempted to become a businessman; in 1828, however, bankruptcy forced him to turn to writing again. *Les Chouans* (1829), a historical novel about Breton peasants, was his first success; in the next 20 years he added over 40 novels to his life's work, the cycle *La Comédie humaine*. In these novels, which included *Eugénie Grandet* (1833), *Le Père Goriot* (1834), and *La Cousine Bette* (1846), he developed new techniques of realism to explore human behavior. Balzac lived extravagantly in Parisian society, constantly in debt and in love, and married his last mistress, Eveline Hanska, during his fatal illness in 1850.

Bamako 12 40N 7 59W The capital of Mali, a port in the S on the Niger River. A center of Muslim learning under the medieval Mali Empire, it had dwindled to a small village by the end of the 19th century, when it was occupied by the French. It became the capital of the French Sudan in 1905. Population (1987): 646,163.

Bamberg 49 54N 10 54E A city in SE Germany, in Bavaria on the Regnitz River. The romanesque cathedral was founded in 1004 and its bishops were princes of the Holy Roman Empire until 1803. Its varied industries include engineering and textiles. Population (1985): 70,400.

bamboo A treelike plant of the tribe *Bambuseae*, native to tropical and subtropical regions, particularly SE Asia. From an underground stem (rhizome) arise hollow woody jointed stems, which may reach a height of 130 ft (40 m) in some species. These are used for building and a variety of other purposes, while the young shoots are eaten as a vegetable. Some bamboos are cultivated in temperate gardens for their graceful foliage. Family: *Gramineae* (grasses).

Bana (7th century AD) Sanskrit writer. He traveled widely in India before becoming court poet of the Buddhist emperor *Harsa. The *Harsacarita* is a prose chronicle written to celebrate his patron's accession to the throne. The prose romance *Kadambari* exploits sophisticated narrative techniques to describe a complex love intrigue.

Banaba. *See* Ocean Island.

banana A palmlike plant of the Old World tropical genus *Musa*, especially *M. paradisiaca sapientum*, cultivated throughout the tropics from prehistoric times for its edible fruit. The "trunk," up to 30 ft (9 m) high, is composed of the overlapping bases of the leaves, which are often 10 ft (3 m) or more long. The tip of the flowering stem bears male flowers and hangs down; clusters of female flowers, further up the stem, develop into seedless fruits, up to 12 in (30 cm) long, without being fertilized. (All cultivated bananas are sterile hybrids: the plants are propagated from suckers arising from the underground rhizome.) Most bananas are eaten fresh, but varieties called plantains are cooked and eaten when still green, forming a staple food in East and West Africa and the Caribbean. Family: *Musaceae*.

Bancroft, George (1800–91) US historian, diplomat, and educator. Originally a teacher and city official in Boston, he was appointed secretary of the navy (1845) under Pres. James Polk. During this time, Bancroft was responsible for the founding of the Naval Academy at Annapolis, Md. Although he served as minister to England (1846–49) and to Prussia and the German empire (1867–74), he is best known for his *History of the United States*, a 10-volume work (1834–74) that earned him the title "Father of American History." Other works include *History of the Formation of the Constitution of the United States of America* (1882).

Banda, Hastings Kamuzu (1905–　) Malawi statesman; president (1964–　). A physician, he worked in the UK and the US before returning home (then Nyasaland) in 1958 to lead the fight against federation with Rhodesia and for independence. On independence (1964) he became president and in 1971, life president.

Bandar Abbas 27 12N 56 15E A town in S Iran, on the Strait of Hormuz. It is a naval base important to the security of the Persian Gulf.

Bandaranaike, S(olomon) W(est) R(idgeway) D(ias) (1899–1959) Sri Lankan statesman; prime minister (1956–59). In 1951 he founded the Sri Lanka Freedom Party (SLFP) and became prime minister as head of an alliance of socialist and nationalist parties—the People's United Front, which pursued a neutral foreign policy and nationalist domestic policies (including the substitution of English with Sinhalese as the official language). He was assassinated by a Buddhist monk and was succeeded as head of the SLFP by his wife **Sirimavo Ratwatte Dias Bandaranaike** (1916–　), the world's first woman prime minister (1960–65, 1970–77). Her socialist coalition with the Marxist party was defeated in 1965 but returned to power in 1970.

Bandar-e Bushehr. *See* Bushire.

Bandar Seri Begawan (former name: Brunei Town) 4 56N 114 58E The capital of Brunei, a port in the NE near the mouth of the Brunei River. Population (1991): 21,500.

Bandeira, Manuel Carneiró de Sousa (1886–1968) Brazilian poet. He was forced by tuberculosis to give up his architectural studies in São Paulo. After meeting the French poet Paul *Eluard while in a Swiss sanatorium, he decided to try a literary career. The originality of his first book, *A cinza das horas*

(1917), was immediately recognized; his modernist style developed more fully in *Libertinagem* (1930) and *Estrêla da Manhã* (1936). He was also an influential critic, translator, and university professor.

bandicoot A ratlike *marsupial mammal of a family (*Peramelidae*; 20 species) occurring in Australia (including Tasmania) and New Guinea. About the size of rabbits, bandicoots are mainly carnivorous, eating insects, worms, and grubs. They are shy creatures and build nests of grass and leaves among thick vegetation.

BANDICOOT *A short-nosed bandicoot (genus* Thylacis *or* Isoodon*), which is 14–16 in (35–40 cm) long (excluding the tail). As in other bandicoots, the pouch opens towards the rear.*

Bandjermasin. *See* Banjarmasin.

Bandung 6 57S 107 34E A city in Indonesia, in W Java. A cultural and industrial center and tourist resort, it was formerly the administrative center of the Netherlands East Indies. Its chief industries are chemicals, quinine, plastics, metal processing, and textiles. It has two universities, established in 1957 and 1959, and a nuclear research center (1964). At the **Bandung Conference** of 1955 representatives of 29 African and Asian countries met to oppose colonialism. Population (1980): 1,462,637.

Banff 57 40N 2 31W A town in NE Scotland, in Grampian Region on the Moray Firth, at the mouth of the River Deveron. It is a resort with fishing and distilling industries, and was the county town of the former county of Banff, covering 630 sq mi (1632 sq km) from the Moray Firth to the Cairngorm Mountains.

Bangalore 12 58N 77 35E A city in S India, the capital of Karnataka. Founded in the 16th century, it fell to the British in 1791. The Institute of Science was established in 1909 and Bangalore University in 1964. An expanding industrial center, Bangalore's many modern industries include aircraft assembly, machine tools, and electronics. Population (1990): 2,650,650.

Bangka (*or* Banka) An Indonesian island in the Java Sea, off SE Sumatra. Its government-owned tin mines are among the world's most productive; other mineral deposits include gold, manganese, and iron. The population is largely Chinese. Area: 4600 sq mi (11,914 sq km). Chief town: Pangkalpinang.

Bangkok (Thai name: Krung Threp) 13 44N 100 30E The capital and main port of Thailand, in the SW near the mouth of the Chao Phraya River. It became a royal city and the capital in 1782. Distinctive features of the city are its canal system and the many Buddhist temples. There has been considerable expansion since World War II. Most of the country's industry and commerce is centered on Bangkok and it has eight universities. Population (1987): 5,609,000.

Bangladesh, People's Republic of A country in the Indian subcontinent, lying between the Himalayas and the Bay of Bengal, in the delta of the Ganges and Brahmaputra Rivers. Bangladesh is the most densely populated country, and one of the poorest regions, in the world, beset continually by famine and floods. The land, which is generally low lying, is on the whole fertile but it has to support a very large population, most of whom are Bengalis. *Economy*: about three-quarters of the inhabitants are occupied in agriculture, rice being by far the most important food crop. Bangladesh produces 50% of the world's raw jute, its main export. Fishing, both freshwater and saltwater, is important not only as a valuable food source, but also for oil and other fish products. Traditional industries include jute milling and textile manufacture but plans for further industrial development are hindered by the comparative lack of mineral resources. Most industry is now nationalized. Communications are greatly aided by the many natural shipping channels that the country's rivers provide. *History*: the area formed part of the kingdom of Bengal, and its conquest by the Afghans in the 12th century led to the growth of the Islamic religion. It was part of British India from 1857 until 1947 when it became independent as a province of Pakistan (East Pakistan). In 1974 floods and famine led to political unrest and terrorism and in 1975 Mujib assumed absolute power on a one-party basis but shortly afterward he and his family were assassinated in a military coup. After several more coups and countercoups, Gen. *Ziaur Rahman assumed power in 1976 and was elected president in 1978 in the first presidential election on a basis of adult suffrage. In 1977 amendments to the constitution established Bangladesh as an Islamic state. General Ziaur was assassinated in an unsuccessful insurrection in 1981. His successor, Abdus Sattar (1906–85), was ousted in a military coup (1982) and replaced by Justice Choudhury. Choudhury, however, was a figurehead president backed by the military regime under Gen. Hossain Mohannad Ershad, who assumed the presidency in 1983. Ershad lifted martial law in 1986, but opposition to his regime grew, and he was ousted in 1990. In 1991 elections, Khaleda Zia, the widow of General Ziaur, became the prime minister. A devastating cyclone in 1991 and Muslim refugees from Myanmar further strained the economy in 1992. Bangladesh became a member of the Commonwealth of Nations in 1972. Official language: Bengali. Official religion: Islam. Official currency: taka of 100 paisa. Area: 142,797 sq km (55,126 sq mi). Population (1990 est): 117,980,000. Capital: Dacca. Main port: Chittagong.

Bangui 4 23N 19 20E The capital of the Central African Republic, a port in the SW on the Ubangi River. Founded in 1889, the port handles goods for both the Central African Republic and Chad; its main exports are cotton and coffee. Its university was established in 1969. Population (1988): 597,000.

Bangweulu, Lake 11 15S 29 45E A lake in E Zambia. Discovered by David *Livingstone (1868), it is shallow and bordered by swamps. During the rainy season its waters cover an area of up to 3783 sq mi (9800 sq km).

Banjarmasin (*or* Bandjermasin) 3 22S 114 33E A port in Indonesia, in S Kalimantan on the Barito delta. Its exports include rubber and timber. Its university was established in 1960. Population (1980): 381,286.

banjo A plucked string instrument of US origin, originally played by plantation slaves. The banjo became popular in minstrel shows, vaudeville, jazz, and folk music. The body of the banjo is a round metal hoop covered with parchment on one side; the fretted fingerboard has four to nine strings, which are plucked with the fingers or with a plectrum.

Banjul (name until 1973: Bathurst) 13 20N 16 38W The capital of The Gambia, a port in the W at the mouth of the Gambia River, founded by the British in 1816. Population (1986 est): 44,200.

Banka. *See* Bangka.

Bank for International Settlements (BIS) A bank in Basle, Switzerland, which acts as a bank for *central banks (mostly European and American) and is governed by representatives of several of them. It was set up in 1930 to coordinate reparations after World War I. Although most of its functions are now performed by the *International Monetary Fund, it has important duties as a trustee.

Bankhead, Tallulah (1903–68) US actress. She won critical acclaim as a stage actress in such plays as Lillian Hellman's *Little Foxes* (1939) and Thornton Wilder's *The Skin of Our Teeth* (1942), but her popularity as a film star owed more to her extravagant lifestyle than to the quality of her performances.

Bankhead, William Brockman (1874–1940) US politician, speaker of the House of Representatives (1936–40). From a family of legislators, he became a lawyer and then was elected to the Congress as a representative from Alabama in 1916. He served the House of Representatives in various capacities until his election as speaker, an office he held until his death. He was the father of actress Tallulah Bankhead.

Bank of the United States Two successive financial institutions established to regulate the economic transactions of the federal government. The First Bank of the US was founded by Secretary of the Treasury Alexander *Hamilton in Philadelphia in 1791. Opposition by state banks led to its dissolution in 1811. After the War of 1812, the finances of the federal government needed reorganization, and the Second Bank of the US was created by Congress in 1816. By the terms of its twenty-year charter, it held all federal assets and was empowered to establish branches in all states. The constitutionality of its activities was upheld by the Supreme Court in the case of *McCulloch* v. *Maryland* in 1819. Pres. Andrew *Jackson opposed the power of the Bank of the US and withdrew all federal deposits in 1833. Jackson later vetoed a plan to recharter the Bank and it ended operations in 1836. *See also* Federal Reserve System.

bank rate. *See* minimum lending rate.

bankruptcy proceedings The legal process by which the property of a person who cannot pay his debts is distributed among his creditors. Bankruptcy is either voluntary or involuntary. A **voluntary** proceeding is initiated by the debtor's own petition to be adjudged a bankrupt and have the benefit of the law. In **involuntary** bankruptcy, the debtor is forced into bankruptcy on the petition of a sufficient number of his creditors.

banks. *See* Bank for International Settlements; Bank of England; Bank of the United States; central bank; commercial bank; International Bank for Reconstruction and Development; merchant bank.

Banks, Sir Joseph (1743–1820) British botanist and explorer. During his most famous expedition, around the world with James *Cook (1768–71), he showed that the marsupial mammals of Australia were more primitive than the placental mammals of other continents and he also discovered many new species of plants. Banks promoted the introduction of economic plants from their native regions to other countries and he was known as a patron of young scientists. He was president of Britain's Royal Society from 1778 until his death.

Banksia A genus of shrubs and trees (about 50 species) all native to dry areas of Australia; some are known as Australian honeysuckles. The flowers are borne in dense spikes and give rise to hard winged seeds. Family: *Proteaceae*.

Banks Island The westernmost island of Canada's Arctic Archipelago, in Franklin district. Mostly hilly plateau, it supports numerous Arctic animals. Area: 23,230 sq mi (60,166 sq km).

Banneker, Benjamin (1731–1806) US surveyor and scientist. The son of a slave, he was for the most part self-educated. He became the first African American ever appointed to an official position by a president when George Washington asked him to assist in surveying the Territory of Columbia, the site for a new national capital. He was also known for his almanacs, the first of which was published in 1792.

Banner System A system of military organization adopted by the Manchu tribes and used by the *Qing dynasty to rule China. It was initiated in 1601 by *Nurhachi, who enrolled his warriors under yellow, white, blue, or red banners. Later four bordered banners were added and all tribesmen were enrolled. Each banner formed an administrative unit, which contributed a quota of men when it became necessary to raise an army and also facilitated taxation. In return bannermen were allocated land. After the Manchu conquest of China and the establishment of the Qing, eight Chinese and eight Mongol banners were added.

Bannister, Sir Roger (Gilbert) (1929–) British doctor and middle-distance runner, who on May 6, 1954, was the first man to run a mile in under 4 minutes (3 minutes 59.4 seconds). In 1975 he was knighted.

Bannockburn 56 06N 3 55W A village in Scotland, near Stirling on the Bannock Burn (a tributary of the River Forth). 1 mi (1.5 km) NW is Scotland's most famous battlefield, where in 1314 the Scots defeated the English, who had come to relieve the besieged Stirling Castle.

banshee (Irish *bean-sidhe*: woman of the fairies) In Irish folklore, a female specter whose weeping announced the imminent death of a person.

bantam One of many breeds of dwarf fowl, possibly named for the district of Bantam in Indonesia, from where they were formerly exported to the West. Bantams generally weigh about 1 lb (450 g).

Banten A region in W Java (Indonesia), which was the center of a Muslim sultanate until 1683 when it became part of the Dutch East Indies. The town of Banten was a flourishing port for the European spice trade from the 16th to the 18th centuries, after which the harbor silted up.

banteng A wild ox, *Bos banteng*, of forests in SE Asia. About 60 in (150 cm) high at the shoulder, bantengs are brown with white socks and a white rump patch and have relatively small horns. They feed on young grass and bamboo shoots.

Banting, Sir Frederick Grant (1891–1941) Canadian physiologist, who, with C. H. *Best, discovered a technique for the successful isolation of the hormone *insulin from pancreatic tissue in 1921. This enabled the successful treatment of patients suffering from *diabetes (caused by lack of insulin). Banting was awarded a Nobel Prize (1923) with J. J. R. *Macleod but he divided his share with Best in recognition of his colleague's achievement.

Bantu A large subgroup of African languages of the *Niger-Congo group spoken over the whole of the S half of Africa by about 60 million people. It includes Zulu, Xhosa, and Kongo; perhaps the most widely known representative is

*Swahili, the language of Tanzania and lingua franca of E Africa. The Bantu languages are tonal, with the exception of Swahili, and make extensive use of suffixes and prefixes. Many use a number of click sounds. The Bantu people are very diverse in culture and social organization and include herdsmen, farmers, hunter-gatherers, and fishers. They probably migrated southward from an area near the Cameroon-Nigeria border, displacing small pygmy and Bushmen tribes, approximately 2000 years ago.

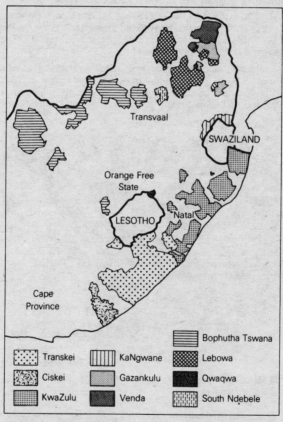

BANTU HOMELANDS *The areas designated as black African territories in South Africa are dispersed over the E and N parts of the country.*

Bantu Homelands (*or* Bantustans) The areas of South Africa designated for the black populations, comprising just over 13% of the land area. Acts of parliament in 1913 and 1936 controlled the extent of African lands and prohibited blacks from holding land in white areas. The Bantu Authorities Act (1951) gave limited administrative and legislative powers to the Bantu authorities, and the Bantu Self-Government Act (1959) divided the black populations into national units, most of them with homelands in several separate areas. Limited self-government was to be granted to these areas; the *Transkei was the first to receive this (1963). The Bantu Homelands Constitution Act (1971) aimed at similar self-government for other areas. Full independence has been granted to Transkei (1976), *Bophutha Tswana (1977), Gazankulu, KaNgwane, *Venda (1979), and Ciskei (1981). Other Bantu Homelands include KwaZulu, Lebowa, and Qwaqwa. The Bantustan policy has been constantly opposed by African leaders (in particular Chief Gatsha Buthelezi of KwaZulu), and many of the territories have resisted moves toward self-government and independence, regarding it as a poor substitute for majority rule in South Africa as a whole.

Banville, Théodore Faullain de (1823–89) French poet. He wrote a technical treatise on French poetry and revived old forms, such as the *ballade and the *rondeau. His best-known collection is *Odes funambulesques* (1857). He helped many young writers, including *Rimbaud.

banyan A tropical Asian tree, *Ficus benghalensis*, related to the fig and reaching a height of 98 ft (30 m). Individual trees commonly grow into impenetrable thickets as the branches produce supporting aerial roots, which grow down to penetrate the soil and subsequently give rise to thorny branches of their own. Family: *Moraceae*.

BANYAN *In India it is regarded as a sacred tree and is carefully tended.*

baobab A tropical African tree, *Adansonia digitata*, with a tapering conical trunk (the base of which may exceed 33 ft [10 m] in diameter) reaching a height of 59 ft (18 m) and bearing branches at its apex. The drab bat-pollinated flowers give rise to fruits that contain a succulent edible pulp surrounded by a tough woody capsule. The bark yields a fiber of local importance, and the trees are grown as ornamentals in some subtropical areas. Family: *Bombacaceae*.

Baotou (*or* Pao-t'ou) 40 38N 109 59E A city in N China, in the Inner Mongolia AR on the Yellow River. It is a major industrial center, with a nuclear power station. Industries include iron and steel, aluminum, sugar, and textiles. Population (1990): 983,508.

baptism A ceremony of initiation, occurring in many religions, involving the use of water as a symbol of purification from sin. In the Christian Church, where it is a *sacrament and is done in the name of the Father, the Son, and the Holy Spirit, it involves the candidate's total or partial immersion in water or the mere wetting of his head. Both the *Baptists and the modern descendants of the *Anabaptists practice adult baptism, but most other Churches prefer infant baptism.

Baptists Protestant Christians who baptize, by immersion, only those old enough consciously to accept the Christian faith. Each Baptist Church is autonomous. The sect was an outgrowth of the Anabaptists of the Reformation period who fled England for Holland. In Britain there were two main types, "General Baptist" Churches, owing their origin in 1612 to John Smyth (c. 1554–1612) and Thomas Helwys (c. 1550–c. 1616), and "Particular Baptist" Churches, founded in 1633 by Calvinists who believed that salvation was only for a particular few. The latter had modified its doctrines by 1891, when both movements merged into the Baptist Union. The first Baptist Church in America was established in Providence, R.I., by Roger Williams in 1639. The majority of Baptists, of whom there are over 30 million worldwide, live in the US and most of them are associated with the Baptist World Alliance.

Baqqarah A cattle-herding Arab people of Chad and the Sudan. As a result of contact and intermixtures with other local peoples they have dark skins and speak a distinct dialect of Arabic. They migrate seasonally between northern wet-season grazing lands and southern dry-season river areas.

bar A unit of pressure equal to 10^5 pascals (0.987 atmosphere). The commonly used unit is the millibar (one-thousandth of a bar).

Baranof Island A US island, off the coast of SE Alaska in the Alexander Archipelago. Area: 1607 sq mi (4162 sq km). Chief town: Sitka.

Barbados, State of An island state in the West Indies, E of the Windward Islands. It is generally low lying except for a district in the NE and is subject to hurricanes. Most of the population is of African descent. *Economy*: high-density agriculture, with sugar cane as the main crop, and tourism are important. The policy of encouraging some small industries has been helped by the discovery of offshore oil and natural gas. Main exports include sugar and sugar products (including rum), petroleum and petroleum products, clothing, and electrical goods. *History*: occupied by the British in 1627, it remained a British colony until 1966, when it became a fully independent state within the Commonwealth of Nations. Prime Minister: Erskine Sandiford. Official language: English. Official currency: Barbados dollar of 100 cents. Area: 166 sq mi (430 sq km). Population (1990): 257,083.

Barbarossa (Khayr ad-Din; d. 1546) Turkish pirate. Barbarossa (Italian: Redbeard) entered the service of the Ottoman Sultan of Turkey to protect his possessions on the Barbary coast of N Africa against Spanish and Portuguese attack. He captured Algiers in 1529 and Tunisia in 1534 and his defeat of Emperor Charles V's fleet in 1538 gave the Turks control of the E Mediterranean.

Barbary A region in N Africa stretching from Egypt to the Atlantic Ocean and from the Mediterranean Sea to the Sahara. It is named for its oldest inhabitants, the *Berbers. In antiquity it consisted of Mauritania, Numidia, Africa, Propria, and Cyrenaica. It was successively conquered by the Romans, Vandals, Arabs, Turks, Spaniards (parts of Morocco), French (Algeria, Tunisia, and Morocco), and Italians (Tripoli). Between the 16th and 18th centuries, Barbary was notorious for its pirates, who caused havoc in the Mediterranean.

Barbary ape A large monkey, *Macaca sylvana*, also called magot, the only *macaque found in N Africa. Barbary apes are tailless and roam in bands over the forest floor, feeding on seeds, leaves, insects, and small animals.

barbastelle A large-eared insect-eating bat, *Barbastella barbastella*, of Europe, S Asia, and NE Africa. About 2 in (5 cm) long, slender, and long-legged, barbastelles fly early in the evening. Family: *Vespertilionidae*.

barbel A long slender freshwater fish, belonging to the genus *Barbus*, that is related to *carp and occurs in clear fresh waters of Asia, Africa, and Europe. It has four fleshy threadlike appendages (barbels) near its mouth, which detect prey, mainly invertebrates, while exploring the river bed. *B. barbus* of Europe is usually 12–20 in (30–50 cm) long.

Barber, Samuel (1910–81) US composer. Two of his works, the opera *Vanessa* (1958) and the piano concerto (1963), won Pulitzer Prizes. His style, although basically lyrical, became increasingly dissonant in his later works. His output includes chamber music, choral works, symphonies, and concertos. His best-known work is the *Adagio for Strings*, an arrangement of the slow movement of his string quartet (1936).

barberry. *See* Berberis.

barbet A small brightly colored forest bird belonging to a tropical family (*Capitonidae*; 76 species) most commonly found in Africa; 3–12 in (8–30 cm) long, barbets have large heavy bills with bristles around the chin and beak and a monotonously repeated call. They feed mainly on fruit but also take insects, lizards, and birds' eggs. Order: *Piciformes* (woodpeckers, etc.).

Barbirolli, Sir John (1899–1970) British conductor of Franco-Italian parents. Originally a cellist, he organized his own string orchestra, and subsequently became conductor of several major opera companies and orchestras.

barbiturates A class of drugs that act by depressing the activity of the brain. Short-acting barbiturates, such as thiopental, are used for inducing *anesthesia. Medium-acting barbiturates, such as pentobarbital, are used as sleeping tablets. Small doses of long-acting barbiturates, such as phenobarbital, are used for daytime sedation and to control epilepsy. As barbiturates are habit-forming and may cause true addiction, with serious effects on the mind and body, their use is now severely limited. They have been shown to be associated with the increased incidence of falls and fractures in elderly patients. Overdosage is a medical emergency and can cause death by inhibiting the breathing center in the brain.

Barbizon school A group of French landscape painters who worked in the village of Barbizon, near the Forest of Fontainebleau, in the 1840s. Truth to nature combined with romantic settings typify the works of the school's founder Theodore *Rousseau, *Daubigny, Narcisse-Virgile Diaz de la Pena (c. 1807–76), and others. Dark trees and ponds betray their debt to Dutch landscape painting but their constant practice of open-air oil sketching to capture light effects inspired the impressionists to paint finished works outside. Fringe members of the school included *Corot and *Millet.

Barbor, John (1316–95) Scottish poet. He became archdeacon of Aberdeen in 1357, studied at Oxford and Paris, and received a royal pension in 1388. In *The Bruce*, a Scottish national epic, he celebrated Scotland's fight for independence under *Robert (I) the Bruce and James Douglas.

Barbusse, Henri (1873–1935) French novelist. His novel *Under Fire* (1916), based on his experiences in World War I, expresses the disillusion that led him first to pacifism and later to communism. *Clarté* (1919) lent its name to a short-lived international movement. Barbusse died in the Soviet Union.

barcarolle A piece of music in imitation of the songs of Venetian gondoliers. It is usually in $\frac{6}{8}$ or $\frac{12}{8}$ time and has a gentle rocking movement. Examples include Offenbach's *Barcarolle* from *The Tales of Hoffman* and Chopin's *Barcarolle* for the piano.

Barcelona 41 25N 2 10E A city in NE Spain, in Catalonia on the Mediterranean Sea. It is Spain's second largest city, its largest port and leading commercial and industrial center. Manufactures include locomotives, aircraft, textiles, and electrical equipment. The country's cultural center and the focus of Catalan art and literature, it has many educational establishments, libraries, and museums; the University of Barcelona was founded in 1430. The city's numerous fine buildings include the palace of the Aragón kings, a cathedral (14th–15th centuries), and a 14th-century monastery. It has several Art Nouveau buildings designed by Antonio Gaudí, notably the Sagrada Familia church (1903–26). *History*: founded by the Carthaginians, it was taken by the Moors in 713 AD and by Charlemagne in 801 AD. In 1137 Catalonia and Aragón united and Barcelona became the capital, rivaling Genoa and Venice as a leading European port. During the 19th century it became important industrially through its cotton industry. The center of the Catalan separatist government, it was the seat of the Catalan autonomous government and later of the Republican government, during the Spanish Civil War (1936–39). In 1939 Barcelona fell to Gen. Franco and the Republican government finally surrendered. In 1992 the city was the site of the summer Olympics. Population (1986): 1,694,000.

Barclay de Tolly, Mikhail Bogdanovich, Prince (1761–1818) Russian field marshal. In 1810, after brilliant campaigns against Napoleon, he became minister of war. Promoted to field marshal (1814), he commanded the army that invaded France in 1815.

Barcoo River. *See* Cooper Creek.

bard In ancient Celtic societies, a poet whose duty was to eulogize heroes and to celebrate notable events, such as victories, and the laws and traditions of the community. Bards constituted a distinct social class with hereditary rights and privileges. The class was at one time subdivided according to functions. In 10th-century Wales the three bardic ranks were *pencerdd* (chief of song), *bardd teulu* (household bard), and *cerddor* (minstrel); an earlier Irish classification was *druid, filid*, and *baird*. Bards ceased to exist in Gaul at an early date, but they survived in Scotland and Ireland to the 18th century and, in a somewhat artificial and diminished role, continue to exist in Wales to the present. Today the term is used to describe any type of poet. *See also* eisteddfod; Welsh literature.

Bardeen, John (1908–91) US physicist, who became professor at the University of Illinois in 1951. He shared the 1956 Nobel Prize for his part in the invention of the transistor (with W. B. *Shockley and W. H. *Brattain) while working at the Bell Telephone Laboratories in 1948. He also shared the 1972 Nobel Prize for his work on the theory of superconductivity (with L. N. Cooper and J. R. Schrieffer). This theory is known as the BCS theory after the initials of its authors.

Bardot, Brigitte (1934–) French film actress. Her films include *And God Created Women* (1956), *Vie privée* (1961), *Viva Maria* (1965), and *Shalako* (1968). She became probably the best-known sex symbol of the 1960s.

Barebones Parliament The assembly, also known as the Parliament of Saints, called by Oliver *Cromwell in July 1653. It consisted mainly of merchants and lesser gentry, nominated by the congregations. In December, the moderates among them resigned their power to Cromwell.

Bareilly 28 20N 79 24E A city in India, in Uttar Pradesh. Founded in 1537, it was a center of the Indian Mutiny. The Indian Veterinary Research Institute was established nearby in 1889. Manufactures include sugar, rope, and furniture. Population (1991): 583,473.

DANIEL BARENBOIM *Conducting the Orchestre de Paris.*

Barenboim, Daniel (1942–   ) Israeli pianist and conductor, who studied in Salzburg, Paris, and Rome. He made his debut in London in 1955. In 1967 he married the cellist Jacqueline *du Pré, with whom he gave recitals. Increasingly active as a conductor in the 1970s, Barenboim conducted the Orchestre de Paris from 1975 until his appointment as musical and artistic director of the Opéra Bastille in Paris (1987–89). He became musical director of the Chicago Symphony Orchestra in 1991.

Barents, Willem (c. 1550–97) Dutch navigator. He led three expeditions (1594, 1595, 1596) to discover a *Northeast Passage, reaching the Novaya Zemlya islands and discovering Spitsbergen (1596). On his last voyage he was forced to winter at Icehaven, where his camp was found in 1871. He died at sea on his return journey. The Barents Sea is named for him.

Barents Sea A section of the Arctic Ocean between Eurasia and Svalbard, Franz Josef Land, and Novaya Zemlya. It covers part of the Eurasian continental shelf, which before the Pleistocene Ice Age was land. It is rich in fish.

Barère, Bertrand (1755–1841) French revolutionary. Initially a moderate in the National Convention, he subsequently became a member of the Committee of *Public Safety during the *Reign of Terror. Imprisoned after the fall of Robespierre (July, 1794), he escaped into exile, returning to France in 1830.

Bar Harbor 44 23N 68 13W A resort town in SE Maine. It is located on Mount Desert Island and is known for its palatial summer homes. Population (1990): 4443.

Bar Hebraeus (1226–86) Syrian bishop and scholar. Bar Hebraeus studied medicine at Antioch and Tripoli. He was consecrated bishop in 1246 and became Primate of the East in 1264. His writings, in Syriac and Arabic, include the *Granary of Mysteries* and the *Chronicle*.

Bari 41 07N 16 52E A seaport in Italy, the capital of Apulia on the Adriatic Sea. It has a cathedral (12th–15th centuries) and a university (1924). Industries include chemicals, textiles, and oil refining. Population (1988 est): 358,900.

barite (*or* barytes) A barium ore consisting of barium sulfate, sometimes called heavy spar. It is colorless when pure, but often white, yellow, or brown, due to impurities. It is used in the manufacture of paint and heavy paper, as a mineral filler in rubber and linoleum manufacture, and in concrete and glass-making. The chief producers are the US, Germany, and Ireland.

baritone A deep adult male singing voice, lower than tenor and higher than bass. Range: G at the bottom of the base stave to G two octaves above.

barium (Ba) A silvery reactive metal that resembles calcium in its behavior. It was discovered in 1808 by Sir Humphry Davy and occurs naturally as barytes ($BaSO_4$) and witherite ($BaCO_3$). The sulfate is used as a white pigment in paint and, because of its opacity to X-rays, is used in X-ray diagnosis. All soluble barium compounds are toxic, the carbonate being used as rat poison. At no 56; at wt 137.34; mp 1338°F (725°C).

bark The dead outer layer of the stems and roots of woody plants, which protects the inner tissues from desiccation, extremes of temperature, pests and diseases, and physical damage. Antiseptic deposits, such as tannins, give the color. Bark may include layers of insulating *cork, which is responsible for the characteristic ridges and patterns on some tree trunks. Small breathing pores (called lenticels) in the bark are conspicuous in many of the smooth-barked trees (such as *Prunus* species) but are hidden in the cracks of rough-barked species. The bark of some trees is of commercial importance, being a source of cinnamon, quinine, and various other products.

bark A sailing vessel with three or more masts. Square sails are set on all masts except the aftermast, which carries fore-and-aft sails. In a **barkentine** only the foremast has square-rigged sails.

bark beetle A hard cylindrical beetle, also called an engraver beetle, belonging to a family (*Scolytidae*; 7000 species) of wood borers. It is usually less than 6 mm long, colored red-brown or black, and causes considerable damage to trees. It burrows underneath the bark to lay eggs that develop into burrowing larvae: the elaborate patterns of tunnels produced are generally characteristic of the species. Certain species also transmit diseases (*see* elm bark beetle) and can be serious economic pests.

Barker, Harley Granville. *See* Granville-Barker, Harley.

Barkhausen, Heinrich (1881–1956) German physicist, who became professor of electrical engineering at the University of Dresden. He discovered (1919) the effect in which ferromagnetic materials placed in an increasing magnetic field become magnetized in small jumps (Barkhausen effect).

barking deer. *See* muntjac.

Barkley, Alben William (1877–1956) US politician, vice president (1949–53). Born and educated in Kentucky, he went to law schools in Georgia and Virginia. A Democrat, he served in the House of Representatives from 1912 until being elected to the Senate in 1927. While a senator he was minority and then majority leader and was a chief supporter of President Roosevelt's New Deal and President Truman's Fair Deal. As vice president, under Truman, he had a more active role than previous vice presidents.

Barkly Tableland An area of Australia, extending SE of the Gulf of Carpentaria, in Northern Territory, into Queensland. It consists of undulating uplands on which beef cattle are raised. Area: about 50,000 sq mi (130,000 sq km).

Bar Kokhba (Simeon bar Kosiba; d. 135 AD) Jewish freedom fighter. In 132 he launched a revolt against Roman rule and attempted to set up an independent Jewish state. He was hailed as Messiah by *Akiba, but did not enjoy widespread support and was killed when his last stronghold, Betar, fell. Some of his correspondence has been recovered from caves in the Judean desert.

Barlach, Ernst (1870–1938) German expressionist sculptor and playwright. First influenced by *Jugendstil*, he only found his mature style after visiting Russia (1906). His bulky figures, usually in wood, with their expressive faces and angular and rigid outlines were inspired both by his studies of Russian peasants and by *gothic sculpture. The Nazis destroyed much of his work.

Bar-le-Duc 48 46N 5 10E A city in NE France, the capital of the Meuse department on the Ornain River. Its manufactures include metal goods, textiles, and jams. Population: 20,516.

Barletta 41 20N 16 17E A seaport in Italy, in Apulia on the Adriatic coast. It possesses a romanesque cathedral and a castle. An agricultural center, it has an important wine trade; chemicals and cement are also manufactured. Population: 75,728.

barley A *cereal grass of the genus *Hordeum*, especially *H. vulgare*, which produces its grain in four rows and can be grown as far north as N Norway; *H. distichon* (two-rowed barley); and *H. hexadistichon* (six-rowed barley). Over 165 million tons of grain are harvested annually in temperate, subtropical, and subarctic regions from the various strains of barley. It is malted and used in the brewing industry, made into food for cattle and pigs, milled to produce pearl and pot barley (used in soups and stews), and used in breadmaking.

Bar Mitzvah (Hebrew: son of the commandment) The ceremony marking the initiation of a Jewish boy into the adult community at the age of 13. At this age he assumes his full religious responsibilities and it is customary for him to read publicly from the *Torah in the synagogue for the first time. In some communities a parallel ceremony (Bat Mitzvah) exists for girls.

Barnabas, St In the New Testament (Acts), a Christian Apostle of the 1st century. After going with St Paul to evangelize Cyprus (his birthplace) and the European mainland, he clashed with him and they parted company. He is traditionally regarded as the founder of the Cypriot Church. Feast day: June 11.

barnacle A marine *crustacean belonging to the subclass *Cirripedia* (1000 species). Some members of the group are parasites, but the typical (nonparasitic) barnacles live attached—head downward—to rocks, ships' hulls, etc., and filter food particles from the water with long feathery appendages, which protrude from the calcareous shell. Goose barnacles (e.g. *Lepas anatifera*)—so called because they were believed in the middle ages to be an immature form of the barnacle goose—are attached by means of a stalk; others, including the acorn barnacle (*Balanus*), are unstalked. Barnacles are hermaphrodite; their larvae are free-swimming, but later settle and become fixed to a surface by means of a cement-like substance secreted by their antennae.

barnacle goose A European *goose, *Branta leukopsis*, which is a regular winter visitor to Britain. It has a distinctive cream face, dark crown and breast, and a white chevron on the tail and grazes on coastal meadows and salt marshes. They were once believed to hatch from barnacles!

Barnard, Christiaan Neethling (1922–   ) South African surgeon, who (in 1967 at the Groote Schuur Hospital in Cape Town) performed the world's first successful heart transplant operation. His patient, Louis Washkansky, received the heart of an accident victim but died 18 days later from pneumonia. In another patient (1974) he implanted a second heart, connecting the circulatory systems to perform as one.

Barnard, Edward Emerson (1857–1923) US astronomer, who became professor at the University of Chicago (1895). He discovered Jupiter's fifth satellite (1892), a total of 16 comets, and **Barnard's Star** (1916) in the constellation Ophiuchus, the star with the most rapid proper motion.

Barnaul 53 21N 83 45E A city in Russia on the Ob River. The center of an industrial and mining area, its industries include engineering, textiles, chemicals, and timber. Population (1987 est): 596,000.

Barnave, Antoine Pierre (1761–93) French revolutionary. A chief spokesman of the *Jacobins, he developed royalist sympathies in 1791 through personal contact with Louis XVI. Advocating a constitutional monarchy, he became leader of the *Feuillants and was executed.

Barnburners A nickname for the radical part of the New York Democratic Party from the early 1840s to the early 1850s. Opposed to the extension of slavery into the territories, they merged with the Free Soil Party, which supported presidential candidate Martin Van Buren. Their opponents, within the Democratic Party, were nicknamed Hunkers.

Barnegat Bay 39 52N 74 07W A bay on the E central coast of New Jersey, sheltered from the Atlantic Ocean by Long Beach Island and Island Beach. It is part of the inland-waterway for small craft. Length: 30 mi (49 km).

barn owl An *owl belonging to a family (*Tytonidae*; 9 species) with a worldwide distribution. Barn owls have heart-shaped faces, long feathered legs, and usually a reddish plumage with pale underparts. The common barn owl (*Tyto alba*), 12–18 in (30–45 cm) long, nests in old barns and belfries and hunts for small rodents.

Barnum, Phineas Taylor (1810–91) US showman. His presentation of such novel exhibits as human "freaks," including the dwarf Tom Thumb, and natural curiosities at the American Museum from 1842 attracted unprecedented crowds. In 1850 he organized the successful US tour of the Swedish singer Jenny Lind. His circus, which he called "The Greatest Show on Earth," established in 1871, merged with that of his rival, J. A. Bailey (1847–1906), to become the Barnum and Bailey Circus in 1881.

Baroda 22 19N 73 14E A city in India, in Gujarat. The siting of an oil refinery at nearby Kouali has helped to promote Baroda's industrial growth and its chief products include petrochemicals, cotton textiles, wood, and tobacco. Population (1971): 467,422.

Baroja, Pío (1872–1956) Spanish novelist. He abandoned a career as a doctor to manage a family bakery in Madrid. His first book of short stories, *Vida sombrías* (1900), was followed by nearly a hundred novels. His early heroes were rebels or reformers embodying his own desire to inspire political action, but the tone of later books—especially *Laura, o la soledad sin remedio* (1939)—was more skeptical and pessimistic.

barometer An instrument for measuring atmospheric pressure. There are two main types: the mercury barometer and the aneroid barometer. In the mercury barometer, atmospheric pressure forces mercury from a reservoir into a vertical evacuated glass tube marked with a scale. The height of the mercury column is directly proportional to the atmospheric pressure. In the aneroid barometer, variations in the atmospheric pressure on the lid of an evacuated metal box cause a pointer to move around a dial. The aneroid barometer is less sensitive than the mercury barometer but it is smaller, more portable, and more convenient to use.

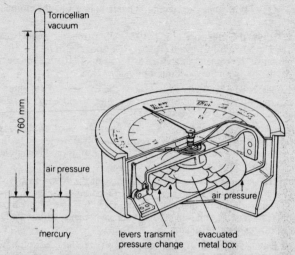

Torricellian vacuum

760 mm

air pressure

mercury

levers transmit pressure change

air pressure

evacuated metal box

BAROMETER *In the mercury barometer the height of the mercury column is directly proportional to the air pressure and is independent of the diameter of the tube. In the aneroid barometer movements of the lid of the evacuated metal box are transmitted to the pointer by the levers.*

Barons' War 1. (1215–17) The civil war between King John of England and his barons. John's failure to honor the *Magna Carta led the barons to offer the English crown to the future Louis VIII of France, who invaded England. John's death and the reissue of Magna Carta (1216) removed many baronial grievances but war continued until 1217 when peace was established and the Magna Carta again reissued. **2.** (1264–67) The civil war between Henry III of England and his barons led by Simon de *Montfort. War broke out following Henry's repudiation of the Provisions of Oxford, which gave the barons much power. Henry was captured at the battle of *Lewes (1264) and England was controlled by de Montfort until his death (1265). Hostilities continued until 1267.

baroque In architecture, a style dominant in European Roman Catholic countries during the 17th and early 18th centuries. The name probably derives from the Spanish *barrueco*, an irregularly shaped pearl. The baroque began in Italy as a reaction against *classicism. It was characterized by curved and broken lines, ornate decoration (which led to the *rococo), and elaborate spatial effects.

In art, the baroque was a style that developed from Italian *mannerism, complementing baroque architecture. Both art and architecture were used to popularize Catholic beliefs during the *Counter-Reformation. Baroque art was characterized by the vivid presentation of stories of saints, miracles, and the crucifixion. Leading exponents of the baroque were the sculptor and architect *Bernini, the architect *Borromini, and the painters *Caravaggio and *Rubens.

In music, the compositions of the 17th and early 18th centuries, from Monteverdi to Bach, are frequently called baroque music. A variety of styles and forms flourished during this period, the use of the term referring to the period rather than a particular style. This period saw the development of *opera, *oratorio, the concerto grosso (*see* Corelli, Arcangelo), and the trio sonata.

Barossa Valley. *See* South Australia.

Barotse. *See* Lozi.

Barotseland A former kingdom in central Africa, now comprising Western Province in Zambia. Inhabited by the *Lozi people, it was put under British protection through two treaties (1890, 1900) by the Lozi chief, Lewanika (d. 1916). The area attempted to break away as a separate kingdom on Zambian independence (1964).

Barquisimeto 10 03N 69 18W A city in NW Venezuela. It is the commercial center of a coffee-growing area and has a university (1963). Population (1990 est): 603,000.

barracuda A shoaling fish of the family *Sphyraenidae* (about 20 species), found in all tropical seas and caught for food and sport. Its body is up to 6 ft (1.8 m) long and bears two dorsal fins. Barracudas feed voraciously on other fish and the larger species are considered dangerous to man. Order: *Perciformes*.

Barranquilla 11 00N 74 50W An important port in NW Colombia, on the Río Magdalena near its mouth on the Caribbean Sea. Its manufactures include textiles, vegetable oils, and chemicals. It has two universities (1941, 1967). Population (1985): 896,649.

Barras, Paul François Jean Nicolas, Vicomte de (1755–1829) French revolutionary. Although he joined the National Convention as a Jacobin, Barras turned against Robespierre and helped to secure his downfall in 1794. As commander of Paris, Barras suppressed a royalist uprising in 1795 by allowing Napoleon Bonaparte to turn his guns on the agitators. A member of the Directory from 1795 to 1799, Barras resigned during Napoleon's coup d'état (1799).

Barrault, Jean-Louis (1910–94) French actor and director. He has directed influential productions of both classical and avant-garde plays and he was director of the Théâtre de France from 1959 to 1968. He is also renowned for his mime, especially in the film *Les Enfants du paradis* (1944).

barrel organ **1.** A musical instrument popular in the 18th and 19th centuries, much used in churches. It consists of a simple organ mechanism operated by a wooden cylinder (or barrel) set with brass pins and turned by a handle, which also works a bellows. **2.** A musical instrument of the 19th century more properly called **barrel piano** and often confused with the barrel organ. A popular street instrument, its barrel and pin mechanism causes leather-covered hammers to strike strings.

Barren Grounds (*or* Lands) The largely uninhabited permafrost plain of N Canada, stretching from about 59°N to the Arctic Ocean and from Hudson Bay to the Mackenzie Valley. Caribou and other animals live on the short grasses and other flowering plants.

Barrès, Maurice (1862–1923) French writer and politician. In the trilogy *La Culte de moi* (1888–91) he described a searching period of self-analysis resulting in his entry into politics. His rigid nationalism was expounded in another trilogy, *Le Roman de l'énergie nationale* (1897–1902), and linked with Catholicism in *La Colline inspirée* (1913). His memoirs, *Mes cahiers* (14 vols, 1929–57), were published posthumously.

Barrie, Sir James (Matthew) (1860–1937) British dramatist and novelist. The son of a Scots weaver, he came to London as a freelance writer in 1885. After two successful novels about Scottish rural life he wrote mostly for the theater. His best-known plays are *The Admirable Crichton* (1902), *Peter Pan* (1904), which has also remained a popular children's book, and *Dear Brutus* (1917).

barrier reef. *See* reef.

Barrow 71 17N 156 47W A village in N Alaska, just SW of Point Barrow, which is the northernmost point in the United States. An Eskimo village, Barrow is mainly a whaling center and serves as a base for the US Navy's Arctic Research Laboratory nearby. Population (1990): 3469.

barrow A prehistoric burial mound, also called a tumulus or cairn. From about 2000 BC earth barrows, concealing stone or timber passages and burial chambers, were built all over Europe for the interment of warrior chiefs. Long (i.e. rectangular or trapezoidal) barrows, such as at West Kennet (S England), were used for Neolithic multiple burials. Round barrows were more usual in Bronze Age cultures. Barrows continued in use in Iron Age Europe, for example the *Hallstatt barrow cemetery at Hohmichele (Germany) on the Upper Danube (6th century BC), and as late as 7th century AD, for example the *Sutton Hoo ship burial.

Barrymore Family Stage and screen actors, descendents of well-known thespians John and Louisa Lane Drew. Their daughter **Georgianna** (1856–1893) wed fellow actor Herbert Blythe (1847–1905), who changed his name to **Maurice Barrymore**. Their three children also went on to prominent acting careers. **Lionel** (1878–1954) studied art in Paris. After achieving success on the stage, he became known as a screen actor in such films as *On Borrowed Time* (1939) and *It's a Wonderful Life* (1946). **Ethel** (1879–1959) acted with Sir Henry Irving in London and became a leading actress in the US, appearing in classical and modern plays and in motion pictures. A New York theater was named for her in 1928. **John** (1882–1942) was a stage success as Hamlet in the 1920s; he was also popular in films, including *Grand Hotel* (1932). He was renowned for his good looks and for his tempestuous private life. His son, **John, Jr.** (1932–   ), had a brief screen career; granddaughter **Drew** (1975–   ) gained prominence in 1982 with the success of *E.T.*

Barth, John (1930–   ) US novelist and academic. His novels, which combine philosophical seriousness with bawdy humor, include *The Sotweed Factor* (1960), *The End of the Road* (1961), *Giles Goat-Boy* (1966), *Chimera* (1974), *Letters* (1979), *Sabbatical, A Romance* (1982), and *The Tidewater Tales* (1987). He often emphasizes the artificiality of fiction by parodying literary conventions.

Barth, Karl (1886–1968) Swiss Protestant theologian. As a pastor during World War I, he became disillusioned with modern liberal theology in the face of extreme suffering. In such influential works as *Epistle to the Romans* (1919) and the four-volume *Church Dogmatics* (1932–67) he returned to the principles of the Reformation and the teachings of the Bible, emphasizing God's sovereignty and man's sinfulness, which necessitates grace. He held professorships at several German universities (1921–35) and at Basle (1935–62).

Bartholdi, Frédéric August (1834–1904) French sculptor, famous for his patriotic monuments. Best known are the Lion of Belfort, commemorating the gallant defense of Belfort during the Franco-Prussian War (1870–71), and the *Statue of Liberty.

Bartholomew, St Christian Apostle. Although mentioned in lists of the Apostles, his name is never connected with any incident from the New Testament. He is sometimes identified with the Nathanel mentioned by John (1.45–51; 21.2). The historian Eusebius tells of his taking the Gospel to India. Feast day: Aug 24.

Bartlett, Josiah (1729–95) US signer of the Declaration of Independence, public official, and physician. He served as a delegate to the Continental Congress (1775), in various court positions in New Hampshire (1779–90), and as governor of the state (1793–94).

Bartók, Béla (1881–1945) Hungarian composer. Bartók studied and taught at the Budapest Academy of Music, where he and *Kodály undertook research into Hungarian folk song. In 1940 he went to live in the US, where he died in poverty. His music blends elements of E European folk music with dissonant harmonies into an astringent and often percussive style. A virtuoso pianist, he composed three piano concertos, a set of progressive pieces for students, entitled *Mikrokosmos* (1926–37), and other piano works. His stage works include the opera *Duke Bluebeard's Castle* (1911) and the ballet *The Miraculous Mandarin* (1919). In his six string quartets and *Music for Strings, Percussion, and Celesta* (1936) he explored unusual sonorities. His most popular work is the *Concerto for Orchestra* (1943).

Bartolommeo, Fra (Baccio della Porta; c. 1472–1517) Florentine Renaissance painter. After training under Cosimo Rosselli (1439–1507), he became a supporter of *Savonarola, whose death moved him to join the Dominican monastery of S Marco (1500) and abandon painting until 1504. His exclusively religious works were close to *Raphael and *Leonardo in style; they include *St Mark* and the *Pietà* (both Palazzo Pitti, Florence).

Barton, Clara (1821–1912) US schoolteacher, who founded the American Red Cross. During the Civil War (1861–65) she helped obtain supplies for wounded soldiers. She later worked for the International Red Cross in the Franco-Prussian War (1870–71) and then established its American branch, serving as its first president (1881–1904).

Barton, Sir Edmund (1849–1920) Australian statesman; Australia's first prime minister (1901–03). He was leader of the Federal Convention in 1897 that drafted the bill to unite the separate states of Australia.

Baruch, Bernard (1870–1965) US economist and adviser to Presidents Wilson, F. D. Roosevelt, and Truman. He helped to coordinate industries during World War I and to draft the economic items of the Treaty of Versailles. He served on the UN Atomic Energy Commission (1946), recommending control of atomic energy production.

baryon A collective term for *nucleons and other elementary particles that have a proton or neutron in their decay products. All baryons have a *quantum number called the baryon number, which is equal to +1. Their antiparticles have a baryon number equal to –1. The baryon number is always conserved in an interaction. *See* particle physics.

Baryshnikov, Mikhail (Nikolayevich) (1948–   ) International ballet dancer; born in USSR. A leading dancer with Russia's Kirov Ballet, he felt a need for fewer artistic restrictions and defected to the West in 1974, while on tour in Canada. After appearing in several productions in Canada and the US, he joined the American Ballet Theatre (ABT) (1974–78) and danced briefly with the New York City Ballet (1978–79) before becoming artistic director of ABT (1980–89). He appeared in movies such as *White Nights* (1985), had an award-winning television special, and made his theater debut in *Metamorphosis* (1989).

barytes *See* barite.

baryton A musical instrument of the *viol family popular in the 18th century. Held between the knees, it had six gut strings and a number of sympathetic wire strings, which could be plucked. Haydn, whose patron Prince Esterhazy was a keen player, wrote many pieces for it.

basalt A volcanic rock of basic composition, typically dark, heavy, and fine textured. It consists essentially of calcic plagioclase feldspar and pyroxene, with magnetite, apatite, and often olivine as accessory minerals. Three broad groups of basalt are recognized: alkali basalt, high-alumina basalt, and tholeiite. The basalts constituting the ocean floor, generated at midocean ridges, are tholeiites. Many volcanoes and huge lava plateaus consist of basalt, which constitutes over 90% of volcanic rocks.

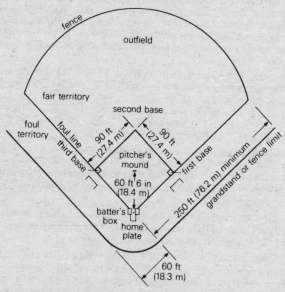

BASEBALL *The dimensions of the field.*

baseball A nine-a-side bat-and-ball game that evolved from *rounders, played mainly in the US, Japan, and Latin America. The object for each team while batting is to score as many runs as possible and while fielding to prevent the other team from doing so; the team with the highest score wins. A team bats until three players are out; one turn at bat for both teams constitutes an inning, of which there are usually nine in a game. The pitcher, standing at the pitcher's mound, throws the ball to the batter, standing at home plate, who tries to hit it into fair territory and run. He scores a home run by making a complete circuit of the bases (first, second, third, and home). A player may strike out (if he misses the ball in each of three attempts), be caught out, tagged out (if he or the base he is running toward is touched by a player with the ball before the runner reaches the base), or be put out by being hit by a batted ball while running.

Basel. *See* Basle.

basenji A breed of dog originating in central Africa. It is lightly built and has a wrinkled forehead, pricked ears, and tightly curled tail. The short glossy coat is usually chestnut with white markings but can be black and white. Height: 16–17 in (40–43 cm).

bases. *See* acids and bases.

Bashkir A Turkic language and people of Russia's Bashkir Autonomous Republic. The language is related to Tatar and Kazakh. The Bashkirs, originally nomads herding mainly horses and sheep, settled in their present territory under Mongol rule (13th–15th centuries). Russian domination of the area after 1551 led to the encouragement of agriculture and village life. Collectivization has obliterated the traditional tribal and clan organization. The Bashkir are either Muslims or Eastern Orthodox Christians by faith.

Bashkir Autonomous Republic of (*or* Bashkiria) An administrative division in E central Russia. The Turkic-speaking Bashkirs comprise some 25% of the population. Bashkiria has large oil and natural-gas deposits, as well as coal, iron ore, and copper and has expanding chemical, coal, steel, and timber industries. Grains are the chief agricultural product. It was the first autonomous Soviet republic (1919). Area: 55,430 sq mi (143,600 sq km). Population (1982): 3,876,000. Capital: Ufa.

Basho. *See* Matsuo Basho.

Basic English A simplified form of the English language, which uses a vocabulary of 850 common English words. It was developed in the late 1920s by the linguist C. K. *Ogden, who intended it to be a simply learned method of international communication and a rival to *Esperanto. The vocabulary divides into 600 nouns, 150 adjectives, and 100 operations, which include verbs. These building blocks are used to form complex ideas without the necessity of complex vocabulary items; for instance the concept "prepare" would be expressed as "get ready," and such combinations can replace 4000 standard English verbs.

Basidiomycetes A large class of fungi (about 13,000 species) that includes many *mushrooms, the *bracket fungi, *puffballs, etc., as well as important microscopic forms, such as the parasitic *rusts and *smuts of crops. They all have the same kind of reproductive organ—a basidium, which is typically club-shaped and produces spores at the tips of stalklike projections.

Basie, Count (William B.; 1904–84) US jazz pianist and band leader. He was influenced by Harlem ragtime pianists, played in vaudeville shows, and formed his own band in 1935. He became famous for his distinctive "big band" style and his piano playing. He recorded many albums, including *Blues by Basie* and *Swingin' Count*.

basil An annual herbaceous plant of the Indian genus *Ocimum*, cultivated as a pot herb. Sweet basil (*O. basilicum*), up to 12 in (30 cm) high, has toothed leaves and small white or bluish flowers. The dried clove-scented leaves are used to flavor various dishes. Family: *Labiatae*.

Basil (I) the Macedonian (d. 886 AD) Byzantine emperor (876–86), who founded the Macedonian dynasty. Of humble origin, Basil became coemperor (867) with Michael III (resigned 842–68) but murdered him in 868. He strengthened Byzantine power in Asia Minor and in S Italy and revived Roman law in a legal text known as the Basilica.

Basil II Bulgaroctonus (c. 958–1025 AD) Byzantine emperor (976–1025). He secured Byzantine conquests in Syria and extended his empire by conquering territory in Georgia and Armenia. He was named Bulgaroctonus (slayer of the Bulgars) after defeating the Bulgarians at Ochrida (1014): he blinded their entire army except for every 100th man, who was left with one eye with which to lead his comrades back to their ruler; the Bulgarian khan died of shock.

basilica 1. A Roman public meeting hall. In imperial times, many had a layout similar to the Basilica of Maxentius in Rome: rectangular ground plan, colonnaded aisles, entrance porch (narthex), and windows in the upper story (clerestory). **2.** A Christian church based on a similar plan (e.g. S Giovanni in Laterano in Rome). The influence of the plan can still be seen in western church architecture.

Basilicata A mountainous region in S Italy. A poor region economically, it is almost entirely dependent upon agriculture producing wheat, olives, vines, potatoes, sheep, and goats. Area: 3856 sq mi (9987 sq km). Capital: Potenza.

basilisk 1. An arboreal lizard belonging to the tropical American genus *Basiliscus*. Up to 24 in (60 cm) long, it has a narrow body, a long whiplike tail, and a flat lobe protruding from the back of its head. It has long hind legs with lobed toes fringed with scales, enabling it to run over the surface of water. Family: *Iguanidae*. **2.** A legendary snakelike creature of ancient Greece and Rome whose glance was believed to be fatal to all living things except the weasel, and later the cock, which both had the power to destroy it.

Basil the Great, St (c. 330–79 AD) Bishop of Caesarea in Cappadocia. His name is usually linked with St *Gregory of Nazianzus and St *Gregory of Nyssa (his brother). Known as the Cappadocian Fathers, they were the chief defenders of orthodox Christian philosophy against *Arianism in the 4th century. Thoroughly educated in both classical pagan and Christian culture, he adopted a monastic life and then lived as a hermit before becoming Bishop of Caesarea in 370. He developed a rule that formed the basis of monasticism in the Eastern Church. He is traditionally considered the author of the liturgy of St Basil, still used on certain days in the Orthodox Church. He wrote many theological works. Feast day: June 14.

basketball A five-a-side court game invented in the US (1891) by James Naismith (1861–1939). The object is to toss or put an inflated ball into the opponents' basket, a net mounted 10 ft (3.05 m) above the floor on a backboard. Players use only their hands, passing the ball or dribbling it by bouncing, and they may not run with it. A professional game has 4 12-minute quarters. The Americans have dominated all Olympic competition, which began in 1936. The premier professional basketball league is the National Basketball Association in the US (founded in 1949) but European professional leagues have grown in popularity. *See also* Harlem Globetrotters.

basking shark A large *shark belonging to the family *Cetorhinidae*. Up to 49 ft (15 m) long, they are gray-brown or blackish and inhabit cold and temperate regions of the Atlantic, Pacific, and Indian Oceans. Basking sharks usually occur in shoals near the surface and float or swim slowly, feeding on plankton.

Basle (French name: Bâle; German name: Basel) 47 33N 7 36E The second largest city in Switzerland, on the Rhine River where the French, German, and Swiss borders meet. A Roman fort originally occupied the site. During the Reformation it became a major literary center and the scholar Erasmus taught at the university (founded 1460). Its notable features include the medieval city gates and the cathedral. Basle is a major commercial and industrial center, strategically positioned in the European railroad system and the chief river port in Switzerland. Industries include chemicals, pharmaceuticals, and engineering. The Bank for International Settlements was established here in 1929. Population (1991 est): 171,000.

Basle, Council of A general council of the Roman Catholic Church summoned by Pope Martin V in 1431 to consider the heretical *Hussites and the nature of papal power. The council, having reaffirmed the principle that general councils are answerable only to God, grew increasingly antipapal and in 1437 Eugenius IV, Martin's successor, moved it to Ferrara. However, a minority of councillors remained at Basle, electing the antipope, Felix V, in 1439. He resigned in 1449 and the council was brought to an end.

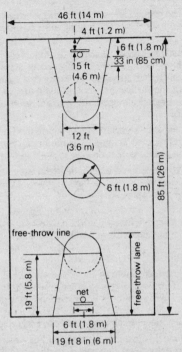

BASKETBALL *Court dimensions for international play.*

Basque A non-Indo-European language spoken by the Basque people of the W Pyrenean areas of Spain and France. Basque is a very ancient language, apparently unrelated to any other and called Euskara by the Basques themselves. It is still spoken by about 500,000 people. The Basques, predominantly farmers and seafarers, are descended from a people known to the Romans as the Vascones. Today there are about 750,000 Basques in Spain and 170,000 in France. They are strongly Roman Catholic and traditionally enjoyed a degree of regional autonomy, forming an independent government (1936–37) at the time of the Spanish Civil War. Nationalism remains a significant force among them in many areas today.

Basra 30 30N 47 50E A city in SE Iraq, on the Shatt (river) al-Arab. It is linked by rail and river steamer to Baghdad; the modern port (Al Ma'qil) was constructed by the British during World War I. Population (1985 est): 617,000.

Bass, Sam (1851–78) US outlaw. He led a gang of bank, stagecoach, and train robbers in the west and was known for giving what he robbed to the poor. He was killed by a Texas Ranger at Round Rock, Texas, in 1878.

bass (fish) One of several perchlike *bony fish of the order *Perciformes*, often valued as food and game fish. The majority belong to the family *Serranidae* (*see* sea bass), which includes the common European bass (*Dicentrarchus labrax*).

This can grow up to 40 in (1 m) long and has a gray or blue back with a white or yellowish belly and silvery flanks. North American freshwater bass belong to the family *Centrarchidae*.

bass (music) **1.** The deepest adult male singing voice. Range: E below the bass stave to E two octaves above. **2.** The lowest voice or instrumental part of a piece of music.

Bassano, Jacopo (Jacopo *or* Giacomo da Ponte; c. 1517–92) Italian painter of the Venetian school, born in Bassano, the son of a painter. In Venice he was influenced by Titian before adopting the elongated figure style of *Parmigianino. He was one of the earliest painters of rustic life, in both secular, e.g. *Pastoral* (Lugano), and religious scenes, e.g. *Adoration of the Kings* (National Gallery, Edinburgh).

Bassein 16 46N 94 45E A port in Myanmar, on the Bassein River. Situated at the terminus of a railroad to Yangon, it is the country's second port exporting chiefly rice, coal, and salt. Population (1983 est): 144,000.

basset horn A woodwind instrument, the tenor member of the *clarinet family. It has a rich velvety tone but lacks the brilliance of the upper range of the A- or B-flat clarinet. Mozart wrote for it.

basset hound A breed of □dog originating in France. It has a long body with very short legs and a narrow face with drooping ears and a mournful expression. The short smooth coat ranges from black to light brown in color with white patches. Basset hounds have a keen sense of smell and were formerly popular hunting dogs. Height: 13–15 in (33–38 cm).

bassoon A musical instrument of the woodwind family. Its conically bored tube is about 8 ft (2.5 m) long and is bent back on itself. It has a metal crook into which a double reed is inserted. Its extensive compass (about three and a half octaves above B-flat below the bass stave) allows it a melodic as well as a bass role. Composers have made much use of its humorous staccato quality.

Bass Strait A channel separating the mainland of Australia from Tasmania. It has valuable oil and natural-gas deposits. Length: 180 mi (290 km). Maximum width: 150 mi (240 km).

basswood A *lime tree, *Tilia americana*, also called American lime or linden, sometimes exceeding 80 ft (25 m) in height. It yields commercially important timber that is especially prized for carving, and a tough fiber derived from the bark is of local importance.

bast fibers Fibers, such as *flax, *hemp, and *jute, that are obtained from the stems of certain plants. The fibers are freed from the stalk by retting (soaking) or mechanical peeling and are used for textiles, sacking, twines, and ropes.

Bastia 42 41N 9 26E A port in France, on Corsica, on the NE coast. Founded by the Genoese in the 14th century, it was the former capital of Corsica and is the island's largest city. Fishing and the manufacture of tobacco and wine are the principal economic activities. Population: 50,100.

Bastille A fortress in Paris, which was a state prison in the 17th and 18th centuries and a symbol of the corrupt and despotic Bourbon monarchy. It was built in about 1370 to protect the wall around Paris against English attack and became a state prison under Cardinal de *Richelieu. The storming of the Bastille on July 14, 1789, is regarded as the beginning of the *French Revolution.

Basutoland. *See* Lesotho, Kingdom of.

bat A flying mammal belonging to the order *Chiroptera* (981 species), distributed in most temperate and tropical regions. There are two suborders: the *fruit bats (*Megachiroptera*; 150 species) and the insect-eating bats (*Microchiroptera*; 831 species). Bats may also feed on pollen, nectar, blood, and small animals. The wings are extensions of skin that are supported between the forelimb, with its very long fingers, the hind limbs, and the tail. Most bats use *echolocation for navigation; this is highly developed in insectivorous bats, which catch prey on the wing whereas fruit bats have large eyes adapted for night vision. Bats can be found roosting in caves and buildings during daytime.

Bataan A mountainous forested peninsula in the Philippines, in W Luzon W of Manila Bay. In a famous action during World War II, US-Filipino forces resisted the Japanese invasion for almost three months here (1942). After their capture, thousands of US and Filipino troops died on the notorious forced Bataan Death March. Length: about 30 mi (48 km).

bateleur An African snake *eagle, *Terathopius ecaudatus*, having very long wings and a short tail. It is highly maneuverable and flies vast distances, preying on snakes, other reptiles, mammals, and carrion, which it seizes with its short rough powerful toes.

Bateson, William (1861–1926) British biologist, whose experiments on inheritance helped found the science of genetics, a term that he first proposed. Bateson investigated the way in which certain traits, such as comb shape in fowl, are transmitted from one generation to the next. His results (1905–08) corroborated the findings of Gregor *Mendel published in 1865. He also found that certain characteristics were inherited together (a phenomenon now known as linkage, due to the occurrence of the controlling genes on the same chromosome), but he refused to accept the chromosome theory proposed by T. H. *Morgan to account for this.

batfish A carnivorous fish, belong to a family (*Ogcocephalidae*; about 60 species) of *anglerfish, found in tropical and temperate seas. It has a slender lumpy-skinned body up to 14 in (36 cm) long and a broad flat head with an elongated upturned snout. Using thickened limblike pectoral and pelvic fins, it crawls on the bottom searching for prey.

Bath 51 23N 2 22W A city in SW England, on the River Avon. A spa town of great architectural interest, it was an early Roman center known as Aquae Sulis because of its hot natural springs. The elaborate Roman baths have survived. Bath became fashionable as an elegant spa town in the 18th century when many of the finest buildings were built. Bath Abbey, mainly 16th-century, lies in the town center. Bath University dates from 1966. Population (1981): 79,965.

Bath, Order of the A British order of knighthood, formed by George I in 1725 as a successor to the Knights of the Bath. It comprises the sovereign and three classes of knights companions: knights and dames grand cross (GCB), knights and dames commanders (KCB), and companions (CB). Women have been admitted since 1971.

batholith A large mass of intrusive igneous rock of unknown depth and often occupying many thousands of square kilometers. They are composed mainly of granite and occur in association with mountain belts. They are often surrounded by a zone of mineralized rocks (metamorphic aureole).

Bathurst. *See* Banjul.

batik Cloth, traditionally cotton, dyed by a special method. An ancient Indonesian craft, developed especially in Java, batik work involves the application of melted wax, later removed, to protect parts of the material from the dye; repeating the process using different wax patterns and several dyeings produces intricate multicolored geometric patterns, symbolic motifs, or stylized pictures of birds, animals, or flowers. Some designs have been passed on in families for a thousand years.

BATELEUR *This African eagle has exceptionally long wings and may fly up to 200 mi (300 km) a day in search of prey.*

Batista y Zaldívar, Fulgencio (1901–73) Cuban statesman, who was president from 1940 to 1944 and, after returning to power in 1952 by means of a military coup, from 1954 to 1958. His authoritarian government generated opposition, notably from Castro's guerrilla movement, by which Batista was ousted.

Baton Rouge 30 30N 91 10W The capital of Louisiana situated on the Mississippi River at the head of oceangoing navigation. It is a major deepwater port with oil and sugar refineries. It has several state institutions, including the Louisiana State University (1860). Population (1990): 219,531.

Battani, al- (Latin name: Albatenius; c. 858–929) Islamic astronomer, born in Haran (Turkey) and noted for his book on stellar motions. Using trigonometric methods, he improved the accuracy of many astronomical measurements, including the length of the year, the precession of the equinoxes, and the inclination of the ecliptic.

battery A cell that can be recharged by passing a current through it in the direction opposite to that of the discharge current, thus reversing the chemical changes occurring during discharge at the electrodes. The most common example is the lead-acid battery used in motor vehicles. This consists, when charged, of a positive lead dioxide electrode and a negative spongy lead electrode, both immersed in sulfuric acid with a relative density of 1.20–1.28. During discharge lead sulfate forms on the electrodes and the acid density falls.

Nickel-iron (NiFe) batteries with an electrolyte of 20% potassium hydroxide are also used. Interest in *electric cars has stimulated battery development in recent years. While lead batteries will deliver up 8×10^4 joules per kilogram, the newer zinc-air battery can produce five times this energy density.

battleship A heavily armored naval vessel designed to combine large size, maneuverability, and extensive cruising range with the most powerful armament. Larger than a *cruiser and smaller than an *aircraft carrier, the battleship was the flagship vessel of a fleet. There have been no new battleships built since World War II, as they have been largely replaced by other more versatile and less expensive vessels.

Batumi 41 37N 41 36E A port in Georgia on the Black Sea. It has an oil refinery, shipping oil piped from Baku, a range of light industries, and there are tea plantations on the city's outskirts. Population (1984): 111,000.

Baudelaire, Charles (1821–67) French poet. He inherited his father's fortune in 1842 and lived extravagantly until what was left of the capital was placed in trust by his family (1844). Forced to earn a living, he began to publish art criticism and poetry and wrote the autobiographical novel *La Fanfarlo* (1847). In 1852 he discovered Edgar Allan *Poe, publishing several translations of his works (1856–65). His only volume of poetry, *Les Fleurs du mal* (1857, revised 1861), contained several erotic poems, which led to his being convicted for obscenity. He became increasingly disillusioned; while in Belgium in 1866 he became paralyzed as a result of venereal disease and died in Paris soon after.

Baudouin I (1930–93) King of the Belgians (1951–93), succeeding his father Leopold III. He was interned by the Nazis in World War II. In 1960 he married Fabiola de Mora y Aragón (1928–　). He was succeeded by his brother Albert.

Bauhaus A German school of design. One of the most important influences on 20th-century art, the Bauhaus enjoyed a short life. Founded in 1919 at Weimar it was closed by the Nazis in 1933. From 1925 to 1932 it was housed at Dessau in a building designed by *Gropius (its director until 1928), itself a work of great influence. Connected with some of the best designers of the age, the Bauhaus sought to produce a practical synthesis of all the arts, from furniture design to architecture, and to develop a coherent style appropriate for the industrial 20th century. The functional style the Bauhaus helped to evolve still has considerable influence in the arts, from the international style of architecture to tubular steel furniture. *See also* Kandinsky; Klee; Mies van der Rohe; Moholy-Nagy.

Baum, L(yman) Frank (1856–1919) US novelist. After working as a journalist, he created in *The Wonderful Wizard of Oz* (1900) a classic children's fantasy land that provided material for 13 sequels and was made into a movie in 1938. In all, he wrote about 60 books, mostly for children.

Baumgarten, Alexander Gottlieb (1714–62) German philosopher, a follower of Christian Wolff (1679–1754) and *Leibniz. In 1740, he became professor of philosophy at Frankfurt-am-Oder. He invented the term *aesthetics and his *Aesthetica* (1750) is a pioneering work on that subject.

Baur, Ferdinand Christian (1792–1860) German Protestant theologian. Baur's early work was concerned with the gnostic background of Christianity. He was much influenced by *Hegel. In 1826, he became professor of theology at Tübingen University, and his later work on St Paul led him to question the authenticity of the New Testament and marked the beginnings of radical biblical criticism.

bauxite The chief ore of aluminum. It is a residual deposit formed by the weathering of aluminum-rich rocks (mainly syenites) under tropical conditions and consists mainly of hydrated aluminum oxide. The main producers are Australia, Jamaica, Surinam, Guyana, Guinea, Sierra Leone, and Yugoslavia.

Bavaria (German name: Bayern) A *Land* of S Germany, bordering on Austria, and the Czech Republic. A third is forested, providing valuable timber resources. Predominantly agricultural, the main crops are rye, wheat, and barley; hops are grown around Munich. Bavaria is a popular tourist area. *History*: a duchy and later a kingdom ruled by the Wittelsbachs from 1180 to 1918, it then became a republic. From the ensuing political unrest Hitler drew much of his early support. Area: 29,232 sq mi (70,547 sq km). Population (1988): 11,083,000. Capital: Munich.

bay A Mediterranean evergreen tree, *Laurus nobilis*, also known as sweet bay and bay laurel, widely grown as an ornamental shrub or pot plant. It can reach a height of 65 ft (20 m), has aromatic dark-green lance-shaped leaves, small yellowish flowers, and blackish berries. The leaves are used to season food. Family: *Lauraceae* (*see* laurel).

Bayard, Pierre Terrail, Seigneur de (c. 1473–1524) French soldier, known as "le bon chevalier sans peur et sans reproche" (the good knight without fear and without reproach). He served in the Italian wars of Charles VIII, Louis XII, and Francis I, gaining particular distinction at Fornovo (1495) and Marignano (1515). Pope Julius II sought unsuccessfully to hire him.

Baybars I (1223–77) Sultan of Egypt and Syria (1260–77) of the *Mameluke dynasty. Brought to Egypt as a slave, he rose in the army and in 1260 he was prominent at the decisive victory over the Mongols at Ayn Jalut. Between 1263 and 1271 he severely reduced the power of the Crusaders in Syria. He became the subject of a popular folk biography.

bayberry A deciduous shrub, *Myrica pensilvanica*, rarely exceeding 10 ft (3 m) in height, bearing flowers in catkins and oblong leaves 4 in (10 cm) long. It is native to E North America and sometimes cultivated in other temperate areas. Family: *Myricaceae*.

The name is also given to the purple-blue berries of the *bay tree.

Bayeux 49 16N 0 42W A city in NW France, in the Calvados department on the Aure River. Its museum houses the famous *Bayeux tapestry and there is a fine 13th-century cathedral. It was the first French town to be liberated by the Allies in World War II (June 7, 1944). Industries include dairy foods and plastics. Population (1983): 15,200.

Bayeux tapestry An 11th-century embroidered linen strip, 231 ft (69 m) long, which depicts the Norman conquest of England (1066). The tapestry, which starts with King Harold's visit to Normandy and ends with the battle of Hastings, is of great historical value. It was probably commissioned for Bayeux cathedral by its bishop, Odo, the half-brother of William the Conqueror, whose wife Matilda is traditionally, though improbably, credited with its making. The tapestry now hangs in the museum at Bayeux (France).

Bayezid II (c. 1447–1512) Ottoman Sultan of Turkey (1481–1512). During his reign Turkish dominions in the Balkans and the Crimea were extended; war with Venice (1499–1503) brought territory in Greece and the Adriatic. Warfare with Egypt and the Safavid dynasty of Persia occupied the last decade of his reign. In 1512 Bayezid abdicated, dying soon afterward.

Bayle, Pierre (1647–1706) French Protestant critic and controversialist. He taught philosophy at Sedan from 1675 until forced into exile in Rotterdam. There he was professor of philosophy from 1781 to 1793, when his contentious religious tracts and determined opponents lost him the chair. Undeterred, he began publication of his masterwork, the *Dictionnaire historique et critique* (1796), a model of scholarship, style, and philosophical skepticism, which was both influential and successful.

Bay of Pigs (Spanish name: Bahia de los Cochinos) A bay on the SW coast of Cuba where on April 17, 1961, about 1200 Cuban exiles attempted to invade the country. Hoping to overthrow the Marxist regime of Fidel *Castro, and supported by the US *Central Intelligence Agency, the invasion was unsuccessful and the US was criticized for its involvement.

bayonet A blade that may be attached to the muzzle of a firearm. The bayonet, which is thought to have originated in the early 17th century in Bayonne (France), replaced the pike. Early bayonets were inserted into the gun, which could not then be fired, a drawback resolved in the 1680s by the development of the socket bayonet. This was attached to a tube that was placed over the muzzle. Bayonets were used in both World Wars.

Bayonne 43 30N 1 28W A city in SW France, in the Pyrénées–Atlantiques department at the confluence of the Ador and Nive Rivers. The chief port of the Basque country, it was formerly famous for its swords and knives; the bayonet was developed here in the early 17th century. Its varied industries include aircraft, distilling, and leather. Population (1983): 125,000.

Bay Psalm Book Probably the first book printed in America, which contained the Psalms in metrical form. It was published in 1640 in Cambridge, Mass., by a group of Congregationalists.

Bayreuth 49 27N 11 35E A city in S Germany, in Bavaria. It is famous as the home and burial place of Richard Wagner, who designed its Festival Theater (1872–76), where his operas are performed annually. Its industries include the manufacture of textiles and machinery. Population (1983): 71,000.

Bazaine, Achille François (1811–88) French marshal, who served in the Crimean War (1854–56), in Italy against Austria (1859), and in Mexico (1863). He was commander in chief in the Franco-Prussian War (1870–71), when he surrendered after being besieged at Metz. For this he was condemned for treason but escaped to exile in Spain.

bazooka Originally a 2.36 inch (60 mm) antitank rocket launcher fired from the shoulder and used by the US army in World War II. It consisted of a 54 inch (1.4 m) breech-loaded tube, open at both ends, firing a 31/2 lb (1.6 kg) rocket to an effective range of about 150 yd (135 m). The term was later applied to all similar weapons. The name came from a tubular wind instrument made famous by Bob Burns, an American comedian.

BCG (*b*acille *C*almette *G*uérin) A vaccine consisting of a weakened form of the tuberculosis bacterium, which is injected to give partial protection against tuberculosis. It acts by stimulating the body's defense system without causing the disease. A successful vaccination produces a lump at the injection site.

Beaconsfield, Benjamin Disraeli, 1st Earl of. *See* Disraeli, Benjamin.

Beadle, George Wells (1903–89) US geneticist, who provided fundamental evidence for the nature of gene function. Working with molds, he proposed the theory that each gene was responsible for the production of a single enzyme, which itself controlled a particular chemical reaction in the cell. He shared a Nobel Prize (1958) with *Tatum and *Lederberg.

beagle A long-established breed of dog originating in England. It has a deep chest, strong shoulders, and drooping ears. The short smooth coat is usually dark brown to light tan with white patches. With their keen sense of smell, beagles have long been used as hunting hounds; more recently, they have become popular household pets. Height: 13–16 in (33–40 cm).

Bean, Roy (c. 1825–1903) US frontier justice of the peace. A saloon keeper in Vinegaroon, Texas (now Langtry), in 1882, he was appointed and then elected justice of the peace and held court in his saloon, making outrageous but shrewd judgments and dispensing appropriate sentences.

bean The seed or fruit of certain herbs, shrubs, or trees of the family *Leguminosae*. They are widely cultivated and not only form a good source of protein for man and livestock but also provide raw material for a wide range of derived products. *See* broad bean; carob bean; French bean; haricot bean; lablab; lima bean; mung bean; runner bean; soybean; tonka bean.

bear A large heavy mammal belonging to a family (*Ursidae*; 7 species) found in Europe, Asia, and America. Bears have a shaggy coat and a short tail and walk flat on the soles of their broad feet. They can stand erect and make good use of their powerful limbs and long curved claws. Eyesight and hearing are poor but bears have an excellent sense of smell; they can exist on any kind of food but most of them are vegetarian. Newly born bears are very small (about the size of rats), blind, and toothless. The female stays in the den suckling her young until they can accompany her outside. Order: *Carnivora*. *See* black bear; brown bear; polar bear; sloth bear; spectacled bear; sun bear.

bearberry A prostrate evergreen shrub of the genus *Arctostaphylos*, native to North and Central America, especially *A. uva-ursi*, which is also widespread in Europe and Asia. The woody stems may reach 7 ft (2 m) in length, sending out roots at intervals. The flowers are white to pink and bell-shaped, and the berries are red. The plant is an important colonist. Family: *Ericaceae*.

bearded lizard An Australian lizard, *Amphibolurus barbatus*, occurring in scrub and desert regions. Up to 24 in (60 cm) long, it has a long head, a whiplike tail, a gray to yellowish spiny skin, and a bright-yellow mouth; a throat pouch swells to resemble a spiny beard during aggressive or courtship displays. It feeds on insects, small lizards, and snakes.

bearded tit. *See* reedling.

bearded vulture. *See* lammergeier.

Beardsley, Aubrey Vincent (1872–98) British illustrator. Virtually self-taught, he achieved notoriety with his grotesque and erotic imagery in periodicals and several books, including Oscar Wilde's *Salome* and Alexander Pope's *Rape of the Lock*. His designs are composed of curved lines, characteristic of *Art Nouveau, which contrast with dense areas of black ink. He died of tuberculosis in France.

beardworm A deep-sea wormlike animal, up to 12 in (30 cm) long, belonging to the invertebrate phylum *Pogonophora* (20 species). Beardworms live in tubes built in the mud of the ocean floor. Their head ends are crowned with tentacles, which protrude from the tubes and are believed to function in respiration and feeding (beardworms lack a digestive system).

Bear Flag Revolt (1846) A revolt of US settlers in California against Mexican rule. A group of American settlers in the Sacramento Valley seized some horses from the Mexican government and raised the "bear" flag over the "Republic of California." It remained until replacement by the US flag a few months later during the *Mexican War.

deep groove
ball bearing

taper roller
bearing

BEARINGS *Common examples of ball bearings and roller bearings.*

bearings A support for a rotating shaft or the interface between a crank and a reciprocating part. Bearings are designed to reduce friction and wear to a minimum and to dissipate the heat generated. In plain bearings, lubrication is achieved by maintaining a film of lubricant between the faces either as a result of their relative motion or by pumping it through channels into the interface. Some small bearings, made of powdered copper or bronze impregnated with oil or graphite, are self-lubricating, while some low-friction plastics (e.g. polytetrafluoroethylene) do not require lubrication. Bearing surfaces or shells are usually made of softer materials (e.g. brass or white metal) than is the shaft.

In **ball and roller bearings** friction between the faces is reduced by replacing the sliding action of a plain bearing by a rolling action. The balls or rollers are usually made from chromium (0.5–2.0%) steels.

bear market A stock or commodity market in which there is a continuing downward movement in prices. An initial fall in prices, caused by adverse economic factors, is often magnified by consequent selling by investors. *Compare* bull market.

Bear River A river that rises in NE Utah in the Uinta Mountains and loops north through SW Colorado and S Idaho before flowing S into NW Utah to empty into the Great Salt Lake near Brigham City. The land at its mouth serves as a waterfowl sanctuary. Length: 350 mi (565 km).

Beas River A river in NW India, flowing mainly W from the Himalayas to the Sutlej River. It forms part of the Punjab irrigation scheme. Length: 290 mi (470 km).

Beatitudes In the New Testament, the eight blessings with which Jesus opened the Sermon on the Mount (Matthew 5.3–12). They describe such Christian virtues as meekness, mercy, and purity of heart (e.g. "Blessed are the meek: for they shall inherit the earth."). The word derives from the Latin of the *Vulgate, beati sunt (blessed are).

Beatles A British rock group, which achieved worldwide popularity during the 1960s. The Beatles appeared at the Cavern Club in Liverpool in 1962 and subsequently recorded "Love Me Do" and "She Loves You," which became top of the Hit Parade in 1963. By this time the group consisted of George *Harrison, John *Lennon, Paul *McCartney, and Ringo *Starr; they toured the US successfully, made two films, and were awarded MBEs in 1965. The most original of the group's subsequent albums were *Sergeant Pepper's Lonely Hearts Club Band* (1967), which reflected the Beatles' experience of drugs and eastern mysticism, and the double *White Album* (1968). In 1970 they disbanded to pursue separate careers. In 1980, John Lennon was murdered.

BEATLES *(From left) Ringo Starr, Paul McCartney, John Lennon, and George Harrison (with bugle).*

Beat movement American literary and social movement of the 1950s that opposed the values of conventional society through art, poetry, and permissive attitudes towards sex and the use of drugs. The movement originated in Greenwich Village in New York City and later centered in San Francisco. Among the most prominent leaders of the Beat movement were the novelists Jack *Kerouac and William *Burroughs and the poets Allen *Ginsburg, Lawrence *Ferlinghetti, and Gregory Corso (1930–   ). Ferlinghetti's City Lights Press in San Francisco became noted for its publication of the works of many writers of the Beat movement.

Beatrix (1938–   ) Queen of the Netherlands since the abdication (1980) of her mother Queen Juliana. Her marriage (1966) to the German Claus von Amsberg (1926–   ) caused some controversy.

beats Variations in the intensity of sound when two tones of nearly equal frequency are heard. The effect is similar to that of *interference. At certain times, the amplitudes of the waves reinforce each other and, at intermediate times, they tend to cancel each other out. The frequency of the beats is equal to the difference in the frequencies of the two notes.

Beauce An area in central France, in the Paris Basin. Consisting of a fertile plain, it is an important wheat-growing area and is known as the "granary of France."

Beaufort scale A scale of wind speed. It is based on easily observable indicators, such as smoke, tree movement, and damage incurred, and was devised in 1805 by Admiral Sir Francis Beaufort (1774–1857).

Beaufort Sea The section of the Arctic Ocean N of North America, between the Chukchi Sea and the Canadian archipelago. It is often covered by floating ice.

Beauharnais, Alexandre, Vicomte de (1760–94) French general, who served in the American Revolution and then became involved in French Revolutionary politics. He commanded in the Rhine (1793) but was guillotined (1794) for failing to relieve Metz. His widow *Joséphine married Napoleon, whom his son **Eugène de Beauharnais** (1781–1824) served in Italy and Egypt. In 1805 he became viceroy of Italy and in 1812 commanded in Napoleon's Russian campaign. He lived in exile after Napoleon's fall. His sister **Hortense de Beauharnais** (1783–1837) married (1802) Napoleon's brother Louis *Bonaparte, King of Holland. Their son was the future Napoleon III.

Beaulieu 50 49N 1 27W A village in S England, in Hampshire. The parish church was formerly the refectory of a Cistercian abbey founded in 1204 by King John. In the grounds of the Palace House, home of Lord Montague, is the National Motor Museum.

Beaumarchais, Pierre-Augustin Caron de (1732–99) French dramatist. Son of a watchmaker, he became rich and famous with *The Barber of Seville* (1775) and *The Marriage of Figaro* (1778), his comedies about the busybodying intrigues of a cunning valet; they inspired operas by *Rossini and *Mozart. He undertook secret missions abroad for Louis XV and Louis XVI, supplied arms to the American revolutionaries, and sponsored the first complete edition of *Voltaire's works. Constantly involved in lawsuits, he wrote *Mémoires* (1773–75) in self-defense.

Beaumont 30 05N 94 06W A city and port in E Texas, on the Naches River. A distribution center since 1835, Beaumont became a center of the oil industry when the famous Spindletop oil fields were opened in 1901. Linked to the Gulf of Mexico by the Sabine-Neches Canal, it is a major shipping center for its petroleum, rice, livestock, sulfur, chemical, rubber, and timber industries. Population (1990): 114,323.

Beaumont, Francis (1584–1616) British dramatist. He studied law at Oxford. From about 1607, he collaborated with John *Fletcher in writing about 12 plays, including *Philaster* (1610) and *The Maides Tragedy* (1611). He was probably sole author of *The Knight of the Burning Pestle* (1607). In 1613 he married and retired from the theater.

Beaumont, William (1785–1853) US physician, who investigated digestion in the human stomach. As an army surgeon in 1822, he treated a trapper named Alexis St Martin for shotgun injuries. These left a permanent opening in his patient's stomach wall and abdomen through which Beaumont sampled the stomach contents. He recognized the chemical nature of digestion, including the importance of hydrochloric acid. His patient lived to the age of 82.

BEAUFORT SCALE

Beaufort number	description of wind	wind speed	
		knots	meters per second
0	calm	<1	0.0– 0.2
1	light air	1– 3	0.3– 1.5
2	light breeze	4– 6	1.6– 3.3
3	gentle breeze	7–10	3.4– 5.4
4	moderate breeze	11–16	5.5– 7.9
5	fresh breeze	17–21	8.0–10.7
6	strong breeze	22–27	10.8–13.8
7	near gale	28–33	13.9–17.1
8	gale	34–40	17.2–20.7
9	strong gale	41–47	20.8–24.4
10	storm	48–55	24.5–28.4
11	violent storm	56–63	28.5–32.6
12	hurricane	≥64	≥32.7

Beaune 47 02N 4 50E A city in E central France, in the Côte-d'Or depart-ment. The center for the wine trade of Burgundy, it has a wine museum and its manufactures include casks, oil, and mustard. Population (1982): 21,100.

Beauregard, Pierre Gustave Toutant de (1818–93) US Confederate general. A West Point graduate (1838) who remained loyal to the South and his native state of Louisiana when the Civil War began, he was appointed brigadier general in the Confederate army in 1861. He was responsible for the bombardment and surrender of Fort Sumter (1861), the first battle of the war, for victory at the first battle of *Bull Run, and for holding back Union troops at Shiloh, Tenn. (1862), Charleston, S.C. (1862–64), and Richmond, Va. (1864).

Beauvais 49 26N 2 05E A city in France, in the Oise department. Its fine cathedral (begun 1227) was damaged during World War II and the factory in which the famous Gobelin tapestries had been made since the 17th century was completely destroyed (the industry was subsequently moved to Paris). Beauvais is a market town, trading in dairy produce, fruit, and cereals. Population (1982): 54,150.

Beauvais tapestry Tapestry produced by the state-subsidized Beauvais factory, in France, established in 1664. The court painter François *Boucher designed pastoral, Italian, and Chinese scenes for the workshops, which spe-cialized in furniture and screen tapestries. Production declined in the 19th century.

Beauvoir, Simone de (1908–86) French novelist and essayist. The constant companion of Jean-Paul *Sartre from their meeting at the Sorbonne in 1929, her writings have explored the implications of *existentialism. Her novels include *The Blood of Others* (1948) and *The Mandarins* (1956). *The Second Sex* (1953) argued for the liberation of women from their traditional roles in a male-domi-nated society. Other works include *The Coming of Age* (1973) and *All Said and Done* (1975).

beaver A large aquatic *rodent, *Castor fiber*, of Europe, Asia, and North America. Over 40 in (1 m) long and weighing up to 88 lb (40 kg), beavers have a dark sleek waterproof coat and a broad flat tail used for balance and swimming. They live in family groups, building a "lodge" of sticks and mud with underwa-ter entrances and dams above and below. They use their large incisor teeth to cut wood for building and bark for a winter food. During the summer they feed on vegetation. Family: *Castoridae*. □mammal.

Beaverbrook, Max (well) Aitken, 1st Baron (1879–1964) British newspa-per proprietor and politician, born in Canada. In 1919 he bought a major interest in the *Daily Express*. In 1921 he founded the *Sunday Express* and in 1929 bought the *Evening Standard* (London). He served in Lloyd George's World War I cabinet and in Churchill's World War II cabinet.

Bebel, August (1840–1913) German socialist leader. Bebel became inter-ested in the labor movement while living in Leipzig, where in 1865 he came under influence of Wilhelm *Liebknecht. In 1869 he helped to found the Ger-man Social Democratic Party, for which he became a leading spokesman in the Reichstag.

bebop. *See* bop.

Beccaria, Cesare Bonesana, Marchese de (1738–94) Italian legal theo-rist and political economist. He achieved international fame with the publication of his *Crimes and Punishments* (1764), the first comprehensive account of the principles behind criminal law. In attacking legal corruption, torture, capital punishment, etc., it was responsible for the reform of penal codes in many countries. Beccaria became a professor of political philosophy at Milan in 1768 and held several important public offices in the Austrian government.

bêche-de-mer. *See* trepang.

Bechet, Sidney (1897–1959) US jazz clarinetist and soprano saxophone player. He achieved wide recognition after a tour of Europe in 1919, subsequently worked with Duke Ellington, and after World War II lived in Paris. He is one of the few jazz musicians to have popularized the soprano saxophone.

Bechuanaland. *See* Botswana, Republic of.

THOMAS BECKET *This drawing from a 13th-century manuscript shows the archbishop arguing with Henry II of England (above) and Louis VII of France (below).*

Becket, St Thomas (c. 1118–70) English churchman. Becket entered the household of Theobald (d. 1161), Archbishop of Canterbury, and in 1154 became *Henry II's chancellor. Succeeding Theobald as archbishop in 1162, Becket resigned the chancellorship and quarreled with Henry. Becket's refusal to swear allegiance to the Constitutions of *Clarendon forced his resignation and exile in France (1164–70). Subsequent attempts to resolve the quarrel failed and on Dec 29, 1170, he was murdered in Canterbury Cathedral at Henry's instigation. Canonized in 1173, his shrine at Canterbury became one of the most important pilgrimage centers in medieval Europe.

Beckett, Samuel (1906–89) Irish novelist, dramatist, and poet. After studying at Trinity College, Dublin, and traveling for several years in Europe, he settled finally in Paris in 1937. He wrote in both French and English. His plays, which include *Waiting for Godot* (1954), and his prose works, such as *Malone Dies* (1956) and *How It Is* (1964), treat human existence with a nihilism tempered by desperate humor. His later works, such as *Breath* (1972) and *Not I* (1973), are notably brief and concentrated. He won the Nobel Prize in 1969.

Beckmann, Max (1884–1950) German expressionist painter, born in Leipzig. His experiences of World War I inspired his grotesque paintings of distorted sometimes mutilated bodies, often indicting German social evils, as in *Night* (1919; Düsseldorf). In later years in Amsterdam and the US he painted a series of triptychs influenced partly by *Bosch.

becquerel (Bq) The *SI unit of activity (radioactivity) equal to the number of atoms of a radioactive substance that disintegrate in one second. Named for Antoine Henri *Becquerel.

Becquerel, (Antoine) Henri (1852–1908) French physicist, who was professor at the Conservatoire des Arts et Métiers in Paris. He discovered radioactivity (1896) by chance, on finding that invisible rays from uranium salts could affect a photographic plate even through a light-proof wrapper. For his fundamental research on these radiations, Becquerel shared the Nobel Prize (1903) with his associates Pierre and Marie *Curie. He also performed research in magnetism and in optics, particularly polarization and absorption in crystals. His grandfather **Antoine César Becquerel** (1788–1878) left the army to join *Ampère in his study of electricity, becoming one of the founders of electrochemistry.

bedbug A flat wingless insect, about 0.2 in (5 mm) long, belonging to a family (*Cimicidae*; 30 species) of blood-sucking parasites. In temperate regions *Cimex lectularius* is the species that most commonly attacks man, hiding by day in bedding, furniture, etc., and becoming active at night. It inflicts a painful bite but does not transmit disease. Order: *Hemiptera* (bugs).

Bede, St (c. 673–735 AD) English historian, known as the Venerable Bede. After 682 he lived at the monastery of Jarrow in Northumberland. His *Ecclesiastical History of the English People* (c. 731), written in Latin and later translated into English under King Alfred, is a great historical work and remains an important source for Anglo-Saxon history from 54 BC to 597 AD. He also wrote poems in English, but only one is extant, his "Death Song." He was the author of many grammatical, scientific, and historical works. Feast day: May 27.

Bedford, John, Duke of (1389–1435) The third son of Henry IV; known as John of Lancaster. He was protector of England and regent of France (1422–35) during the minority of his nephew Henry VI. He pursued the *Hundred Years' War and procured the execution of Joan of Arc (1431).

Bedfordshire A county in the South Midlands of England. It is chiefly low lying, rising to the Chiltern Hills in the SW, and is drained by the Great Ouse River. Agricultural products include wheat and vegetables. The chief industries, centered on Luton, Dunstable, and Bedford, are motor vehicles, agricultural engineering, and electrical manufactures. Area: 477 sq mi (1235 sq km). Population (1981): 504,986. Administrative center: Bedford.

Bedlam The popular name for the Bethlehem Royal Hospital, a mental hospital located from 1815 until 1931 in London. Founded in 1247, it was transferred to Beckenham, in Kent in 1931. "Bedlam" has passed into the English language as a synonym for "madhouse."

Bedlington terrier A breed of dog originating in Bedlington, N England, in the early 19th century. It has long legs and a long narrow face and is a sporting dog. The thick coat may be blue, blue and tan, liver, or sandy. Height: about 16 in (40 cm).

Bedouin The nomadic *Arab tribes of the Syrian and Arabian deserts and other desert regions of the Arab world. Their economy is based on camels, sheep, and goats. At present they are found within the political boundaries of Saudi Arabia, Yemen, the United Arab Emirates, Kuwait, Iraq, Jordan, Israel, Egypt, and the *Maghrib states. The policies of these countries are to restrict the movements of the nomadic population and induce them to take up a settled existence. Courageous fighters, the Bedouin played an active role in the early Arab conquests.

bedsore An ulcer that develops in areas of skin subject to continuous pressure, such as may occur in elderly or other bedridden patients who are unable to change their position frequently. The pressure reduces the blood supply to the affected part. Patients at risk require careful nursing, with frequent changes of position and massage to prevent bedsores from developing.

bedstraw A weak, often climbing, plant of the widely distributed genus *Galium* (300 species), common in damp places. Lady's bedstraw (*G. verum*), native to Europe, is a weedy perennial, up to 30 in (75 cm) tall, with small yellow flowers. Its name derives from the legend that Mary rested on a bed of these plants while giving birth to Christ. Family: *Rubiaceae* (madder family). *See also* cleavers.

Bedworth 52 28N 1 29W A market city in central England, in Warwickshire. It has coal mining, brick making, and light engineering industries. Population (1981): 41,991.

bee A four-winged insect 0.4–1.2 in (10–30 mm) long belonging to the superfamily *Apoidea* (about 12,000 species), of worldwide distribution. Bees feed on pollen and nectar from flowering plants using well-developed tongues and are important pollinators, transferring pollen on their hairy bodies and broad back legs. The ovipositor is used to sting attackers and in some species is barbed, remaining in the wound.

Most solitary bees nest in soil, hollow trees, or wall cavities. Some, however, tunnel into wood (*see* carpenter bee) or construct nests using earth (*see* mason bee) or leaves (*see* leafcutter bee). The female lays one or more eggs in a nest that is then sealed, leaving the larvae to develop. The social bees (families *Apidae* and *Halictidae*) live in communities organized into castes—workers (infertile females), drones (males, developed from unfertilized eggs), and a queen (a fertile female). Colonies are established in trees, walls, or cliffs (*see also* honeybee). Order: *Hymenoptera*.

Beebe, Charles William (1877–1962) US explorer and naturalist. As head of tropical research for the New York Zoological Society (1916–52) he conducted numerous expeditions and, in 1934, made a record undersea descent of 3028 ft (923 m) in a bathysphere. He wrote many books describing his observations and adventures, including *Monograph of the Pheasants* (1918–22) and *Galapagos* (1923).

beech A tree of the genus *Fagus* (10 species), native to N temperate regions. Beeches have smooth gray bark and a broad dense crown, occasionally reaching a height of 130 ft (40 m). The leaves are oval, pointed, and toothed, the flowers are unisexual and inconspicuous, and the fruits are nutlike seeds enclosed in husks (beechnuts or mast). The common beech of Europe and Asia is *Fagus syl-*

vatica, the timber of which is used for furniture and flooring, while that of North America is *F. grandiflora*. Family: *Fagaceae*.

In the S hemisphere beeches are represented by a related genus (*Notofagus*; 14 species) and differ in being evergreen and having separate trees bearing male or female flowers. Some are of importance for their durable timber, edible nuts, or ornamental value.

Beecham, Sir Thomas (1879–1961) British conductor. He used his inherited fortune for the advancement of English musical life. He was a memorable interpreter of Haydn and Mozart and championed the works of Richard Strauss, Sibelius, and particularly Delius, whose friend and biographer he became. He founded the London Philharmonic Orchestra (1932) and the Royal Philharmonic Orchestra (1947).

Beecher, Henry Ward (1813–87) US Congregational preacher and author. He was the son of a distinguished preacher, and brother of Harriet Beecher *Stowe. He was a pastor first in Indianapolis and then for 40 years in Brooklyn, New York, where his sermons and his writings, in which he advocated the abolition of slavery and women's suffrage, were widely influential.

Beecher, Lyman (1775–1863) US preacher, educator, and father of Henry Ward *Beecher and Harriet Beecher *Stowe. He became well known for his sermons while minister of Congregational churches in Litchfield, Conn., (1810–26) and Boston (1826–32) and president of Lane Theological Seminary (1832–50) in Cincinnati. An advocate of Calvinism, he made speeches against dueling, slavery, and the use of alcohol that were widely circulated.

bee-eater A brightly colored bird belonging to a family (*Meropidae*; 24 species) occurring mainly in tropical Old World regions. Bee-eaters have pointed wings, long central tail feathers, a slender curved bill, and, commonly, a black eye stripe. They nest in burrows and feed in flight, chiefly on bees and wasps. Order: *Coraciiformes* (hornbills, kingfishers, etc.).

beefwood. *See* Casuarina.

beekeeping (*or* apiculture) The rearing of colonies of *honeybees in hives either for their *honey or *beeswax or for pollinating flowers. Sheets of wax in wooden frames (starter combs) are hung vertically inside the hive. Onto these the bees build wax cells that they fill with honey and seal. When a frame is full it is removed, the honey is extracted, and the comb is reused. A colony makes about 71 lb (32 kg) of honey in a summer, but 31 lb (14 kg) of this is needed by the bees for food during the winter; following a bad summer they must be fed sugar syrup. About 10,000–20,000 bees survive the winter; during the spring, when a colony has increased to over 50,000, a large group is likely to leave the hive (i.e. it swarms). The beekeeper collects the swarm and puts it into an empty hive.

beer and brewing Beer is an alcoholic drink made from fermented malt flavored with hops. Brewing is the process of making beer. Barley, or other grain, is first malted by being allowed to germinate, the resulting malt being dried (kilned), ground, and heated with water (mashed). Starch in the grain is converted into soluble carbohydrates by enzymes in the malt. The resulting liquid wort is boiled with hops to concentrate the wort and utilize the bitter flavor of the hops. The wort is then filtered and cooled and is ready for fermentation. Yeast is added and the carbohydrates in the wort are converted into alcohol. The liquid is drained and stored. Different brewing methods and types of ingredients produce different varieties of beer. Beer was drunk in ancient Egypt and has been enjoyed in a great many countries ever since. **Ale** was originally a stronger drink than beer, brewed without hops. The terms are now interchangeable, although ale is sometimes reserved for stronger brews fermented at higher temperatures. **Mild** beer is made with fewer hops than **bitter** and a darker malt is used to impart color. **Lager** is traditionally a light beer matured over a long period at low temperature. **Stout** is made from a blend of roasted barley and malts.

Beerbohm, Sir Max (1872–1956) British caricaturist and writer. He published several collections of essays, caricatures, and brilliant parodies during the 1890s. His only novel, *Zuleika Dobson* (1911), is an ironic romance set at Oxford University.

Beersheba 31 15N 34 47E A city in S Israel, the largest in the Negev. In World War I it was the scene of a British victory over the Turks. Beersheba has a university (1965) and manufactures chemicals and glass. Population (1990 est): 114,000.

beeswax A substance produced by bees to build honeycombs. It is collected by heating the honeycomb in water (after removing the honey) so that the floating wax can be separated after solidification on cooling. Beeswax is used in high-quality polishes, etc.

beet A herbaceous plant, *Beta vulgaris*, native to Europe and the Mediterranean region, stemless but sometimes exceeding 40 in (1 m) in height. Several varieties are widely cultivated in temperate areas, the most important of which is the *sugar beet. The taproot of the red or garden beet is eaten as a vegetable, while the mangel-wurzel (*B. vulgaris vulgaris*) is an important fodder variety. The spinach beet is grown for its leaves, used as a vegetable. Family: *Chenopodiaceae*.

Beethoven, Ludwig van (1770–1827) German composer, born in Bonn. His father, a court musician, attempted to exploit him as a child prodigy. Often boorish and temperamental, he nevertheless won a considerable following for his piano playing and compositions in Vienna, where he settled in 1792 after studying there with Haydn. At the age of 30 he began to go deaf, an experience that increased his loneliness and eccentricity, but did not stop him composing. His later years were plagued by illness and by his adoption of his troublesome neph-ew Karl. About 600 of Beethoven's works survive, among them 9 symphonies, 5 piano concertos, 1 violin concerto, 16 string quartets, 10 violin and piano sonatas, 32 piano sonatas, 2 ballets, 2 masses, 1 opera, and about 200 song settings. His early masterpieces, influenced by Mozart and Haydn, include much chamber music, piano works, and the first and second symphonies. During his middle years he produced the *Emperor* piano concerto (1809), the *Kreutzer* sonata (1803), the opera *Fidelio* (1805–14), and the rest of the symphonies, up to the eighth. His last most intense works include the *Missa Solemnis* (1818–23), the ninth symphony (1817–23), and the innovative late string quartets.

beetle An insect belonging to the largest order (*Coleoptera*; about 278,000 species) of the animal kingdom. The forewings are specialized as hard structures (called elytra), which cover the functional hindwings when these are not in use. The elytra and the thick cuticle provide protection against predation and desiccation and enable aquatic species to trap a store of air. Beetles occupy a wide range of habitats and have exploited all possible food sources—many feed on plants or animals or scavenge their remains and a few are parasitic.

Many beetles are of great economic importance: some species are serious pests of crops, timber, textiles, and stored grains and cereals; others are useful by preying on insect pests or by speeding up the process of *decomposition. *See also* weevil.

Begin, Menachem (1913–92) Israeli statesman; prime minister (1977–83). Born in Poland, he led the Polish Zionist youth movement until the outbreak of World War II and from 1942 commanded the militant *Irgun Zvai Leumi* in Palestine. After the establishment of the State of Israel in 1948, he founded the Freedom (Herut) Movement and became the leader of the parliamentary opposition. In 1973 he became joint chairman of the Likud coalition and then prime minister with the victory of Likud in the 1977 elections. Under the auspices of Pres. Jimmy *Carter, Begin held negotiations with Egyptian President Anwar *Sadat that led to the Camp David Accords and the signing of a peace treaty between Egypt and Israel in 1979. Begin and Sadat were jointly awarded the Nobel Peace Prize in 1978. In the aftermath of Israel's invasion of Lebanon in 1982, Begin resigned from office and retired to private life.

LUDWIG VAN BEETHOVEN *This portrait of Beethoven as a young man is considered to be one of the best likenesses of him.*

Begonia A genus of generally succulent herbaceous plants (about 1000 species) native to the tropics. They are widely grown as ornamental pot or garden plants for their attractive, often brightly colored flowers with pink, yellow, or white "petals" in two unequal pairs (as in *B. semperflorens*) or for their variegated leaves (as in *B. rex*). The underground parts are long lived and may be tuberous, fibrous, or rhizomatous. Family: *Begoniaceae*.

Behan, Brendan (1923–64) Irish playwright. His first play, *The Quare Fellow* (1954), and his autobiography, *Borstal Boy* (1958), were based on his years of detention and imprisonment for Irish Republican Army (IRA) activities. His best-known play, *The Hostage* (1956), treated a basically tragic situation with characteristic liveliness and boisterous comedy.

behaviorism A school of psychology, founded in the US by J. B. *Watson in the early 20th century, in which the emphasis is on describing and predicting observable behavior: unconscious ideas, feelings, and the process of thinking are regarded as unimportant. The behaviorist concentrates on understanding the laws relating a stimulus to a response, how responses are built up into complex behaviors, and how *conditioning affects behavior. The approach was successful in describing how animals learned tasks in the laboratory but has been limited in its ability to account for such complex processes as emotion, language, and interpersonal relationships. *Behavior therapy was developed from behaviorism and is an established psychiatric treatment.

behavior therapy A method of treating mental disorders that is based on the view that psychological problems are the result of faulty learning. It was developed mainly by H. *Eyzenck. Sometimes *conditioning is used to teach new behavior, such as better ways of relating to other people, or to eliminate undesirable behavior, such as excessive drinking (*see* aversion therapy). It includes treatment for *phobias, in which repeated exposure to the feared object or situation gradually reduces the subject's fear of it. *See also* behaviorism.

Behrens, Peter (1868–1940) German architect. Coming to architecture from the *Arts and Crafts movement, he erected his most influential buildings before World War I. He occupies a transitional period in architectural development, evolving a modernistic style that echoed a functional classicism and was notable for its complete lack of ornamentation in design. His most important building was the AEG turbine works in Berlin (1909–11), which was one of the first industrial buildings to be evaluated as a work of architecture.

Behring, Emil Adolf von (1854–1917) German bacteriologist, who produced an antitoxin that conferred passive immunity against tetanus. By 1882 Behring and Paul *Ehrlich had developed a serum that provided effective immunity against diphtheria and also aided its treatment in established cases. He was awarded a Nobel Prize in 1901.

Behrman, S(amuel) N(athaniel) (1893–1973) US dramatist, noted for his comedies. His first, *The Second Man*, was produced on Broadway in 1927, and was followed by *Serena Blandish* (1928), *End of Summer* (1936), *Wine of Choice* (1938), and *No Time for Comedy* (1939). Other works include *Meteor* (1929), *Brief Moment* (1931), and *Fanny* (in collaboration with Joshua Logan; 1954).

Behzad (c. 1455–c. 1536) Persian painter, regarded as one of the greatest of Islamic miniaturists. As director of the academy at Herat he was an influential teacher and the many imitators of his richly colored and dramatic style have made his works—few of which are signed—difficult to identify.

Beiderbecke, Bix (Leon Bismarck B.; 1903–31) US jazz cornetist and pianist, famous for the purity of his cornet tone and such songs as "Singin' the Blues." Toward the end of his short life he played with Louis Armstrong and in the band of Paul Whiteman (1891–1967). The originality of his own compositions is evident in "In a Mist" (1927) for piano.